Legality, Ideology
and
The State

LAW, STATE AND SOCIETY SERIES

Editors

Z. BANKOWSKI, *Department of Public Law, University of Edinburgh, U.K.*
M. CAIN, *Institute of Criminology, University of Cambridge, U.K.*
W. CHAMBLISS, *Department of Sociology and Anthropology, University of Delaware, Newark, U.S.A.*
M. McINTOSH, *Department of Sociology, University of Essex, Colchester, U.K.*
P. FITZPATRICK, *Darwin College, University of Kent at Canterbury, U.K.*

Legality, Ideology
and
The State

Edited by

DAVID SUGARMAN

Middlesex Polytechnic, London, England

1983

ACADEMIC PRESS

A Subsidiary of Harcourt Brace Jovanovich, Publishers
London · New York
Paris · San Diego · San Francisco · São Paulo
Sydney · Tokyo · Toronto

ACADEMIC PRESS INC. (LONDON) LTD.
24/28 Oval Road
London NW1

United States Edition published by
ACADEMIC PRESS INC.
111 Fifth Avenue
New York, New York 10003

British Library Cataloguing in Publication Data

Legality, ideology and the state. — (Law
state and society; 11)
1. Sociological jurisprudence
I. Sugarman, D.   II. Series
340′.115   K370

ISBN 0-12-676080-2
LCCN 83-70336

Phototypeset by
Dobbie Typesetting Service, Plymouth, Devon

Printed by
T. J. Press (Padstow), Ltd, Padstow, Cornwall

Preface

It is often asserted that the systematic exploration of the linkages between law, economy and society is a relatively recent phenomenon in Britain. Although such a view is oversimplistic, it is undoubtedly true that until the last decade, with few exceptions, the relation between law and other aspects of the socio-economic order was either ignored or treated in a relatively unproblematic manner.

Since the 1960's, however, the development of critical criminology, law in context, the social history of crime and punishment, and the emergence of the sociology of law as a discrete discipline have all served to emphasize the importance of the inter-relation between law, economy and society within the social sciences and allied areas. This, in turn, has spawned a host of new courses and a rich and diverse literature which to a significant extent cuts across the boundaries separating traditionally defined subject areas.

One aspect of the recent renaissance in the sociology of law has been an understandable concern to excavate the sociology of law that has developed in a variety of directions since the eighteenth century. In particular, the work of Marx, Weber and, to a lesser extent, Durkheim on law, economy and society have been afforded increasing attention. Useful summaries of or extracts from many of the classic texts now exist. Moreover, considerable energy has been expended on the grounding of analysis in classic writers or texts.

This collection seeks to provide students and teachers with a *different* set of resources. It explores the relationship between law, economy, ideology and the state both historically and theoretically from a variety of perspectives. Each essay provides an introduction and guide to the work of a major twentieth century theorist or a body of literature which, whilst important in furthering our understanding of the linkages between law, economy, ideology and the state, has been relatively neglected until very recently.

In addition to this expository aim, each essay includes a re-appraisal of a particular literature or an aspect of a theorist's work. Indeed, the development of new theories, the conceptual clarification of major questions, arguments for different priorities and attempts to provide new answers are also to be found in this collection. As a whole, then, the collection is Janus-like. On the one hand, it looks back and re-appraises the intellectual products of earlier analyses. On the other hand, it looks forward and seeks to introduce new questions and to formulate new arguments, theories or priorities.

A brief explanation concerning the use of the term 'legality' in the title of this collection may be in order. 'Legality' rather than 'law' appears in the title because a major theme underlying several of the essays is the complex co-existence of a variety of systems for ordering and organizing in society of which the state legal order is but one instance. Now we are not the first to emphasize that the state has no monopoly over ordering and organization in society. In preparing this book, however, we have tried to pay greater attention to the consequences of this thesis for both historical and theoretical work than perhaps has tended to be the case to-date. Thus as a whole, the focus of the collection is wider than the state law order; it also examines the place of ordering and organization in the analysis of social networks and Third World or socialist contexts.

It is hoped that this book will contribute towards the growing body of work which seeks to transcend 'left idealism' and to foster a lively and richer history and sociology of law.

It is also hoped that it will prove of value to students and teachers in schools of social science, law, history, and social work, and will be of interest to all those concerned about the relationship between law, economy and society. In order to aid further reading, each chapter is appended by an annotated bibliography.

May 1983   David Sugarman

Acknowledgements

I am grateful to Brian Hipkin for his assistance with the preparatory stages of this anthology, and to those who commented on earlier drafts of the papers— principally Bill Chambliss, Roger Cotterrell, Peter Fitzpatrick, Bob Spjut and Ronnie Warrington. I would also like to express my appreciation to Maureen Cain and Peter Fitzpatrick for their support and encouragement. Besides my fellow contributors, I would like to thank Léonie Sugarman for her positive assistance. Finally, I am grateful to Millicent Wolmark for her excellent typing and to those publishers who gave me permission to reprint or use extracts from the following works:

Academic Press Ltd., for permission to reproduce extracts from A. Hunt, "A Radical Critique of Law", *International Journal of the Sociology of Law*, Vol. 8, pp. 34-46, 1980 and to reprint R. A. Warrington, "Pashukanis and the Commodity-Form Theory", Vol. 9, pp. 1-22, 1981.

Edward Arnold Ltd., for permission to reproduce extracts from *State and Capital* Ed. by J. Holloway and S. Picciotto.

Heinemann Educational Books and Beacon Press for permission to reproduce extracts from the following works of J. Habermas: *Towards a Rationalist Society, Theory and Practice, Legitimation Crisis* and *Communication and the Evolution of Society*; from *Sociology as a Skin Trade* by J. O'Neill; and from *Aspects of Sociology* Ed. by Adorno and Dirks.

Jonathan Cape Ltd. for permission to reproduce extracts from *Letters From Prison* by Antonio Gramsci, Ed. by L. Lawner.

Lawrence Wishart Ltd. for permission to reproduce extracts from *Selections from the Prison Notebooks* of Antonio Gramsci, Ed. by Q. Hoare and G. N. Smith; and Capital, Volume One by K. Marx.

Macmillan Publishing Co. Inc. for permission to reproduce extracts from *Knowledge and Politics* by R. M. Unger.

Monthly Review Press for permission to reproduce extracts from *Anarchism* by D. Guerin.

J. O'Neill for permission to reproduce extracts from *Sociology as a Skin Trade.*

Ink Links for permission to reproduce extracts from *Law and Marxism* by E. B. Pashukanis, Ed. by C. Arthur.

Martin Robertson and Co. Ltd. for permission to reproduce extracts from the *British Journal of Law and Society.*

New Left Books for permission to reproduce extracts from *Essays in Self Criticism* by L. Althusser.

Routledge and Kegan Paul Ltd. for permission to reproduce extracts from *The Institutions of Private Law and their Social Functions* by K. Renner; *Marxism* by G. Lichtheim; and *From Max Weber* Ed. by H. H. Gerth and C. W. Mills.

The University of Chicago Press for permission to reproduce extracts from *Law, Legislation and Liberty, Vol. 1* by F. A. Hayek; and to reprint "State, Civil Society and Total Institution" by M. Ignatieff, from *Crime and Justice* Ed. by N. Morris and M. Tonry.

Contributors

Zenon Bankowski *Lecturer in Jurisprudence, Department of Public Law, University of Edinburgh, Old College, South Bridge, Edinburgh EH8 9YL, Scotland*

Maureen Cain *Visiting Scholar, Institute of Criminology, University of Cambridge, 7 West Road, Cambridge CB3 9DT, England*

Roger Cotterrell *Senior Lecturer in Law, Faculty of Laws, Queen Mary College, Mile End Road, London E1 4N, England*

Peter Fitzpatrick *Senior Lecturer in Law and Interdisciplinary Studies, Faculty of Social Science, Darwin College, The University of Kent, Canterbury CT2 7NY, England*

Michael Ignatieff *Senior Research Fellow, Kings College, Cambridge CB2 1FT, England*

Richard Kinsey *Lecturer in the Sociology of Law, Department of Jurisprudence, Edinburgh University, Old College, South Bridge, Edinburgh EH8 9YL, Scotland*

David Sugarman *Reader in Law, School of Law, Middlesex Polytechnic, The Burroughs, London NW4 4BT, England*

Colin Sumner *Lecturer in Criminology, Institute of Criminology, University of Cambridge, 7 West Road, Cambridge CB3 9DT, England*

Ronnie Warrington *Senior Lecturer in Law, School of Law, Middlesex Polytechnic, The Burroughs, London NW4 4BT, England*

Contents

1 Introduction and Overview

David Sugarman

The essays in this collection cover a wide range of historical and theoretical material. As a whole, the collection is concerned with the theme of legality, ideology, and the state. The majority of papers were written especially for this collection and are here published for the first time. Whilst they may seem superficially disparate and are not the work of a specific 'group' or 'school', there are linkages between and convergencies within them.

Much Marxist and other socialist writing on legality, ideology and the state has traditionally tended to succumb to what has been called 'left idealism'. By 'left idealism', following Young (1979), I mean the tendency of the left not to take liberal and conservative theory seriously. Law is reduced to a wholly dependent variable, a superstructure merely reflecting a capitalist-economic base; a brutalizing coercive injunction from above; simply an ideology in the sense of 'a trick' or false consciousness. Real political advance is equated with the withering away of law and the state. In its most extreme form left idealism subscribes to the ". . . wholesale dismissal of *all* laws and *all* police and sometimes . . . the soppy notion that all crime is some kind of displaced revolutionary activity". In this latter form it ". . . is unable to distinguish the factory from the prison, education from brainwashing, the anti-social from the social, fascism from democracy" (Young, 1979, pp. 12-13 and 16).

In recent years there has been an increasing awareness on the left that left idealism must be transcended and that the role of law and state in capitalist societies is both complex and contradictory. In one sense the essays in this anthology spring from this new sensitivity, and seek to build upon some of the important work that it has fostered. Not surprisingly, economic and political events have played an important part in the left's repudiation of overly-functionalist accounts of law, state and society. The ruthless tenacity of fascist

Law, State and Society Series: "Legality, Ideology and the State", edited by D. Sugarman, 1983.
Academic Press, London and New York.

regimes and the horrors of Stalinism and other Eastern bloc oppression have heightened the need to limit the exercise of ordering and organization in society by means of the law and processes of democratic accountability. Less visibly, hard won rights and practices are being eroded by increasingly powerful corporate organizations (private and public) and the growth of new technologies sanctioned in the name of progress and cost-effectiveness. However, the need to treat the problems of ordering and organization more seriously has taken on an immediate urgency in view of the run down of vital public services and the right-wing authoritarianism of the Thatcher and Reagan administrations in Britain and the United States. The rapid deterioration of the world economic climate has made it impossible for governments to hide the fact that economic growth, the *sine qua non* of post-war Western governments, can no longer be guaranteed.

Together, the essays in this collection posit a variety of ways by which the theory and politics of the left may be advanced beyond the traditional left idealist conceptions of legality, ideology and the state. Two common themes can be detected in the essays as a whole. Firstly, it is recognized that, both theoretically and politically, law and state in capitalist societies are complex, double-edged and deeply fissured institutions. Law, society, economy, state and ideology cannot be treated as static, undifferentiated monoliths. Instead, they constitute heterogeneous entities, whose external and internal relations are characterized by continuity *and* discontinuity, function *and* disfunction, mediation, refraction and reinforcement. This renders problematic the relation between law, state, economy and society. Thus the essays by Bankowski, Fitzpatrick, Ignatieff, Sugarman and Warrington all, in different ways, demonstrate the plurality of ordering and organization in society; that the state and the state legal order has no monopoly over ordering and organization; and the complex semi-autonomous co-existence of sometimes competing, sometimes complementing, state law, semi-state law and indigenous norms.

A second common theme grounds several of the papers in this collection. A signal error of left idealism is its failure to take seriously the form and content of the law both during and after the transition to a socialist society. This is part of a wider absence in the theory and politics of the left. The actual properties of a socialist society and the nature, form and scope of ordering and organization in that society has tended to be given short shrift. Not surprisingly therefore, it could be argued that: ". . . at the very centre of Marxist theory there is, indeed, a void: the nature of the 'classless' society . . . What is missing is any developed analytical treatment of the distribution of power and the division of labour that could match the attainment of 'classlessness' in an advanced industrial society." (Downes and Rock, 1979, p. 15)

Notions about the withering away of law and state have done much to foreclose important avenues, sustain political impotence and the pessimism of legal nihilism. Most dangerously of all, perhaps, socialist society and its institutions are equated with consensus. The essays by Bankowski, Cain and Kinsey in this anthology begin, albeit in different ways, to prepare for what Kinsey calls ". . . a jurisprudence of the ends, uses and limits of legal intervention . . ." both during and after the transition to socialism. They recognize that socialist society requires ordering and organization; and, therefore, the analysis of socialist legality is vital in order to evaluate norms, practices and institutions, now and in the future.

It is important to stress that this position accepts both the importance of the Rule of Law in capitalist societies *and* the need to think about the nature, form and content of socialist law, ordering and organization and the politics of their construction, that is to go beyond defending the Rule of Law and posit a more just and practical alternative form of ordering and organization. A brief consideration of some of the major arguments in each essay will clarify the ways these and other related themes are handled.

There was a time when Karl Renner's major work, *The Institutions of Private Law and their Social Function* was regarded by some as the exemplar of a materialist analysis of law. Yet Renner's work on the politics of law and socialism has received scant attention. In recent years it has been passed over, perhaps, in favour of the work of Pashukanis. Indeed, Pashukanis's stress on the relation between the form of law and the economic form of capitalist society could be read as discrediting Renner and as exposing his 'revisionism'. In the first essay in this collection, Richard Kinsey presents a spirited defence of Renner's enterprise. Usually Renner's contribution to a materialist analysis of law has been assessed solely in terms of the efficacy or otherwise of his examination of the changing functions of the legal institution of private property. The novelty of Kinsey's essay derives in part from his claim that Renner's principal virtue was that, unlike Pashukanis, he took the form of socialist law seriously. Kinsey locates Renner's work in the general context of Austro-Marxist theory and politics and describes the relation between this context and Renner's particular conception of socialist legality and the uses of law in the transition to socialism. Renner's views on socialism and the nature of socialist society and the transition between capitalism and socialism are contrasted with those of Marx and the political and theoretical implications of their differences are described and evaluated. Kinsey argues that Renner's work constitutes both a seminal Marxist analysis of law and is of great contemporary relevance. This is because almost alone within an identifiably Marxist tradition, Renner grappled with the role and function of law, ordering and organization in the transition to socialism and the problems of socialism legality. Although Renner failed in his efforts, his importance, argues Kinsey, lies in his attempt to explicate the material possibilities and the desired alternatives to the present. Kinsey criticizes those within conventional social science and on the left who refuse to speculate about possible and alternative forms of ordering and organization. Kinsey's arguments closely accord with other recent valuable work which underlines the importance of ". . . creating a set of demands for alternative and socialist arrangements in every area in which the state imposes itself on the citizens of our . . . society." (Taylor, 1981, pp. xviii–xix)

Renner's great adversary was the Bolshevik jurist, Evgeny Pashukanis. The current renaissance of Marxist analyses of law, the gradual recovery of the heritage of Bolshevik thought repressed during the Stalinist era and the appearance of a readable English translation of Pashukanis's work have encouraged the rediscovery of Pashukanis's jurisprudence. Why have Pashukanis's ideas met with an often enthusiastic response from the left? First, unlike many Marxist analyses of law, he transcended a simplistic reduction of law to the coercion of the dominant economic class, i.e., he stressed the consensual as well as the coercive nature of law in capitalist societies. Second, he drew an important distinction between the *content* and the *form* of law. The content of the law includes particular case law or legislation, facilitating or prohibiting specific behaviour. This may be distinguished from the form of law, that is, its general structure, its categories, methods and procedures. Radical legal, historical and sociological analyses of law and state have been very largely devoted to explaining which historical causes or motives grounded particular legislation or judicial decisions. In other words, they have largely adopted an instrumentalist method by which to de-code the relation between law, state and economy. One of the flaws of an instrumentalist focus is that it concentrates so much on the particular content of the law that the legal form or structure within which that content was constructed tends to be ignored. The legal system embraces a variety of discrete facets and facilities which need to be differentiated. Pashukanis's work sensitizes us to the important role played by the form of law, in shaping the content of the law over long periods of time. Third, and most controversially, perhaps, Pashukanis discerned a strong, intellectual or structural parallel between the form of law and the economic structure of society. In capitalist society, following Marx's stress on the commodity form of capitalist society, the form of law is seen as the product of commodity relations. In this way, Pashukanis could argue that both the content and form of law were decisively shaped by the economy. Ronnie Warrington's essay provides an exhaustive account of the objects and method of Pashukanis's commodity form theory as well as a detailed critique. Warrington argues that it is Pashukanis's overwhelming theoretical commitment to the withering away of law, rather than his commodity form theory, which is the cornerstone of his jurisprudence. The logic of his position caused him both to overstate the influence of the economic structure on law in capitalist societies and to conclude that only commodity production societies had legal systems. Thus, the form and content of ordering and organization in a socialist society was a non-issue. As Pashukanis's tragic death testifies, the road to socialism requires the conscious articulation of the objects, uses and limits of organization and ordering in a socialist society; that is a conception of socialist legality.

It is widely recognized that Weber's sociology of law ". . . is the most important and substantial contribution to the sociological movement of law." (Hunt, 1978, p. 130). The importance that is rightly attached to Weber's sociology of law and the work and debates it has stimulated does not, of course, necessarily imply a whole-hearted acceptance of his substantive analysis of law nor his methodologies. What is clear, however, is that ". . . Weber provides the central point for theoretical encounter within the tradition of the socio-logical movement in law. It is through engaging with Weberian sociology of law, that advances are possible both theoretically and in the direction of empirical enquiry" (Hunt, 1978, p. 131). Weber's work on legality and political legitimacy cuts across his exploration of the linkages between economy and law, state and law and domination and law. Roger Cotterrell's paper argues that Weber's conceptual framework for the systematic analysis of the role of law in securing political legitimacy constitutes an essential starting point for an analysis of the ideological importance of law. Weber tackled important questions such as: when can law provide political legitimacy; what were the historical conditions which favoured the particular form of law associated with legal domination; what exactly is the nature of the belief that sustains *law* as the basis of legitimacy under legal domination; and what attributes does law possess which enables it to provide ideological support for political legitimacy? Cotterrell places special stress on Weber's ideal-type of legal domination. Weber argued that the system of political rule in modern society obtains its legitimacy from a system of rationally made legal rules. In modern society, therefore, legality and political legitimacy become almost identical. As Cotterrell points out, in this light, legal domination becomes self-sustaining and mechanical; the rational form of law as opposed to its content or morality becomes paramount for the purposes of political legitimacy. Cotterrell goes on to relate Weber's notions of legality and political legitimacy to his conception of the modern state and formal logical legal rationality. Cotterrell describes both the utility and limits of Weber's analysis. In particular, he points to Weber's failure to examine the conditions under which legal domination may become problematic and the impact of changing class relations on legal domination.

In Weber's work, the law's ideological dimensions become exclusively associated with rationalization and the need for order. Human agency, the importance of political choices, and the tension between order and justice are minimized. As a result, argues Cotterrell, Weber's conceptual framework cannot explain the relevance of law's ideological functions for political action and social change. The existence of competing systems of values and beliefs tends to be smothered by the conceptual structure of Weber's sociology and his ideal-type method. The tension between order and justice, formal vs substantive rationality, is treated as abnormal rather than as endemic. These tensions and their relevance for political action and social change constitute an important *locus* for future work on legality, ideology and the state.

Antonio Gramsci's writings have been extremely influential both within and beyond Marxism. Maureen Cain's essay examines the differing contradictory ways Gramsci used the concept of the state in order to secure a better understanding of law. Now this task cannot be undertaken without an understanding of Gramsci's notions of intellectuals, civil society and the state. Cain's essay begins, therefore, with an introduction to these components of Gramsci's conceptual schema. Here, Cain distinguishes two distinct conceptions of the state in Gramsci's work: what she calls an "extended" and a "narrow" conception, and evaluates their respective merits and de-merits. This section of the paper concludes with a description of Gramsci's suggestive, but highly schematic discussions of the functions and importance of law. Gramsci stressed law's double-edged qualities, its consensual and coercive dimensions and its educational and norm creative tasks. Gramsci eschewed the view that lawmaking and ordering were the monopoly of the state. For Gramsci, behaviour associated with the state's legal order (coercion, norm generation, enforcement, education, legitimation etc.) could be found in all the diverse institutions of civil society. Control of the law was therefore a vital task in the reconstitution of society. Cain argues that the efficacy of Gramsci's theory of law and state derives from its political down-to-earthness. But what of the critique of Gramsci's theory of knowledge (his historicism)? Cain examines the epistemology which grounds his theory and assesses Althusser's attack on Gramsci on the grounds of historicism. She explains why it is that this 'battle of the giants' still matters both theoretically and politically.

In the final section of her paper, Cain presents her own views as to the political and theoretical relevance of Gramsci's theorization. Gramsci's work encourages us to think of the state in new ways. Cain provides examples of its potential as well as possible ways of clarifying Gramsci's conceptualization of the state.

Jurgan Habermas has been particularly associated with those theories which suggest that the expansive role now played by the state in contemporary capitalist societies necessarily generates changes in the character of legal ordering and beliefs about law and society. The contradictory demands on law and state tend to mean that state resources are dysfunctionally distributed. This in turn generates a crisis of legitimacy for law and state which requires either the construction of a new legitimizing ideology or the buying off of the most powerful social groups. Beyond Habermas's ideas on 'legitimation crises', however, there is much in his work about law which, surprisingly, has received hardly any attention within the sociology of law. Colin Sumner's essay contains a detailed exposition of Habermas's work on law, as well as his critique of Weberian and Marxian analyses of law. The significance of Habermas's theories for contemporary debates concerning the form of law, the value of the Rule of Law, the erosion of civil liberties by the modern state and the linkages between ideology and state, are conveyed by Sumner's paper. Sumner's essay also contains an extensive critique of Habermas's ideas on law which it would be impossible to do justice to in the context of a brief overview. Sumner's essay does much to make Habermas's difficult work more widely accessible as well as suggest a number of important qualifications to his ideas on legality, ideology and the state.

In the last decade, especially with the eruption of a sizeable body of social history, the regulation of *social* behaviour through the instrumentality of the law has been afforded special attention. Some of this work has been at pains to explore the law as a mode of organizing beliefs and values (influenced in part by Gramsci's notion of 'hegemony') and as a means of 'social control' — in addition to law as a directly coercive weapon. In particular, the history of policing and punishment has undergone a profound paradigm shift. Until recently the history of policing and punishment was written as the story of progressive reform, enlightenment and good intentions. However, a new revisionist historiography has pointed to the complex motives of the reformers; and in particular the social control functions of the new disciplinary institutions. These, in turn, have been related to certain political, economic and social changes in the eighteenth and nineteenth centuries. The so-called progressive reform spawned, the revisionists argued, far more harmful modes of behaviour control than existed before. However, the revisionists' emphasis on social control and the linkages they posited between changes in punishment, policing, economy and society soon came under attack. In an early and important critique Gareth Steadman Jones pointed out that:

> . . . a casual usage of 'social control' metaphors leads to non-explanation . . . There is no political or ideological institution which could not in some way be interpreted as an agency of social control. It is as if . . . the masses . . . were simply a blank page upon which each successive stage of capitalism has successfully imposed its imprint. (Jones, 1977, pp. 163-164)

Michael Ignatieff's history of the emergence of the prison in England in the period from 1770 to 1840 (Ignatieff, 1978), together with the work of Michel Foucault (Foucault, 1978) and David Rothman (Rothman, 1971), best embody the revisionist current as far as histories of punishment are concerned. In his essay in this collection, Michael Ignatieff explains the context and motives which helped generate a new revisionist history of punishment; and the core theses which underpinned those histories. He argues that the attack on revisionist histories for over-schematizing a complex story and for reducing intentions to conspiratorial class strategies has put into question the viability of both Marxist and structural-functionalist theory and history, not only in the area of prisons but by extension in other areas of research. These larger implications make the revisionist anti-revisionist debate of interest to readers beyond the historians' parish. Ignatieff's paper is in part an essay in self-criticism. In essence, he argues that the revisionists argument contained three basic misconceptions: that the state enjoys a monopoly over punitive regulation; that its moral authority and practical power are the major binding sources of social orders; and that all social relations can be described in the language of subordination. This does not, by implication, make the counter-revisionist position correct. Ignatieff's paper includes a significant critical evaluation of Foucault's work on punishment, power and the problem of agency. Especially suggestive, is Ignatieff's thesis that by describing all social relations as relations of domination, Foucault neglects the large aspect of human sociability, in the family and in civil society generally, which is characterized by norms of co-operation, reciprocity and the 'gift relation'.

The recent explosion of a social history of crime and punishment has had an immense impact on the development and refinement of the sociology of law as well as the theory and politics of the left. By contrast, the history of private law such as that regulating contracts, property, companies and families, has received very little attention from both historians and sociologists. David Sugarman's essay examines some of the major issues and subject-matter underlying the historical sociology of the relationship between law, economy and the state in England, 1750–1914. A wide range of literature and subject-matter is surveyed. Some of the topics considered include: the importance of private law in the economy; freedom of contract; the rise of absolute private property; the plurality of law; the ideological dimensions of law; the popular legitimacy of the law; inter- and intra-class conflict and the law; law, the state and the rise of capitalism; the modern state, public law and regulatory agencies; the intellectual history of law; the relative autonomy of law and the state; and the relation between the legal professions, the state and dominant economic interest groups. It is argued that the relation between law, economy and the state was often much more complex and contradictory than has tended to be assumed. The essay suggests a variety of ways in which overly-functionalistic theses and methodologies might be transcended.

Sugarman's essay questions the assumption that modern (i.e. post-1750) contract, property and commercial laws were essential in securing certainty in commercial transactions. This is not to say that private law was unimportant. In particular, it is argued that facilitative laws, such as the laws of contract, land and property, afforded the parties concerned the opportunity to make their own law (private law-making) and even the opportunity to by-pass or attenuate the state's legal order. This is one instance of a wider phenomenon, namely the role of private law in the facilitation and legitimation of a plurality of semi-autonomous realms. The law simultaneously exemplified such a realm and defined and reproduced a mode of thought and practice which promoted a variety of semi-autonomous realms with powers that in some respects resembled those of the state.

Peter Fitzpatrick's *Law and State in Papua New Guinea* (Fitzpatrick, 1980) has been widely praised since its publication as an important theoretical and empirical study of the relation between law and under-development in the third world. In his contribution to this collection, Fitzpatrick builds upon his earlier work to describe the value of a radical theory of legal pluralism in both the first world and third world context. Law is seen as constituted largely by the interaction between the state legal order and the plethera of other systems of indigenous ordering within the family, the work place and social networks. It is argued that indigenous ordering cannot be reduced to the state legal order. It is also contended that they cannot be reduced to forces such as the capitalist mode of production.

In the first part of his essay, Fitzpatrick explains why it is that legal scholarship has tended to ignore the diversity of ordering in society. Pioneering work on the family and "informal command ordering" are briefly considered. The essay then examines the plurality of law in the Third World. After a review of theories of underdevelopment, Fitzpatrick explains how one such theory—namely, the articulation of modes of production—can be used so as to illuminate the symbiotic but semi-autonomous relation between modes of production and the plurality of law. Finally, the author describes the implications of his essay for the analysis of law and legal plurality in First World nations.

Zenon Bankowski's essay constitutes a defence of a socio-anarchist view of law and details its strengths relative to Marxist analyses of law. He criticizes two kinds of Marxist analyses of law: the work of E. P. Thompson and Alan Hunt on the efficacy of the Rule of Law and their critique of instrumentalist theories of law; and certain form of law theories inspired by the work of Pashukanis. In essence, Bankowski's argument is that they cannot coherently explain what is wrong with law. He also questions the way some Marxists reduce the questions of organization and ordering to the economic character of society. For anarchists believe that the key problem is one of organizing to prevent the authority and control of the few; whereas for Marx, at times, and Marxists more generally, the problem has always been one of abolishing private ownership of the means of production—once that is done everything else will follow. But of course it does not.

Bankowski claims that socialist-anarchism does not espouse "no order", but is concerned with how to organize society on a free and equal basis. It, therefore, has much to contribute to an alternative conception of ordering and organization in society. In his conclusion, he briefly describes what these alternatives would entail.

Taken together, the essays in this book explore the problems of legality, ideology and the state from a variety of methodological and theoretical perspectives. The collection is offered as a contribution towards the movement to transcend the deficiencies of left idealism and to foster a lively sociology and history of law in this country. In the pursuit of such an enterprise we would do well to bear in mind that:

> In the formulation of historico-critical problems it is wrong to conceive of scientific discussion as a process at law in which there is an accused and a public prosecutor whose professional duty it is to demonstrate that the accused is guilty and has to be put out of circulation. In scientific discussion, since it is assumed that the purpose of discussion is the pursuit of truth and the progress of science, the person who shows himself most 'advanced' is the one who takes up the point of view that his adversary may well be expressing a need which should be incorporated, if only as a subordinate aspect, in his own construction. (Gramsci, 1971, pp. 343-344)

References

Downes, D. and Rock, P. (Eds) (1979). *Deviant Interpretations.* Martin Robertson, London.

Fitzpatrick, P. (1980). *Law and State in Papua New Guinea.* Academic Press, London.

Foucault, M. (1978). *Discipline and Punish.* Penguin Books, London.

Gramsci, A. (1971). *Selections from the Prison Notebooks.* Lawrence and Wishart, London.

Hunt, A. (1978). *The Sociological Movement in Law.* Macmillan, London.

Ignatieff, M. (1978). *A Just Measure of Pain.* Macmillan, London.

Jones, G. S. (1977). "Class exploration versus social control?" in *History Workshop,* No. 4, pp. 163-170.

Rothman, D. (1971). *The Discovery of the Asylum.* Little Brown, Boston.

Taylor, I. (1981). *Law and Order: Arguments for Socialism.* Macmillan, London.

Young, J. (1979). "Left idealism, reformism and beyond" in *Capitalism and the Rule of Law* (B. Fine *et al.*, Eds), pp. 11-28. Hutchinson, London.

2   *Karl Renner on Socialist Legality*

Richard Kinsey

Introduction

A comprehensive exposition of the functions fulfilled by the legal
institutions at every stage of the economic process has been given in *Das
Kapital*, Marx's principle work. No other investigator, either before him or
after him, was more aware of their importance for even the most intimate
details of this process. (Karl Renner, 1949, p. 58)

Karl Renner's *Institutions of Private Law and their Social Function* is an
underrated yet fundamental document of Marxist theory.[1] Renner's claim was
no less than to have synthesized Marx's economic writings and in effect to have
written up the theory of law, which Marx, though trained in law and jurisprudence, never actually produced.

There is of course good reason to doubt the reliability of any such claim.
Indeed, in crucial respects Marx and Renner are at variance, and the implications
of these differences are substantial. However, although we may dispute Renner's
analysis of the role and function of legal institutions in the development of
capitalist forms of social production, in other respects his work is of singular
importance — namely as an attempt to construct a socialist jurisprudence. Almost
alone within an identifiably Marxist tradition, Renner took seriously the problems of socialist legality and the role and function of law in the transition to
socialism. Although he was to move further to the right in his later political career,
even in the second edition of the *Institution* Renner's commitment to the Austro-
Marxist conception of social revolution cannot be doubted. Suggestions that the
text is 'revisionist' or 'reformist' are as unjustified as they are vague and unhelpful.

Law, State and Society Series: "Legality, Ideology and the State", edited by D. Sugarman, 1983.
Academic Press, London and New York.

The object of this essay is not however to give an account of Renner's analysis of the development of bourgeois law, so much as to examine his conception of socialist legality and the role and political uses he attributes to law in the transition to socialism.

This approach is much in accord with Renner's own project. Renner did not see his own work as 'academic' in intent. The *Institutions* was written as a political statement and intervention in the construction of socialism. As such its production was consistent with the political philosophy of Austro-Marxism which, as we shall see, emphasized discourse and demonstration as essential elements in promoting social revolution.

So saying, it must not be forgotten that the book was written for a particular political constituency. The analysis is based upon a series of interlocking theoretical assumptions and political purposes which were common to his audience and for that reason remained largely unstated. Self-evidently this can now cause problems in reading Renner's work and very easily lead to misinterpretation of its significance. To that end in this essay, I have attempted to draw out those assumptions, to look at some of the difficulties they entail, and in particular to emphasize the politics of law to which Renner was committed and through which his analysis of bourgeois legal institutions was directed.

It has been suggested that such an endeavour is of no more than marginal historical interest. Louis Althusser, for example, dismisses Austro-Marxism with an irritated scratch of the philosopher's pen:

> The 'Austro-Marxists' were merely neo-Kantians; they produced nothing that survived their ideological project. (Althusser, 1970, p. 77)

There are no doubt others who would afford Renner a more generous paragraph in the history of socialist ideas, even if only as the foil to the cutting edge of Pashukanis, whose analysis of the form of law might be said to have taken on and discredited Renner's 'revisionism' in its entirety.

In certain respects of course Renner and Pashukanis were bitterly opposed. Renner's political judgement of Bolshevism — he referred to it as the 'idolatory of the decree' — undoubtedly provoked Pashukanis as much as it did Trotsky, who was to write in his autobiography that:

> An Austro-Marxist too often revealed himself as a philistine who had learned certain parts of Marxist theory as one might study law, and had lived on the interest that *Das Kapital* had yielded him. (Trotsky, 1975, p. 215)

One can see very much the same virulent dislike of 'Karner' in Pashukanis's work, however Renner and Pashukanis avoided overt confrontation on the terrain of revolutionary strategy.[2]

At the level of theory, however, the confrontation is explicit in Pashukanis and tacitly present in the footnotes and revisions to the second edition of Renner's work. Without going into the detail here, much of the relevance and power of Pashukanis's critique of Renner turns upon the emphasis placed upon his conception of the 'bourgeois form of law'. However, it is one thing to refer to the 'form of bourgeois law' and another to infer that 'all law is bourgeois in its form'. Whilst Renner's analysis is, in my view, open to Pashukanis's criticism that he failed to recognize that the form of bourgeois law is problematic, in so far as Renner took the problem of the 'form of socialist law' seriously his work is of singular importance and for that reason an advance over that of Pashukanis.

In this respect it is important to emphasize that the Austro-Marxists were not 'revisionists' in the sense that they opposed the revolutionary seizure of state power in favour of a gradualist programme of democratic achievements. Rightly or wrongly, the Austro-Marxists believed that victory was theirs already. Their problem was not how to gain political power, but how to use it. As they saw it, theirs was a problem of social, not political revolution. Renner's critique of Bolshevism was not then an attack on the concept of revolution, but on the viability of a political revolution where, in Renner's terms, the 'economic substratum' had not 'evolved' sufficiently to maintain a socialist mode of production.

In the industrialized regions of Austria the radical democratic-socialism of the Austro-Marxists did indeed seem to promise the future. Consequently the approach of their work constantly places an optimistic emphasis upon the progressive aspects of capitalist social order as the basis of socialist reconstruction and transformation. They perceived themselves to be actively engaged in the construction of socialism, and it is as such that the problems of legal intervention and the nature of socialist legality were questions of immediate social and political relevance.

It is very easy with the benefit of hindsight to dismiss the historical experience and the theory of the Austro-Marxists for failing to recognize the threat of fascism and to provide a political organization and disciplined party structure adequate to defend the working class movement. It is however a strange imagination which suggests that their project was merely an exercise in neo-Kantian metaphysics as the deaths of many workers and the ruins of the co-operative housing schemes bear witness. Neither proposition should be allowed to obscure the commitment of their movement nor the practical value of their ideas.

Nonetheless, the physical and political destruction of 'Red Vienna' requires us to stop short and to reflect upon the one-sided optimism of their analyses. In discussing Renner's work I have taken his analysis of the legal form of the joint stock company, which he regarded as a major vehicle of socialist transformation, as an instance of such theoretical shortcomings which, perhaps, led ultimately to political defeat.

Having said this much, I must make it clear that I do not regard Renner's work as 'merely' of historical or philosophical interest. In the first place, historical awareness of revolutionary socialism (be it 'political' or 'social' revolution) is frequently ignored in the name of philosophical purity and 'science'. All too frequently this serves as a disguise for dogmatism. But secondly it would seem that the questions posed by the Austro-Marxists and especially by Renner, have again a political significance, even if they are now informed by pessimism rather than optimism.

In a peculiar way, it was the very fascism which destroyed Austro-Marxism which was to preserve Renner's ideas and ensure his contemporary relevance. The legacies of fascism, and also Stalinism, have served in different ways to direct socialist enquiry away from the problems of law and socialist legality. For the British Labour movement at least, the experience of fighting Spanish, Italian and German forms of fascism, allied to manifest Soviet oppression in 1956, 1968 and now the events in Poland—certainly as much, probably more than any beliefs in a radical past and the rights of the 'Free-born English'—have served to confirm a profound political realism which asserts the need to limit the exercise of power by means of the law and democratic procedures of accountability. For such reasons the political desirability and necessity of a 'rule of law' is understandably and rightly placed beyond question. The converse of this, however, is that questions of the nature of 'form' of law and legal regulation appropriate to *socialist* organization have not been raised. There is in other words no (post-war) tradition of a socialist jurisprudence.

Where questions have been asked of the legal system the emphasis has been placed primarily upon the ideological significance of law as a means of maintaining and reproducing the 'order' of capitalist production. The importance of the work of the radical criminologists and radical lawyers during the sixties and seventies, the more general resurgence of interest in the work of Pashukanis, and the major contribution of the social historians cannot be understated in this respect. Such work has been critical to the intellectual conditions which now prevail, and, crucially, has clarified understanding of the present operation of 'the most intimate details' of the legal process. Put bluntly, without such work we would not know where we had come from, let alone where we are going to.

The political conditions of the present, however, urgently demand the elaboration of a socialist jurisprudence. In the face of what Stuart Hall (1979) has referred to as the rise of 'popular authoritarianism' and the drift to a 'law and order society', but also in relation to the less visible development of corporate forms of economic power, the legal and democratic mechanisms of accountability, which for so long have been taken for granted, are increasingly stripped away in the name of efficiency and necessity.

In such conditions it is no good simply 'defending legality' if there is no conception of what socialist regulation should, and as importantly, could entail. Socialism is more than a moral promise, it must be a practical solution. As many as his failures may be, this was Renner's starting point.

The object of this essay, however, is necessarily limited. I hope firstly to place Renner's work in the general context of Austro-Marxist theory and politics, and then to draw out the taken-for-granted theoretical principles which structure and inform Renner's analysis. In the next section I look at how these assumptions predispose Renner to a particular conception of socialist legality and the uses of law in the transition to socialism. Following that, Marx and Renner are compared on questions of socialism and the nature of socialist society and forms of organization. In particular I emphasize the major differences in their respective methods of historical analysis and their political implications. These problems are then focussed, firstly, in a more detailed consideration of Renner's 'science of positive law' and then in a more substantive examination of his analysis of the role of the joint stock company as the vehicle of socialist transition. Here again comparison is made of Renner's method with that of Marx in order to display the political as well as the theoretical and methodological weaknesses of Renner's position.

In writing this essay I have felt constrained by the need to unravel Renner's thought. As a result I have no doubt over-simplified his work which on re-reading becomes increasingly complex, if not contradictory. Given the approach I have adopted all I can hope is to provide a guide to be read in conjunction with Renner's own work. To that extent the essay is not intended to stand on its own. However, in the conclusion to this paper, so as to draw together some of the points raised, I outline very schematically some of the more general reasons why I believe Renner's work still to be of relevance to contemporary politics and the problems of socialism, even if it is by way of his failures rather than successes.

The Basic Theoretical Structure of the Institutions

Born in 1870, Renner was to witness at first hand the economic and political transformation of the Habsburg Empire. By the time of its final collapse, he was a leading member of the Social Democratic 'Austro-Marxist' Party and by 1919 he had become the first Chancellor of the new Austrian Republic. It was very much out of this history that the theory and practice of Austro-Marxism, and Renner's work in particular, developed and was articulated.

By the end of the 1914–18 war, Renner had already published prolifically— over 100 articles and books dealing with the main questions of law, nationalism and the state as they confronted the socialist movement. He was established as a leading theoretician of Austro-Marxism as early as 1904 when the first edition of the *Institutions* was published in the Party journal, *Marx-Studien*.[3]

By 1929, when the second edition of the work was published, the Social Democratic Party had maintained its position as the single largest parliamentary party and political force in Austria for a decade, even though it was never to obtain an outright majority and after 1920 had refused to enter coalition government. 'Red Vienna' however was under full control of the social democrats, and remained the 'showpiece of European Social Democracy' until clerical fascism usurped the democratic process in 1934.

The strength of the party as a mass movement was equally remarkable. Unlike its German counterpart, the Austrian party was not to suffer immobilizing division between left and right, nor was it to face any meaningful challenge from the Communist Party. In part at least this strength can be attributed to the pre-war development of Austro-Marxist theory and its sensitivity to the specific problems of the transformation of the old empire.

In the period leading up to the war, the immediate questions posed by the various separatist and national movements, economic development and modernization together with the broader issues of imperialism, democratization and socialization of the state and the economy were examined by the Austro-Marxists in a series of theoretical and empirical studies, of which Renner's *Institutions* formed one element.[4] Through this work a distinct conception of 'Marxism between revolution and reform' was elaborated. Politically this emphasized that conditions appropriate to and necessary for radical social change could be accelerated but not created by direct political or legal intervention. The democratic organization of the labour process, education and extended socialization of the means of production were seen as elemental steps towards social revolution, but not as a substitute. Furthermore, within established capitalism, political revolution without such a basis would never amount to more than a spontaneous gesture.

For the Austro-Marxists neither the decree via the seizure of state power, nor the Bernsteinian moral programme of socialism as a social condition of ethical autonomy provided an acceptable programme of political initiative.[5] The concrete economic, cultural and social problems of the old order required a theoretical statement and political programme which emphasized unity, development, (re-)organization and political intervention. Theoretically these concerns were reproduced in the basic Austro-Marxist concepts of *political power*, *socialized man* and *social evolution*. These three concepts, in combination, were to provide Austro-Marxism with its specific theoretical identity.

In Renner's *Institutions* the three concepts are fused to provide an analysis of the limits of legal intervention within capitalism and an implicit conception of socialist legality. By taking each in turn we can reconstruct the principal dimensions of his analysis.

Political power: Renner and the imperative form of law

Imperatives, says Renner:

> . . . are the elements of the legal order. They are addressed to the individual and claim his obedience. Aiming at the will they limit or enlarge, break or enhance the individual will (autonomy), and hence confront it as an extraneous will. This relation of wills is fundamental to the law, there is little or no mystery about it, nothing metaphysical, supernatural or divine. (1949, p. 46)

Law is thus posed explicitly as a direct relation of power. It is experienced as such, as an external limitation to action. In this way Renner makes a strict separation between the form and the content or 'function' of law.

Renner's 'command theory' should not however be confused with the Austinian theory of illimitable sovereign power. According to Renner the power relation does not obtain between individual wills, conceived as a relation between a political superior and a political inferior. There is, says Renner, this 'mysterious difference' between the law of the state and the imposition of the highway robber:

> In modern times all law is laid down, in the name of all citizens, by the state conceived as an entity. Instead of one man's will prevailing over the will of another, the common will is regarded as imposed on that of the individual. (1949, p. 47)

It is central to Renner's analysis of law that the social reality of the common will is acknowledged, although by and large it appears to be taken for granted in the text:

> Let it suffice that the legal order is in fact imposed upon the individual will of the citizens as a unified common will, and that in actual fact it operates as a unified whole . . . this analysis does not form part of our present task. (1949, pp. 47–48)

Here Renner draws upon the second of the shared assumptions of Austro-Marxism, namely the conception of socialized man. In precis, we might represent Renner as saying: what appears as the will of individuals is in reality only the will of the supra-individual entity—i.e. socialized man. In this way Renner is able to constitute the sovereign as exercising not an individual but a social power.

Socialized man and the power of command

According to Renner it is a necessary condition of social order that the law-maker acts as the 'agent' of society, he is the 'trustee' of 'organised society' (1949, p. 73). Thus Renner tells us:

> Wherever the community has the power of command as it has in every society, it exercises this power by means of individuals *acting as its organs*. (1949, p. 71, emphasis added)

The power exercised is a social power in that it is necessary to the organization of social production and collective existence. However it can only be experienced, and as such 'exist', as a relation between individual wills:

> . . . the total will does not exist outside the individuals, though its embodiment in writing as a code gives it an appearance of independence, since *society's consciousness of itself as an entity cannot exist but within the consciousness of individuals*. It is individuals who are the exponents of the total will, they are the bearers of power, and it is to them that the will of the individual is subject. The formula: total will—individual will *can only be conceived as:* will of the power—will of the subject, that is to say *it can only exist* as a relation between two wills. (1949, p. 254, emphases added)

The social power of command cannot be assumed or exercised arbitrarily, however. It is limited in range and efficacy by the level of 'social evolution' (see *infra*), by the social requirements of particular forms of organized social production, and by what Renner refers to as the 'technical relation' obtaining between man and nature. As such the limits to legal power are external to the imperative form of law which for its efficacy depends upon the greater or lesser consciousness or 'rationality' of the *social* actor.

Thus, for Renner, law is the means by which modern society—'conscious of itself'—*organizes* the *social* relations of production. Such social organization must be expressed in terms of *commands*, which will necessarily be *experienced* as power relations obtaining between individual wills. The sovereign power of the state or legislator is not the power of the individual but the power of socialized man.

Law and social evolution

Central to Renner's thesis on the possibility of legal intervention is the conception of social evolution and the extent to which society is 'conscious' of the requirements of social organization. This in turn depends upon the evolved state of material conditions and forces of production. Organization through the imperative form of law is characteristic of a modern society, which is at least partially conscious of its own needs. It follows that in a fully self-conscious socialist society law will reach its zenith.

Even the simplest societies, however, presuppose socialized man and organization in production, thus Renner writes:

> Every social system pre-supposes socialised man. He must have arrived at the stage where language and tools . . . have already been developed in the tribe. Furthermore, the tribe must have developed into a community that is conscious of its own existence. We will refer to this type of community as an organisation. This term clearly expresses the *consciousness of co-operation*, differentiating itself from the concept of organism. (1949, p. 69, emphasis added)

Thus, for Renner, both the concept and the actual existence of society imply the cognitive-rational appropriation of nature and the laws of natural evolution in a gradual process whereby man becomes conscious of the natural laws governing his social existence and the ends which those laws serve. Thus the 'natural law' of preservation of the species (social man) dictates organized production, distribution and consumption of the social product. These Renner terms the economic functions of society. The greater the conscious appropriation of nature in production and reproduction the more "the natural laws of the preservation of the species are gradually transformed into social conventions and eventually into a code of conduct" (1949, p. 69). As the laws of society 'finally evolve' this code of conduct:

> . . . re-formulates and consciously remoulds what had been the process of natural cause and effect into teleological imperatives addressed to the individuals in the name of the community. It now determines their actions with the same precision as previously instinct and inherited disposition had determined them. This code of conduct is the foundation of social life and brings about the order of society. (1949, p. 69)

Only in a socialist society is there a conscious recognition and rational organization of the invariable economic functions. Within socialism this 'order of power' will be articulated in a law as an 'order of goods', an 'order of succession' and an 'order of labour'.

In pre-socialist society, however, there is at best only a partial 'consciousness of co-operation'. Thus in capitalist society it *appears* that there is only an order of goods; in fact, however, private property conceals and contains an irrational order of labour, whilst denying the social basis of power. As a result bourgeois society has "successfully developed the illusion that labour is not a social duty but a private affair for which no regulation of labour is required" (1949, p. 72).

Nonetheless, in bourgeois society the collective consciousness of the social basis of production is heightened as the division of labour and the social differentiation of capitalist production increases. As it does so, 'society' becomes increasingly aware of the functional inadequacies of the mode of its organization, i.e. private property and the related institutions of private law. Indeed very often a 'functional transformation of the norm' occurs, as it were, behind the backs of men, without it being present in consciousness. In such cases the law may well fall into disuse or else it must be rationalized and re-formed after the event to match the needs of the changed 'economic substratum'. Thus the *political* purpose of Renner's analysis of the institutions of private law was to demonstrate that this point in capitalist development has been reached: the functional inadequacy of private property as a means of social organization is apparent for all to see as the productive potential of society renders centralization and state regulation of the economy *demonstrably* necessary: i.e. present in the consciousness of society. State regulation and public law will supersede the institutions of private law as the functionally necessary means of rational social organization.

Renner on the Limits of Law in the Transition to Socialism

In socialist society the development of the material conditions of production allows full consciousness of co-operation. The common will thus realized is 'personified' in the organizing power of the state as legislator. Law and legal intervention cannot dictate the development of social production which renders this possible, for, Renner tells us, it is premised upon it. Further, the legal order can address its commands to human beings only, not to nature, so that:

> ... the relation between the individual and the natural object, the technical power of man, the productive capacity of the individual, all these develop under the eye of the law but not by means of the law. (1949, p. 255)

On this theoretical basis Renner concludes from this survey of the development of private law that:

1. fundamental changes in society are possible without accompanying alterations of the legal system,
2. it is not law that causes economic development,
3. economic change does not immediately and automatically bring about changes in the law,
4. development by leaps and bounds is unknown in the social substratum, which knows evolution only, not revolution. (p. 252-253)

The power of legal intervention on the social economic order—the 'efficacy of the norm' in Renner's terms—is thus constantly subject to external limitation. This, of course, significantly affects the conditions of possibility of revolution. Revolution, which can obtain only at the level of political institutions—the economic substratum knows evolution only—will in the transition to socialism take the form of a legal revolution in which there occurs a cognitive re-appropriation and normative re-ordering of the social relations of production. It is a revolution of re-form.

On the basis of the foregoing we can say that, as a logical consequence of Renner's theoretical position, socialist legality will display the following features:

1. The state will engross and perform those economic functions—the organization of production, distribution and consumption—presently fulfilled by the owner of private property. This will take legal form in an order of goods, of labour, of power and of succession. Public law will displace private law as:

   > All of a sudden it has become apparent to us that property has developed into a public utility. (1949, p. 129)

2. The state as legislator will be the fully conscious rational embodiment of the common will. State and society become one, the state *is* social regulation:

   > Legal institutions designed to regulate the order of labour and of power and the co-ordination of individuals have an organising function in that they integrate the individual into the whole. (1949, p. 71)

3. The state will be all-powerful. Its laws will take the form of commands addressed to individuals. As the embodiment of reason, however, the state will recognize the limits of the law and regulate itself.

   > The development of law gradually works out what is socially reasonable. (1949, p. 122)

Marx and Renner on Socialism and Socialized Man

Renner's defence of legality and the imperative form of law relies upon:
1. the 'necessity' that social relations are expressed and experienced as relations between individual wills; and
2. the 'necessity' of organization/regulation of production in all forms of society, including the socialist mode of production.

As such the imperative form of law is neither capitalist nor socialist, on the contrary, it is 'as neutral as an algebraic formula'. The specific forms of law—

or *legal institutions*—are no more than 'empty frames' given content in their application; law is an instrument at the disposal of society as legislator. All too easily, however, the function of law in capitalist society obscures these fundamental, supra-historical qualities. Thus Renner tells us:

> A social criticism which rejects contracts of sale and employment as unsocialistic on the grounds that they serve capitalist exploitation is quite mistaken. *It confuses legal form and social function.* (1949, p. 135, emphasis added)

Clearly in making such claims Renner differs substantially from Pashukanis, whose analysis of the form of bourgeois law and legal institutions leads to diametrically opposed conclusions as to the characteristics and qualities of modern law and to its place in the transition to socialism. But, more fundamentally, it needs emphasizing that Renner's 'instrumentalism' and his positivist analysis of the neutral form of law are both rooted in a conception of socialism and, in particular, of 'socialized man' which is significantly at variance with Marx's analysis in *Capital* and the *Grundrisse*. Renner was undoubtedly aware of the following passage from *Capital*:

> . . . the realm of freedom actually begins only where labour which is determined by necessity and mundane considerations ceases; thus in the very nature of things it lies beyond the sphere of actual material production. Just as the savage must wrestle with Nature to satisfy his wants, to maintain and reproduce life, so must civilised man, *and he must do in all social formations and under all possible modes of production.* With his development this realm of physical necessity expands as a result of his wants; but at the same time, the forces of production which satisfy these wants also increase. *Freedom in this field can only consist in socialised man, the associated producers, rationally regulating their interchange with Nature, bringing it under common control.* (Karl Marx, 1974, Vol. 3, p. 820)

Despite the obvious similarities of language there are crucial conceptual differences between Marx and Renner, particularly in relation to the notion of socialized man. Earlier we saw that socialized man is presumed in the very idea of society, be it feudal, capitalist or socialist. For Marx, on the other hand, capitalism creates only the possibility of fully socialized man, i.e. the conditions of possibility for a material transformation of the social relations of production. Thus, Marx emphasizes that it is the increased productivity of labour, brought about by the drive to secure greater surplus value, which in capitalism

> . . . creates the material means and embryonic conditions *making it possible in a higher form of society* to combine this surplus labour with a greater reduction of time devoted to material labour in general. (Marx, 1974, Vol. 3, p. 819, emphasis added)

Despite the qualitative differences between them, however, Marx recognizes the common points between the socialist and the capitalist modes of production. In particular both need to create "a large quantity of disposable time apart from the necessary labour time of society generally" (Marx, 1973, p. 708). In this sense socialism of course presupposes organized social labour, as does capitalism and indeed all pre-socialist, class societies. However, in *class society* the organization of social labour is always the servant of the appropriation of surplus labour by the economically dominant class. Thus under capitalism, for example, the reduction of necessary labour—through economies of scale, the rationalization of the labour process, etc.—and the creation of 'disposable time', only occur to the extent that by doing so surplus value is maximized. This of course requires the continued opposition of capital and labour in so far as the private appropriation of surplus social labour remains the motive force underlying the social organization of production. Despite the exploitative basis to the process however, capitalism exhibits a potential, which although restrained and ultimately negated by the need to secure surplus value, is nonetheless progressive. Thus Marx sees the "uniting of labour with the natural sciences" (1974, Vol. 3, p. 266), technological innovation and the consequent rise in the productivity of labour as one of the "civilising aspects of capital" (1974, Vol. 3, p. 819). This is so precisely because, potentially, such developments provide 'room for the development of the individuals' productive forces, hence those of society also'—i.e. the realization of socialized man—whereas, 'this creation of non-labour-time appears at the stage of capital, as of all earlier ones, as non-labour-time, free time, for a few'—i.e. the negation of socialized man. Thus for Marx, the condition of fully socialized man is yet to be achieved, and requires the qualitative transformation of the social relations, that is the class relations upon which capitalist production for private appropriation is based.

For Renner however, as we have seen, 'socialized man' is a universal feature of all social formations, given in the *objective* condition of dependence and inter-dependence in production. The difference between socialism and all previous forms of society is that man becomes *subjectively* aware of his condition and the natural laws which govern it and thereby capable of giving rational order to his present existence—i.e. developed capitalism—and of reconstituting it as socialism. Thus it is that in the concentration of capital, the growth of state intervention and the development of legal institutions within capitalism we can, as it were 'read out' the shape of socialism, as the *social* basis—i.e. the objective interdependencies—of capitalist production distribution and consumption becomes self-evident. Furthermore, class relations of production, based on private property, have with evolution of the economic substratum become no more than an artificial impediment, *marginal* to the real business of social production and crying out for rational re-organization:

Every society requires a regulation of power and labour. Why do we not set out to create it directly? Why do we not appoint skilled teachers to be masters of our apprentices, why does society accept blindly everyone who takes over an enterprise by the chance of birth or inheritance, although he may be totally unfit to instruct? . . . why is it that the fortuitous heir may still succeed into an important economic enterprise which is responsible for the good or bad fortune of a thousand workers, and, maybe for the adequate supply of certain goods to the whole of society? Anyone can see that society is in immediate need of a regulation of appointments. Our exposition has shown that the real successor who serves the economic functions of a concern is appointed by contract of employment, so that the heir need only play the part of possessor of a title to surplus value without performing any function. (1949, pp. 294-295)

I have quoted this passage at length because I think it gives the clearest indication of what Renner thought was really wrong with capitalism. At root for Renner capitalism is *morally* intolerable. But not only is it unfair that one parasitical section of the population should by accident benefit at the expense of others, it is *technically irrational* and *inefficient* in that the best qualified— i.e. rationally equipped—to put production into effect on behalf of society are excluded by private property. Such much is methodologically self-evident to the observer of social events—and ultimately to anyone who cares to look. It is the role of the theorist to make knowledge of the course of events available to all.

In sum, we might say that, for Marx 'socialized man' refers to a potential condition which is to be actualized in socialism, whilst Renner is referring to an actual condition which is to be, and now can be realized cognitively. Whereas for Marx socialism is achieved through and in class conflict, for Renner socialism is a condition of 'pure' knowledge, to be achieved through critical reflection. This is in essence the basis of what has been termed the 'neo-Kantian' epistemology of Austro-Marxism. Lichtheim gives the clearest summary:

In short, Marxian sociology was fully compatible with Kantian philosophy. More than that: Marx's analysis of social reality in *Capital* (a work not accidentally sub-titled *Critique of Political Economy*) had been essentially Kantian in spirit, seeing that his method consisted in isolating the logic of the economic process by abstracting from the surface phenomena present to mere uncritical reflection, and thus penetrating to the reality concealed behind them. For Marx as for Kant, the world of experience was not simply 'given', but mediated by the human mind. His theory was a 'critique' in the Kantian sense, specifically a critique of *society*. The latter was to be understood as a living totality of material forces and ideal (psychological) strivings, the social organism being subject to historical 'laws' (processes) which in the last resort yield a rational harmony of individual and social interests. Human activity (practice) realises the aims of philosophy, the latter being nothing but the ideal norms of human nature correctly understood, i.e. nature actuated by reason. (Lichtheim, 1961, pp. 305-306)

This reading of Marx was of enormous importance to Renner's analysis of law and the problem of transition which becomes one of the movement from largely unconscious organization to conscious regulation. Until the advent of socialism, 'actuated by reason', Renner tells us that: "Human society, unconscious or only half conscious of its own needs, drags itself forward, driven on by obscure urges." (p. 122)

From Renner's point of view we see that the transition to socialism is thus to be understood as the transition from organization to regulation, that is, from partial understanding to science, and in particular to the science of positive law.

Renner's Instrumentalism and the Science of Positive Law

For Renner and the Austro-Marxists knowledge of the natural sciences and knowledge of the normative order are analogous and methodologically compatible. As we have already seen, for Renner knowledge of the rational order (regulation) is rooted in the historical evolution of the objective social process, which, studied inductively, reveals its logic and telos:

> To decide the function of law in general we have to study inductively all social orders as they appear in the course of history, from the most primitive to the most highly developed. By this method we obtain the general categories of social order and at the same time the general functions of law. (1949, p. 59)

Order—in particular the orders of power, labour, goods and succession—is *a priori*, the concept is assumed in the very fact of social existence. In modern society the objective reality (organization/unconscious order) is given rational existence in the law. In the form of law and legal institutions what is rational becomes real and open to scientific investigation as a social fact. The *a priori* categories of social order are thus revealed in the 'inherent nature' of law. Thus Renner maintains that the study of 'legal science' has three separate parts: the study of the origin or evolution of law; the study of its social effects or function; and 'positive legal analysis' (1949, p. 54). Positive legal analysis is 'that part of legal theory' of which the object

> is to analyse the legal norms contained in the sum total of positive legal provisions, arranging them in accordance with their inherent nature, and to reduce them to a system. . . . We have to classify norms according to their constituent elements, which we will call 'legal characteristics'. (1949, p. 48)

Legal norms are thus 'things', to be identified and classified according to their implicit rational structure which ultimately accords with the rational ordering of society. Nonetheless law is to be considered as a system with its own independent structure, and the subject of particular technical competences, for

> However interesting these social repercussions (of law) may be to the lawyer as a side-line, they are the province of the economist and the sociologist. They lie outside the province of systematic legal analysis, just as the economic use of the tobacco leaf lies outside the province of botany. (1949, p. 48)

Of course, Renner recognizes that the law is a human product, made by people for the purpose of regulating their relations and dependencies. Yet, like its analysis, the positive law is itself independent of those relations. It is a mechanism at our disposal, to be set in motion and "co-ordinated" "like a cog to the whole machinery of social events" (p. 55). In short, *in its application*, the problem of law is that of technical-rational social engineering.

Renner's legal positivism thus occupies a particularly important place within the overall structure of his work. Firstly, it reinforces his contention that the problem of capitalist appropriation is entirely separate from that of the organization/regulation of the objective dependencies and inter-dependencies of man in society in general. So to say, it completes the separation of form and function, complementing his treatment of the imperative form of law as a-historical, a-social and neutral. Secondly, positive legal analysis — through critical reflection — provides the tools of socialist regulation. Thirdly, the reification of law which this entails, allows Renner to treat developed legal 'forms' or institutions of modern society — such as the 'legal association' and the contract of employment — as falling within the category of those 'material means and embryonic conditions', which as we saw earlier, Marx considered necessary to the creation of a socialist mode of production. This enables Renner to posit such institutions as analogous to any other product of applied science. The development of the science of law is thus one of 'the civilizing aspects of capital' just as Marx considered 'the uniting of labour with the natural sciences' to be. The problem is one of application of law, for

> . . . nearly all the legal forms which would be applicable in a socialist commonwealth are already now in existence, though their functions have not been fully developed. (1949, p. 83)

One such legal institution or legal form upon which Renner places particular significance is the legal association in the shape of the joint stock company:

> This previously insignificant legal institution has . . . deprived property of all functions connected with social production and reproduction, making property itself an inoperative and anti-social institution, to which only one function is left, that of obstructing the future development of society. (1949, p. 220)

Association and Regulation: Marx and Renner on The Joint Stock Company as The Form of Socialist Production

So far we have looked at the various assumptions which inform Renner's analysis. We have seen that for Renner regulation is a necessary feature of all societies and that this requires the expression of social relations as power relations between individual wills. The more the economic substratum has developed or 'evolved' the greater is the possibility of 'conscious' or rational regulation of social relations in the form of law. The problem of transition is then that of articulating the 'social power' through the state and dispossessing the capitalist as 'trustee' of that power.

For Renner the possibility of social revolution rests in the combination of economic/technical 'evolution' and rational regulation by society (i.e. the state). The most important problem faced in transition then is the transference of the *power* which is vested in the capitalist by virtue of ownership of private property to the state. The abolition of private property is critical as it signals the abolition of the private, irrational exercise of social power.

For Renner the development of the Joint Stock Company is the most significant movement in this direction. It represents the redundancy and ultimately the transcendence of the power of the *individual capitalist* and the implementation of a progressively more rational system of regulated production. This instances the optimistic emphasis placed in Austro-Marxist work upon the progressive aspects of capitalism and the belief that material conditions for socialist transformation were already present at the time.

In this section we shall see how Renner emphasizes the *power* of the individual capitalist, rather than *social relations* of capitalist production, and thereby plays down the need for a transformation of the *class* relations of capitalist society in the transition to socialism. In its place he promotes rational regulation — embodied in the development of 'public' institutions which displace the property related institutions of private law. Rational regulation, as instanced in the legal form of the joint stock company, thus becomes a condition precedent to socialism rather than a product of a classless social order.

For Marx on the other hand, the development of the Joint Stock Company is an instance of the *social* basis of capitalist production becoming more apparent, but it is no more *socialist* for all that. So long as the basic social relation of capital (the continued existence of a class of capital and a class of labour) remains the basic structuring force, the Joint Stock Company remains no more than a specific form of capitalist organization. For Marx the transition to socialism entails much more than an alternative mode of *regulating* production. It is not a question of *who* exercises the 'social' power, but under what social conditions that power is exercised. Capital is then a *social relation* rather than a simple *power relation*.

In this section we shall look in detail at the analyses given by Marx and Renner of the Joint Stock Company in order to bring out these differences. The argument is quite complex, and of relevance to a number of issues of wider political importance, particularly the whole question of so-called 'people's capitalism', and worker participation and control in industry. It has direct implications for the theoretical argument variously employed that the movement from 'gesellschaft' to 'bureaucratic-administrative' forms of law represents a fundamental shift from one 'type' of society to another. The analysis in this section could be elaborated to question such ideas. Indeed Renner's thesis has been drawn on to justify precisely this line of argument as put forward strongly by amongst others Kamenka and Tay.[6] Space precludes any such consideration here, and I simply draw attention to the implication of the argument in that connection.

The purpose here however is less ambitious. It is simply to counterpose to Renner's concern with political power and the use of law, an emphasis upon the social relations of capitalism and to claim a priority for the latter in terms of achieving transition. Concentration on rational regulation at the expense of considering the social relations upon which and within which political power is and can be effective, runs the risk of leaving the class forces of capital out of the equation. At the same time, however, changes in the form of the legal and political regulation of capitalist production relations must not be neglected.

Throughout his work, Renner points to the supercession of private ownership of capital by the Joint Stock Company, to the extension of credit, loan facilities and banking, to the co-operative movement etc. as empirical evidence of the rationalization of social production. In each case he emphasizes that such developments serve to display (1) the implicit social basis of capitalist production as demonstrative of the empirical reality of socialized man, and (2) the functional redundancy of both private property to organized production and the capitalist as the 'trustee' of the 'social power of command'.

In his analysis of legal development Renner maintains that the functional efficiency of capitalist production requires the continuing elaboration of complementary legal institutions—such as the various forms of contract as described in Chapter 2, ii—if private property is to extend beyond its original functional limitation to the 'own and patrimony' of simple commodity exchange. The different forms of credit—mortgage, bailment, loan—are central to this process in the later period of *laissez-faire* capitalism, but still complementary to the institution of private property. The progressive concentration of capital and the increased scale of the economic enterprise, however, ushers in the period of finance capitalism and with it private property becomes functionally redundant as a means of organizing production, in so far as the scale of social production has broken beyond the limits of personal wealth and property. Under such conditions the Joint Stock Company is (correctly) identified by Renner as the cornerstone of extended capitalist accumulation and reproduction. Thus the joint stock company functions to bring together the 'particles' of the total social capital, which were previously aggregated through the market mechanism. It is then one of the two mechanisms whereby capitals attract—the other being take-over and merger in the market—which demonstrate the tendency even within capitalism to establish production as explicitly social.

At this point Renner introduces a distinction—crucial to his analysis—between what he terms 'legal' and 'economic property'. Thus the *shareholders*, who exercise *economic ownership*,

> ... without having the right of ownership, utilise a part of the functions of property for their own purposes. The legal institution of property no longer comprises its whole material content. The contract of obligation, [the shareholders' right is contractual—R.K.] itself an institution complementary to ownership (formally), absorbs property by taking over its principal functions, thus opening and revealing the true character of property as a mere title to surplus value. This example shows us that economic ownership is clearly distinguishable from its original form, that of legal property. (1949, p. 276)

Thus, whilst the shareholders' economic property—'title to surplus value'—is now secured through a contractual right to a share in the profits of the enterprise, legal property is vested in the joint stock company.

Bearing in mind the differences in terminology, there is also a very different emphasis in Renner's work from the notion current today of the myriad of small shareholders who are deemed to 'own' but not to 'control' the enterprise. For Renner—writing at the turn of the century—the significance of the joint stock company was two-fold. On the one hand, it is to be seen as an association of *capitalists*, whose economic property takes the form of shareholdings. Whilst on the other hand Renner recognizes the formal or legal property right of the company which is to be construed in terms of the *organising function* of paid managerial staff. The functions of organization of production and appropriation are thus clearly separated and distinguished in the division of legal and economic property.

The identification of shareholder and capitalist is of the essence to Renner's argument that the capitalist, and thereby capitalism, has become redundant. The formation of the joint stock company, according to Renner, is primarily a means of bringing together relatively large units of capital, which, individually, are nonetheless insufficient for the purposes of extended capitalist production. These 'shareholder-capitalists' are, quite simply, too small to exist *in their own right*; if they do not combine, they will be swallowed up in competition. Furthermore, from the point of view of the capitalists themselves, the 'association' has the added attraction that, in giving up 'legal' ownership to the company, they are also rid of the requirement to dirty their hands with the mundane tasks of day-to-day management. The capitalist is no longer a functioning capitalist. In Renner's terms, the 'social power of command' has been given over to the salaried manager, who by virtue of the institution of the contract of employment, becomes the new trustee of power. The capitalist on the other hand is revealed for what he is—a parasite, sucking the surplus value out of the system of social production for his personal use. For all practical purposes then, the 'shareholder-capitalist' is redundant, and the rational organization of production is identified with management and the 'technical expert' (1949, p. 283).

The assumptions which guide Renner's analysis can be itemized:
1. the joint stock company is functionally necessary in conditions of extended capitalist production;
2. the functions of organization and appropriation are divided in practice, the latter being divorced from 'legal property';
3. the capitalist is identified as shareholder—the owner of 'economic property' —and a parasitic 'class of associated capitalists' comes into being (p. 286).

Class relations are external to production, so that, even within the capitalist mode of production itself, the abolition of capitalism requires no more than the dispossession of the capitalist. It is within this framework that Renner interprets Marx's statement that the joint stock company announces 'the abolition of private capital within the framework of capitalist production itself' (Marx, 1974, Vol. 3, p. 436). Thus Renner writes:

> The social function of property where it is held by the joint stock company, is in the first place to deprive the economic owner himself of his functions and to expose his superfluity; secondly to bring about the self-abolition of property even within a capitalist system of production, for even to the law the owner is either no longer owner or merely one among a multitude of owners without influence; and finally to transfer the capitalist function to paid managers, so that the contract of employment . . . takes over the last remaining function of general service to the community as a whole, of those fulfilled by the institution of property. (1949, p. 220)

Each of the propositions put forward may be contested empirically and with hindsight each is at best dubious.[7] However, a more fundamental objection can be made, which goes to the root of Renner's analysis: namely, that the formation of the joint stock company and the transfer of 'power' from the capitalist to the salaried manager, in no way presupposes or facilitates a transformation of the class relations upon which capitalist production rests. As we shall see, with the advent of joint stock, production is merely released from the control of private property in the market. It is nonetheless capitalist production.

In *Capital III*, in the chapter on 'The Role of Credit in Capitalist Production', Marx analyses the place of the joint stock company in the development of capitalism. This very short and conceptually dense chapter is of particular significance as it also provides Marx's most comprehensive statement on the transition to socialism within the context of his analysis in Capital. We shall see that there are major differences between Renner and Marx on the question of the role of the joint stock company in the transition to socialism, and that these rest in Renner's conflation of three distinct aspects of Marx's analysis. Thus, we shall see that Marx seeks, firstly, to place the historical development of joint stock in the particular conditions and contradictions of *commodity circulation*, and not in the organization of capitalist production as does Renner. It was in respect of commodity circulation that Marx wrote of "private production without the control of private property" (1974, Vol. 3, p. 438). Secondly, once Marx has analysed the role of credit and joint stock as a means of escaping the limits of personal wealth as a market regulator, he then considers their effect in terms of the *subsequent* development of capitalist production and the *concentration* of capital. In this context Marx refers to joint stock as "the abolition of capital as private property" — elsewhere *"private capital"* — "within the framework of capitalist production itself" (1974, Vol. 3, p. 436). We should note that nowhere does Marx suggest that the abolition of capital as private property amounts to the abolition of the capitalist mode of production. Finally, Marx considers the possibilities for transition unfolded in the consequent changes internal to capitalism. Here he speaks of the joint stock company as setting conditions for a potential "reconversion of capital into the property of associated producers, as outright *social property*" (1974, Vol. 3, p. 437).

Marx thus raises three different conceptual problems relating to changes in the form of property and capital: (1) the change from private property to joint stock; (2) the change from private capital to social capital; these pave the way for (3) a fundamental and revolutionary transformation of social capital to social property.

Renner's analysis serves a very different end. By concentrating upon the legal form solely as a mode of regulation, Renner can view the joint stock company as a *post hoc rationalization* of the advanced capitalist 'method of production'. Whereas Marx sees joint stock as a particular form of capital, Renner regards the legal form as an autonomous, rational construct which is 'neither capitalist, socialist nor feudal', 'private capital' and 'social property' and takes various statements and propositions out of context to justify his own conception of the 'abolition of the capitalist method of production', namely through the dispossession of the individual capitalist.

Reduced to its bare elements, Marx's analysis of the role of credit and the joint stock company in relation to commodity circulation is as follows. Throughout *Capital* Marx sought to demonstrate and analyse the processes whereby, *inter alia*, capital strives to maintain the continuous and uninterrupted flow of the production process. This is a necessary 'movement' of capitalist production for the simple reason that surplus value is created only in production. Any interruption of the production process is therefore to be avoided or at least minimized. However, in so far as surplus value in the form of the commodities produced must be realized in the market (circulation) before it can be returned into the production process as capital (the metamorphosis of commodities), the total process is subject to repeated hiatus. To this end, there will be the constant endeavour to reduce time 'wasted' in circulation—time is money. In the best of all capitalist worlds there would be circulation without circulation time, but clearly this can never be more than a fiction.

The provision of credit, however, is a step in this direction. By raising credit *against the time* when market conditions are—or are hoped to be—most advantageous, realization of surplus value can be delayed, whilst allowing the production process to continue *meantime*. Of course, ultimately, that surplus value must be realized, but in the short term at least, *capital is released from the immediate control of private property in the market-place*. This then is the basis to Marx's reference to 'private production without the control of private property'. However, one unintended consequence of relevance here relates to the question of management. For, Marx observes, where credit is advanced on any large scale:

> . . . a large part of the social capital is employed by people who do not own it and who consequently tackle things quite differently than the owner, who anxiously weighs the limitations of his private capital in so far as he handles it himself. (1974, Vol. 3, p. 441)

We shall look at the significance of the distinction between private and social capital presently; for the moment let us note that, whilst credit "helps keep the act of buying and selling further apart in time" (p. 436) it serves at the time to:

> . . . develop the *incentive* of capitalist production, enrichment through exploitation of others, to the purest and most colossal form of gambling and swindling. (1974, Vol. 3, p. 441, emphasis added)

i.e., through reckless speculation both by those who raise and by those who give credit. Thus, in respect to the incentive of capitalist production, Marx more than relies upon Adam Smith's criticisms of the management of joint stock companies:

> The directors of such companies . . . being the managers rather of other people's money than their own, it cannot well be expected that they should watch over it with the same anxious vigilance with which the partners in a private co-partnery frequently watch over their own. Like the stewards of a rich man, they are apt to consider attention to small matters as not for their masters honour, and very easily give themselves a dispensation from having it. Negligence and profusion, therefore, must always prevail, more or less, in the management of such a company. (Smith, 1819, Vol. 3, p. 141)

Marx's echo of Smith's comments clearly sits uneasily with Renner's treatment of what he terms the manager's "gift" — "the art of giving orders and of managing men and things, the ability to make quick decisions are the result alike of natural endowment and of efficient training" (p. 143). It should be noted, however, that by the time Renner was writing, the legal form of the joint stock company had itself been developed to counter fraudulent misuse and in this respect to act as a substitute for the control of private property. Thus the powers, rights and duties of company directors in relation to shareholders were defined with more or less precision, and procedures designed to secure accountability to shareholders, public disclosure etc. were implemented giving at least a semblance of order to the stock company as a means of raising credit.[8] This of course in no way changes the central role of the stock company, which, as with the entire credit system: ". . . rests on the necessity of expanding and leaping over the barrier to circulation and the sphere of exchange" (Marx, 1973, p. 416). For Renner, on the other hand, 'private production without private property' signalled the end of capitalism itself, heralded by the rise of managerialism.

Once the joint stock company has been established as a means of raising credit on the promise of a future share of surplus-value yet to be realized in the market, Marx points out that it sets the conditions for "an enormous expansion of the scale of production and of enterprise that was impossible for individual capitals" (1974, Vol. 3, p. 436). Through this process of concentration, individual capitals are aggregated as joint stock. As such, *capital*, Marx tells us, is:

> . . . directly endowed with the form of social capital . . . *as distinct from* private capital, and its undertakings assume the form of social undertakings *as distinct from* private undertakings. (1974, Vol. 3, p. 436, emphases added)

Marx's point here is that capital is dissociated from personal wealth and no longer appears to be identical to the person of the individual capitalist or entrepreneur. The capitalist is no longer the personification of capital; capital has assumed the form of social capital, which Marx also refers to as 'the capital of associated individuals'.

It is at this point that we should emphasize that for Marx *capital* must not be regarded as a 'thing' to be owned and controlled by any particular individual or group of individuals. That which is owned and controlled is the means of production, and they only become capital when set to work, or rather *put in use* under particular social conditions; capital is a social relation, not a simple power relation.

> Whatever the social form of production, labourers and means of production always remain factors of it. But in a state of separation from each other either of these factors can be such only potentially. For production to go on at all

they must unite. The specific manner in which this union is accomplished distinguishes the different economic epochs of the structure of society from one another. (1974, Vol. 2, pp. 36-37)

Marx describes in detail this process whereby, under capitalism, social relations appear as things, in his analysis of the fetishism of commodities. However, this need not delay us at this point, beyond reiterating the main point that capital is not a thing but a *social relation*, and the determining question is not 'who, in particular, owns (or controls) the means of production', but 'how are workers united with the means of production'. Hence Marx tells us that "the separation of the free worker from his means of production is the starting point" (1974, Vol. 2, p. 37). Thus, capital may assume the form of 'private capital' or 'social capital'—i.e. as a possession or property of individuals or associated individuals—precisely because the nature of the union of workers and the means of production in the wage form remain unchanged.

In relation to Renner's analysis it is important to emphasize that when Marx says that capital is endowed with the form of 'social capital or associated producers', he says nothing to suggest that the social relation of capital or, in Renner's terms, 'the capitalist method of production' has been abolished. Furthermore, from the point of view of capital as a social relation, it matters not whether the individual capitalist is separated from the enterprise or is an actually functioning capitalist who manages the enterprise on his own behalf. What, for Marx, *is* significant about the form of capital as social capital, however, is the enormous expansion of production which it engenders. Yet, in this respect, precisely because Renner sees the joint stock company as an *effect of* the concentration of capital, he misses its real significance in relation to the transition to socialism.

As well as advancing the material means of production necessary to a socialist mode of production, Marx argues that the concentration of social capital in the form of joint stock serves to heighten awareness of the class basis of the capitalist mode of production. Thus profit, in the form of dividends and interest:

> . . . appears . . . as a mere appropriation of the surplus-labour of others, arising from the conversion of means of production into capital, i.e. from their alienation *vis-à-vis* the actual producer, from their antithesis as another's property to every individual actually at work in production, from the manager down to the last day labourer. (1974, Vol. 3, p. 437)

It is in this context that Marx refers to the joint stock company as "the ultimate development of capitalist production", the *result of which* is "a necessary transitional phase *towards* the reconversion of capital into the property of producers, although no longer as the private property of the individual producers, but rather as the property of associated producers, as outright social property" (1974, Vol. 3, p. 437, emphasis added). Note here that the stock company is only the precursor to a transitional phase—which Marx identifies as the workers co-operative—and that this itself is only a step towards the conversion of the means of production into social property. In so far as the stock company represents capital as social capital:

> . . . the conversion (of the social means of production) into the form of stock still remains ensnared within the trammels of capitalism; hence instead of overcoming the antithesis between the character of wealth as social and as private wealth, the stock companies merely develop it in a new form. (1974, Vol. 3, p. 440)

Thus we can see that for Marx the change of the legal form (the joint stock company) does indeed represent a qualitative change in the form of property. The legal institution of *private* property is displaced by the joint stock company which requires alternative forms of regulation. The contradiction between private and social wealth continues in the appropriation by *capital* of the surplus social product and as such remains unresolved; for the reason that the social relation of capital remains untransformed. We can see from Renner's treatment of the Joint Stock Company how, as a consequence of his analysis of the legal relation simply in terms of power (i.e. as a relation between individual wills, rather than upon the social relation obtaining between class forces), he underestimates the nature and extent of social transformation. The problem is reduced to one of the power of the individual capitalist. In his analysis he tends to assume that once productivity rises as a result of a developed technological infrastructure and division of labour, a transfer of power is all that is required to ensure 'rational regulation'. The state (the order of power) serves to guarantee the rational division of labour both in society and in the workplace (the order of labour) and to secure a planned distribution of the social product (order of goods). As such the necessary and sufficient conditions of socialism are realized.

Conclusion: The Open Questions of Jurisprudence

Renner concludes the *Institutions* with the following appeal:

> Given that, like all else under the sun, norms have their causes, wherein do these lie? Given that they enjoy a real existence what are its characteristics, what is the mode of their existence and how do they change? Given that their origin lies in the conditions of life of the human race, that they are nothing more than a means of preserving society, what part do they actually play in the existence and development of our own generation?

> These are the open questions of jurisprudence. The time has come to engage in an attempt at their solution. (1949, pp. 299-300)

My main purpose in this essay has been to draw out the basic axioms of Renner's work with the aim of rendering a key Marxist text more accessible to criticism. It is remarkable that so little attention has been paid to Renner's work over the past 10 or 15 years, especially given the renewed interest in Marxism and the law. In part at least this must be due to the inaccessibility to English readers of the basic texts of Austro-Marxism, in part to the density and twists of Renner's own approach in the *Institutions*, and in large part, as I suggested earlier, to the particular shape of post-war European labour politics. Given the tone of my own comments and the unfavourable comparisons I have made with Marx's analyses in *Capital*, it may seem even more surprising that I should insist that Renner's work should nonetheless be considered as a key Marxist text— however imprecise the term 'marxist' may be.

So, to conclude this essay, I want to emphasize the more positive contribution Renner has made, and to be more generous in support of his conception of the general role and place for a socialist jurisprudence. For reasons which I hope by now are self-evident, the particular questions asked of jurisprudence in the passage cited above are inadequate. However, at the more general level my reason for claiming that Renner's work remains 'marxist' is not hard to find. Quite simply, it boils down to what I think both Marx and Renner shared, even though it directed their analyses in critically different ways: namely, a shared commitment to and vision of a socialist future which from beginning to end informs their respective works.

Conventional social science frowns upon such statements. More importantly, so do many Marxists. Marxism, we are frequently told, is also a 'science'; it does not speculate or provide 'blue-prints for the future'. But, what is the value of a critical and radical theory if it has no explicit conception of material *possibilities* and desired *alternatives* to the present? These are prerequisites of intervention. They dictate that theory elaborates standards against which to evaluate present conditions, future possibilities and immediate political practice. In terms of the Marxist analysis of law, Renner more than any other writer, attempts to provide such criteria. He fails and we should be aware of how and why he fails, but his importance lies in the attempt to politicize legal theory, jurisprudence and the law. In this his work is exceptional.

I would emphasize, then, that my criticisms of Renner have centred in the main upon the inadequacies of his analysis of bourgeois law and its uses in the transition to socialism. Thus, despite the many deficiencies in analysis, I would be less than critical of Renner's concept of law were its application restricted to the specific problems of socialist organization and to the political tasks of socialism. In this respect the particular value of Renner's work is, I think, to have articulated a concept of law which is appropriate to and adequate to the needs of a transformed mode of production, although, as we have seen, in practical detail—for example, democratic institutions of law enforcement—the work is woefully inadequate.

To an extent, however, this can be seen as a side issue. If we accept the main thesis of Renner's work that socialist society requires regulation in the form of law, and that, within socialism, law and its enforcement requires the 'conscious' exercise of political power, then a jurisprudence of the ends, uses and limits of legal intervention is a self-evident necessity. The disasters and self-created impotences of leftist beliefs in the withering away of the law and the state are in themselves adequate justification of such assumptions. Once we follow Renner's lead, however, the questions facing Marxism are not simply those of exposing the class interests and biases embodied in the law, nor even of displaying the more complex class form of bourgeois law. If we accept that socialism requires the regulation of production and, as Marx put it, that 'freedom begins only where (not when—RK) labour which is determined by necessity and mundane considerations ceases' then the problems of a socialist jurisprudence and the uses of law are of unique importance in the construction of the material base to such freedom.

Within this framework the Austro-Marxist conception of socialism and Renner's concept of law is one in which socialized man is realized as a *political* actor. In the last section we saw the limitations of such an approach when applied to the analysis of the historical development of capitalist regulation. But if applied to a socialist mode of production, what is entailed is a vision of the future in which conflict and contradiction are not resolved by the dawn of socialism—socialism is not to be equated with consensus. Rather socialist forms of organization are presented as a process in which *political* struggle has displaced *class* struggle and in which the choice of alternative ends rather than the class control and disposal of means dictates the character of the political-legal process itself. The object is not the resolution of all differences, but the politicizing of disputes through direct mass democracy. This, I believe to be at the root of Renner's otherwise rather alarming equation of state and society.

The broad aims of Renner's jurisprudence can thus be seen to fall into three related categories, though it should be said again that these are implicit and need to be read out of his work. It should also be re-emphasized that in arguing for the necessary presence of a socialist jurisprudence within contemporary Marxism, in my view, the particular questions of bourgeois law addressed by Renner would have no place.

Firstly, then, Renner is right, in my view, to emphasize that the starting point must be the material need for socialist forms of regulation and control, and the rejection of idealist claims, that with the advent of socialism, law and legal regulation will be redundant. Secondly, a socialist jurisprudence would assert the priority of a *political* concept of law, its use and its enforcement as a central feature of a socialist mode of production. In the 'mundane' field of production choices and decisions will remain, policies and programmes will require to be implemented and enforced in detail and in the face of opposition. This would require the implementation of procedures and the elaboration of criteria of political evaluation—not merely those of technical rational calculability. Thus, thirdly, a socialist jurisprudence would provide at the same moment the criteria and standards against which to evaluate the possibilities and inadequacies of bourgeois law and modes of regulation. Only then can present questions of, for example, the protection of individual rights or the implementation of systems of public accountability be formulated as socialist demands.

All of these aims Renner attempts to fulfil in the *Institutions*. Indeed if the book is read from this point of view, rather than as an account of the role of law in the development of capitalist social relations, then all which is good, as well as all that is bad in the work, surfaces very clearly. For what we see is that Renner was not really concerned to analyse the institutions of bourgeois private law so much as to project and legitimate the Austro-Marxist conception of socialism and his own conception of socialist legality. Thus in his analysis, Renner is trying to demonstrate the extent to which the development of bourgeois law is in accord with and supports his own preconceptions. His teleogical account of the necessary evolution of regulation thus masks his initial commitment to a socialist future. In consequence we are presented with a highly selective empirical history of bourgeois law, which, methodologically suspect from the outset, emphasizes the non-contradictory, progressive aspects of the law at the expense of historical contradiction. In short, Renner misuses the implicit criterion of socialist legality to ride roughshod over history and to demonstrate the inevitability of socialism itself.

On the other hand, we see that in order to break out of the unconscious movement of historical progress and the political impasse in which he finds himself Renner invokes rationalist criteria of legal intervention—again but inconsistently by reference to his conception of socialist legality—against which to judge and to assess the immediate practical implications of the 'emergent' rationality of bourgeois legal institutions. This permits him to speak not only of the unconscious misuse of law, but also the rational use and deliberate abuse of law.

In doing so, however, Renner at least provides a guide to immediate political action and attempts to forge the elusive link between theory and practice. In this his work can usefully be counterposed to the more sophisticated, yet politically nihilist analyses of Pashukanis, whose work suffers precisely because of his refusal to countenance any place for jurisprudence within Marxist 'science'. Yet clearly Renner has provided neither an adequate analysis of bourgeois law, nor in consequence has he grounded his jurisprudential project within an historical analysis of persuasive value. Put crudely this is precisely *the* open question of a socialist jurisprudence: Historical materialism, if it is to lay claim to the political future, must generate from within its analyses of bourgeois law an understanding of the form and criteria of socialist legality. Renner realized the necessity, but lost his way. Marx frequently pointed out that capitalism both civilizes and brutalizes. Bourgeois justice constantly reveals this to us. Renner chose only to see the good.

Notes

1. The *Institutions of Private Law and their Social Function* was first published under the title 'Die Social Funktion des Rechtsinstitute' in *Marx-Studien, Blätter zur Theorie und Politik des wissenschaftlichen Sozialismus*, Vol. 1, Wienervolksbuch-handlung, (Vienna 1904). It was revised in 1929 and republished as *Die Rechtsinstitute des Privatrechts und ihre Sozial Funktion*, Wienervolksbuchhandlung, 1929. This edition was published in English in 1949, edited with an introduction and notes by Otto Kahn-Freund and reprinted in 1976.
2. The first edition of the *Institutions* appeared under one of Renner's pseudonyms, 'Karner'. Renner also published under the names of 'Rudolf Springer' and 'Josef Hammer'. Renner utilized such pseudonyms not for fear of political repression, but on account of his position in the civil service.
3. See note 1. above.
4. Cf. Bottomore and Goode (1978), especially the Introduction by Tom Bottomore.
5. This is obviously too bald a statement. Throughout their history, but especially after the war, party unity was a recurrent problem and theme of SDP conferences. The reconciliation of left and right, and the satisfaction of the more radical interests and aspirations of the industrial workers as well as those of the more conservative rural and urban SDP constituencies, was always high on the political agenda. The degree to which this realpolitik was effective can perhaps be gauged by the lack of support obtained by the Communists in the industrial areas.

   By 1929, when Renner revised the *Institutions*, he had lost considerable ground in the leadership to the more left politics of Otto Bauer. Bauer, whose commitment to the democratic process again cannot be in any doubt, nonetheless urged a strategy of revolutionary politics where democratic gains were threatened by counter 'social' revolution. By this time however Renner was politically committed to 'legitimate' constitutional means alone, and on many occasions was roundly condemned by the left. This rightward drift did not however substantially affect the theoretical structure of the *Institutions*. Clearly certain revisions evidence a strengthened emphasis upon the potential of law reform but nonetheless within the limits of 'efficacy' as originally analysed. Equally a detailed textual comparison of the second edition of Bernstein (1879) reveals that Renner was not unsympathetic to aspects of Bernstein's work, but in the main body of the text at least he remains faithful to the tenets of Austro-Marxism.
6. See the series of essays by E. Kamenka and A. Tay, reproduced in the 'Ideas & Ideologies' series, Edward Arnold, 1978.
7. Cf. Hirst (1979), pp. 96-176.
8. The legal definition of directors' powers has always remained problematic. Proverbially in 'hard cases' reference is made to 'reasonable business practice', which in itself builds into legal restriction an openness to 'acceptable' entrepreneurial risk-taking. In this context the elaboration of business ethics in Stock Exchange regulations must be seen to supplement case law and legislative controls.

References

Adler, M. (1904). *Kansalitat und Teleologie in Streite un die Wissenschaft*, Marx-Studien, Vol. One.
Adler, M. (1908). *Marx als Denker*, Berlin.
Adler, M. (1925). *Kaut und Marxismus*, Berlin.
Althusser, L. (1970). *Reading Capital*. New Left Books, London.
Bauer, O. (1910). *Die Nationalitaten Frage und die Sozialdemocrazie*. Marx-Studien, Volume Two.
Bernstein, E. (1899) (1961). *Evolutionary Socialism*. Schoken Books, New York.
Bottomore, T. and Goode, P. (1978). *Austro-Marxism*. Oxford University Press, Oxford.
Buttinger, J. (1954). *Twilight of Socialism*. Weidenfeld and Nicholson, London.
Fisher, F. (1974). *An Opposing Man*. Allen Lane, London.
Follis, C. (1961). *The Austrian Social Democratic Party, June 1914-November 1918*. Stanford University Doctoral Thesis.
Friedmann, W. (1950). "The Function of Property in Modern English Law", *British Journal of Sociology* 240-259.
Gulick, C. (1948). *Austria from Habsburg to Hitler*. University of California Press, Berkeley.
Hall, S. (1979). *Drifting Into a Law and Order Society*. The Cobden Trust, London.
Hannak, J. (1965). *Karl Renner und seine Zeit*. Vienna.
Hilferding, R. (1910) (1981). *Finance Capital*. Routledge and Kegan Paul, London.
Hirst, P. (1979). *On Law and Ideology*. Macmillan, London.
Kahn-Freund, O. (1949). "Introduction" in Renner, K. *The Institutions of Private Law and Their Social Function*. Routledge and Kegan Paul, London.
Lenin, V. I. (1901). *Materialism and Empirico-Criticism*, Collected Works, Volume XIII.
Leser, N. (1965). "Karl Renner, Ban und Lehrmeister" *Zukunft* 10.
Leser, N. (1968). *Zwischen Reformismus und Bolschewismus, Der Austro Marxismus, Als Theorie und Praxis*. Europa Verlag, Vienna.
Loew, R. (1979). "The Politics of Austro-Marxism", *New Left Review* **118**, 15-51.
Marx, K. (1973). *Grundrisse*. Penguin Books, London.
Marx, K. (1974). *Capital*, Three Volumes. Lawrence and Wishart, London.
Renner, K. (1901). *Staat und Parlament* (Pseudonym, Rudolf Springer). Wienervolksbuch-handlung.
Renner, K. (1904). *Die Sozial Funktion der Rechtsinstitute*, Marx-Studien, Volume One.
Renner, K. (1914). *Die Nation als Rechtsidee und die Internationale*. Wienervolksbuch-handlung.
Renner, K. (1916). *Österreichs Erneuerung. Politische-programmatische Aufsatze*, Two volumes. Franz Deuticke, Vienna.
Renner, K. (1917). *Marxismus, Krieg und Internationale*. J. H. W. Dietz, Stuttgart.
Renner, K. (1929). *Die Rechtsinstitute des Privatrechts und ihre Sozial Funktion*. Wienervolksbuchhandlung.
Renner, K. (1946). *An der Wende zweier Zeiten: Lebenserinnerungen*. Danubia Verlag, Vienna.
Renner, K. (1949) (1976). *The Institutions of Private Law and Their Social Functions*. Routledge and Kegan Paul, London.
Robson, P. (1977). "Renner Revisited" in *Perspectives in Jurisprudence* (Attwooll, E., Ed.). Glasgow University Press, Glasgow.
Smith, A. (1819). *The Wealth of Nations*. Edinburgh.
Trotsky, L. (1975). *My Life*. Penguin Books, London.

Further Reading

There is surprisingly little available in English on Renner's work in particular and on Austro-Marxism in general. For many years, Renner (1949) remained the only Austro-Marxist text to have been translated, although Hilferding (1910) (1981) has recently been published in an English language version.

General texts on Austro-Marxism available in English

Bottomore and Goode (1978)
This is the most comprehensive Austro-Marxist 'reader' available. It contains extracts from many of the most significant contributions from the leading theorists of the movement, including Max Adler, Otto Bauer, Hilferding and Renner. Tom Bottomore's introduction provides a very useful introduction to the theory of the 'neo-Kantians' Marxism, and emphasizes the methodological assumptions common to the school.

Buttinger (1954)
This work describes Buttinger's first hand experience of the collapse of the Social Democratic movement and the response of the left to Dolfuss's fascism.

Fischer (1974)
Fischer experienced the Austro-Marxist movement from the outside both as a left intellectual and as a member of the Communist Party. This autobiography gives an extremely sensitive, impressionistic account of the culture and politics of Vienna throughout the period.

Follis (1961)
An extensive analysis of Austro-Marxism, which provides detailed material on the social background of the movement and its leaders.

Gulick (1948)
This history of the Republic provides the most detailed account of the period available. It provides a reasonable outline of the theory of the Austro-Marxists, but goes on to document in extraordinary detail the implementation of policy and the politics of compromise into which the Party was frequently forced. Renner's individual political role is described fully. Of particular interest is his closeness to Hans Kelsen.

Lenin (1901)
Although not directed exclusively against the Austro-Marxists, in this very substantial work, Lenin attacks the attempt to build into Marxism Mach's

conception of evolution and history which informs the Austro-Marxist conception of economic development and social evolution.

Loew's critique (1979) considers Austro-Marxism to be a harbinger of Euro-communism.

Selected Austro-Marxist texts

Two works in particular were crucial to the formulation of Renner's ideas in the Institutions, both of which were in preparation and appeared contemporaneously:

Adler (1904)
In this work, Adler provides the philosophical analysis of neo-Kantian Marxism which informed Renner's derivation of the 'categories of order'. Substantial parts of this essay are extracted in Bottomore and Goode (op.cit.).

Hilferding (1910) (1981)
This work also appeared in Marx-Studien, Vol. 1 alongside Renner (1949) and Adler (1904). Theoretically however Hilferding stands apart from other Viennese Marxists; and methodologically he remains much closer to Marx. The significance of Hilferding's work for Renner rests primarily at the empirical level.

Other works of general interest include: Adler (1908) and (1925); and Bauer (1910).

Major texts of Karl Renner

Renner (1901), (1904), (1914), (1916), (1917), (1929), (1949), (1976) and (1946).

Commentaries on Renner (1949) available in English

Friedman (1950); Hirst (1979), pp. 96–176; Kahn-Freund (1949); and Robson (1977).

Biographical and other accounts

Renner (1946); Hannak (1965); Leser (1965) and (1968).

3 Pashukanis and The Commodity Form Theory

Ronnie Warrington

Introduction

Surprising though it now seems, just prior to the worst years of Stalinism, a startling success was achieved by a Bolshevik jurist who argued, quite literally, that law was about to be made superfluous. E. B. Pashukanis was the undisputed leader of the Soviet legal theorists of the 1920's and early 1930's and though little progress was actually made in transforming the legal practice of the period up to 1930 and beyond, Pashukanis, Krylenko and their colleagues worked ceaselessly towards the goal of a future society not dependent on legal control. They annually produced draft criminal codes consistent with the aim of the withering away of law, though none were taken up (Sharlet, 1978, p. 181). But the effect in the law schools of the Pashukanis movement was more than theoretical. The law schools were purged of bourgeois influences and the disarray in legal studies was remarkable. Students were instructed to write essays on the pointlessness of their own studies, and in the somewhat rarified atmosphere of those law schools that existed, a real prospect of the imminent end to legal studies overwhelmed both student and teacher. Nowhere was the "theory/practice distinction" more marked, and it is therefore necessary to distinguish between "the salient characteristics of the real or actual legal process in place in Soviet Society at a given time and those characteristics associated with the Marxian ideal of 'withering away' of law" (Sharlet, 1977, pp. 157-158).

The "paens of praise" (Sharlet, 1974, p. 111) with which Pashukanis's *General Theory* was received in the 1920's in Russia, when each new edition seemed, "to call forth a more positive response" (Sharlet, 1974, p. 110) have been matched

Law, State and Society Series: "Legality, Ideology and the State", edited by D. Sugarman, 1983. Academic Press, London and New York.

by the enthusiastic rediscovery in the West of this powerful, but enigmatic work. This rediscovery was fuelled by the publication of readable translations of his work (Pashukanis, 1978, 1980[1]). This paper is a further contribution to the debate on Pashukanis. It attempts to restate the important facets of Pashukanis's theory, and outline some evaluations. The four sections of the paper examine Pashukanis's object and method, his commodity form theory, some criticisms of the theory and finally Pashukanis's commitment to the withering away of law.

It is sometimes forgotten that the *General Theory* always remained a preliminary draft. The turmoil of the period in which it was written, Pashukanis's own prodigious output of other work and ultimately the political repression which destroyed him, all prevented Pashukanis preparing the more definitive text to which the *General Theory* was supposed to be a mere prelude. But the limitations of Pashukanis's work do not vitiate his whole enterprise. The problems of the theory do not destroy some interesting insights.

Section 1: The Object of the Theory and Pashukanis's Method

History and object

Pashukanis saw legal theory as an historical enquiry, historical in at least two important senses. It was historical in that an understanding of bourgeois forms of law required a historical approach to the question of law because law was a result of a specific stage of social development only. Much of Pashukanis's work was based on this historical premise, though unfortunately, Pashukanis's historical assumptions often turn out to be untenable. But Pashukanis's theory is also historical in a second, perhaps more fundamental sense. Pashukanis saw the function of the jurisprudence of his day as more than mere development of legal concepts. For Pashukanis, the task of Marxist theory of law was to demonstrate that law was only to exist for a limited time and that it would shortly begin its final process of withering away. The legal form, writes Pashukanis, "only encompasses us within its narrow horizon for the time being. It exists for the sole purpose of being utterly spent. The task of Marxist theory consists of verifying this general conclusion and of following up the concrete historical material" (Pashukanis, 1978, p. 133). Pashukanis's enquiry was then in no sense an attempt at an 'objective' theory of law; it was very definitely overlaid with the political demands of orthodox Bolshevism. It was designed to meet a purely political end, the speeding of the revolution which he saw as being in process, the revolution to end property relations entirely.

Pashukanis based his view of the revolution on the two stages outlined by

Marx (1971 especially), as developed by Lenin (1975). This view of the proletarian revolution specifies first the introduction of a transitional society broadly characterized by the slogan 'from each according to ability, to each according to work': the 'dictatorship of the proletariat'. It would be in the second stage of the revolutionary process only that the narrow confines of bourgeois right could be transcended and the slogan 'from each according to ability, to each according to need', become social practice. As an orthodox "Old Bolshevik" (Sharlet, 1978, p. 170) Pashukanis assumed that 1917 had commenced the process of the revolution by introducing the first stage. The arguments were really as to the length of time this stage would take, and the correct method of theorizing the political and economic forms appropriate to this stage.

According to the orthodoxy of his day (to which Pashukanis adhered with unhealthy rigidity) there were at least two reasons for the revolution proceeding in two phases. One was in order to bring the productive forces to the required stage where it would be unnecessary to restrict access to wealth in society by the restraints of bourgeois or quasi-bourgeois legality. The second reason was to enable the traces of bourgeois mentality to be eradicated. The second stage of the revolution, introducing a harmonious co-operative society, would only be possible when bourgeois attitudes (not just to property) had been overcome. As an academic jurist, Pashukanis's function was to overthrow bourgeois attitudes in general, and the hegemony of the bourgeois jurists in particular. As late as 1929 Pashukanis wrote: "Even now, the struggle against the bourgeois legal view of the world represents a task of pressing importance for the jurists of the Soviet Republic today" (Pashukanis, 1978, p. 33).

It is on this latest point that Pashukanis faced a contradiction which he never resolved and which resulted in his liquidation. Pashukanis argued that the form of law in the Soviet Union after 1917 was still bourgeois. All juridical thought, he argued, was characterized by abstract general definitions, and it was his belief that the law of the transition was no different. Thus he said: "The fundamental, or formal juridical concepts have a continued existence in our statute books and the corresponding commentaries. Also still with us is the method of juridical thought with the procedures peculiar to it" (pp. 48-49). Thus for Pashukanis, Russia in the 1920's was still dominated by a recognizable bourgeois legal system.

In 1930, Pashukanis wrote a paper which can be seen as a landmark in the development of both Russian legal theory and of Pashukanis himself. In this paper Pashukanis struggled to make his theory fit the new facts of the increasing power of a dictatorial state. The paper in no way succeeds, and for the next six years, Pashukanis tried to resolve the contradictions in his own position by sticking to his theory, and protesting his adherence to the new regime. Amongst the arguments in this paper is an assertion that socialized production had not been achieved (Pashukanis, 1951, pp. 270-271). Three years earlier, Stuchka had also written that Russian society was still class divided (Stuchka, 1970, p. 213) and that therefore a bourgeois legal system was still needed if only to deal with the problems of distribution. Pashukanis never overcame the problem of categorizing the new regime in a form acceptable to the post-1930 Russian state. In so far as Pashukanis's theory was not changed by the pressure of outside political events that left him far behind, he saw the law of the transition period as thoroughly permeated by bourgeois concepts. Paradoxically, this gave Pashukanis his own 'legitimacy', his own justification for working on and teaching legal theory. The desire finally to overcome the bourgeois world view was sufficient justification for his work.

Theory and reality

Despite the apparent political naïvety of Pashukanis and his abject failure to perceive the tide of events, his theory is obsessed with 'facts'. Contemporaries, Stuchka included, accused Pashukanis of being too abstract yet Pashukanis prided himself on his theory's sound link with reality. "Scientific, that is theoretical study can reckon only with facts" (Pashukanis, 1978, p. 88). The argument he continually employed against the bourgeois theorists of his time (especially Kelsen) was that his own theory matched up to reality, whilst theirs did not. Thus Pashukanis saw his theory as being 'sociological' rather than pure-ly 'juridical'. "My aim was this: to present a sociological interpretation of the legal form and of the specific categories which express it" (Pashukanis, 1979, p. 107).

Thus, not surprisingly, normative theories of law were totally unacceptable:

> To assert the objective existence of law, it is not enough to know its normative content, rather one must know too whether this normative content materialises in life, that is in social relations . . . When the legal dogmatist has to decide whether or not a particular legal form is valid, most often he makes no attempt at all to ascertain whether a certain objective social phenomenon is present or absent, but only whether or not there is a logical connection between the given normative proposition and the more general normative premise. (p. 87)

Natural law theory, state and will theory are similarly condemned because the picture they paint "in no way corresponds to reality" (p. 145). Even Renner, whom Pashukanis attacks in scathing terms, is unable "to comprehend the concept of law in its actual workings . . ." (p. 56). For Pashukanis legal theory has to discover what exists in the same way that political economy studies something which actually exists (p. 59).

Pashukanis's concern with 'facts' appears far more problematic now than it must have done to his contemporaries. To Marxists working in the 1920's theories of law must have seemed completely out of touch with the everyday workings of bourgeois law. Yet Pashukanis's insistence on facts solves very few problems, if only because Pashukanis's downfall itself can be seen as a triumph of fact over theory. Whilst Pashukanis was trying to overplan the non-legal future, the ground was being cut from under his feet; a greater awareness of fact would not have come amiss. More important, Pashukanis himself treats facts as totally unquestionable, forgetting that what is fact for Pashukanis may be loaded interpretation, for example, for Kelsen. Othello actually thought he saw the handkerchief he gave Desdemona in another's hand. He thought he 'saw' a 'fact'. The problem was how to interpret it.

Whilst the contract of employment is, for a Marxist, concerned with the 'fact' of exploitation, the sale of labour power for an equivalent which is precisely not an equivalent, for bourgeois theorists a contract of employment is the 'fact' of the free meeting of minds of equally uncoerced parties. These two 'factual' positions cannot be reconciled, and they may be equally valid from the position they occupy within their own theoretical systems. What is at stake for Pashukanis is the validity of his own theoretical structure. Thus merely because "Kelson had to admit that some part of real life, that is to say of people's actual behaviour, must in some way be injected into the ideal normative system" (p. 86) tells us nothing about the validity of theories of Kelsen or Pashukanis.

Form and substance

Nonetheless, Pashukanis's method did represent at least one major breakthrough for Marxist analysis of law; it emphasized the need to examine form as well as substance. There was, and still is, an almost inevitable tendency for Marxist theory, whether of law, economics, politics or history to concentrate on the substantive inequality that capitalism produces, to highlight the gross differences in different historical groups. This is clearly a valid part of any Marxist analysis. But what Pashukanis attempted in his theory was to show that the form of law as well as its substantive workings, was inherently bourgeois. Thus for Pashukanis, unlike many quasi-Marxist theories, there was no possibility of retaining the existing form of law, whilst revolutionizing its substantive content. The form of law itself demanded that the new society had to transcend law in its entirety, a point to which I return in the final section of this paper.

Section 2: The Commodity Form Theory and the Legal Subject

Pashukanis considered his most important contribution to jurisprudence to be the development of a commodity form theory. Both at the time the theory was published and since, this has been taken to be the centre of his critique. Some writers, such as Balbus (1977) have even argued that the commodity form theory has been the only worthwhile product of Marxist legal theory, and it is on the basis of the commodity form theory that Edelman (1979, p. 24) proclaims the necessity at last, of recognizing the genius of Pashukanis. Put simply, the theory argues that the legal form is the parallel ("homology" according to Balbus) of the commodity form. Law arises out of the needs of the commodity form of production. The commodity is the cell form of legal relations because capitalist society consists of producers of commodities. These commodities when produced are exchanged. All law is concerned with the process of the exchanging of commodities between subjects who act as the 'guardians' of commodities and are created by law in order to enable the commodity production form of society to function. Law is thus the 'philosophy of the subject'. In order to appreciate this categorization of law, the theory can be explained as based on two premises, i.e. logical and historical.

The logical premise

"Every legal relation" proclaims Pashukanis, "is a relation between subjects" (Pashukanis, 1978, p. 109). Therefore, he says, the logical starting point for analysis is the subject. Property, says Pashukanis, is the basis of the legal form, but only property that can be disposed of in the market, that is, capitalist property. The subject in law is the expression of the freedom of property, that is, the freedom to alienate property. Thus the key to understanding law is the contradiction between things (commodities) and subjects. Commodities according to Marx relate to each other as values, that is exchange (buying and selling) takes place on the basis of equivalent amounts of labour-time embodied in commodities passing between buyers and sellers. (Unfortunately, here as elsewhere Pashukanis's failure to follow Marx's arguments beyond the 'simple' beginnings of Vol. 1 of *Capital* causes problems; I discuss this further in Section 3 below.) For this to operate commodity owners must recognize that they stand towards each other in a relation of equals, where each is entering into a process of uncoerced exchange. "Exchange or the circulation of commodities is predicated on the mutual recognition of one another as owner by those engaged in exchange" (p. 161). The exchange is uncoerced in the double sense that neither party is forced to exchange and that when the transaction is completed, both parties are satisfied. Exchange then operates on the principle that the parties to the exchange are gaining mutual advantages in an uncoerced harmonious process.

> For the products of human labour to be able to relate to each other as values,
> it is necessary for people to relate to each other as autonomous and equal

personalities . . . Man as a moral subject that is as a personality of equal
worth, is indeed no more than a necessary condition for exchange according
to the law of value. Man as a legal subject, or as a property owner, is a
further necessary condition . . . The economics of value relations provides
the key to an understanding of the juridical and ethical structure, not in the
sense of the concrete content of legal or moral norms, but in the true sense
of the form itself. (pp. 151-152)

It follows that for Pashukanis contract is both logically the central legal
premise on which all other aspects of law are based, and also the highest form of
expression of the commodity owning subject. This is because it is the relations of
contract that are crucial for commodity production society since the contract is
the necessary legal expression of commodity owners' ability to use their
commodities in the market, i.e. to trade with them. For Pashukanis, all other
forms of legal relations in capitalism flow from this, since without the exchange
of commodities persuant to legal contracts, society itself would not continue in
its capitalistic form. The commodity owners' legal relation is presented in two
'absurd' forms, that is the form of the value of commodities and the form of the
capacity to be the subject of rights. The former is the inherent 'right' of the
commodity expressing itself through the market 'independently' of the
individual. The latter is the 'legal' proprietor, the personification of the abstract
notion of a bearer of rights. As such they dominate commodities since legally
they are the commodities' 'guardians'. The absurdity (contradiction) for
Pashukanis lies in the paradox that economically the commodity dominates; the
individual subject, glorified in the capacity to exercise rights, is no more than the
necessary appendage of the cell form of the unit of wealth in capitalist society.

The historical premise

Pashukanis's historical premise for his theory is even more fundamental than his
logical premise. In his overwhelming desire to produce a theory based on history
rather than on abstract notions of justice, equality etc., Pashukanis is determined
to prove that the commodity form theory is almost the necessary outcome of a
historical development from petty commodity production to capitalist production
proper.

For Pashukanis, the fully developed form of exchange society, which Marx
analysed, grew out of prior modes of petty commodity production. The
commodity form of exchange historically precedes the legal system which
emerges from it. It is this which expands and becomes the universal form as
commodity production takes over. But it is not merely that the commodity form
produces the legal form; it is that the commodity form exists prior to the legal
form and that only with the full development of the commodity form is there the

possibility of a fully developed abstract legal form at all. "Only when bourgeois
relations are fully developed does law become abstract in character" (Pashukanis,
1978, p. 120). This potential for abstraction (in terms of rights, subjects etc.)
arises out of the logic of the commodity form as that form extends. "Historically,
however, it was precisely the exchange transaction which generated the idea of
the subject as the bearer of every imaginable legal claim. Only in commodity
production does the abstract form see the light; in other words, only there does
the general capacity to possess a right become distinguished from concrete legal
claims" (p. 118). The legal subject becomes an "abstract owner of commodities
raised to the heavens" (p. 121). Commodity production is developed through
trade. Trade helps break the barriers of pre-capitalist production, and the law
itself develops out of the increasing importance of trade. Trading nations
required laws because they dealt in commodities (although within a society
where commodity exchange was the exception). As trade expanded, the development of the particular legal form associated with the commodity expanded with
it.

Pashukanis also examines the development of law in relation to contractual
disputes. In summary, Pashukanis argues that commodity owners, on the basis
of the 'recognized' reciprocity of equals, almost exchange without laws. The law
steps in when disputes arise between parties to transactions which require a legal
system capable of arranging settlements on a basis that does not violate the
principles of equivalent exchange. Thus as exchange develops, so disputes
increase and the necessity arises of a developed legal system to cope with
disputes. "It is disputes, conflicts of interest, which creates the legal form,
the legal superstructure" (p. 93). But the implications of this development
are that commodity exchange historically (and logically) is prior to law and,
in some pure theoretical sense (but here not in any actual historical instance),
exists independently of a legal system. "Thus the economic relation of
exchange must be present for the legal relation of contracts of purchase and
sale to arise . . . the existence of a commodity and money economy is the basic
precondition without which . . . concrete norms would have no meaning"
(p. 93).

Fetishism as summary

One method of summarizing Pashukanis's commodity form theory is to point to
its relationship with Marx's theory of fetishism—an approach recently adopted
by Balbus. Marx argued that the commodity was a fetishized form because the
formal equality that the commodity form postulated was only an apparent
equality. Balbus has argued that what is at stake is the distinction between
equality in law and inequality in fact (Balbus, 1977). He argues that all citizens

are formally equal before the law and find no overt discrimination in the law. Balbus says the commodity form encompasses two aspects, i.e. the use value of the commodity and its exchange value. But when the commodity appears on the market, the "memory", as Balbus calls it, of the use value is extinguished, and instead all that concerns people is the equivalent amounts of labour-time which are exchanged. The commodity therefore, says Balbus, appears as a fetishized form because the commodity's connection with human origins is masked. This "gives rise to the appearance, the ideological inversion, that commodities have living human powers" (Balbus, 1977, p. 574). Balbus says it is possible to construct a similar theory of law from Marx's writings. Thus, he says, citizens also take on a two-fold form; that is, substantially they are unequal but they enter into formal relations of equals, which is the concern of the law. The 'blindness' of the legal form to substantive human differences is the parallel of the blindness of the commodity form to the substantive differences in use value. Ultimately, Balbus argues, the legal form (as commodity form) exists independently of the will of the individual. The illusion is produced "that the law—as the universal political equivalent—has a life of its own" (p. 584).

Section 3: Some Criticisms of the Commodity Form Theory[2]

Pashukanis has probably had more vilification and abuse heaped on his head than any other twentieth century legal theorist (see Fuller, 1949). But one thing that has united both hostile and sympathetic critics is that the commodity form theory was Pashukanis's central insight. However, despite the merits of the theory, the neat parallel it presents with aspects of Marx's analysis, and its powerful commitment to attacking bourgeois notions of the hegemony of legal systems, the *General Theory* has some major defects which lessen its appeal. Ultimately these flaws may be so strong as to make the theory unusable. What follows is necessarily only a brief and outline account of some of the problems raised by Pashukanis's theory.

The priority of commodity exchange

Pashukanis's argument that the commodity exchange form of social relations exist both historically and logically prior to law is extremely suspect. Although Pashukanis is consistent here in that he applies his notion to all forms of property, holding in effect that property itself only takes on a juridic form after the development of capitalism, the consistency does nothing to strengthen the argument. The problem is that Pashukanis has ignored the difficulty of conceptualizing and defining any form of developed property relations without using law. Although the legal form does not exhaust the concept of property, the property form itself is inchoate without the legal form. Whilst Pashukanis is right to criticize Renner's somewhat simplistic notion of property as a relation between people and things, Pashukanis's concept of property existing prior to law is unacceptable.

In discussing violations of the law, Pashukanis traces the problem of criminal law back to blood vengeance. Developing the theme of law arising out of disputes between already existing (factual) relations, he says: "Historically, the specific traits of legal intercourse were acquired primarily as a result of actual violations of the law. The concept of theft arose before the concept of property" (p. 167). This argument is again the logical product of Pashukanis's commitment to the historical development of the laws of capitalism but it is no less problematic for that and left Pashukanis open to some fairly penetrating attacks from the bourgeois theorists he so despised, such as Kelsen (1955, p. 93) (and see also Lapenna, 1964, p. 26 and Schlesinger, 1945, p. 151). The problem is to explain the concept of theft without having a developed concept of property. Theft must involve the appropriation of property, since if an object or person is not regarded as property there is no way it, or he or she, can be appropriated wrongfully. Thus the problem with the Robinson Crusoe analogy of the classical economists, was not that Crusoe did not appropriate objects, but that mere appropriation does not turn objects into property. Property is a social concept, incorporating in part at least, the concept of the exclusion of others. It has nothing to do with, say, a primitive people (and Pashukanis is trying to trace his concept from primitive tribes) using or improving natural resources etc., where the tribe or community or whatever hold those resources communally. Where property develops it does so on the basis of certain sections of the community being able to exclude other sections from what would otherwise be enjoyment of the particular object/person in question. Pashukanis argues that in contrast to other theories "Marxist theory considers every social form historically" (p. 111). It can be argued that Pashukanis produced a most unhistorical work.

One possible defence of Pashukanis is that despite concentrating on history, Pashukanis's thesis is definitely not historical. Pashukanis focusses on an explanation of commodity production society only and make no genuine attempt to be historical. Whilst Pashukanis assumed that laws were only necessary for particular forms of society, and thus quite unjustifiably tried to argue that feudal or slave societies were not legal, it can be suggested that this is not fundamental to his argument. If Pashukanis really had set out to write a historical analysis then he failed. But Pashukanis's theory should be judged on its applicability to developed capitalism; in effect, it is this only which is analysed.

The dominance of exchange

Pashukanis's theory concentrates on the exchange of commodities. That is, it focusses on the law's concern to see that the requirements of the free exchange of commodities are guaranteed. Law develops for this purpose and overcomes the practical problems that will arise where the free exchange of commodities is violated. Ultimately it serves to guarantee to the capitalist the ability to enter into that most important of 'free' contract, the purchase of labour-power. In this contract, according to Marx's analysis, the worker both receives a 'fair' exchange in that equivalents of value are passed between the contracting parties, and at the same time the capitalist is able to receive a surplus by the exploitation of the worker. This surplus is the source of all profits, and the source of funds for accumulation which serve to reproduce the conditions under which this process is repeated.

However, the process of exchange is not all that is involved. Capitalism is a process of production, and exchange is merely a part of that process. Legal theory must be as concerned with production as with exchange. Yet Pashukanis appears to have written production out of the law. This is unacceptable for Pashukanis. Historically the commodity form system is based on the development of the forces and relations of production to a particular stage where the commodity form becomes the dominant form. But this is the result of a specific process of technical and social development which encompasses a complete transformation of the production process. Legal theories which attempt to be historical cannot just bypass this process. Pashukanis has failed to make the logical allowances necessary for the importance of the production process itself in the development of a social system. Legal theories which attempt to base themselves on 'social reality', as Pashukanis claimed, most incorporate the production process into their legal analysis or make sufficient allowances for its importance in relation to the legal system as a whole. Pashukanis's theory is based on a society of commodity production, yet almost eliminates the process of production from history.

The generality of commodity form

Not only does Pashukanis apparently ignore the central influence of production on law, his legal theory is not based on capitalist commodity production at all. Pashukanis assumed that the commodity form itself produced legal relations but that this form did not do so at any specific stage in social development. He assumes that the legal form of pre-capitalist commodity production merely expands and develops as the commodity form of production becomes, in time, the dominant world form. What he ignores is the transformation commodity production undergoes in the process of development into the modern world system. Thus the theory can be criticized for being applicable to petty commodity production only, though even here Pashukanis's concepts are of doubtful historical validity.

The absence of coercion

The historical period in which Pashukanis was writing makes the absence of coercion in the theory a puzzle, something contemporaries such as Stuchka (1970, p. 230) commented on. The dominant Leninist view of the time included the conception that all law is but the expression of the will of the ruling class to crush other classes and that in the revolutionary period of the dictatorship of the proletariat the role of law was to help crush the bourgeoisie. Krylenko wrote that revolutionary law was ultimately concerned with the forceful crushing of the class opponents of the dictatorship of the proletariat. "Thus revolutionary law is one of the weapons and one of the manifestations of the dictatorship of the proletariat" (Krylenko, 1933, p. 6). The extent to which Marxist theories of law should incorporate coercion is the subject of much debate. But some notion of law as a forceful action, as a weapon which despite enormous and sometimes quite unexpected contradictions, is part of the means for ruling class control, ought to be incorporated into Marxist legal theory. Yet Pashukanis excludes coercion almost by definition. As legal relations are but the expression of commodity exchange, and as by definition commodity exchange for Pashukanis takes place on the basis of the free meeting of minds, coercion must be relegated to a very minor role if not eliminated entirely. Indeed, Pashukanis writes of coercion actually contradicting the conditions necessary for the free and equal exchange of commodities and of exchange value ceasing to be such if its ratios are determined by an authority situated outside of the market (Pashukanis, 1978, p. 143).

Although Pashukanis does not totally ignore the role of force (the chapter on the state in particular brings in aspects of the coercive nature of the state), and although he can be seen as reacting against classic Marxist theories which overemphasized the role of force in legal theory, he has failed to incorporate an important element. It is possible that some of Pashukanis's recantations on this area represent a genuine desire to reject untenable positions. In 1932 Pashukanis wrote of his error in identifying law solely with exchange as this did not bring in the coercion and personal subordination which were essential elements of all legal systems (Pashukanis, 1970, p. 235). Whether or not this and similar recantations are genuine, the lack of coercion in the theory can be linked to the question of class. Very broadly, Pashukanis ignores class relations in his concentration on bourgeois notions of equivalents. Whilst Pashukanis critiques capitalist society, his legal theory ignores the division of that society into classes.

The use value/exchange value distinction

Pashukanis's theory in part relies on Marx's distinction between the two aspects of a commodity, use value and exchange value. He argues that just as the market almost ignores use values and concentrates on the socially embodied labour-time in a commodity, where equivalent amounts of labour time are exchanged, so law operates in a similar manner. The law, he said, deals only with the formal equality of citizens (i.e. the analogue of the exchange value) and ignores the substantive inequalities between citizens (i.e. the analogue of the use value).

The problem with this analysis is that it might be quite misleading. In one sense law can be seen as essentially concerned with substantive differences (i.e., for the purpose of the analogy, use values). As Pashukanis regards contract as the most important legal category and as he regards contract as the highest expression of the commodity owning subject (Pashukanis, 1978, p. 121) the best method of explanation here is to use contract. From Pashukanis's analysis it would be argued that when a dispute arises over the exchange of commodities (contracts) then the court merely looks to the form of the transaction and ignores substantive elements. The fact that one party is rich, the other poor, one employer, the other employee, are all, it is said, irrelevant.

This may be incorrect. First, in many areas (landlord-tenant, mortgagor-mortgagee, supplier-consumer etc.) statute has intervened in most common law countries to try to redress the substantive imbalance, at least to an extent. In landlord and tenant cases, for example a vast amount of legislation since before 1914 has altered the purely common law balance between the parties. Though the parties are clearly very differently placed prior to the contract being made where in many cases (though perhaps not all) the power and wealth of the landlord overwhelms the tenant in terms of bargaining strength, thus making a mockery of classic contract theory, once the contract is actually made the law attempts to impose substantive contractual inhibitions on the landlord in favour of the tenant. The law then does not actually disregard substantive differences in many areas. Even in the most important and sensitive arena of employer-employee contracts, the law is by no means always the formal, impartial, but therefore hopelessly loaded creature Pashukanis claims.

Second, and more important, given Pashukanis's nineteenth century assumptions as to classic freedom of contract, assumptions which may be doubtful (see Atiyah, 1979, part 2 especially), there is an argument for saying that the analysis is inapplicable. In contract cases the one aspect with which the court is actually most definitely concerned is use value, i.e. the substantive subject matter of the contract. In English law, especially on the breakdown of a contract, the court specifically excludes enquiry into the exchange value of the commodity asusming that the parties, if of full age etc., have made a bargain knowing what they were doing. The rule that the court (subject obviously to exceptions) does not enquire into the adequacy of the consideration means that in the average contract case the court is very much concerned with the use value of the contract, i.e. the substantive different items that are exchanged. If this were not the position, the court's function in contract disputes would be almost superfluous. In strict contract theory the court looks to the substantive different objects that are being exchanged (i.e. usually commodities for money). In that sense, then, Pashukanis's argument breaks down completely. The object of contracts is not actually the exchange of equivalent exchange values, i.e. equal sums of money (a pointless exercise), but the passing between the parties of different use values. The court is and must be concerned with this substantive aspect of contract if legal mediation is to be of relevance. In contractual disputes courts try to place the parties in the same financial position that they would have been in had the contract been fully performed. But this operation, to be meaningful, must be related to the passing of different use values.

Even with employment contracts, where the analogy and argument of Pashukanis are at their strongest, there are problems. It can be argued that the court, in classic contract terms, ignores the fact that one party is employer with all the substantive advantages that entails and that the other is employee with the corresponding disadvantages. Here the argument is that the law does 'fetishize' the unequal relations and produces an inherently 'biased' or 'unfair' system under the guise of equality. However, what Pashukanis and his adherents ignore is that substantively the law does recognize employer and employee as such. That is, it takes into account the fact that two parties only appear before it because they are in the substantive and legal relation of employer and employee and therefore the law inevitably accommodates their factual position. Pashukanis is perhaps only saying that the court itself does not change the substantive inequality of capitalist society. The intricacies of the commodity form theory are hardly necessary for such a result.

Ultimately, one of the difficulties here is that Pashukanis is confusing the specific realm of the legal with the different realm of the economic. By taking a fairly unsophisticated approach to the base-superstructure metaphor Pashukanis, in effect, ignores the potential of law for shaping economy and reduces law to the mere reflex response of the given economic. Law should be seen as having its own specificity, albeit that specificity is not to be seen as in any way purely independent of the 'economic'. Whilst arguments over the relative autonomy of law seem relatively endless, one theoretical advance that has been made since Pashukanis, arguably a point that both Marx and Engels anticipated, is the recognition of the effect of law on the economic. Pashukanis's theory conflates the two, thereby seriously misjudging the importance of law in bourgeois society. Whereas, "the work of Marx and Engels as a whole does not subscribe to essentialism, that is, to the view that all social phenomenon can be reduced or derived from the economic" (Sugarman, 1981, p. 81).

The misreading of Marx

Arguments as to 'correct' readings of Marx must almost inevitably be sterile. Marx is open to an infinite variety of readings and even if a 'correct' reading could be shown this does not of itself in any way guarantee the validity of the argument. On the other hand, if a writer justifies a theory by the claim in some way to 'apply' Marx, then if the writer completely misunderstands Marx, the conclusion might be drawn that this indicates defects in the thesis. Pashukanis regarded his object as the mere applying of Marx's economic analysis in the field of law. "The material pre-conditions for the community of law or for trans-actions between legal subjects are specified by Marx himself in Vol. 1 of *Capital*, albeit only in passing, in the form of fairly general allusions" (Pashukanis, 1978, p. 111).

Pashukanis's task is impossible. Analysis designed for one field of enquiry cannot merely be appropriated and 'applied' to a different field. "What is legitimate for a study of political economy is not legitimate for a study of legality. . . ." (Fine, 1979, p. 36). The form and substance of law have to be analysed from concepts which may be linked to the economy, and to a particular economic analysis, but cannot merely be the economic analysis as such.

In fact, Pashukanis has seriously misread Marx's economics. That is, given Pashukanis's own theoretical premises he has failed in the task he set himself. In summary, Pashukanis's error is similar to the problems of concentrating on the process of exchange noted above. He takes up Marx's opening remarks in *Capital* and treats these as the totality of Marx's economic theory. The beginning of *Capital* presents an examination of the individual producer and above all the individual exchanger of commodities. In some detail, Marx examines the process of individuals exchanging commodities to show that, on the face of it, equivalents of labour time are exchanged. Therefore, the source of wealth (profit) for the capitalist is not to be found in the sphere of individualistic exchange. The source of wealth, Marx argues, is in the production process itself. Labour-power is shown to be that unique commodity which (fortunately for capital) is capable, whilst being productively consumed, of reproducing its own value and an all important surplus. Volumes 2 and 3 of *Capital* are concerned with circulation and distribution of this surplus. Marx's economics is an analysis of the production, circulation and distribution of this surplus in a particular form of class society.

But it is just the aspect of socially produced surplus that is missing from Pashukanis's work. Pashukanis centres his analysis on isolated individuals who might have been valid subjects for analysis of pre-capitalist commodity production, but who are much less important (except possibly for the purposes of preliminary explanations as in *Capital*) when it comes to the laws of the social production of surpluses in the developed capitalist form. So when Pashukanis writes "commodity exchange presupposes an atomised economy" (1978, p. 85), he can be accused of misunderstanding the theory on which he relies. Commodity exchange in its world dominant stage presupposes a highly developed socially intertwined state and eventually world economy. Dobrin pointed out that Pashukanis, having taken up theories of German jurisprudence, worked on the basis that: "All law is conditioned by relations between individuals" (Dobrin, 1936, p. 413). Pashukanis summarized this analysis when he wrote, "The legal system differs from every other form of social system precisely in that it deals with private isolated subjects" (1978, p. 100). But this is not the way capitalist society functions, it does not 'represent' Marx's analysis of it, nor is it a suitable starting point for approaching the complexities of legal relations; the atomization of capitalism and its laws, at the best, can only be a part of any jurisprudential analysis.

Fine has pointed out that Pashukanis's work only applies to simple commodity production, and in effect to the exchange of commodities in simple commodity production (Fine, 1979, p. 41). For Marxists, Fine argues, it is necessary to take the analysis into production, which Pashukanis fails to do. However, even this criticism does not go far enough since it is not merely the need to follow Marx into production that is missing from Pashukanis, but the recognition that exchange is merely a part of the (socialized) production cycle itself, that the commodity form that Pashukanis analysed is only one particular aspect the commodity passes through in its cycle of production, circulation and distribution as a whole. Picciotto comes nearer to the fundamental critique of Pashukanis that needs to be made here. He points out that one problem with Pashukanis is that he fails to appreciate the development that takes place when labour power itself becomes a commodity, i.e. capitalist production becomes dominant (Picciotto, 1979, p. 170). In a sense, this is correct, in that the domination of capital, its establishment as a world system, ultimately requires legal theory to go beyond the simple exchange of commodities.

Section 4: The Withering Away of Law

In 1927 Stuchka wrote that "Communism means not the victory of socialist law, but the victory of socialism over any law, since with the abolition of classes with their antagonistic interests, law will die out altogether" (quoted in Berman,

1963, p. 26). In essence this summarizes Pashukanis's view. It can be argued it is his most important contribution to legal theory, and therefore his commitment to the withering of law is more important than his commodity form theory. If this is correct, the flaws of his commodity form theory, although not unimportant, do not totally detract from Pashukanis's overall importance as a Marxist jurist. However a theory which argues that the object of legal study is to work towards the annihilation of law is almost bound to contain contradictions. I wish to outline both Pashukanis's commitment to withering of law and some of the contradictions in his position in this final section. In 1929 Pashukanis reaffirmed this fundamental precept: "The Problem of the withering away of law is the cornerstone by which we measure the degree of proximity of a jurist to Marxism" (Pashukanis, 1980, p. 268). Dobrin (1936, p. 405) accurately summarized Pashukanis when he wrote of his work: "Either—or; either socialism or law."

No law prior to capitalism

Pashukanis held that law was a peculiarly capitalist problem. This is a result of his commodity form theory. As Pashukanis defined all law as merely the outgrowth of the exchange of commodities, it follows that to be consistent, social arrangements prior to the commodity form of society were not legal. Thus he wrote of the middle ages having "no abstract concept of the legal subject" (p. 170) and of slavery not being a legal relation and thus requiring no specifically legal formulation (p. 110).

Pashukanis acknowledged the gross oversimplification of this argument soon after the *General Theory* was first published, and continued to acknowledge it in later works. Untenable though the position is, its theoretical force is that it enhances his commitment to the abolition of all forms of law as a means of social organization. Pashukanis's argument is, in effect, presenting bourgeois theory with an example of forms that are non-legal in the bourgeois sense. Pashukanis argues from this the inevitable conclusion that non-legal forms are both a possibility and something to be immediately worked towards.

No proletarian law

The most heated legal debate in the 1920's in Russia related to the characterization of the legal system of the transition period. The view that eventually prevailed was that just as previous forms of society had their own specific forms of law, so too did the dictatorship of the proletariat. On the other hand, Pashukanis's view was that the transition period, because of its flexible character, did not have a form of law appropriate to it, and that the form of law in the transition period was still inevitably stamped with its inherent bourgeois characteristics. There was therefore no such thing as proletarian law. In 1930 Pashukanis wrote of the theoretical bedevilment of proletarian law and expressed his "deep regret that even Stuchka employs this term . . ." (1951, p. 269).

Pashukanis's objection to proletarian law was that it completely misled Marxist theories of law. Pashukanis explained that on the face of it, the call for concepts specific to proletarian law would appear to be "revolutionary par excellence" since it seemed to develop further Marxist theory in the field of law by use of an appropriate new theoretical tool. "In reality, however, this tendency proclaims the immortality of the legal form, in that it strives to wrench this form from the particular historical conditions which had helped to bring it to full fruition, and to present it as capable of permanent renewal" (Pashukanis, 1978, p. 61). Thus the call for proletarian law was inherently reactionary. The mere fact that bourgeois forms were still in use in Russia was not, for Pashukanis, a reason to change that form. He explained:

> The proletariat may well have to utilise these forms, but that in no way implies that they could be developed further or be permeated by a socialist content. These forms are incapable of absorbing this content and must wither away in an inverse ratio with the extent to which this content becomes reality. (p. 160)

> The withering away of certain categories of bourgeois law (the categories as such, not this or that precept) in no way implies their replacement by new categories of proletarian law . . . The withering away of the categories of bourgeois law will, under these conditions, mean the withering away of law altogether, that is to say the disappearance of the juridical factor from social relations. (p. 61)

The move towards developing concepts of proletarian law were for Pashukanis inherently backward looking. They sought to solidify the existing relations of society, whereas Pashukanis's position was that in a transitional society, by definition, no forms were immutable. He therefore argued that Soviet jurists must not hold back development with "any system that has been frozen into immobility even though it be dubbed proletarian law" (Pashukanis, 1951, p. 280).

Pashukanis's refusal to countenance proletarian law has been criticized as a two-edged weapon. Some commentators (such as Binns, 1980 and Beirne and Sharlet *in* Pashukanis, 1980, pp. 28-29; but contrast Sharlet, 1977) have argued that Pashukanis's attitude paved the way for Stalinism. But Pashukanis tried, however inadequately, to produce a theory that would reach beyond the confines of the restraints of all forms of legality. It seems a little unfair to blame Pashukanis's theory for the terror that followed merely because Pashukanis himself was politically inept, and later even wilfully blind. Only by assuming that if a society shakes off the need for law that it must then regress to a dark age is it possible to see Pashukanis's *General Theory* as a step towards arbitrary power. Pashukanis's last 6 years as a jurist are another matter.

The abolition of property

Ultimately for Pashukanis, revolutions concerned property. He was of the view that the distinction between previous forms of revolution and the form of revolution that he thought he was helping to build, was the different relation with property. Thus for Pashukanis previous revolutions merely replaced one form of property society with another. They:

> did not shake the foundations of private property, the economic framework linking economic units through exchange. The same people who had rebelled against property had no choice but to approve it next day when they met in the market as independent producers. That is the way of all non-proletarian revolutions. (Pashukanis, 1978, p. 124)

But future revolutions, revolutions that were to establish full communism, would be about the replacing of property entirely. The object of the revolution was the abolition of property relations, the abolition of commodity exchange social relations. Pashukanis thought that with the revolution, relations of property would "be historically absolutely done for . . ." (p. 130) property being abolished (p. 98). Thus property can be see as the key to Pashukanis's understanding of his own and future society and the crucial barrier that had to be surmounted for full communism to be achieved. In as much as he saw the commodity form of property as the highest form, he also saw it as a final form. And as he saw the commodity form of property as the 'creator' of laws, the transcendence of property meant the transcendence of laws.

Morality, state and crime

It is not possible to present a full discussion of Pashukanis's views on this area but in summary, Pashukanis linked morality, state and crime to commodity production society. It therefore follows that for Pashukanis all three concepts are historically limited in that the completion of the revolutionary process would make these concepts redundant. "One must, therefore, bear in mind that morality, law and the state are forms of bourgeois society" (Pashukanis, 1978, p. 160).

However, Pashukanis is not totally consistent in his argument that the full development of law meant the complete disappearance of crime, state and morality. His discussion of criminal law exposed the ambiguity. On one level Pashukanis is clear. Criminal law is a requirement of capitalist society only. It is related to the fundamental principle of equivalence of bourgeois society, in that the requirements of punishment are calculated by means of a trade off—severity of crime being equalled by the severity of punishment. However, the equivalent relation itself is only an aspect of bourgeois society. The categorizations of crime and criminal punishment are derived from the overwhelming requirements of the law of exchange of equivalents. "Conversely, the characterisation 'criminal law' becomes utterly meaningless if the principle of the equivalent relation disappears from it" (p. 176).

This argument then points to the future society where relations are not dominated by the threat of the criminal process. Yet as Korsch (1978) and others have pointed out, Pashukanis contradicts himself. Thus Pashukanis writes: "Only the complete disappearance of classes will make possible the creation of a system of penal policy which lacks any element of antagonism" (p. 175). Pashukanis is calling for a society that has transcended the requirements of criminal law and yet talks of criminal punishment in that new society. The sentence following the one just cited states that it is doubtful whether there will be any necessity for a penal system in the new society. But Pashukanis does not explain how he contemplates penal systems the results of commodity societies, in the future society of which he speaks.

One possible excuse for Pashukanis here is that criminal law, even more than history, fits uncomfortably into Pashukanis's project. Pashukanis's theory is really concerned with private civil law and the chapter on criminal law is only added to attempt a spurious theoretical consistency. Pashukanis merely tries to apply his commodity form theory which had a certain logical force for private civil law, to criminal law, where in the formulation of Pashukanis at least, it clearly has no place. The theory of equivalent punishments is faintly comic, and is very different from insights given elsewhere in the *General Theory* and in other works, in which Pashukanis displays a far more sophisticated approach to criminal policy. It is of course the result of trying to apply his theory (or as he thinks Marx's theory) mechanistically. It is consistent only in so far as Pashukanis pushes the equivalent principle to its illogical conclusion; but Pashukanis from time to time draws back from the full implication of his own argument.

Law versus plan

Ultimately, Pashukanis argues that law is not something that can be seen as socially useful and that is why it is necessary to call for its complete abolition.

Pashukanis fulminates against the view that law can be socially beneficial or used in the revolutionary process.

> But there is absolutely no formula, be it even drawn from the writings of the most progressive Western European jurists imaginable, which can transform the legal transactions arising out of our Civil Code into socially useful transactions, and can transform every property-owner into a person performing social (sic) functions. Such an abolition of private economy and private law on paper can only serve to obscure the perspective of its real abolition. (p. 98, footnote)

But if for Pashukanis law was now socially a restraint, 'planning' was the basis of the future society which would enable the transcendence of the 'narrow horizons of bourgeois right' (see Kamenka and Tay (1971) on the importance of the plan for Pashukanis). Indeed he berated legal theorists to the extent of suggesting all their work is unnecessary. "Only when the individualistic economic system has been superseded by planned social production and distribution will this unproductive expenditure of man's intellectual energies cease" (p. 80). The inevitability of legal intercourse is a product of the relations of commercial exchange. "The ultimate victory of planned economy will transform their relationship into an exclusively technical expedient, thereby doing away with their 'legal personality'" (pp. 134-135). Legal relations are characterized by Pashukanis as the opposite of the planned rational economy of the new society he worked for, but which never arrived. Whilst Pashukanis's concept of the plan is full of problems (see Kamenka and Tay (1970) for a discussion of some of the difficulties here), the commitment to the abolition of law which it entails is beyond question.

Conclusion: The Ultimate Commitment to Withering Away

The thesis that law would wither away was obviously unacceptable to the authoritarian Soviet state. Though the evidence as to Pashukanis's recantation is somewhat confusing, different writers suggesting different conclusions and citing inconsistent texts, Pashukanis did abandon his thesis.

However, Pashukanis's overwhelming theoretical commitment to the ultimate evanescene of law, and the importance of that thesis to his theory cannot be overstated. The withering away of law is the logical conclusion of the commodity form theory. If the commodity form theory is to be coherent, it must postulate that only commodity production society has legal systems. If, therefore, the object of 1917 was to go beyond the requirements of commodity production, and the straightjacket of bourgeois relations and bourgeois thought, as Pashukanis and the 1917 Bolsheviks assumed, then the conclusion must follow that legal relations were to be overtaken. The moves by Pashukanis to abandon this thesis represented the ultimate defeat, the withering of his life's work.

By 1936 the critique of Pashukanis was universal, though most of the criticisms were restatements of the new orthodoxy rather than genuine attempts to discuss the failings of his works. Pashukanis himself joined in the tirade of vilification as eagerly as most (see Pashukanis, 1967, p. 321 and the final extracts in Pashukanis, 1980) but these abject obeisances were of no avail. On January 20th 1937 Pravda declared Pashukanis an enemy of the people (the most serious criminal category). Pashukanis disappeared without trace, trial or confession (see Sharlet, 1977, p. 169), but his own withering away represented more than another personal tragedy. It started the period when legal theory was no longer allowed to pursue wild flights of fancy, when legal academics became tied to the formality and professionalism of the new Soviet legal order. The fact that the very same legal order that Pashukanis asserted was withering away became what Sharlet (1977) has called the "jurisprudence of terror" is another story.

Notes

1. For reasons explained in the Further Reading (below) I have used the 1978 translation of the *General Theory* throughout this paper.
2. For the fullest discussion of Pashukanis's contemporary Russian critics see Sharlet (1968). For further criticisms see Redhead (1978), Kinsey (1978) and some of the essays in Fine *et al.* (1979). Arthur (1976, 1978) presents some of the most fullsome praise of Pashukanis. As some of the materials published in the Beirne and Sharlet anthology (Pashukanis, 1980) show, Pashukanis recanted on many aspects of his work, at times abandoning parts of his thesis in necessary but unseemly haste. Whilst many, if not most, of the recantations were the result of other than theoretical pressures, some might represent genuine attempts to develop the theory.

Acknowledgements

David Sugarman's patient encouragement with and undeserved suffering from this paper have both been great. Amongst the many other people who have commented on the various drafts of this paper I have derived considerable help from Viv Brown, Hugh Collins and Michael Freeman. My thanks also to Peter Fitzpatrick and Jerry Palmer for some stimulating criticisms.

References

Arthur, C. (1976). Towards a Materialist Theory of Law *Critique* 7.
Arthur, C. (1978). "Editor's Introduction", *in* Pashukanis 1978.

Atiyah, P. (1979). *The Rise and Fall of Freedom of Contract*. Clarendon Press, Oxford.

Balbus, I. (1977). Commodity Form and Legal Form: An Essay on the Relative Autonomy of the Law, *Law and Society Review*, Vol. 11, No. 3. (Reprinted in Reasons, C. E. and Rich, R. M. (Eds) *The Sociology of Law*. Butterworths, Toronto.)

Berman, H. (1963). *Justice in the USSR: An Interpretation of Soviet Law*. Harvard University Press, Cambridge, Mass.

Binns, P. (1980). Law and Marxism. *Capital and Class* **10**.

Dobrin, S. (1936). Soviet Jurisprudence and Socialism. *Law Quarterly Review* **52**.

Edelman, B. (1979). *Ownership of the Image: Elements for a Marxist Theory of Law*. RKP, London.

Fine, B. (1979). Law and Class. In *Capitalism and the Rule of Law: From Deviancy Theory to Marxism*, Chapter 2 (Fine *et al.*, Eds). Hutchinson, London.

Fuller, L. (1949). Pashukanis and Vyshinski: A Study in the Development of Marxism Legal Theory. *Michigan Law Review* **47**.

Kamenka, E. and Tay, A. (1970). The Life and Afterlife of a Bolshevik Jurist. *Problems of Communism* **19**.

Kamenka, E. and Tay, A. (1971). Beyond the French Revolution: Communist Socialism and the Concept of Law. *University of Toronto Law Journal* **21**.

Kelsen, H. (1955). *The Communist Theory of Law*. Stephens & Son, London.

Kinsey, R. (1978). Marxism and the Law: Preliminary Analysis. *British Journal of Law and Society*.[5]

Korsch, K. (1978). An Assessment. *In* "Pashukanis 1978".

Krylenko, N. (1933). *Revolutionary Law*. Co-operative Publishing Society of Foreign Workers in the USSR, Moscow.

Lapenna, I. (1964). *State and Law: Soviet and Yugoslav Theory*. The Athlone Press, London.

Lenin, V. I. (1975). *The State and Revolution*. In *Selected Works*. Progress Publishers, Moscow.

Marx, K. (1971). *Critique of the Gotha Programme*. Progress Publishers, Moscow.

Pashukanis, E. B. (1951). The Soviet State and the Revolution in Law. In *Soviet Legal Philosophy* (Babb, H. and Hazard, J. N., Eds). Cambridge, Mass.

Pashukanis, E. B. (1967). State and Law Under Socialism. In *Soviet Political Thought* (Jaworski, M., Ed.). Johns Hopkins Press, Baltimore.

Pashukanis, E. B. (1970). Exchange and Law. In *Ideas and Forces in Soviet Legal History* (Zile, Z., Ed.). College Printing and Publishing Inc., Madison, Wisconsin.

Pashukanis, E. B. (1978). *Law and Marxism: A General Theory*. Ink Links, London.

Pashukanis, E. B. (1980). *Selected Writings on Marxism and Law* (Beirne, P. and Sharlet, R., Eds). Academic Press, London.

Picciotto, S. (1979). The Theory of the State Class Struggle and the Rule of Law. In *Capitalism and the Rule of Law: From Deviancy Theory to Marxism* Chapter 11 (Fine, B. *et al.*, Eds). Hutchinson, London.

Redhead, S. (1978). The Discrete Charm of Bourgeois Law: A Note on Pashukanis. *Critique* **9**.

Sharlet, R. (1968). *Pashukanis and the Commodity Exchange Theory of Law 1924-1930*. Indiana University PhD Thesis 1968.

Sharlet, R. (1974). Pashukanis and the Rise of Soviet Marxist Jurisprudence. In *Soviet Union* Vol. 1, No. 2.

Sharlet, R. (1977). Stalinism and Soviet Legal Culture. In *Stalinism: Essays in Historical Interpretation* (Tucker, R. C., Ed.). W. W. Norton & Co. Inc., New York.

Sharlet, R. (1978). Pashukanis and the Withering Away of Law in the USSR. In *Cultural*

Revolution in Russia 1928-1931 (Fitzpatrick, S., Ed.). Indiana University Press, Bloomington, Indiana.

Schlesinger, R. (1945). *Soviet Legal Theory: Its Social Background and Development.* Kegan Paul Trench Trubner, London.

Stuchka, P. (1970). My Journey and My Errors. In *Ideas and Forces in Soviet Legal History* (Zile, E., Ed.). College Printing and Publishing Inc., Madison, Wisconsin.

Sugarman, D. (1981). Theory and Practice in Law and History: A Prologue to the Study of the Relationship Between Law and Economy from a Socio-historical Perspective. In *Law State and Society* (Fryer, B. *et al.*, Eds). Croom Helm, London.

Further Reading

There are three versions of the text of Pashukanis's *General Theory* in English, that is those listed in the references above at Pashukanis (1951, 1978 and 1980). The 1978 translation although from a German edition is preferable to the 1980 edition because the German edition used for the 1978 version is a translation of Pashukanis's third edition, whereas the 1980 edition translates the first Russian edition which is a much less complete work. However, Pashukanis (1980) contains several other interesting Pashukanis works translated into English for the first time. Further translations of other Pashukanis works can be found in the collections at Pashukanis (1951, 1967 and 1970).

The best introductions to Pashukanis are those by Beirne and Sharlet in Pashukanis (1980), and those by Sharlet (1974, 1977 and 1978). Sharlet (1968) is still almost certainly the most complete discussion of Pashukanis's life and work in the English language, but is not yet generally available. In addition to other works referenced above the following provide useful introductions to Pashukanis:

Kamenka, E. and Tay, A. (1970): this explains Pashukanis's decline from grace and partial rehabilitation.

Cotterrell, R. (1980): Review of Pashukanis 1980 (in *British Journal of Law and Society* **9**); this is a very useful brief introduction to Pashukanis's work and the reasons for the revival of interest in him. There is also a helpful review article by the same author at: Cotterrell, R. (1981): Conceptualising law: problems and prospects of contemporary legal theory (in *Economy and Society* **10**); this article surveys four modern texts of legal theory with various attitudes to Marxism; Cotterrell situates the relationship between these texts and Pashukanis's work. There are numerous studies of the Soviet Legal System, but most of these tend to treat the Pashukanis movement as an aberration rather than a serious contribution to legal theory. Classic examples can be found at: Schlesinger, R. (1945).

Gsovski, V. (1948): *Soviet Civil Law: Private Rights and their background under the Soviet regime* (2 vols) (Ann Arbor, Michigan).

Berman, H. (1963): *Justice in the USSR* (Harvard University Press, Harvard). In addition to the above J. Hazard has published extensively on the post 1917 Russian legal system of which he was a student in Moscow during the period of Pashukanis's disappearance. A full bibliography of Hazard's work can be found in:

Barry, D. (*et al.*, Eds) (1974): *Contemporary Soviet Law: Essays in Honour of John N. Hazard* (Martin Nijhoff, The Hague). The most sympathetic development of Pashukanis's commodity form theory is Balbus (1977). Edelman (1979) whilst claiming adherence to Pashukanis develops a theory with which Pashukanis would not necessarily have agreed. The revival of interest in Marxist studies of law and state has resulted in a rapidly expanding literature that takes account of Pashukanis's contribution. Some of these contributions are surveyed and discussed critically in:

Jessop, B. (1980): On Recent Marxist Theories of Law, the State and Juridico-political Ideology (*International Journal of the Sociology of Law* 8). In addition to the contributions mentioned in Note 2 above an extended critique of Pashukanis can be found in:

Hirst, P. (1979): *On Law and Ideology* (MacMillan, London). Hirst claims that Pashukanis is unable to account for the development of the corporate form of ownership and that an unjustifiable superior place is given to judge-made law at the expense of statute law. A contributor to this volume, Colin Sumner also criticizes Pashukanis in:

Sumner, C. (1979): *Reading Ideologies: an Investigation into the Marxist Theory of Ideology and Law* (Academic Press, London). Sumner, as part of his development of a theory of law and ideology, suggests that Pashukanis was partly responsible for allowing the development of bourgeois law in Russia. A variant of this critique is given by Binns (1980). Several of the essays in *Capitalism and the Rule of Law: From Devianey Theory to Marxism* (Fine, 1979) critically assess Pashukanis's work, the most interesting contributions being those of Fine and Picciotto.

For a strongly expressed critique of the views set out in this paper, and a vigorous defence of the merits of Pashukanis, see Norrie, A. (1982): Pashukanis and the 'Commodity Form Theory': A Reply to Warrington (in *International Journal of the Sociology of Law* 10).

4 Legality and Political Legitimacy in The Sociology of Max Weber

Roger Cotterrell

Introduction

Some years ago A. P. D'Entrèves wrote that the relation between legality and political legitimacy—that is, the successful assertion by holders of power of their "title" to rule and "right" to be obeyed—"finds no place among the topics normally discussed by jurists" (D'Entrèves, 1967, p. 142). Times have changed, however, and when the authority of law and state seems ever more problematic as a practical matter it presents itself as a theoretical issue not only in the perennial forms of political philosophy but in the changing elaborations in legal reasoning of ideas of 'sovereignty' and the 'rule of law' and in increasingly pressing sociological inquiries into the bases of power in society and the structure of the modern state.

Max Weber, "the greatest of German sociologists" (Aron, 1964, p. 67), and, with Marx, the major founder of twentieth century sociological analyses of capitalist development and its conditions and consequences, provided, amongst other elements of his political sociology, a conceptual framework for systematic analysis of the role of law in securing political legitimacy. The significance of this conceptual framework lies partly in the fact that it both reflects and promotes a view of legality and legitimacy which has been profoundly influential in the development of the sociology of law (cf. Treves, 1974, p. 203) and in modern political and legal theory. But, in addition, its key concept, that of 'legal domination', is elaborated in the context of Weber's important analyses of the

Law, State and Society Series: "Legality, Ideology and the State", edited by D. Sugarman, 1983. Academic Press, London and New York.

character of modern law and the sociological significance of legal history, as well as his detailed studies of the development of the modern state. Thus, in Weber's writings the relationships between law and power are analysed with the combination of a lawyer's insights into the character of legal ideas and a great sociologist's synthesizing vision of patterns of economic, political and social development in history.

If, as D'Entrèves suggests (1967, p. 142), the word 'legitimacy' sounds rather obsolete today this is because it is a term associated with the deliberate elaboration of ideologies to support or question the claims of political authority. Today we seek to look at ideology 'from the outside', considering from a sociological point of view the importance of its content in securing the sociological conditions for the exercise of power. We seek knowledge of the conditions under which ideologies develop, are sustained and disintegrate because of the sociological and politically practical significance of this knowledge. Hence, while moral and other evaluations of claims to legitimacy are far from unimportant, the conditions of legitimacy are a matter for sociological analysis as well. In modern terms this matter is part of the study of structures of ideology and their social significance.

Weber's analysis of legitimate domination remains one of the most important and detailed *sociological* studies of political legitimacy and, coupled with studies which make up his sociology of law, it provides at least a starting point for modern analysis of the ideological importance of law. For these reasons the concept of legal domination in Weber's writings is one which any rigorous contemporary social theory of law must confront.

Like all Weber's other fundamental concepts for social analysis, legal domination is an ideal type, that is, a conceptualization which is not a generalization from experience but a logically formulated idea intended as a useful basis for constructing models of socio-historical development and social processes with the aid of which data from experience can be interpreted. The concept of legal domination does not, therefore, imply a description of actual historical circumstances—for example, those in which modern states exist in developed capitalist societies. But, in Weber's view, structures of authority in complex industrial societies have come to approximate more and more the type of legal domination. The form of legitimacy which it represents has become the essential meaning content of the sociological fact of acceptance of authority in modern societies.

In essence therefore, the claim which the concept of legal domination allows Weber to make is that political domination, the system of political rule, in modern states obtains its legitimacy from the existence of a system of rationally made legal rules which designate powers of command exercisable in accordance with the rules. The rules specify also the procedure and the agency by which they may be altered. Authority is recognized in so far as it is exercised in accordance with the requirements of these rules. And, in Weber's view, this form of legitimacy is the essential basis of all stable authority in modern society —in the large business enterprise as in the agencies of state administration. Rationally created and systematically ordered rules officially define the scope of power and provide its legitimacy.

The importance of this concept of legitimacy is in what it deliberately excludes. In Weber's view, in order to understand political legitimacy under conditions of legal domination it is not necessary to evaluate the content of the law. The existence of law—in particular conditions and in a particular form—provides its own ideological basis whatever its substantive content. And the action of the state, in accordance with law, derives legitimacy from law. Legal domination does not, therefore, depend on the law's reflection of values to which those who accept its legitimacy are committed. As long as state action conforms to legal requirements it can adopt any policies or reflect any values without disturbing the basis of its legitimacy.

In an important sense legal domination is self sustaining. Having no dependence on fluctuating value choices it relies only on the formally rational character of its legal basis. Under legal domination, society is governed essentially by technological choices not ideological ones. Moral criticism cannot shake the fundamental basis of law's legitimacy. Whatever its content, law's rational, systematic character gives it the continuing ability to successfully claim obedience. In modern societies, the relationship between legality and legitimacy is, therefore, one of virtual identity. Law not only provides the technical apparatus for exercise of state power but also the ideological foundation of authority.

The relations of law and legitimacy were far from unexplored when Weber wrote at the beginning of the twentieth century. They are a recurrent theme in the history of legal and political theory and, in particular, in the history of natural law theory, a topic which exerted endless fascination for Weber (see Honigsheim, 1968, p. 53) and which the elaboration of his concept of legal domination required him to confront. Weber's treatment of the relationship between legality and legitimacy is particularly important because of its sociological, rather than philosophical, treatment of the question of legitimacy and because it is supported by the important insights of his sociology of law which clarify the sociological conditions under which law can provide political legitimacy and the historical conditions which have favoured the particular form of law associated with legal domination.

In considering the relation of law and legitimacy we are considering one aspect of the ideological significance of law, and it will be argued here that Weber's analysis of legal domination takes us some way towards an understanding of the functions of legal ideology even though the conceptual structure of his sociology and the ideal type method could not provide the basis for an adequate analysis.

Legitimate Domination

Power, in the most general sense of the possibility of imposing one's will on the behaviour of others, can exist in the most diverse forms. Within this diversity Weber identifies two broad categories of domination (*Herrschaft*): domination by virtue of a constellation of *interests*, such as that by which a monopolist, or partial monopolist, dominates trading conditions in the market; and domination by virtue of *authority*, involving power of command and duty to obey (Weber, 1954, p. 324). Although one form of domination can shade into the other and both are inevitably present in social life,[1] their analytical separation is a consequence of the conceptual framework of Weber's sociology. Sociology for him is concerned with the understanding of social action, that is to say, behaviour subjectively meaningful to the actor and which takes into account experience of, or expectations of, the conduct of others. Weber's sociology is predicated on the ability of individual actors to choose courses of conduct. Power in the sense of market domination can be considered, in Weber's terms, *conceptually* as no more than a cluster of considerations which the dominated actor takes into account in choosing a course of action.

Domination may however operate in a different way. It may operate not merely as part of the calculation on the basis on which the actor chooses a course of action but as an actual overriding of the independent will of the actor so that his "conduct to a socially relevant degree occurs as if [he] . . . had made the content of the command [addressed to him] the maxim of [his] . . . conduct for its very own sake . . . this situation will be called *obedience*" (1954, p. 328). Insofar as the will of the actor is overborne his behaviour cannot be analysed without considering the specific reasons why he submits himself to the will of another. To the extent that he does so submit himself voluntarily he recognizes the legitimacy of the domination exercised over him. What is involved here is thus a form of relationship in which the behaviour of the dominated is, at least partially, explicable only in terms of the social action of *submission*—and continued submission—of will to the source of command. As Paul Hirst has shown, it is the necessary logical consequence of the structure of Weber's sociology that the behaviour of the dominated becomes invisible to this sociology insofar as domination is accepted by them as legitimate and their conduct is determined by it (Hirst, 1976, p. 87). They cease to be individuals attaching subjective meaning to freely chosen courses of action. Their behaviour choices are made for them.

The concept of *legitimate* domination is thus an essential one in Weber's sociology. Systems of domination, insofar as they are stabilized, depend on effective claims to legitimacy and all such claims, Weber argues, can be analysed in terms of three types: charismatic domination, traditional domination and legal domination. The first two are forms of personal authority. *Charismatic authority* "is the authority of the extraordinary and personal *gift of grace* . . . the absolutely personal devotion and personal confidence in revelation, heroism, or other qualities of individual leadership", the leadership of the prophet, the elected warlord, the plebiscitarian ruler, the great demagogue or the political party leader (Gerth and Mills, 1948, p. 79). *Traditional authority* is that of "the 'eternal yesterday', *i.e.* of the mores sanctified through the unimaginably ancient recognition and habitual orientation to conform": the authority of the patriarch and the patrimonial prince (*ibid*). Obedience is founded on the sacredness "of that which is customary and has always been so and prescribes obedience to some particular person" (Weber, 1954, p. 336).

In contrast to these personal forms of legitimate domination stands the impersonal authority of *legal domination*. Here the 'validity' of a power of command is expressed

> in a system of consciously made *rational* rules (which may be either agreed upon or imposed from above), which meet with obedience as generally binding norms whenever such obedience is claimed by him whom the rule designates. In that case every single bearer of powers of command is legitimated by that system of rational norms, and his power is legitimate in so far as it corresponds with the norms. Obedience is thus given to the norms rather than to the person. (Gerth and Mills, 1948, p. 79)

Each of these legitimations of domination is associated with a *structure* of domination; patriarchalism in traditional domination, the rule of the personal charismatic leader in charismatic domination and, under legal domination, the typical structure of domination is *bureaucracy*.

Law as The Basis of Legitimacy in The Modern State

What exactly is the nature of the belief that sustains *law* as the basis of legitimacy under legal domination? What attributes does law possess which enable it to fulfil this role in providing ideological, and not merely repressive, support for domination? We can try to answer these questions, first, by drawing inferences from the logic of Weber's concepts, second, by reference to the historical conditions of the development of the state and, third, by examining Weber's analysis of the character of modern law.

The relationships between ideal types

The first of these approaches leads to ambiguities which have engaged the attention of commentators and which are centrally important in the analysis of legal domination. The social action by an individual of submission of his will by acceptance of a power of command exercisable over him is the basis of legitimate domination. The subjective 'meaning' of this action for the actor is, presumably, capable of analysis in the manner in which all social action is understandable: by means of four ideal types of action which underlie the whole of Weber's sociology. Action may be *purpose rational*, that is, oriented towards the achievement of the actor's own rationally desired and considered aims. Second, it may be *value rational*, that is, undertaken without reference to any aim but because of a belief in the worth of the action in itself, measured against some system of values or ideals. Third, action may be determined *affectually*, by feelings and emotions and, fourth, it may be *traditionally* oriented, through "the habituation of long practice" (Weber, 1947, 104 ff.).

There is only a partial correlation between the types of social action available for analysis of the act of submission to authority and the types of legitimate domination. The third and fourth types of action correspond with charismatic and traditional domination. But how does legal domination relate to the remaining first and second types of action? Is the act of submission purpose rational, value rational or a combination of both, or can it be of either type?

This ambiguity is perhaps partly resolved by yet another scheme of typifications which Weber provides in the schematic outline of his fundamental sociological concepts set out at the beginning of his posthumously published *Economy and Society*. Here Weber provides a four-fold typification of the bases of legitimacy of orders (1947, 119 ff.; 1954, pp. 8-9). Legitimacy may be based, first, on tradition, second, on affectual attitudes, third, on a rational belief in the absolute value of the order and, fourth, because the order has been established in a manner recognized to be *legal*. This strongly suggests that, in Weber's view, the acceptance of legality as the basis of legitimacy is to be understood as an act of submission whose subjective meaning for the actor is *purpose rational*, that is, not in any way oriented to acceptance of values but to a calculation of necessary means to the actor's rationally chosen purposes. Although attempts have been made to argue that, in fact, Weber's concept of legal domination implies the acceptance of certain values as he formulates it, the argument seems hard to sustain (see Bendix, 1966, p. 419; Beetham, 1974, p. 264; Mommsen, 1974, p. 86; Habermas, 1976a, pp. 99-100).

It seems reasonable to suppose that the final formulation of the three pure types of legitimate domination deliberately excludes the possibility of value rationality as a general basis for acceptance of the legitimacy of domination, not merely because of sociological insights derived from study of the development of the modern state, modern forms of law and the fate of natural law — all of which we shall consider shortly — but also because the three-fold typification is adequate to cover all forms of submission to authority as legitimate if legal domination is taken to be based on purpose rational submission.

Weber's elaboration and use of concepts implies that value adherence is, in itself, too vague, variable, uncertain and scientifically impenetrable to be recognized sociologically as a basis of legitimacy. Ultimately adherence is to the will of persons whose authority is accepted for a variety of reasons which may or may not include commitment to the values espoused by or associated with those persons; or adherence is to an order which commands allegiance irrespective of its value orientations and because its structure provides an accepted basis for fulfilment of the purpose rational activities of those subject to it. Weber's sociology of law has as its primary objective the explanation of, first, how modern law *does* provide this basis through its formal rationality and, second, what economic, political and other conditions have promoted a historical development of law which has made this possible.

The development of the modern state

Weber defines a state as "a human community that (successfully) claims the monopoly of the legitimate use of physical force within a given territory" (Gerth and Mills, 1948, p. 78). Historically, defence of, and forcible dominion over, a territory and its inhabitants have often been maintained not by a single (political) community but by several, e.g. kinship groups, neighbourhood associations, warrior fraternities, religious organizations. The existence of a separate political community is indicated by communal action, with physical force available to support it, regulating interrelations of inhabitants of a territory in matters not restricted to satisfaction of common economic needs (Weber, 1954, pp. 338-339). The ability of this community to apply coercion (including its power of life and death), its gradual permanent institutionalization allowing for the development of a rational order for the administration of coercion, and the constant emergence of new or more complex forms of social and economic interests requiring protection and able to obtain it only through the "rationally regulated guarantees which none but the political community was able to create", (1954, p. 341) established the steadily increasing dominance of the political community and created the idea of its legitimacy based in *rational order*.

This belief "in the specific legitimacy of political action can, and under modern conditions actually does, increase to a point where only certain political communities, viz., the 'states', are considered to be capable of 'legitimizing', by virtue of mandate or permission, the exercise of physical coercion by any other community" (ibid.). The modern state is characterized by the highest development of the rational order on which its legitimacy is based, so that it has broken free of dependence on personal traditional ties of authority as the basis of stability. This state "in the sense of a political association with a rational, written constitution, rationally ordained law, and an administration bound to rational rules or laws, administered by trained officials" is specifically the consequence of the unique patterns of cultural development of the West (Weber, 1927, Ch. 29; Weber, 1930, pp. 16–17). Legitimacy based substantially on *law* is thus the consequence of particular historical developments.

Of crucial importance is the idea that the legitimacy of the state centres on the *exclusion of arbitrariness* in the exercise of power. While the evaluation of state policies and the advocacy of values and interests which should be reflected in state action may be infinitely various among those whose allegiance the state claims, it increasingly depends for its 'title' to rule on the rationality of exercise of power through formally structured rules. Equally important historically is the fact that the increasing complexity of state administration demands the highest technical forms of administrative organization, and ensures the state's eventual total dependence on a form of administration organized on the basis of a system of formally logical rules. Ultimately the requirements of legitimacy and the requirements of administrative organization combine in the same demand: for a legal order based on what can be called, following Weber's terminology, formal logical legal rationality.

Formal legal rationality

Weber's definition of law is in terms of an order (not necessarily a set of rules) guaranteed by agencies of enforcement. Law is *rational* to the extent that its operation is guided by general rules, rather than by subjective reaction to the individual case (empirical law finding) or by irrational formal means such as oracles and ordeals. But legal rationality may be understood in terms of two contrasting types. *Substantively rational* law is guided by general rules determined by the principles of an ideological system other than the law itself, e.g. ethics, religion, political values. *Formally rational* law is guided by general rules in such a manner that "in both substantive and procedural matters, only unambiguous general characteristics of the facts of the case are taken into account". Legally relevant characteristics of the case may be formally determined either by reference to rigidly stipulated tangible requirements, e.g. certain forms of words spoken or written, a signature, etc., or in the case of *formal logical legal rationality* "the legally relevant characteristics of the facts are disclosed through the logical analysis of meaning and . . . accordingly, definitely fixed legal concepts in the form of highly abstract rules are formulated and applied" (Weber, 1954, p. 63).

In general, the *process* of rationalization in legal development can take two forms: first, *generalization*, the synthetic construction of general conceptualizations of legal relations by determining which aspects of a typical situation or course of action are to be considered legally relevant and in what logical manner the aspects are to be linked in legal analysis; and, second, *systematization*, which only appears "in late stages of legal modes of thought" and, as understood in modern law, involves "an integration of all analytically derived legal propositions in such a way that they constitute a logically clear, internally consistent, and, at least in theory, gapless system of rules under which, it is implied, all conceivable fact situations must be capable of being logically subsumed lest their order lack an effective guarantee" (1954, p. 62).

The important point to note about these processes — generalization of concepts and systematization — is that both can be purely 'internal' orderings and developments of legal material carried out through the use of a logic which does not demand guidance from 'external' interest claims, codes of values or political policies. This is so even though, historically, the tendencies towards generalization and systematization have, Weber argues, been promoted by the needs of the developing state and also by the demands of particular groups, particularly those interested in the development of the market and in security of economic transactions.

The synthetic construction of legal concepts through generalization does not necessarily produce systematization of the law. The two rational processes are essentially separate and, indeed, in many legal systems have been to some extent incompatible. Legal domination depends on a *legal order* which is internally consistent and therefore provides a total, self-sufficient code to specify unambiguous criteria of legitimacy (i.e. lawfulness) of action in whatever context legitimacy might be challenged. Ultimately a 'gapless', unambiguous legal order makes questions of legitimacy purely *technical* and politically uncontroversial. Thus systematization is the key process of rationalization for the creation of such a legal order. And systematization, in such a manner as to create a self-sufficient internally coherent legal order which can be seen as providing its own 'internal' rational justification and hence a self contained basis for political legitimacy, is only possible when the dominant mode of legal thought utilized in organizing the material of law is formal logical legal rationality.

Alan Hunt remarks that Weber "makes the leap" of associating formal logical legal rationality with legal domination and adds "The danger in so doing is that it obscures the relationship between the two different theoretical constructs which then tend to be used interchangeably" (Hunt, 1978, p. 115). But the association of these concepts is dictated by the logic of Weber's scheme of analysis. For Weber, *substantive* legal rationality — the development and interpretation of law by reference to ethical or other systems of values existing 'outside' the law itself, leads to forms of law which, if they are systematic, are so only because of the common reference points of all the rules in external values. Such law derives the systematic interrelationship of its rules not from their intrinsic logical interconnections but from their common orientation to an outside value source. In such a system it is clear that law itself cannot provide legitimacy for domination. Legitimacy will depend on affectual or traditional attachment to the value source which it reflects.[2] Thus a charismatic basis of legitimacy may ensure the authority attaching to the revelations of a prophet, the natural law invocations of a judge, or the will of a political leader (see the discussion of the "charisma of reason" in Roth and Schluchter, 1979, Ch. 3).

Legal domination presupposes the dominance of formal logical legal rationality in the legal order upon which it is based. Weber remarks that every system of law is based on either formal or substantive principles of organization of legal precepts (Weber, 1927, p. 342). Formal and substantive legal rationality are ultimately in perpetual opposition to each other. The development of the systematization of law necessary to support legal domination *necessarily* makes it quite impossible for the law to consistently reflect any set of ultimate ethical, political or other values. Rational order and technical precision are the only values which could conceivably be attributed to modern law as the basis of its capacity to provide legitimacy for the actions of the state. Otherwise modern law exists in an environment characterized by the "rationally irresoluble pluralism of competing value systems and beliefs" (see Jaspers, 1965; Habermas, 1976a, p. 100).

The rational formalization of law which is so important to legal domination has come about in a long process of historical development and through a unique combination of factors arising in western civilization. Weber stresses the importance of Roman law (not as regards its content but its formal reasoning), the early influence of the church in promoting formalization and promoting a separation of secular law and religion, the intellectual concerns of the Continental jurists of the universities, and the alliance between rulers and jurists to make good the claims of the modern state to power and the suppression of competing sources of authority. The claims of the developing state could only be fulfilled through rational administration which, in turn, presupposed rational calculable law. Finally, at all times economic interests have pressed for security and they gradually sought calculable law to guarantee the growing complexity of market relations. Hence at a certain crucial historical conjuncture bourgeois interests pressed upon the law similar demands for formalization and predictability to those which arose from the state's need for rational administration.

The Twilight of Natural Law

The fourth type of legitimation originally mentioned by Weber—orientation to ultimate values—was quite clearly included by him primarily to deal with the historical significance for political legitimacy of natural law. Weber's discussion of natural law shows that for him its significance was as a unique ideological development in particular historical circumstances and not as an example of a typologically distinct basis of legitimacy. As he makes clear it is an example of *charismatic* transformation.[3] But the discussion of natural law is important because it leads us towards more general problems of the analysis of legal ideology which Weber's method of conceptualization cannot confront, and, because of its marginality within the conceptual framework of the analysis of legitimate domination, it shows why the pure types of legitimate domination cannot ultimately provide a sufficient basis for analysis of legal ideology and its sociological significance.

Natural law seemed to Weber to be the only form of consistent value orientation which could be coherently elaborated to provide basic ideals of a system of rational law. To the extent that natural law embodied 'reason' it could be consistent with the demand of reason for consistency and systematization within a legal system. Secular natural law allowed the systematic promotion of values in legal form contributing towards the generalization of contract as a legal concept and uniform conceptions of legal liberties and responsibility. These characteristics allow Weber to draw a distinction between formal and substantive natural law, the former contributing towards rationalization of the law through conceptual generalization reflecting individualistic values. Natural law in this form developed from a variety of intellectual sources including religious influences from the rationalistic non-conformist sects, English ideas of inherent rights traceable back to the symbol of Magna Charta, the concept of nature of the Renaissance and, mainly, the rationalistic enlightenment of the seventeenth and eighteenth century. But no reference to material sources is made in Weber's general discussion of the origins of this form of ideology. He writes that natural law is the "specific and only consistent type of legitimacy of a legal order which can remain once religious revelation and the authoritarian sacredness of a tradition and its bearers have lost their force" (Weber, 1954, p. 288). Yet, in his view, it has not remained and positive law has become its own justification.

When Weber wrote, formal natural law had given place to many varieties of substantive natural law making substantive demands for justice through law incompatible with the formal, individualistic principles of earlier natural law. Socialist theories contributed in particular to this development. More generally, Weber writes:

> In consequence of both juridical rationalism and modern intellectual scepticism in general, the axioms of natural law have lost all capacity to provide the fundamental basis of a legal system. The disappearance of the old natural law conceptions has destroyed all possibility of providing the law with a metaphysical dignity by virtue of its immanent qualities. In the great majority of its most important provisions it has been unmasked all too visibly, indeed, as the product or the technical means of a compromise between conflicting interests. (1954, pp. 297-298)

Thus the 'charisma of reason' has passed and the basis of the legitimacy of the modern capitalist state has approximated more and more the pure type of legal domination. This is not merely the consequence of the historical development of rational law through the activities of jurists and others combining the satisfaction of professional intellectual needs for systematization and generalization with the accommodation of demands from the state and bourgeois interests. The modern state cannot, in Weber's view, derive stable authority either from tradition or charisma. Natural law, in his analysis, has been an agency of change and development of major significance. Yet its changeability and controversy make it quite unable to provide a stable basis of legitimacy. It infused new ideas and values into the rationalizing Western law which became stable through processes of formalization with which natural law had only temporarily and incidentally been allied. As it developed in new forms, natural law challenged the formal qualities of the law and hence parted company with the essential foundations of legal domination.

For Weber, legal domination is the *essential* foundation of the bureaucratic administration on which not only the modern state but also modern capitalism depends. Bureaucracy is technically superior to any other form of administration and, in Weber's view, it is the only form suitable for managing the complexities of modern societies. Hence Weber's clear opinion is that natural law cannot emerge again as a unified system of values to reshape the law in a manner that sets it free from its ever more formal and systematic qualities and leads it according to systematic value-rational principles.[4] Thus, only at a certain point in history did the substantively rational ideas of 'reason' in natural law coincide with the requirements of systematization in Western law.

Natural law is the only form of 'legal ideology' Weber recognizes. Its historical importance and relatively coherent and systematic value orientation at particular times in Western history tempted him to provide a specific place for it in his typology of legitimacy. Yet its transience convinced Weber quite properly that it could not be representative of a fundamental type of political legitimacy having an explanatory significance similar to that of the other concepts in his typology of legitimate domination. Once natural law had been analysed out of Weber's typology, all possibility of systematically confronting the ideological functions of law disappeared and, with it, all possibility of systematic analysis of the conditions under which legal domination may become problematic.[5]

Escape from the tyranny of the ever more detailed and all enveloping web of 'value neutral' technical rules can come only from the emergence of a charismatic leader who imposes new values to direct the law according to substantive principles and policies and lead society into new paths until the inevitable process of routinization sets in again. The role of the citizen is to obey the law and perhaps, in periodic elections, to confirm the choice of leaders whose election gives them the power to enact into law whatever policies they see fit, guided only by expediency, personal vision and the legal restraints of the constitution which, if adhered to, confer unchallenged legitimacy on the leaders' acts. Weber's analysis seems to suggest that it will never be possible to foresee conditions in which tensions in society directly threaten the basis of legal domination. The providential emergence of the charismatic leader is a precondition of change. And such a development—the irrational 'outburst' of charisma—defies theoretical analysis. It is the inexplicable irrationality for which a place is carefully preserved in Weber's rational science.

The only destination of change which *is* predictable is ever increasing bureaucratization of politics, economy and society in a technically rational world which has seen the "end of ideology" (cf. Parsons, 1967, p. 100). Legal domination is, therefore, not a concept which allows us to reach an analysis of law's ideological functions which could explain their relevance for political action and social change. It sees these functions in a single dimension, that of rationalization. Rationalization is the sole consistent and ubiquitous motor of change, removed from all human choice and struggle.

Thus society becomes, for Weber, an "iron cage" imprisoning men who increasingly "need 'order' and nothing but order, who become nervous and cowardly if for one moment this order wavers, and helpless if they are torn away from total incorporation in it" (Weber in a 1909 speech, quoted in Mayer, 1956, pp. 127-128). The sociology which begins from the conception of social action as the choices of the free will of individuals leads to a view of society in which, for almost all, there are no politically important choices to be made.

Legal Rationality and Legal Ideology

In this essay it is appropriate only to consider how far the use of the concept of legal domination and the view of modern law on which it is based provide an acceptable basis for the analysis which leads Weber to adopt this view of present and future society. This will be done, first, by re-examining the idea introduced earlier, that purpose rational submission is the basis of legal domination; second, by making some general comments on the nature of legal ideology; and, third, by reintroducing the concept of legal values and relating certain 'ultimate' values to Weber's typology of legal rationality.

It is obvious that in 'normal' circumstances of political stability legal domination usually exists in the form Weber describes. Legal or other rationally established norms do often provide the necessary and sufficient 'title' to power of command and produce sociologically significant ideas of 'duty' in those who are to be influenced towards compliance with the dictates of holders of power who are designated by the norms. Governments change without change in the political system within which they operate. At all levels of structures of political authority officials come and go but the structures remain. Do they become, as Weber suggests, ever more permanent? Is legal domination in important respects self perpetuating? Contemporary society hardly reflects the 'end of ideology' heralded by some sociologists more than two decades ago (see e.g. Bell, 1960). Competing systems of values and beliefs proliferate yet, as Ernest Gellner has suggested, it is possible to see these ideological currents of Western life today as merely superimposed ineffectually over a technological world with its own dynamics and which is too essential for modern life to be fundamentally challenged, whatever the ideological basis of the challenge (Gellner, 1975, pp. 192-193).

If, as suggested earlier, in Weber's analysis submission to the authority of law is a type of submission of will corresponding to the type of purpose rational social action, then legal domination exists as legitimate domination because it provides the framework of regulation which is seen as appropriate for the fulfilment of rationally chosen individual purposes. Individuals accept legal domination as legitimate because they consider their interests are best served by the continued existence of a system of rational law in the society in which they seek to fulfil their chosen purposes.

As an analysis of the ideological conditions of social order this is no more adequate than, for example, Herbert Spencer's conception of society as the consequence of the free interaction of self seeking individual wills. Hence Durkheim's famous criticism (Durkheim, 1933) that the Spencerian contract between individuals presupposes a regulation of the contract which is social— supra-individual—and the expression of a 'moral consciousness' within society or, as we might now put it, a certain ideological climate.

Purposes are rationally chosen by individuals within the constraints of what is, for them *conceivable* as a rational purpose. This conception depends in its turn, to a considerable extent, on how social relations are perceived and on general cognitive and evaluative judgments about the nature of society. These judgments, which involve certain conceptions of justice and social order, enable the individual to define his actual and ideal place in society and thus also his social expectations which provide parameters for the purposes he seeks to achieve. Hence, the purpose rational action, which takes place within the security of legal domination and so justifies individuals in accepting such domination as legitimate, is chosen within an ideological climate which influences the scope of conceivable choices and expectations.

It will be argued here that while Weber is correct in pointing out the partially self-sustaining character of legal domination in certain circumstances, this is not a consequence of the inevitability of rationalization as an unchallengeable necessity removed from influence by human will, but is, to a significant extent, the consequence of ideological effects of law which help to create conditions under which the range of choices of action and the expectations of individuals are normally seriously conceived only within the limits of the conception of society and social relations embodied in legal ideology.

In a recent paper Duncan Kennedy has tried to relate preferences for formalism or substantivism in legal reasoning to particular *value* preferences, centred on, respectively, individualistic and altruistic ethics (Kennedy, 1976). His method of doing so is, in some respects, rather impressionistic yet it is vital to affirm that Weber's distinction between formal and substantive rationality is not adequate to parcel value considerations out of formally systematized law. The concept of formal logical law is the essential basis of Weber's claim that legal domination makes no reference to values in the law, hence that it sustains itself through its purely technical utility for the fulfilment of purpose rational conduct of those subject to authority. But, in reality, formal and substantive considerations are inextricably related in all legal systems made up of rules intended to influence behaviour, and the development of law, of whatever kind, expresses certain value orientations or, at least, implies certain value preferences reflected in legal rules and principles.

A 'pure' formally rational legal system or a 'pure' substantively rational legal system is realistically an impossibility. A system of fundamental values elaborated according to purely substantive criteria could not produce law (in the sense of rules or intelligible, workable guides for a system of social order) at all but only a private ethical code requiring each situation to which the code is to be applied to be analysed in all its aspects (not just those picked out as relevant by formal criteria in a legal system) and ultimately in terms of a unique subjective determination of how fundamental values may be best realized in all the circumstances. This would involve a process of introspection which could not give rise to a predictable and practical system of legal control.[6] Conversely a purely formal system making no reference to substantive purposes or situations of human beings could only be a system of quasi-mathematical logic, assessing logical relations between concepts bearing no relation to actual experience or human objectives. Such a system could not be a legal system since it would be incapable of connecting its logic with meaningful conduct in social life and hence would be wholly irrelevant to any legal purposes of social control of whatever nature. It is clearly impossible to create a pure formal logic of legal rules (cf. Kennedy, 1976, p. 1724), just as it is impossible to create a system of rules of law on the basis only of a subjective elaboration of substantive values. Formal rationality and substantive rationality cannot therefore represent different types of *legal* thought but only different facets of legal thought. Both are necessarily present in any legal system made up of rules aimed at regulation of social life.

Yet, in Weber's sociology of law, formal logical legal rationality tends to take on a life of its own. In this way it becomes the basis of a 'value free' or 'value neutralized' technology of social order. But even when a rule is applied by mechanical processes of deduction, its meaning is given only by reference to human purposes or human conduct. Even mechanical jurisprudence, as Roscoe Pound called it, which purports to be blind to everything except the logical requirements of formal elaboration of existing concepts, creates value implications either by 'unthinkingly' carrying the values embedded in legal rules to new situations by merely applying such rules, or, by altering the value orientations of an area of the law by mechanically applying legal concepts or rules to new situations where the substantive effect of application is quite different from substantive effects in areas where the legal concepts or rules have previously been applied. Of course such value implications may often be extremely ambiguous. The fact that they may be unrecognized by the judge does not affect their existence for those affected by or aware of the relevant law.

Weber was, of course, well aware of this but he could not analyse it within his framework of ideal types because the value implications of formally systematized and generalized law are necessarily highly complex, historically specific and often seemingly self-contradictory. They cannot be the subject of a typology. They make up part of a rich tapestry of ideology created in the law and developed in modern legal systems to form modes of cognition and evaluation of virtually all important recurrent social relations and of the institutions and processes in which social action is patterned.

Legal ideology in the sense used here refers, therefore, to the structures of values and cognitive ideas presupposed in and expressed through legal doctrine developed by courts and other practical law finding or law creating agencies and in the work of legislators and jurists in so far as these ideas and values serve to influence the manner in which social roles and relationships are conceptualized and evaluated.

Processes of generalization which have been referred to earlier are naturally promoted by a legal profession monopolizing the organization and application of law in stable conditions. Thus, although legal ideology in a secular highly systematized legal order cannot attain consistency in its value orientations, processes of legal development often allow certain value implications in rules or concepts to be developed into quite broad value orientations: partly through 'internal' rationalizing legal processes, particularly those of generalization of concepts and principles; and partly through the effects of identifiable 'external' pressure sources (administrative, order-maintaining requirements of the state, particular demands of classes and groups, etc.) influencing the legal system.

Legitimacy and Personal Values

Legal ideology is sociologically significant in so far as it influences the manner in which individuals conceptualize and evaluate social relations and their place and aspirations within society. In Weber's terms, it is important in so far as it helps to fix the limits within which rational purposes of social action are chosen. Within the limits of this essay only a few aspects of this matter can be touched upon.

It can be noted that even in the most formally systematized legal orders, two values are regularly associated with law in general. These are the values of 'justice' and 'order, both of them so ambiguous that they can be supported in some form by individuals espousing the most varied beliefs and ideals. It is unnecessary here to ask what these values 'really' import. Our concern, in analysis of legal ideology, is with recurrent themes in discussion of these values and with the way in which law regularly interprets them and promotes its interpretation as socially significant and essentially definitive. Order implies the subjection of all phenomena (natural and social) to rational control. *Justice* implies fair treatment of individuals, groups, etc. within this system of rational control. Fair treatment is not necessarily equal treatment. Fairness depends on a judgment of circumstances. Here then is a crucial ideological task of the administration of justice: to fix values which determine what circumstances should be weighed in the balance and to promote conditions under which these values are accepted as necessary and sufficient. Part of law's ideological function is to determine the content of justice in social relations: to promote definite conceptions by individuals of what is their 'due'; what is an acceptable return for effort; what obligations can be considered to be attached to oneself and others in the circumstances in which one finds oneself, and in a broad sense, what is to be expected from life.

The value of *order* in law implies consistency, certainty, stability and specifically, the maintenance of predictable patterns of action by officials and others (cf. Barkun, 1971, p. 134). Order implies the stability of existing institutions and structures of social relations whatever their substantive content. 'Order' is contrasted with 'chaos' and is thus associated with human capacity to rationally control the conditions of life in its natural and social environment. It is, of course, no coincidence that the deeply ambiguous values of order and justice are related to Weber's categories of formal and substantive legal rationality. Both polarities reflect the essential duality of law which has been recognized as long as legal philosophy has existed.

Weber's primary failure was in failing to develop a mode of analysis which would emphasize the permanent fusion of these elements in all law and all legal systems. What is understood by values of justice and order varies greatly in different societies and at different times. The content of legal ideology in this sense varies greatly, and the demands made on legal institutions vary correspondingly in so far as these demands are structured by legal ideology. Nevertheless, the tension between these values can, in certain circumstances, determine directions of political change and perhaps also conditions under which political legitimacy based on rational law may be threatened.

In modern societies sophisticated mechanisms are employed to ensure that as far as possible the content of justice and order in legal ideology is accepted as the basis of general social conceptions among members of society. Even in patently undemocratic regimes the consistent appeal to 'the people's will' is used to reinforce acceptance of legal conceptions of justice. In developed legal systems, rigorous formal adherence to legal procedures especially in trial is encouraged, even where — as in political show trials — formal procedures have no relevance to the actual consequences of the trial. The value of order is consistently promulgated in elaborate charades. In many legal systems, the appeal to democratic will and the insistence on procedural propriety are genuine contributions to the safeguarding of legal values. In all systems their ideological significance is not to be underestimated.

How are these matters related to the concept of legal domination and the relationship between law and political legitimacy? Legal ideology, elaborated within legal institutions, and supporting, in so far as it permeates popular consciousness, the view that law is a 'common sense' embodiment of reason and the technically necessary framework for purpose rational social action, exists as a relatively identifiable ideological form only in certain societies. It exists only to the extent that legal institutions possess a degree of autonomy, rather than merely reflecting in a direct manner ideological inputs from political or religious powers. The conditions of this autonomy are partly explored by Weber in his analysis of the development of Western law through the interaction of state interests, the interests of client groups, particularly the rising bourgeoisie, and the professional interests of lawyers seeking to establish a rationally organized body of technical legal knowledge.

Where such conditions are satisfied and a stable development of legal ideas, particularly through processes of generalization, is supervised by an organized legal profession ensuring doctrinal continuity and resistance to rapid uncontrolled change in the content of legal ideology, then legal ideology may well be enabled to gradually permeate a developing society and powerfully influence more general ideological currents within it (see Cotterrell, 1981). To the extent that law can be portrayed as the rational compromise of interests promoted by 'enlightened' rulers or representative democracy, it may come to be seen as a 'harmony of conflicting wills', the necessary regulation which actually *constitutes* and defines all significant characteristics of society itself (cf. Weber's criticism of Stammler's legal-ideological conception of society. Weber, 1977, 98 ff.).

Legal ideology contains detailed elaborations of both conceptions of justice and conceptions of order. In so far as the former define the 'proper' expectations individuals may have in their relations with each other they purport to fix general conceptions of social relations. In so far as the latter define the range of choice of action available to individuals, they specify in ideology the scope of human personality and its expression, the relation between the individual and 'society' and the nature of individuality.

The connotations of order and justice therefore imply a 'continuum' of values which extend far beyond procedural values directly reflected in the forms of adjudication and application of law. It can be suggested that legal legitimacy depends ultimately on the belief of individual actors that law promotes, within the limits imposed by its 'essential' nature as a consistent and comprehensive rational *system* of regulation, what is most fundamental among the actor's values of justice and order, thought of not merely as procedural elements in law, but *social* values.

Conclusion

Various writers have suggested theories of a 'legitimation crisis' based on particular conceptions of contradictions within modern capitalist societies (see especially Habermas, 1976a). To attempt to evaluate such theories would take us too far from Weber's themes and too far from the specific concerns of this essay. Nevertheless, as Jürgen Habermas and others have noted, the greatly increased scope of state activity in contemporary capitalist societies necessarily produces major changes in the nature of legal regulation and its impact on individuals and their beliefs about the society in which they live. For various reasons differential access to law as between sectors and classes in society has diminished with the development of new forms of legal representation, legal aid and other institutions. And, with the increase in state intervention, "taken-for-granted cultural factors which previously were fringe conditions of the political system are now drawn into the administrative field of planning" (Habermas, 1976b, p. 378). Law is brought to the direct attention of individuals in their experience far more extensively and in far more varied contexts than previously. Hence the relationship between the specific content of legal ideology and the detailed experience of individuals and groups is made increasingly apparent to the broad mass of individuals in a wide variety of situations. Consequently, increasing demands are made on the law from all quarters, and established legal conceptions of justice and order are challenged.

This in itself poses no threat to legal legitimacy as long as these demands for particular values can be considered by those making them to be capable of being met without compromising other values of justice or order which provide fundamental justifications of the existing legal system. Even where this is not so there will be no threat as long as the law's legitimating values are considered ultimately more fundamental than the values demanded. In such a case demands will not be pressed to the point of challenging the legitimacy of the legal system as a whole.

It may be suggested in conclusion that legal domination begins to become problematic when two conditions are met: first, the values demanded are seen by those demanding them as ultimately more important than values, considered to be embodied in the legal system, which provide the basis of any claim to legitimacy it may have; and, second, it is considered that the legal system cannot embrace the values demanded and those which found its legitimacy in a sufficiently rationally consistent manner to maintain the systematic character of law on which legal domination depends.

Western law has been dependent on the apparent fusion within a *rational system of rules* of carefully circumscribed values of justice and order. The centring of both of these sets of value orientations primarily on procedural matters and their substantive implications has made this rational harmony possible. And, as Thurman Arnold pointed out many decades ago, the ideological significance of much broader value implications in the law has often depended on the obscuring of practical incompatibilities between them when they are invoked in legal practice (Arnold, 1935). To the extent then, that legal ideology has not actually constrained demands upon the law for satisfaction of values incompatible with the requirements of its systematic rational nature, it has 'neutralized' these demands by continuing to proclaim adherence to broad fundamental values which in fact are not, and cannot be, realized in legal practice. As increasing demands are made on the law and increasingly wide experience of the 'illusion' and 'reality' of its value orientations is made available to individuals, the problem of maintaining the rational order of the legal system and the hegemony of legal ideology may become a particularly serious one.

These considerations do not destroy the utility of Weber's concept of legal domination. They indicate, however, that the highly complex ideological elements of law must be analysed in ways that cannot utilize the ideal type method, if conditions of legitimacy are to be understood in relation to social change. Weber's interpretation of political legitimacy in modern states reflects, perhaps, not only the distinct ideological conditions within which the conception of the German *Rechtsstaat* developed[7] but also a form of legal positivism—the German *Begriffsjurisprudenz*—which, far from being the natural mode of legal thought in modern societies, appears increasingly to have been the product of particular historical conditions and the preserve of a particular tradition of Continental European scholarship in law. The combination of formal and sub-stantive considerations in perpetual tension seems to be the continuing legacy of legal history for today's law. In this tension lies both stability and impetus to change in law. And because law's ideological content changes and can be changed, Weber's 'iron cage' is less secure than he thought. Action on and through the law is one of the necessary, though not sufficient, means for breaking out of it.

Notes

1.   Weber explicitly denies the possibility of popular democracy in normal conditions for reasons which are familiar in the tradition of 'elite theory' in political sociology (Weber, 1954, p. 334).

2. I.e. charismatic or traditional domination. Hence attempts to argue for a fourth category of legitimate domination — based on belief in validity of ultimate values — seem to miss the point of Weber's analysis (cf. Spencer, 1970; and see Albrow, 1972).

3. See Weber's closely related discussion of democratic ideologies in terms of the type of charismatic domination (Weber, 1947, 354 ff.).

4. It is relevant to note here that, particularly in the late nineteenth century, the anti-absolutist tendencies of natural law had been effectively dissolved away in German thought, so that the state was made to appear the guardian of liberties rather than their potential enemy. "Natural law lost its status as an independent source of social norms. Positive law was redefined as an offshoot or an ally of eternal ethical principles. The idealized state became a moral agent, an educational institution, and the freedom from external restraint was transformed into the inner freedom of the ethically self-directed individual" (Ringer, 1969, p. 114; and see Troeltsch, 1934, p. 214). This view of natural law which sees it *absorbed* into the conception of the modern state rather than discarded, and which was current in Weber's time, suggests why for him the idea of a significant revival of natural law seemed untenable. The modern state has superseded natural law and in absorbing it has drawn strength from it. Hence the conception of the German *Rechtsstaat* which is reflected in Weber's concept of legal domination (cf. e.g. Haines, 1930, 246 ff.). Compare the idea of the 'rule of law' in English constitutional theory which is usually held to import definite *values* governing the exercise of legal authority. See e.g. Finnis, 1980, 270 ff. Cf. Kirchheimer, 1967, for a typically provocative analysis.

5. As David Beetham suggests (1974, p. 259), while the static quality of the types of legitimacy prevents such systematic analysis in Weber's sociology, his writings on specific political developments do explore conditions of change particularly in terms of the relations of classes. See J. G. Merquior's extremely negative judgment on the use of Weber's typology (Merquior, 1980, 131 ff.) and compare Talcott Parsons' dramatically different assessment in his introduction to Weber, 1947, p. 77.

6. On the relationship between legal rules and ultimate values in a legal order oriented primarily to substantive rationality in Weber's sense, see e.g. Schacht, 1964, 77 ff., 201; Coulson, 1964, Ch. 3 and Ch. 6.

7. Cf. Arthur Mitzman's more general judgment: "At the heart of Weber's vision lies only the truth of his epoch, his country and his station, the truth of a bourgeois scholar in Imperial Germany" (Mitzman, 1970, p. 3) and see footnote 4 *supra*. Weber's conception of legitimate domination in the modern state reflects what appear to be deep rooted political assumptions recurrent in German society. Cf. Julien Freund's remarks on a failure of German sociology to confront Weber directly "as though the author's ideas might prove embarrassing on closer inspection" (Freund, 1968, p. 288). And for detailed discussion of German political reactions to Weber, see Roth, 1965. On recent German studies, however, see Kalberg, 1979, and especially his comments on p. 137.

References

Albrow, M. (1972). Weber on Legitimate Norms and Authority: A Comment on Martin E. Spencer's Account. *British Jo. Sociol.* **23**, 483-487.

Arnold, T. (1935). *The Symbols of Government.* Yale University Press.

Aron, R. (1964). *German Sociology.* (M. and T. Bottomore, transl.) Greenwood reprint 1979. Westport.

Barkun, M. (1971). Law and Social Revolution: Millenarianism and the Legal System. *Law and Society Rev.* **6**, 113-141.

Beetham, D. (1974). *Max Weber and the Theory of Modern Politics.* George Allen and Unwin, London.

Bell, D. (1960). *The End of Ideology.* Free Press, Glencoe.

Bendix, R. (1966). *Max Weber: An Intellectual Portrait.* Methuen, London.

Cotterrell, R. (1981). The Development of Capitalism and the Formalisation of Contract Law. In *Law, State and Society* (B. Fryer, A. Hunt, D. McBarnet and B. Moorhouse, Eds), pp. 54-69. Croom Helm, London.

Coulson, N. J. (1964). *A History of Islamic Law.* Edinburgh University Press.

D'Entrèves, A. P. (1967). *The Notion of the State.* Clarendon Press, Oxford.

Durkheim, E. (1933). *The Division of Labour in Society* (G. Simpson, transl.). Macmillan, New York.

Finnis, J. (1980). *Natural Law and Natural Rights.* Clarendon Press, Oxford.

Freund, J. (1968). *The Sociology of Max Weber* (M. Ilford, transl.). Allen Lane, London.

Gellner, E. (1975). *Legitimation of Belief.* Cambridge University Press.

Gerth, H. H. and Mills, C. W. (1948). Eds and transl. From *Max Weber: Essays in Sociology.* Routledge and Kegan Paul, London.

Habermas, J. (1976a). *Legitimation Crisis* (T. McCarthy, transl.). Heinemann, London.

Habermas, J. (1976b). Problems of Legitimation in Late Capitalism (T. Hall, transl.). In *Critical Sociology* (P. Connerton, Ed.), pp. 363-387. Penguin, Harmondsworth.

Haines, C. G. (1930). *The Revival of Natural Law Concepts.* Harvard University Press.

Hirst, P. Q. (1976). *Social Evolution and Sociological Categories.* George Allen and Unwin, London.

Honigsheim, P. (1968). *On Max Weber* (J. Rytina, transl.). Free Press, New York.

Hunt, A. (1978). *The Sociological Movement in Law.* Macmillan, London.

Jaspers, K. (1965). *Three Essays: Leonardo, Descartes, Max Weber* (R. Manheim, transl.). Routledge and Kegan Paul, London.

Kalberg, S. (1979). The Search for Thematic Orientations in a Fragmented Oeuvre: The Discussion of Max Weber in Recent German Sociological Literature. *Sociology* **13**, 127-139.

Kennedy, D. (1976). Form and Substance in Private Law Adjudication. *Harvard Law Rev.* **89**, 1685-1778.

Kirchheimer, O. (1967). The *Rechtsstaat* as Magic Wall. In *The Critical Spirit: Essays in Honor of Herbert Marcuse* (J. Barrington Moore *et al.*, Eds), pp. 287-312. Beacon Press, Boston.

Mayer, J. P. (1956). *Max Weber and German Politics.* Second ed. Arno reprint 1979. New York.

Merquior, J. G. (1980). *Rousseau and Weber: Two Studies in the Theory of Legitimacy.* Routledge and Kegan Paul, London.

Mitzman, A. B. (1970). *The Iron Cage: An Historical Interpretation of Max Weber.* Knopf, New York.

Mommsen, W. J. (1974). *The Age of Bureaucracy: Perspectives on the Political Sociology of Max Weber.* Blackwell, Oxford.

Parsons, T. (1967). Evaluation and Objectivity in Social Science: An Interpretation of Max Weber's Contribution. In *Sociological Theory and Modern Society* pp. 79-101. Free Press, New York.

Ringer, F. (1969). *The Decline of the German Mandarins: The German Academic Community 1890-1933.* Harvard University Press, Cambridge.

Roth, G. (1965). Political Critiques of Max Weber: Some Implications for Political Sociology. *Amer. Sociol. Rev.* **30**, 213-222.

Roth, G. and Schluchter, W. (1979). *Max Weber's Vision of History.* University of California Press.

Schacht, J. (1964). *An Introduction to Islamic Law.* Clarendon Press, Oxford.

Spencer, M. E. (1970). Weber on Legitimate Norms and Authority. *British Jo. Sociol.* **21**, 123-134.

Treves, R. (1974). Co-operation Between Lawyers and Sociologists: A Comparative Comment. *British Jo. Law and Society* **1**, 200-204.

Troeltsch, E. (1934). The Ideas of Natural Law and Humanity in World Politics. In O. v. Gierke, *Natural Law and the Theory of Society.* (E. Barker, transl.). Cambridge University Press.

Weber, M. (1927). *General Economic History.* (F. H. Knight, transl.). George Allen and Unwin, London.

Weber, M. (1930). *The Protestant Ethic and the Spirit of Capitalism* (T. Parsons, transl.). George Allen and Unwin, London.

Weber, M. (1947). *The Theory of Social and Economic Organization* (A. M. Henderson and T. Parsons, transl.). William Hodge and Co., London.

Weber, M. (1954). *On Law in Economy and Society.* (E. Shils and M. Rheinstein, transl.). Harvard University Press, Cambridge.

Weber, M. (1977). *Critique of Stammler.* (G. Oakes, transl.). Free Press, New York.

Further Reading

Literature in legal and political theory on the nature of authority is immense but, inevitably, much of it considers the basis of legitimacy primarily in terms of philosophical justification rather than sociological analysis. See especially the essays in Carl J. Friedrich (Ed.) (1958) *Authority* (American Society of Political and Legal Philosophy: Nomos 1), Harvard University Press, Cambridge. Friedrich's brief but scholarly (1972) *Tradition and Authority*, Pall Mall, London, stresses rational bases of authority and is strongly critical of Weber. See also C. W. Cassinelli (1959) "The 'Consent' of the Governed", *Western Political Quarterly*, **12**, 391-409, which denies any rational basis of acceptance of authority and canvasses both sociological and philosophical ideas.

Weber's views on rationality and the basis of order in contemporary Western societies have provided a foundation for an extensive critical literature. See especially: Herbert Marcuse, "Industrialization and Capitalism in the Work of Max Weber" in his (1968) *Negations—Essays in Critical Theory*, Allen Lane, London; Jürgen Habermas' various works, particularly "Technology and Science as 'Ideology'" in his (1971) *Toward a Rational Society*, pp. 81-122, Heinemann, London, and (1976) *Legitimation Crisis*, Heinemann, London: Karl Loewith, "Weber's Interpretation of the Bourgeois-Capitalist World in Terms of the Guiding Principle of 'Rationalization'" in D. Wrong (Ed.) (1970) *Max Weber*, Prentice Hall, Englewood Cliffs. See also Georg Lukács (1971) *History*

and Class Consciousness, Merlin Press, London, particularly the essay
"Reification and the Consciousness of the Proletariat" (pp. 83-222) in which the
discussion is strongly influenced by Weber and offers a critique, by implication,
of Weber's central themes on rationality and modern society. On Lukács'
critique of Weber, David Plotke's discussion in (1975-76) *Berkeley Journal of
Sociology* **20**, 192-230, is useful. See, generally, the essays in Otto Stammer (Ed.)
(1971) *Max Weber and Sociology Today*, Blackwell, Oxford, and the works by
Mommsen, Mayer, and Roth and Schluchter referred to in the text. Weber's
bleak vision of the oppressive, socially pervasive consequences of increasing
rationalization and technological advance is mirrored and transformed in central
themes of the Frankfurt School of critical theory: see especially Max Horkheimer
and Theodor Adorno (1973) *Dialectic of Enlightenment*, Allen Lane, London.
For a recent study of Weber's conception of political legitimacy see J. G.
Merquior (1980) *Rousseau and Weber*, Routledge and Kegan Paul, London.
Merquior's book summarizes major criticisms of Weber, offers an extremely harsh
judgment on his work on political legitimacy as a whole (see especially pp. 135-
136) and seeks to explain its defects primarily in terms of the effects of Weber's
cultural milieu. Among other critiques, see P. M. Blau (1963) "Critical Remarks
on Weber's Theory of Authority", *American Political Science Review* **57**, 305-
316; R. Grafstein (1981) "The Failure of Weber's Conception of Legitimacy",
Journal of Politics **43**, 456; and, for a useful attempt to clear up terminological
confusions, A. Swidler (1973) "The Concept of Rationality in the Work of Max
Weber" *Sociological Inquiry* **43**, 35-42. A much more intricate and wider ranging
analysis of Weber's concept of rationality is contained in S. Kalberg (1980)
"Max Weber's Types of Rationality: Cornerstones for the Analysis of Rationalization Processes in History" *American Journal of Sociology* **85**, 1145-1179.

   Among numerous discussions of contemporary problems of political
legitimacy the following provide interesting contrasts: Alan Wolfe (1977) *The
Limits of Legitimacy*, Free Press, New York; Claus Offe, "Structural Problems
of the Capitalist State" in K. v. Beyme (Ed.) (1974) *German Political Studies*
Vol. 1, pp. 31-57, Sage, London; R. P. Wolff (Ed.) (1971) *The Rule of Law*,
Simon and Schuster, New York; E. V. Rostow (Ed.) (1970) *Is Law Dead?*, Simon
and Schuster, New York; George Kateb (1979) On the 'Legitimation Crisis'
Social Research **46**, 695-727.

   From a position of almost total neglect in Anglo-American literature a few
years ago, Weber's sociology of law has now emerged as a major focus of analysis
in legal theory. For recent general discussions see: Alan Hunt (1978) *The
Sociological Movement in Law*, Ch. 5, Macmillan, London; Maureen Cain, "The
Limits of Idealism — Max Weber and the Sociology of Law" in S. Spitzer (Ed.)
(1981) *Research in Law and Sociology* Vol. 3, JAI Press, Greenwich — stressing
methodological issues; and Piers Beirne, "Ideology and Rationality in Max
Weber's Sociology of Law" in Vol. 2 (1979) of the same series — providing a

concise sketch of Weber's intellectual background and of major aspects of his sociology of law. One of the most incisive brief studies is Martin Albrow's (1975) "Legal Positivism and Bourgeois Materialism—Max Weber's View of the Sociology of Law", *British Journal of Law and Society* **2**, 14-31; and Max Rheinstein's typically thoughtful and scholarly introduction to his (1954) edition of *Max Weber on Law in Economy and Society*, Harvard University Press, Cambridge, is a still valuable guide. I have briefly discussed Weber's analysis of contract in "The Development of Capitalism and the Formalisation of Contract Law" in B. Fryer *et al.* (Eds) (1981) *Law, State and Society*, Croom Helm, London.

For Weber in the context of his times, Marianne Weber's criticized but fascinating (1975) *Max Weber—A Biography*, Wiley, New York, provides much illumination. See also the essay on Weber in Carlo Antoni (1962) *From History to Sociology*, pp. 119-184, Merlin Press, London. Fritz Ringer's (1969) *Decline of the German Mandarins*, Harvard University Press, Cambridge, describes the intellectual and political climate in which Weber wrote; and Paul Honigsheim's reminiscences (1968) *On Max Weber*, Free Press, New York, briefly discuss Weber's relations with the German jurists of his time—a matter of some importance given the orientation of his sociology of law.

While it is often still convenient to approach Weber's magnum opus *Economy and Society* through separately published parts, the complete work is published in two volumes by the University of California Press (1979). For Weber's work as a whole, Reinhard Bendix's (1966) *Max Weber—An Intellectual Portrait*, Methuen, London, remains, despite the proliferation of more recent studies, one of the best introductions in English. Given the continuing significance of Weber's writings for so many issues of contemporary social and legal theory, it seems unlikely that the flood of secondary literature will abate in the near future. Contemporary writers continue to explore what Donald McRae has aptly termed "the liquid and evasive richness which is the secret of Weber's strongest sorcery over all his successors."

5 Gramsci, The State and the Place of Law*

Maureen Cain

If you're not able to understand real individuals, you can't understand what is universal and general. November 19, 1928. (LFP, 136)

Introduction

Antonio Gramsci was born in 1891 in Sardinia, the son of a petty rural official. As a child he was set apart from his fellows as much by his physical weakness as by his intelligence. As a student in Turin and in the years immediately following, when with four socialist colleagues he established the *Ordine Nuovo*, he knew extreme poverty, which both exacerbated his poor health, and strengthened his determination to overcome it. Later he became Secretary General of the Italian Communist Party (PCI), of which he was also a founder member. He was imprisoned by the Fascists in 1926, having returned two years before to Italy from Moscow, where he had spent two years working in the Comintern as representative of the Central Committee of the PCI. He had returned to Italy because as an elected member of parliament he had legal immunity from arrest. None the less, he was deemed too dangerous to go free. "We must prevent this brain from functioning" was the obscene remark of the prosecutor at Gramsci's trial (Adamson, 1980, p. 101). He died in 1937, after 11 years in prison, just four days after his release.

*An earlier version of this paper was presented to a Conference on Critical Legal Studies at the University of Kent, Canterbury, on 30th March-3rd April, 1981.

Law, State and Society Series: "Legality, Ideology and the State", edited by D. Sugarman, 1983. Academic Press, London and New York.

There are four main English language sources of Gramsci's writings. There are his contributions to *Ordine Nuovo* and other journals; his speeches, letters, and interventions in the political debates in the PSI (Italian Socialist Party) and, following the split, in the PCI; the letters which he wrote from prison to political comrades, family, and friends; and the notebooks in which he elaborated his theoretical position during his years in prison. These latter are the main source for this paper.

Gramsci's work is special because, like Marx, he elaborated his most telling concepts from analyses of particular historical events, in the main events of French and Italian history, and the Russian Revolution. He sought also to understand, historically, the different social structure and continuing economic and political disadvantage of southern Italy, and this dual perspective on his own country, of industrial north and quasi feudal or peasant south, adds a richness to his conceptual elaborations, and guarantees his reluctance to solve the problems of theory and history with facile generalizations. Finally, his political experiences, particularly his heavy involvement with the failed factory council movement in Turin in 1919-1920, and the failure of the left to mobilize the masses in the way the fascists subsequently did, provided the problems with which he grappled theoretically. Gramsci's theory is thus deeply rooted in the concrete, although he stressed the importance of the war of ideas on the plane of the elaborated philosophies as well as on the plane of common sense, and contributed more than any other Marxist scholar to our understanding of the place and function of intellectuals.

In recent years there have been published a number of scholarly and politically insightful interpretations of Gramsci (Anderson, 1977; Mouffe (Ed.), 1979; Adamson, 1980; Buci-Glucksman, 1980; Sassoon, 1980a). These have greatly influenced my own reading of Gramsci, and certainly they have confirmed my sense (Cain, 1977a) that Gramsci used the concept of state in a number of different and, indeed, contradictory ways. I am indebted to all these interpreters. My justification for again approaching this topic is that none of these scholars has read Gramsci in order to achieve a better understanding of law. In giving law a minor place they have remained faithful to Gramsci, for whom, as we shall see, it was but one of many pedagogic devices. In this paper, I focus attention on the place of law in Gramsci's conceptual schema because I believe that correct theorization is reciprocally a part of correct political action (Cain and Finch, 1981), and I believe with Mathiesen (1981) that the manipulation of legality is one of the most important techniques deployed by the late capitalist state in its strategy of absorbing incipient conflict in such a way as to conserve the *status quo*. Therefore it is important to understand law.

The discussion starts with Gramsci's analyses of intellectuals, of the state and civil society, and of law; it then considers the epistemology which underpins this theory, and seeks to appraise Gramsci's contribution in the light of the massive attacks on him which were levelled by Althusser in 1970; the final section departs from Gramsci and presents my own views as to how his theorization might most usefully be elaborated.

The Intellectuals, State and Civil Society

Gramsci's conception of the intellectual is related to his theory of knowledge, and made necessary by it (although he produced the conception of the intellectual first). For Gramsci, knowledge is both temporally specific and class specific. Intellectuals constitute the structures which generate, promulgate, and 'verify' class specific knowledges. This paper is not about the intellectuals so I will briefly say that according to Gramsci intellectuals are both conceptive ideologists in Marx's sense, that is, those whose practice it is to think creatively the advance of a class, *and* those who do the organizing and administrative work of a class. They are the "thinking *and organising* (my italics) elements of a particular fundamental social class" (PN, p. 3). Thus the organic intellectuals of the bourgeoisis are not simply lawyers, as I have argued elsewhere (Cain, 1976), but also managers, technicians and state officials. In fulfilling these two functions organic intellectuals are of crucial importance in establishing the knowledge of a class. Because knowledge is (reciprocally) important in achieving and securing political power intellectuals provide a dynamic element in the state-civil society relation.

The third function of intellectuals is the propagation of that knowledge which they have established within their own class, to class allies, and ultimately to enemy classes in order to create and sustain class hegemony of knowledge and ultimately an historical bloc (relatively stable social formation). In Gramsci hegemony involves political as well as ideological domination, a point which is often overlooked: the two are *welded* in the concept of hegemony. While either is possible without the other, their unity in hegemony is an object of class struggle, since it is a stabilizing factor. Full hegemony is not achieved until *after* the revolution, but the objective of hegemony gives an immediate direction to struggle.

I will not deal here with traditional, that is autonomous, intellectuals except to say that they may be used by and allied to a class in the early stages of its movement to hegemony, but are regarded by Gramsci as unreliable as compared with the organic intellectuals whose places and practices develop as a class moves forward.

Intellectuals therefore constitute a crucial link between levels of structure and also within the revolutionary party. They are crucial because for Gramsci an historical bloc involves the consent of many classes to the dominance of one, in alliance with others. The political and ideological generation and maintenance of such consent is hegemony.

The state as superstructure

It is necessary here to quote Gramsci's formulation, which is used by Buci-Glucksman in particular as the basis of her discussion of Gramsci's expanded concept of the state (1980, p. 69). Having pointed out that the identification of the state with government represents a "confusion between civil society and political society" Gramsci continues "For it should be remarked that the general notion of the state includes elements which need to be referred back to the notion of civil society (in the sense that one might say that State = political society + civil society, in other words hegemony protected by an armour of coercion)". This discussion proceeds to a consideration of the possibility of an ethical state or civil society in which the coercive element has withered away. In this conception

> one will have to pass from a phase in which 'State' will be equal to 'government' and 'State' will be identified with civil society (a phase in which state is both, M.C.) to a phase of the State as nightwatchman — i.e. of a coercive organisation which will safeguard the development of the continually proliferating elements of regulated society, and which will therefore progressively reduce its own authoritarian and forcible interventions . . . . (PN, 263)

Elsewhere (in his discussion of "statolatry", PN, p. 268) Gramsci speaks of "the two forms in which the State presents itself in the language and culture of specific epochs, i.e. as civil society and as political society". Later in this discussion too he emphasizes the need "to develop and produce new forms of State life, in which the initiative of individuals and groups will have a 'state' character".

As a final example, in a letter to his sister-in-law in 1931 Gramsci offered the following formulation in which he both clearly delineated his conception of the state as superstructure, and argued that this expanded formulation gave a special place within the state to intellectuals.

> This research will also concern the concept of the State, which is usually thought of as political society — i.e. a dictatorship or some other coercive apparatus used to control the masses in conformity with a given type of production and economy — and not as a balance between political society and civil society, by which I mean the hegemony of one social group over the entire nation, exercised through so-called private organisations like the Church, Trade unions, or schools. For it is above all in civil society that intellectuals exert their influence. (LFP, 204)

It seems that (1) in using his expanded, inclusive superstructural concept of the state Gramsci is identifying a function of control/consent which can be performed by non-governmental institutions; (2) he draws a distinction between passive consent and active participation (PN, 195). This distinction is implicit in all his discussions of a transformed civil society; (3) he uses his expanded conception for at least two purposes: (a) to point a political direction (a state without coercion is not a contradiction in terms), and (b) to link his conception of the state with his immediate political strategy which involves the formation/ development of institutions within which a counter hegemony can be formulated.

This interpretation, namely, that in the expanded conception, state is identified with the two main forms of control by a dominant class and its allies, and processually with the assumption of control to such a class, is borne out further by his assertion (in the context of a discussion about the relationship between Marx and Lenin) that "the foundation of a directive class (i.e. of a state) is equivalent to the creation of a Weltanschauung" (PN, 381).

State and civil society: the narrow conception

The clearest expression of the narrow conception of the state is to be found in Gramsci's *Notes on Italian History*. He writes:

> The historical unity of the ruling classes is realised in the State . . . But it would be wrong to think that this unity is simply juridical and political . . . the fundamental historical unity, concretely, results from the organic relations between State or political society and civil society . . . . (PN, p. 52)

Here then State is equated with political society, and distinguished from the non-political. There are two recurrent themes when Gramsci is working with the narrow conception of the state. The first is that the function of the state and of political society is coercion; that, indeed, coercion is their definitive characteristic. The second theme is that civil society provides a protective layer between the infrastructure and the state or political control. It seems that Gramsci is not consistent on this point, but the main thrust of his arguments in this regard is that the conquest of civil society (a moment towards the establishment of an alternative hegemony) is a prerequisite for the final conquest of political society (the state) as ultimately expressed (if necessary) in a war of movement. The apparent inconsistency occurs because Gramsci is not making a statement about what empirically must be done first, before, as it were, a political thrust is started. He is trying to link his two conceptions in a theoretical statement that political control is not *by definition* gained until consent or ideological control is achieved. The moment of both political and ideological control is hegemony.

(The confusion is also in part metaphoric: civil society is variously presented as the ditches before the walls, and the bastions protecting the retreat of the defeated class, and so delaying the moment of hegemony.)

I must back these assertions with some evidence before I move on. The first piece of evidence is a long quotation from Gramsci's essay on *The Intellectuals*:

> What we can do, for the moment, is to fix two major superstructural "levels": the one that can be called "civil society", that is, the ensemble of organisms commonly called "private", and that of political society or "the State". These two levels correspond on the one hand to the function of "hegemony" which the dominant group exercises throughout society and on the other hand to that of "direct domination" or command exercised through the State and juridical government . . . The intellectuals are the dominant group's "deputies" exercising the subaltern functions of social hegemony and political government. These comprise:—
> 1. the spontaneous consent given by the great masses of the population . . .
> 2. the apparatus of state coercive power which "legally" enforces discipline on these groups who do not "consent" either actively or passively. This apparatus is, however, constituted for the whole of society in anticipation of moments of crisis . . . . (PN, p. 12)

Elsewhere he argues

> the massive structures of the modern democracies both as state organisations and as complexes of associations in civil society, constitute for the art of politics as it were the "trenches" and the permanent fortifications of the front in the war of position. (PN, p. 243)

Thus when Gramsci is operating with the narrow conception of the state as political society, as organized coercion, and distinguishing it from civil society, he uses a narrow conception of hegemony as well. In this narrow conception hegemony is something like ideological control or control within civil society; in the expanded conception hegemony, like the state, is both civil and political: it is a way of saying that a class is in superstructural dominance.

Comparative evaluation

The narrow conception has weaknesses, which must be noted. Civil society is depoliticized, or alternatively put, politics is reduced to state coercion. So, while the narrow conception too points up the immediate political strategy of undermining established apparatuses of hegemony by creating alternatives, these apparatuses are in this view purely ideological, whereas in the expanded conception of civil society they are also political. Moreover, the expanded conception supplies a long-term objective, the demise of coercion coupled with a democratic (active participation rather than passive consent) form of regulation, whereas while the narrow conception supplies a strategy, a general direction, a state without coercion, cannot be derived from it theoretically, because this would be a contradiction in terms. Because of this inability to indicate an overall direction, the narrow conception generates defensive rather than progressive approaches. Finally, the expanded conception is consistent with Gramsci's view of hegemony as being both political and ideological, and therefore expresses the necessary temporal unity of these two moments of control by a directive class. According to the narrow conception, political and civil control may be separated. One may be conceived without the other. Tactics will be affected, because it will therefore seem that one may be achieved without the other.

The expanded conception also has weaknesses, however, for if the state is conceived as all forms of domination by a directive class there is no way of theorizing the *process* of penetration of civil society by agencies of government, e.g. a stronger role for central government in devising school curricula, to give a recent British example. Secondly, there is no way of theorizing what is special about non-governmental forms of control, for example by the church, or the Girl Guides, or the family.[1]

Law

Gramsci referred to the educative function of law frequently, but in a tantalizing and untheorized way. He emphasized the importance of law, but it did not occupy a specific place in his political strategy, or a significant place in his theory.

Gramsci defined the 'juridical' problem as that of "assimilating the entire grouping to its most advanced fraction". He continued:

> It is a problem of the education of the masses . . . this is precisely the function of law in the state and in society; through "law" (in inverted commas in Gramsci's original, M.C.) the State (in its expanded sense of political and ideological control, M.C.) through "law" the State renders the ruling group "homogeneous", and tends to create a social conforming which is useful to the ruling group's line of development . . . . (PN, 195)

Thus law plays a part in the creation of both the political and the ideological elements of hegemony, first by unifying the emergent directive class and its allies, and then by bringing the masses to conformity. Presumably the same analysis could be applied to law in the bourgeois state, but all Gramsci's relatively extended (two page) discussions of law are in the context of his analyses of revolutionary developments. His question is 'what can law do for us' — a positive and open approach.

Law, it becomes clear, has the advantages that it can be used both coercively (through courts and so on) and persuasively. It is persuasive because it assists the directive group by *creating* a 'tradition' in an active and not in a passive sense (PN, 195). Law has an umbrella effect whereby the standards and ways of thought embodied in it penetrate civil society and become a part of common sense. Thus:

> the general activity of law (which is wider than purely State and governmental activity and also includes the activity involved in directing civil society in these zones which the technicians of law call legally neutral — i.e. in morality and in custom generally) serves to understand the ethical problem better in a concrete sense. (PN, 196)

Law produces "a correspondence" between individual conduct and the "ends which society sets itself as necessary so that these ends are accepted in a 'spontaneous and free' way" (1930-32).

Later (in 1933-34) Gramsci picks up the theme again, arguing that for the new directive class led by the industrial workers a new conception of law "must be developed so that it is suitable for such a purpose" — a purpose which it will share with the school system and, Gramsci vaguely tails off "other institutions and activities". What is specific about law, it seems, is its double face—the fact that it is also coercive in its practices, although Gramsci does not return to this or consider it worth elaborating.

More important is his grasp of the positive, norm creative, task of law; this is the aspect which he elaborates in his discussions of the tasks of the revolutionary classes as they advance towards hegemony and the building of a stable historical bloc expressing their dominance. For Gramsci, norm creation is legal, and practices directed towards securing compliance with norms are legal. Thus legal behaviour can be found in all the institutions of civil society. It is not a prerogative of government.

> Every man, in as much as he is active, i.e. living, contributes to modifying the social environment in which he develops (to modifying certain of its characteristics or preserving others); in other words, he tends to establish "norms", rules of living and of behaviour. . . . A father is a legislator for his children, but the paternal authority will be more or less conscious, more or less obeyed, and so forth. . . .
>
> In general, it may be said that the distinction between ordinary men and others who are more specifically legislators is provided by the fact that this second group not only formulates directives which will become a norm of conduct for others but at the same time creates the instruments by means of which the directives themselves will be "imposed" and by means of which it will verify their execution. . . . If everyone is a legislator in the broadest sense of the concept, he continues to be a legislator even if he accepts directives from others—if, as he carries them out he makes certain that others are

carrying them out too; if, having understood their spirit, he propagates them as though making them into rules specifically applicable to limited and definite zones of living. (PN, pp. 265-266)

The last sentence shows why Gramsci argues that the main task of law is educational. It also explains why he sees law as continuing in the non-coercive, regulated state which he sees as the long-term goal of the revolutionary class. The revolutionary task in civil society is therefore very much a struggle for the control of law, that is, *a struggle to achieve authoritative, norm creating positions.* In a society based on active rather than passive consent we should describe these as positions of respect and authority, rather than thinking in more confined, institutional terms. This last point is worth reiterating, for it is a crucial point of articulation between the party of the revolutionary classes and the masses. If the struggle for legislative control is interpreted as gaining the respect of the masses, in their various private groupings, then a society can be envisaged which organically expresses democratic concerns, a society in which consent is active and participatory. If the struggle for legislative control in civil society is interpreted solely as a struggle to gain positions of institutional significance and authority then no organic links between the party and the masses can be created, for the institutions may be pre-given by the existing society and not organic creations of the masses of the revolutionary classes: in such a case a merely passive consent will be generated, and the party, divorced from its mass navigators, will lose its correct direction.

Gramsci makes no distinction between legal and other norms. Elaborating his position beyond the point to which his discussion takes it, it can be argued that this is because norms, like other forms of knowledge, have an existence which is rooted in a class standpoint. In bourgeois society the form in which the norms of the subaltern classes confront those of the dominant classes may have the form of a clash of morality or tradition vs law. Gramsci was concerned, however, with creating active, new, traditions in civil society; with using political society to abet this task; with eliminating the distinction between law and morality by making both political and civil society function in terms of the norms of the revolutionary classes; and so with the gradual diminution of coercion and the creation of an 'ethical society'.

The strength of Gramsci's theory of the state, and of the place of law within it, is its political realism. He acknowledges the importance of coercion and analyses its forms. Indeed, it is this analysis and recognition which enables him to identify a political direction. The section left out of the immediately previous quotation reads as follows:

Of this second group (those who can 'impose' directives, M.C.), the greatest legislative power belongs to the state personnel (elected and career officials), who have at their disposal the legal coercive powers of the state. But this does not mean that the leaders of "private" organisms and organisations do not have coercive sanctions at their disposal too, ranging even up to the death penalty. The maximum of legislative capacity can be inferred when a perfect formulation of directives is matched by a perfect arrangements of the organisms of execution and verification, and by a perfect preparation of the "spontaneous" consent of the masses who must "live" those directives, modifying their own habits, their own will, their own convictions to conform with those directives and with the objectives which they propose to achieve. (PN, 266)

Gramsci's Historicism

Gramsci's theory has been forcefully attacked on the grounds of historicism. Since Gramsci himself claimed that his position was that of an "absolute historicism" and that "Marx is essentially a historicist" (cited in Buci-Glucksman, 1980, p. 349), and since his main critic, Louis Althusser, believed with Gramsci (PN, p. 344) that the opponent occupying the strongest position should always be selected for critique, the attack is unsurprising. But it is not unimportant. Although it occurred a decade or more ago (Althusser, 1970), this battle of the giants still matters both politically and theoretically: politically because it bears on the question of whether the left can be led by experts or specialists in pure thought; theoretically because it bears on the questions of whether such expert thinkers are possible and if not of how a belief in such an expertise can be explained structurally. For us too it is important because Gramsci's theory of knowledge (his historicism) is integrally related to his theory of the intellectuals and therefore to his theory of the state and of hegemony as well as to his formulation of the role and structure of the vanguard party. In the final section I argue that Gramsci's concept of the intellectual is a potential and needed growth point for the modern theory of the state: this concept falls if historicism falls. An analysis and defence of Gramsci's historicism is therefore called for.[1]

The crux of the debate is whether Marxism is a science, which can therefore be distinguished from ideological forms of knowledge by the application of rational criteria concerning its form and its mode of production (Althusser's position); or whether all knowledge, including that styled scientific and that of the Marxist, has the same status theoretically, though not politically (Gramsci's position). This summary statement does justice to neither theorist: it is necessary to examine their positions more closely. Here it must be recorded that only Althusser's critique of Gramsci will be examined: an appraisal of his influential positive contributions to a theory of knowledge merits at the least another paper.

The impetus for Gramsci's work on a theory of knowledge was a political need for a theory, not a logical one. He needed to explain the rise of fascism, to devise a strategy which would undermine advanced capitalism, and to devise a form of organization which would be effective in a revolutionary sense, that is, a form of organization which would transcend the contradiction between discipline and democracy. His theory of the intellectuals played a key part in these enterprises, and his conception of the intellectual was developed before his theory of knowledge was made explicit.

Whenever Gramsci describes to his friends and family his projected intellectual enterprise for his years in prison he emphasizes his wish and intention to study the history and structures of (a) the intellectuals, and (b) language (LFP, 79-80; 86; 183-184; 200). He also constantly bemoans the fact that he cannot do so adequately for lack of access to a research library with its facilities for systematic work. However, he turned this position to good account, for the seven or eight books a week which he did manage to read in the early years of his imprisonment (LFP, 116), covered all manner of topics, and made him aware of the need for a theory of common sense knowledge as well as for a theory of the productions of the recognized intelligentsia (LFP, 145).

When he was first imprisoned he claimed:

> A few books are sent to me from outside, and I read whatever books I happen to get from the prison library every week. I'm blessed with the capacity for finding something of interest even in trash like *feuilletons*. (popular serials, M.C.) 8th August, 1937 (LFP, 93)

Four months later he wrote to his mother:

> I've learned a number of things I would have gone on not knowing about otherwise. 2nd January, 1928 (LFP, 113)

Gramsci's studies of the structure (forms of organization) and influence of intellectuals in Italian history, his complementary understanding of everyday knowledge, and his growing political concern with the modes of articulation between the two, a concern with " 'crucibles' where the unification of theory and practice takes place" (PN, p. 335), led him to formulate a theory of knowledge which transcends the distinction between absolutism and relativism. In rejecting all claims to absolute knowledge he also disregards the verifying claims of reason: indeed, if there is no absolute knowledge there can be no truth. However, correct knowledge is possible and necessary: alternative knowledges are not equal as in relative accounts.

In an earlier work (Cain, 1977a, pp. 21-25), I discussed at length the connections between the various elements of Gramsci's theory of knowledge. The argument has profoundly influenced my own position (Cain and Finch,

1981). Because these fuller and more systematic accounts are available the main elements of Gramsci's theory are simply asserted here.

    i. All knowledge is philosophy, because "even in the slightest manifestation of any intellectual activity whatever, in 'language' there is contained a specific conception of the world". (PN, p. 330)

    ii. Philosophy is distinguished from other knowledge only by its class consistency and appropriateness. (PN, pp. 327; 350; 435–436 esp.)

    iii. The true philosopher is the man of action, and conversely action is the best expression of philosophy. (PN, p. 326; 352)

    iv. Causal, undialectual, and unilinear explanations are not acceptable (PN, pp. 467)

    v. All knowledge is human centred. (PN, p. 446)

    vi. There are no timeless truths. (PN, pp. 445; 455)

    vii. There is no privileged category of the human: "the nature of the human species is not given". (PN, p. 355)

    viii. Correct knowledge is class specific. (PN, pp. 352; 408; 455)

    ix. The promulgation of class specific knowledge is possible and important: forms of knowing are objects of class struggle. (PN, pp. 327; 393)

    x. Class knowing is an organic activity, grasped initially by class instincts for correct action, which must be formulated, and which are capable of recognition as having been correct or not only retrospectively. (PN, p. 327)

Thus Gramsci regards correct knowledge as historically specific and class specific. *An analysis at most can be correct for a time and for a class.* Yet Gramsci also warns against the "primitive infantilism" (PN, 407) of claims that forms of knowledge can mechanically be derived from class structure, and not only because language itself, both in its structure and form, provides a value laden mediation (PN, p. 450). For a Marxist, then, in knowing as in politics there are no certainties, but there can be errors. It is an uncomfortable, but a profoundly open and anti-totalitarian, position.

Importantly, therefore, Gramsci saw no distinction between science and other forms of knowledge, and no essential distinction between philosophy and other forms of knowledge. Indeed, he argues strongly against the purported elevation of Marxism to the status of science, which he regards as a peculiarly retrogressive step.

> Separated from the theory of history and politics philosophy cannot be other than metaphysics, whereas the great conquest in the history of modern thought, represented by the philosophy of praxis, is precisely *the concrete historicisation of philosophy and its identification with history.* (PN, p. 435) my italics.

However, the internal structure of any developed theory renders it more persuasive than mere 'common sense', which is typically layered with concepts and objects from previous historical periods, and is an amalgam in which the elements are not systematically linked and may, indeed, be inconsistent.

Thus for Gramsci science, and philosophy, including Marxist science and philosophy, are (i) temporal and (ii) human productions. Their correctness relates to their use-values. There is no outside-time rationality which can arbitrate between theories; nor does the number of people thinking in terms of a particular form of knowledge guarantee its correctness, even in a temporal sense (PN, pp. 327; 410). Thus, there can be no denying Gramsci's claim that his theory represents an absolute historicism. For this reason Althusser was correct in selecting Gramsci as his prime target in his attack on historicism, and in his attempt to establish the privileged status of Marxist theorizing.[2]

After detailing the ways in which Marxist texts lend themselves to an historical reading, Althusser (1970) begins his appraisal of and attack on Gramsci. In two senses he regards Gramsci's historicist insistence as acceptable (p. 127). First, he acknowledges that "Marxism cannot claim to be the theory of history unless even in its theory it can think the conditions of this penetration into history", i.e. its penetration into people's practical lives, as a way of living and of thinking one's way of living. Secondly, he expresses sympathy with Gramsci's "vigorous protest against . . . aristocratism of theory and of its 'thinkers' ", p. 129.

However, on the negative side Althusser points out (1) that Gramsci does not distinguish between historical and dialectical materialism and (2) that Gramsci fails to distinguish Marxist theory from "ideological conceptions of the world". These failures, according to Althusser, give rise to a number of serious errors, namely a collapsing of the levels of structure, empiricism and humanism.

In Gramscian Marxism, says Althusser, there is no longer any privileged present, for all presents are privileged to the same degree. The effect of this is to 'flatten out' the essential section of contemporaneity in each present. In other words, the presents of the separate instances of structure are diverse, and variously articulated. Historicism forces them to coincide in accordance with a contemporaneous reading. More simply expressed, Althusser says that Gramsci makes it impossible to analyse how a class and that class's way of knowing are related together. He argues that Gramsci implies only one possible relationship, i.e. that class knowledge is treated as an inevitable consequence of class position, so that two levels of structure, the economic and the ideological, are put together or conflated. Althusser's concern is that this leaves no space for the relative autonomy of knowledges. Gramsci, says Althusser, collapses the theory or knowledge of history into real history and reduces the (theoretical) object of the science of history to real history. This confusion between the object of knowledge and the real world is empiricism.

By this process, and also because Gramsci argues that a philosopher is in the last instance a politician, Althusser says theoretical practice in Gramsci loses its specificity and becomes historical practice. "Deprived of any object of its own, Marxist philosophy loses the status of an autonomous discipline." This loss of an autonomous knowledge, and "the reduction of all knowledge to the historical social relations" means that "a second, underhand reduction can be introduced by treating the relations of production as mere human relations". History becomes the transformation of human nature which is its subject, p. 137.

These errors, says Althusser, are not peculiar to Gramsci, but are endemic to historicisms, which, as a result of them, are inevitably fatalist (knowledge is determined), voluntarist (because this is the only possible political escape from fatalism), and humanist, that is, fundamentally dependent upon an idealist problematic which treats human nature as trans-historical (p. 138).

In his subsequent work (1976) Althusser reconsidered not his critique of historicism, but his earlier (1969) attempt to specify the unique character of scientific knowledge and of its means of production. However, given the criticisms outlined above, the main thrust of Althusser's *auto-critique* is relevant. As he summarized it (1976, p. 196):

> ... I was led to give a rationalist explanation of the 'break', contrasting *truth* and *error* in the form of the speculative distinction between *science* and *ideology*, in the singular and in the general. The contrast between Marxism and bourgeois ideology thus became simply a special case of this distinction. Reduction + interpretation: from this rationalist-speculative drama the class struggle was practically absent.

He also emphasizes:

> ... the primacy of the practical function over the theoretical function in philosophy itself. . . . It is not a Whole, made up of homogeneous propositions submitted to the verdict: truth or error. It is a system of positions (theses), and, through these positions, itself occupies positions in the theoretical class struggle (p. 143).

The remaining task in this section is to see to what extent Althusser's criticisms as revised apply to the work of Gramsci. This will enable us the better to assess Gramsci's contribution and its political relevance. Again, because this paper is primarily about law and state, I will try to summarize.

At the most general level Althusser jettisons his distinctions between truth/error and science/ideology. He comes closer to Gramsci in abandoning the possibility of the concept of error, and substituting that of "correctness" which "must be continually reworked", pp. 142-143. This process of reworking is and results from "the class struggle in theory". The aim is to defend (and presumably to advance) "positions useful to Marxist theory and to the proletarian class struggle: against the most threatening forms of bourgeois ideology". . . . p. 146. Thus now in Althusser as in Gramsci a theory is to be judged in terms of its use-value from a proletarian standpoint. This use-value is specific in time and space: it has no fixity.

However, also at the general level Althusser continues to insist that Marxism is an *autonomous* science. It is indeed a science which revolutionaries can use, but it is more than that: it is "a science which they can use because it rests on *revolutionary class theoretical positions*". This distinguishes Marxism from all other sciences (and ideologies). But unfortunately the phrase is ambiguous. Are these the theoretical positions held by the revolutionary class? That would be an even more empiricist theory of knowledge than that of Gramsci, who devoted much thought to how the revolutionary class could be educated to realize itself as such. Certainly in this society (the UK) the proletariat (revolutionary class) seems bent on consensus politics, and alleges to pollsters that it is tired of extremes! But if both the empirical (past) and utility (future) tests are ruled out as (i) empiricist and (ii) insufficient, respectively, in what sense is Marxism a revolutionary class theoretical position? Are we not back to identifying the appropriateness of the theory to the revolutionary class by some internal characteristic of the theory, are we not returned, that is, to a rationalism/theoreticism? Either the answer is yes, and Althusser falls by his own arguments, or he is saying the same as Gramsci is saying, and is himself reinstating utility, and moving in the direction of historicism, for utility must be a spatially and temporally specific criterion, i.e. an historicist one.

Since Althusser's more specific criticisms derive from his most general ones they too should fall with the above argument. None the less, it will aid my delineation of Gramsci's position to go through them one at a time.

Conflation of structural levels

While Gramsci's important concept of the 'historical bloc' identifies a specific unity "of economy and culture and culture and politics" (Texier, 1979), this concept depends on prior analytic distinctions between these elements. The theory of superstructures must be also, and is in Gramsci, a theory of the modes of articulation between infrastructure and superstructures, or, as he put it in *The Modern Prince*: "It is the problem of the relations between structure and super-structure which must be accurately posed and resolved if the forces which are active in the history of a particular period are to be correctly analysed" (PN, p. 177). Later, when Gramsci discusses the three moments of revolution the practical implications of this distinction are elaborated and here also (a) distinctions between the political and hegemonic moments are elaborated and (b) the possibility—indeed probability—of disarticulation between these instances is discussed. A similar close attention to the complex and contradictory structures of specific social formations (not Gramsci's term) is apparent in his historical analyses of fascism and of the Risorgimento. Certainly there is little sign of the simple expressivity of levels which Althusser's critique advised us to expect.

Empiricism

Gramsci's emphasis on the need for the subaltern classes to develop their own knowledge (theory) of their situation, and then to promulgate this first to their class allies and then to their enemies suggests that he did not confuse knowledge with its object. His eschewing of truth as a standard of judgement also suggests this. But does Althusser's criticism hold from the standpoint of a single class? It is fair to say that Gramsci did not think through the distinction, and that his adages that "the real philosophy of each man is his political action" and that "the real philosopher is, and cannot be other than, the politician" (1971, p. 352) —and the theory of knowledge which they express—prevented him from seeing the need to think it through. None the less (a) his theory of knowledge does transcend the absolutism/relativism dichotomy, which empiricism fails to do; (b) he argued the necessity of critically and systematically examining and ordering one's class "intuitions", and argued further that "this elaboration must be, and can only be, performed in the context of the history of philosophy" (PN, p. 327); (c) in so far as empiricism concerns the derivation of knowledge from human experience, Gramsci regarded both humanity and experience as problematic.

Humanism

First, it is clear that for Gramsci human nature is not a static essence, but something historically specific. Secondly, it is equally clear that for Gramsci human nature and human experience is collective. What is less clear is whether human nature is an object/outcome of class struggle or (as Althusser argues of historicisms) is a changing class nature conceived as a permanently transforming collective subject. There are two difficulties in the way of an answer to this question, one being that Gramsci did not develop a theory of the individual or of interpellation, nor did he direct his attention to the fine but important distinction between class struggle as the motor of history and classes as subjects creating history. I am prepared to give him the benefit of the doubt, because it is clear that he does not regard classes as pre-given. In his analyses of the intellectuals, and also of Italian history, it is clear that he sees classes constantly forming and being formed at each instance of structure, and as historically specific (viz. his analysis of the Southern petty bourgeoisie as compared with the Northern managing and administrative classes, some of the organic intellectuals of capital). If there are no pre-formed classes there cannot be classes-as-subjects.

Secondly—and most important—*within* Gramsci's own theory as well as a point of external critique, Gramsci does not explain philosophically *the category of experience*. We may accept the (undeveloped) notion of class instinct, and the concept of organic class action — a class knowing and doing what is right for itself. But Gramsci's theory of knowledge does not tell us how this is possible. On the other hand this category of experience carries an important if often hidden burden in Gramsci's practice and theory of politics as well as of knowledge. Upon the category of experience depends the possibility of a counter hegemony, developed indeed through the establishment of pre-figurative institutions (Adamson, p. 231) in and by means of which new cultural and political forms can be generated. But both the recognition of this as a necessary action, and the ongoing political/ideological creative work depend heavily on and are made posisble by the notion of the experience of the subaltern classes.

In sum, while Gramsci may not properly be called a humanist, there are serious gaps in his theory at the point where a full defence against the charge of humanism would have to be elaborated. On the other hand, he may be exonerated from the charges of conflation of structure and of empiricism.

How Should One Think The State?

Both in his illustrative examples and in his concrete analyses Gramsci indicates that he is very well aware of structural and organizational differences within and between both ideological and political agencies. The intellectuals who, in Gramsci's formulation constitute these agencies have variously organized structural links, or none, with various classes and class segments and fractions. Thus Gramsci's concept of the intellectual as organizer/administrator as well as thinker/legitimator provides the seed from which an elaborated theory of state agencies could be developed. The need for such an elaborated theory has been recognized at least since I argued, somewhat polemically (Cain, 1977b) that the treatment of the state as a monolithic structure either stultified or pragmatised political action.[3] But in terms of consistency with an entire theory of knowledge and politics, and in terms of its potential for guiding revolutionary action, a Gramscian theory of the state agencies as constituted by intellectuals action, a Gramscian theory of the state agencies as constituted by intellectuals generating class specific common senses, and having organizational relationships with classes and agencies external to themselves is as yet unmatched. Both further elaborations (say, of the structure of intra-agency relationships) and concrete specification are required. But Gramsci has made a unique and consistently overlooked contribution here. Furthermore, this argument holds whether one chooses the expanded or the narrow conception of the state, although the latter focusses attention better on the tasks and effectivities of intellectuals operating from theoretically distinguished sites within the structure, and, of course, on the relationships between them.

Broadly speaking, Gramsci used an expanded conception of the state, indicating an empirically necessary unity of forms of control, when discussing *revolutionary tactics, strategies and directions*. The concept of a directive class exercising state control in a non-coercive way shaped his theory and his politics. However, when discussing the *forms of resistance* which the revolutionary classes will meet, Gramsci tended to use a narrow conception of the state as political society, as governmental institutions even, in order to emphasize that the conquest of these governmental institutions would not be sufficient for the foundation of a new historical bloc. Both purposes are important, and both theoretical elaborations with their political consequences need to be retained. It is, therefore, not a choice between concepts which is required, accepting one formulation and rejecting the other. Nor even is a new theoretical elaboration required at this point, although elaborations of all theories are needed as situations change. Analysis reveals that the elements of the two Gramscian formulations are often the same, and never incompatible. Since these constituents give the conceptions their value, what is needed is simply a re-naming of some of the conceptual packages. This modest task can be completed rather briefly.

The expanded conception of the state involves the unification of forms of control/consent under a directive class and its immediate allies. But the conception of civil society plus political society does not leave space for elements of civil society which are not or are not yet controlled by such a class. Constructing the concept 'state' in this way obscures a distinction which is politically as well as theoretically important. The narrow conception of the state, on the contrary, facilitates the task of analysing the growing penetration of civil society by the state, and consequent hidden unification of apparently dispersed centres of power (cf. Santos, 1980). Using the narrow conception we can identify interlocking arrangements between the state and the class bloc which controls it and each of its apparatuses, we can identify struggle for control of each apparatus within and between classes, and we can examine interfaces between state and civil society which become sites of law (norm creation/application) in Gramsci's sense and which therefore propagate the forms of knowing of the directive classes. Community policing as advocated by Alderson (1979) might be seen as such an interface. The example also makes clear why hegemony is a political as well as an ideological practice: the creation of community police officers is a political move which makes possible and expands in conjunction with the ideological penetration.

Thus the narrow conception enables relationships which are of crucial current concern to be investigated. Unwittingly, Gramsci has provided us with an incipient theoretical apparatus with which to examine struggles for the control of television, of radio wavelengths, and the press; of workers' co-operatives and schools; of women's movements, youth movements, children's movements, and pensioners' movements. His concepts enable us to examine both disjunctions and concordances between structural levels, and at the same time the state/civil society distinction means that *within* each of these levels the modes of achieving order may be examined.

So it is suggested that the narrow conception of the state is more useful for the analytic tasks which the subaltern classes presently have to accomplish. But the major insights made possible by the expanded conception must not be lost. To achieve this the term *order* must be substituted for the expanded conception of the state. To achieve the social order of a directive class and its allies it is indeed necessary to conquer both political and civil society. And order based on regulation through civil society, without coercion, can indeed be seen as possible in the long term. Both the direction and the strategy can be maintained.

The concept of state can itself be rendered more specific. I would go beyond Gramsci's narrow conception in this respect, and identify as also constitutive of the state the power to raise a compulsory levy—of labour, of 'money' (surplus value), or of 'goods' (use values).

The aim here is not to seek for a definitive or definitional characteristic in the sense of bourgeois science. Such an idealist practice would profoundly contradict Gramsci's own methodological principle of the historicity (temporal specificity) of theory. Theory, as we have seen, is historic in terms both of its constitution (it may be correct for a class at a time) and in terms of its applicability. Concepts which are elaborated must take account of the historical specificity of that conceived.

Secondly, the aim is not, in a few tail end paragraphs, to elaborate a complete theory of the state, taking account of significant historical and political variations, but rather to indicate an additional dimension along which such detailed elaborations may be made.

The notion of the compulsory levy as a power which becomes possible when particular constellations of class forces occur is necessary to get away from the legalism or constitutionalism in the 'governmental agencies' notion which tends to dominate the narrow conception of the state.

Thus the new conception enables the identification of emergent states, e.g. in compulsory billeting by conquering armies, or levies of supplies by guerilla troops and others. The political threat inherent in protection payments is laid bare—and the 'new narrow conception' has the additional merit (from the standpoint of a traditional intellectual) of opening up new areas for research. For the first time the customary emphasis on the allocative and distributive tasks undertaken by states could be balanced by a theorization of their forms in terms of that which they have to distribute and how it is obtained. For the first time it should be possible to theorize taxation law, the conflict between central and local states about the rates, and even conscription.

Elaborations of our conceptions of the state along this additional dimension will, of course, vary according to which historically specific forms of the state are under examination. It is argued that these elaborations will be consistent with Gramsci's conception of legislation as dispersed rather than as emanating solely from governmental agencies. For example, if a feudal state were being considered the levying power would appear as both dispersed and stratified. The state would be seen to be embodied in heads of households, heads of religious houses, and so on. The state form would be dispersed in specific ways. Secondly, that which is levied would have to be considered: direct labour, or, in later years, commutations for this; on occasion, military labour. Thirdly, perhaps, the style of the levy might have to be analysed: the extent of compulsion and/or compliance and types of sanctions.

All three sub-dimensions would, of course, vary both within and between modes of production. And the final and arguably the most important consideration would be their manner of articulation with other aspects of state power as constituted in various structures and 'agencies', and their articulation with the other levels—the economic and ideological levels—of the total structure.

Such an elaboration is consistent both with Gramsci's narrow conception of the state, and can arguably be harnessed to it, and with Gramsci's conception of legal and other powers as capable of being either dispersed or centralized, controlled by one class or another. The conception can also be used to analyse aspects of the articulation between civil and political society in the present day, and the desired direction for this relationship.

There are problems of course—the long-term direction is not to a civil society penetrated by political society, giving rise to passive consent, but to an order in which *the organic organizations of civil society will take over and become political society.* But this reunification of civil and political society must not be the same as their pre-bourgeois unification. The repoliticization of civil society, as Gramsci saw, will require practice, failure, continuous experimentation, just as the bourgeoisie, especially in the century preceding the English revolution, experimented with the form of parliament and its powers. To prevent a situation in which order is created by a directive class in a dispersed and organic way from becoming an arbitrary order new forms of guarantees will be required. So it is necessary to construct pre-figurative institutions to practice with organic and democratic forms at each level of structure, including, of course and most important, the economic. Gramsci believed that the revolutionary class would know by experience when a correct form and direction was found. He could not adequately theorize this belief, and neither can I. But we must adopt it pending theorization because it is politically necessary to do so. Perhaps when we have a fully organic philosophy, it will no longer be a question.

Acknowledgements

I am grateful to Bill Chambliss, Peter Fitzpatrick, Anne Sassoon, David Sugarman and Colin Sumner for comments on the first draft, and to the London School of Economics which made possible my continuing work in this area. The elaboration of the notion of the compulsory levy owes a great deal to the comments of Mark Benney.

Notes

1. A similar criticism has been made of Althusser's (1971) conception of ideological state apparatuses, a conception which owes much to Gramsci's expanded concept of the state. The critics (Hall *et al.*, 1977), however, fail to identify Gramsci's two usages, and therefore argue that Althusser was departing from Gramsci by abandoning the distinction between state and civil society which is found in Gramsci's narrow conception.
2. A paper by Hall *et al.* (1977) attempts to absolve Gramsci from Althusser's charge of historicism. However, it does so by arguing that Gramsci was not a fully fledged historicist rather than by accepting Gramsci's own claim that he was a historicist and arguing that the negative consequences delineated by Althusser do not *necessarily* follow from this position. The paper is necessary reading, however, if only for the illuminating way in which 'the structuralist appropriation of Gramsci' is presented.
3. "What must be achieved is a theory which enables one to look at all the state agents and agencies, the military, the civil service, the police, the workers in nationalised industries, the judges, in terms of the mediations effected by both vertical and horizontal differentiations and rifts in structure. . . . We have to go a bit beyond telling each other that they are all state agents, and we have to go beyond it *theoretically*, . . . we have to make a quilt which does justice to the sophisticated shapes and colours of the raw materials." (Cain, 1977b, p. 164)

References

SPN. See Gramsci, 1971.
SPW I and II. See Gramsci, 1977; 1978.
LFP. See Gramsci, 1979.

Adamson, W. (1980). *Hegemony and Revolution*. University of California Press, Berkeley.
Alderson, J. (1979). *Policing Freedom*. MacDonald and Evans, London.
Althusser, L. (1969). *For Marx*. Penguin, Harmondsworth.
Althusser, L. (1970). "Marxism is not a historicism" in Althusser, L. and Balibar, E. *Reading Capital*. New Left Books, London.
Althusser, L. (1971). *Lenin and Philosophy and Other Essays*. New Left Books, London.
Althusser, L. (1976). *Essays in Self Criticism*. New Left Books, London.

Anderson, P. (1977). "The Antinomies of Antonio Gramsci: "in *New Left Review* **100**, Nov-Jan.

Buci-Glucksman, C. (1980). *Gramsci and the State*. Lawrence and Wishart, London.

Cain, M. (1976). "Necessarily out of touch: thoughts on the organisation of the English bar" in Carlen, P. (Ed.) *Sociological Review Monograph* **23**: *The Sociology of Law*. University of Keele, Staffordshire.

Cain, M. (1977a). "Optimism, law, and the state: a plea for the possibility of politics" in *European Yearbook of Law and Sociology*. Nijhoff, The Hague.

Cain, M. (1977b). "An ironical departure: the dilemma of contemporary policing" in *Yearbook of Social Policy in Britain, 1976*. Routledge and Kegan Paul, London.

Cain, M. and Finch, J. (1981). "The rehabilitation of data" in Abrams, P. *et al.* (Eds) *Practice and Progress: British Sociology 1950-1980*. Allen and Unwin, London.

Davidson, A. (1977). *Antonio Gramsci: towards an Intellectual Biography*. Merlin Press, London.

Gramsci, A. (1971). *Selections from the Prison Notebooks*. Lawrence and Wishart, London.

Gramsci, A. (1977). *Selections from Political Writings I, 1910-1920*. Lawrence and Wishart, London.

Gramsci, A. (1978). *Selections from Political Writings II, 1921-1926*. Lawrence and Wishart, London.

Gramsci, A. (1979). *Letters from Prison*. Quartet Books, London.

Hall, S. *et al.* (1977). "Politics and Ideology: Gramsci" in Centre for Contemporary and Cultural Studies, *On Ideology*. Hutchinson, London.

Jessop, R. (1982). *Theories of the Capitalist State*. Martin Robertson, London.

Joll, J. (1977). *Gramsci*. Fontana, London.

Mathiesen, T. (1981). *Law, Society and Political Action*. Academic Press, London.

Mouffe, C. (Ed.) (1979). *Gramsci and Marxist Theory*. Routledge and Kegan Paul, London.

Santos, B. de S. (1980). "Law and community: the changing nature of state power in late capitalism." In *International Journal of Sociology of Law* **8**, 4.

Sassoon, A. Showstack (1980a). *Gramsci's Politics*. Croom Helm, London.

Sassoon, A. Showstack (1980b). "Gramsci: a new concept of politics and the expansion of democracy" in Hunt, A. (Ed.) *Marxism and Democracy*. Lawrence and Wishart, London.

Texier, L. (1979). "Gramsci, theoretician of the superstructures" in Mouffe, C. (Ed.) *Gramsci and Marxist Theory*. Routledge and Kegan Paul, London.

Further Reading

Newcomers to Gramsci's work will meet the man best by reading his *Letters from Prison* (1979). However, there is no escape from reading *Selections from the Prison Notebooks* (1971), since the most comprehensive and insightful commentary (that of Buci-Glucksman, 1980), while essential reading, is rather less accessible than the texts themselves, and presumes the prior comprehension of a considerable Marxist and philosophical literature. A simpler introduction by Joll (1977) is available, but it is a better strategy for the student to start with Gramsci and proceed to Joll rather than the other way round.

Within the *Prison Notebooks*, the sections on "The Intellectuals" and on

"State and Civil Society" are of first importance for the student of the topics dealt with here, although a major discussion of law is contained in "The Modern Prince". Gramsci's crucial distinctions between active and passive revolution, his seminal discussion of the three moments of revolution, as well as his concepts of wars of movement or of position and of "caesarism", are to be found in his "Notes on Italian History". Part III of the *Notebooks* deals with the problems of knowing touched on here. Those interested in the role of the organic intellectuals of the subaltern classes (mentioned briefly on p. 103 of this paper) should consider Sassoon's (1980) work on *Gramsci's Politics*. Gramsci's theory of knowledge is considered in the opening pages of my earlier paper (Cain, 1977a), although the later arguments of that work describe my own thoughts at the time rather than those of Gramsci. Part V of Buci-Glucksman's work (op. cit.) gives a full and clear exegesis of this aspect of Gramsci's work, which situates his developing position in relation both to his contemporary Italian philosophers and to antecedent and contemporary Marxist theorists. Hall *et al.* (1977) deal extensively with Gramsci's relationship with modern structuralist Marxists.

Since this paper went to press an extensive discussion of both Gramsci and "neo-Gramscianism" has appeared: see Jessop, 1982, Chapter 4.

6   Law, Legitimation and The Advanced Capitalist State: The Jurisprudence and Social Theory of Jurgen Habermas

Colin Sumner

> Marx, with his critique of ideology applied to the bourgeois constitutional state and with his sociological resolution to the basis of natural rights, went beyond Hegel to discredit so enduringly for Marxism both the idea of legality itself and the intention of Natural Law as such that ever since the link between Natural Law and revolution has dissolved. (Habermas, 1974, p. 113)

Introduction

For Habermas, the fundamental weakness in the whole of Marxian social theory is its unclear normative basis. Marx did not renew the ontological claims of classical natural law nor did he sustain the hopes of the new, positivist social sciences; instead through his analysis of capital he critically revealed the normative content of bourgeois political economy and jurisprudence. He thus bequeathed an explosive tension between science and critique, analysis and evaluation. Habermas regrets that it was supplanted by waves of Marxist scientism. Stalin codified historical materialism and the objectivist theory of history negated its bourgeois counterpart. A void was thus created: moral justification for political praxis (or strategic action) became unnecessary and disappeared into the black hole of historical logic.

Law, State and Society Series: "Legality, Ideology and the State", edited by D. Sugarman, 1983. Academic Press, London and New York.

> In the meantime, bourgeois consciousness had become cynical; as the social sciences—especially legal positivism, neoclassical economics, and recent political theory—show, it has been thoroughly emptied of binding normative contents. However, if (as becomes even more apparent in times of recession) the bourgeois ideals have gone into retirement, there are no norms and values to which an immanent critique might appeal with (the expectation of) agreement. (Habermas, 1979, p. 97)

In reconnecting politics to a transcendental moral reason, Habermas sustains the Frankfurt tradition of 'critical theory', and brings law, justice and morality to the forefront of his political philosophy and social theory. He attempts to develop, and to justify as universally valid, a moral political yardstick with which we are to supplement our analytic-empirical sociology of law. The Enlightenment is to be restored to Marxist critique; or is it vice versa? Sociological exposé is politically insufficient: theory has to be linked with praxis.

An aversion to the scientistic reduction of questions of justice also pervades Habermas's attack on conventional Marxist theories of the state as an instrument of valorization. Habermas explores the nature of the interventionist post-war state, welfarism and the changing nature of bourgeois legality to raise some sharp questions for commodity-exchange theories of law, for the base-superstructure conception and for theories which give law a strong role in legitimation. He claims that a technocratic dirigisme "of pure control and manipulation", has arisen which cannot be met by theories and strategies which are out of date, which are rooted in the assumption that the state is accountable to the civil rights and public opinion of nineteenth century, laissez-faire capitalism. The advanced capitalist state has moved on; its policies are no longer 'normed' in that sense anymore—a gap has emerged between a scientized state instrumentalism and the civil privatism of a depoliticized public. This distance means that only the resurrection of ethical/political, public debate will suffice to renew the search for democracy and social justice.

By the same token, Habermas conducts a challenging critique of Weber. The latter's concept of legitimacy is said to be merely descriptive and therefore useless for criticizing the ideological content of political self-justification. Habermas also believes that Weber's concept of purposive-rational action does not grasp the extent to which instrumentalism has grown at the expense of symbolic interaction and rational communication. These two deficiencies would amount to a damaging weakness in Weber's sociology of law which supposes that a public reason is at the heart of rational-legal domination.[1] When we also consider that Habermas would question Weber's nineteenth century view of the state as a guarantor of an autonomous, free enterprise economy, we realize that Habermas presents a substantial challenge to Marxian and Weberian sociologies of law. If only for this reason, his work ought to be given more attention by researchers in this area.[2]

The critical theory of the Frankfurt school is itself a tradition which has suffered much criticism over recent years (see e.g. Therborn, 1970; Slater, 1977; Giddens, 1979; Connerton, 1980). Although it has changed over time, it contains certain constant basic themes:

1. A sense of critique as the reconstruction of the subjective conditions of knowledge-constitution (Kant) and as the emancipation of consciousness from illusions (Hegel, Marx).

2. A belief in the potential for regression in human history, and that the truth of critical theory is not to be confirmed in the historical action of the proletariat.[3]

3. A sense of the growth of an over-arching state apparatus and of the decline of meaningful public debate, leading naturally to a concern with the super-structure rather than the infrastructure.

4. A rejection of commodity-fetishism theories of ideology and the development of a theory which focusses on the media and its capacity to reduce the distance between internal needs and externally suggested desires.[4] This naturally entailed a concern to reveal the depth of the superstructural invasion into the individual psyche.

5. A view of the decline of 'practical' reason in the face of a bloated technological capacity and a rampant 'instrumental' reason. Rather than posing irresoluble problems for the relations of production, technology and its fruits have become their *raison d'être*, their legitimating ideology.

Clearly these themes reflect the German experience of fascism (see Connerton, 1980, Ch. 8). They certainly carry forward into Habermas's work and form the background to his ideas about law as described in the next three sections of this essay.

Rationalist Natural Law and The Growth of The Advanced Capitalist State

In the Aristotelian conception, politics was the doctrine of the good and just life — ethics, custom and law were inseparable, all being part of prudent direction. Such *praxis* was quite separate from *techne*, "the skillful production of artefacts and the expert mastery of objectified tasks" (Habermas, 1974, p. 42). Politics was about the cultivation of character not the technical accomplishment of the correct state: "the order of virtue" not "the regulation of social intercourse" (p. 43). As such, politics and practical philosophy must be separated from rigorous science since they "lack ontological constancy as well as logical necessity" (p. 42) and can only attain a prudent understanding of a specific situation. There lies Habermas's heart. It rests with an ancient Greek notion of democracy and rational discourse: the notion permeates all his arguments.[5]

According to Habermas, the order of the Greek *polis* "was actualised in the participation of the citizens in administration, legislation, justice and consultation" (1974, p. 48). In that polis, the nature of man was realized; the law was natural and necessary for an order of freedom. Labourers and slaves, of course, did not count in this noble political calculus. Habermas often forgets this, as though it has no bearing on Aristotelian thought.

Aquinas, however, did count labourers as political units and the focus of political philosophy began its long shift away from the quality of governance to the technics of domination. Politics, in Aquinas, became a philosophy of a social order which aimed, not for freedom, but for peace and the preservation of morally differentiated, social rankings. The "discipline of law" was the answer to those who did not share man's "natural aptitude to virtuous action" (Aquinas, quoted in Lloyd, 1979, p. 113). Law and order acquired a new purpose: to preserve the life of stratified natural virtue and to repress the threat from those of "evil disposition". With Machiavelli and More, political philosophy moved further in this direction, reflecting the changes in political society. A state of (internal and external) war became "the fundamental pre-supposition of politics" (Habermas, 1974, p. 50) and politics became the art of asserting one's own power. Law was separated from the achievement of virtue and became a technique for organizing society to ensure the reproduction of necessary goods and institutions and the subordination of the enemy (internal and external). Domination, argues Habermas, was extricated from its ethical context:

> The normative sense of the laws is, to be sure, emptied of its moral substance by the reduction to underlying structures, be they those of political domination or those of economic exploitation. (1974, pp. 54, 55)

On the other hand, as Habermas makes clear but underemphasizes, political society was also seen to include all. Society as a total structure became the new object of the art of political manipulation.

With the advent of Hobbes, art became science, says Habermas. The practical knowledge necessary for domination and survival became technical-scientific knowledge necessary to reflect accurately the "laws of civil life" (Hobbes). Reflecting the development of empirical-analytic procedure by men such as Bacon, Galileo and Descartes, Hobbes asserted a causal link between the laws of nature and the laws of government. The law that had once been seen as ethical and desirable in both process and product now became "rational" in its natural necessity, as an organizing technique. So, says Habermas, Hobbesian political theory marked the 'positivisation" of Natural Law. Laws were now the formal and positive ordinances imposed by individuals upon each other by contract; "and justice now designated no more than respect for the validity of these contracts" (Habermas, 1974, p. 62).

> Such formal law corresponded to objective conditions insofar as the two great processes which fundamentally changed the interconnection of *dominium* and *societas* asserted themselves within the territorial states of the sixteenth century: that is, the centralisation and at the same time the bureaucratisation of power within the modern state apparatus of the sovereign national governments, as well as the expansion of capitalistic trade in commodities and the gradual transformation of the mode of production, till then bound to household production. (Habermas, 1974, p. 62)

Alongside the national and territorial economies, oriented toward the 'market', the modern state began to endure and to specify the structure of those economies using the modern legal categories, technically applied for the precise regulation of social intercourse.

Hobbes's physicalist/behaviourist conception of human nature, in the war of all against all, is contradicted however by his view that our reason demands legal order. This tension in Hobbesian theory between located practical reason and the technical dictates of the laws of nature is extremely significant for Habermas since, ultimately, Hobbes's liberal conception of the responsibilities of the sovereign (welfare, freedom and protection) was severely restricted by his notion of the sovereign's *absolute* power. For only the sovereign could decide whether his 'practical' laws corresponded to the Natural Law of the social contract; he could never, therefore, do injustice. Such absolutism 'devours' Hobbes's liberal justification of the state. Due process (emanating from normative reason) must always be outweighed by penal law (necessitated by the causal laws of human nature). Similarly, Habermas points out, the technicians of the 'correct' order will also always be members of the faulty order of nature, objects as well as subjects, and their reason must therefore always be subject to their self-interest.

Fundamentally flawed from the beginning, both in theory and reality, the liberal capitalist state grew with the aim of producing the good life via the legally protected enjoyment of freely disposable property. Locke continued this trend by formulating the civil law of bourgeois society as Natural Law, by making the bourgeois property order the basis of state power. The eighteenth century political economists rounded it off by declaring bourgeois property norms to be the natural laws of social development. That gave us a natural order of capitalist economics and despotic state government. But also in that century we see the growth of the concept of 'public opinion', a pivotal notion in Habermas's thought. Significantly, he defines its original form as:

> . . . the enlightened result of the common and public reflection, guided by the philosophers as the representatives of modern science—a reflection on the fundamental bases of the social order . . . . (1974, p. 77)

In this (physiocratic) form, public opinion was to be the practical complement to scientific political theory, it was to mediate the monarch's insight into the natural laws of society; thus mitigating Hobbesian absolutism. The Scottish moral philosophers built this mediating role into their 'natural history of civil society' so that the public-political sphere unfolded historically along with the unfolding of the natural laws of the market. Historical evolution thus, in their view, guaranteed the harmony between economy and public politics; Habermas describes this as a "facile evolutionism".

The problem we inherit from the Scottish philosophers and their French contemporaries is simple: if scientific social philosophy wants to integrate the 'practical consciousness of politically active citizens' into its theory of history then it cannot remain in the positivist realm of rigorous science and must clarify the relationship between the technical control of society and the practical action of an intersubjectively constituted public (which is the object of such control). "The moderns achieved the rigour of their theory at the cost of access to praxis" (1974, p. 79).[6] A scientific social philosophy is now necessary which "will correspond to a clarification of practical consciousness" whilst retaining that rigour which is "the irreversible achievement of modern science" (p. 79). This is the very core of Habermas's methodology. He has expressed it another way: the rationalization of labour involved in the fine-tuned, modern phenomenon of purposive-rational action must be matched by the rationalization of communication systems of symbolic interaction systematically distorted during the growth of the capitalist social formation. Only a theory which grasps that contradiction, and serves to resolve it analytically and practically, will do. Neither Weber nor Marx are sufficient. Weber elevated purposive-rational action onto a pedestal, thus glossing the whole problem; Marx failed to theorize the internal logic of consciousness and therefore to explain adequately why capitalist crises should result in socialist progress.

Habermas's assessment of the relationship between rationalist natural law and the bourgeois revolution, like his analysis of earlier political philosophy, focusses on history's philosophical self-understanding rather than the social processes and class struggles which constituted that history and philosophy. His premise is that the philosophy of the bourgeois revolution was vitally effective in structuring subsequent reality. This philosophy took natural law as one of its key concepts and saw the revolution as its positive realization.

As opposed to classical natural law with its norms of moral and just action oriented towards the virtuous life of the citizenry, modern natural law of the enlightenment allows a neutral sphere of personal choice where each citizen can egoistically maximize his (her?) own satisfaction, i.e. dispose of private property, live free from harm, etc. All acts not prohibited are thus morally neutral, free "from the motivations of internalised duties" (1974, p. 84). Penal law secures the realm of private autonomy through coercion and obedience; legality becomes divorced from moral obligation. The revolutionary self-understanding countered the danger of absolutism by positing a reorganization of state power based on the General Will, 'the will of all free individuals guided by a common and rational insight'. As Habermas puts it, social contract philosophy had matured, grown conscious of itself, and understood itself as the positivization of natural rights. The declarations of fundamental rights in America and France were not statements of the sovereign's duties but statements of the rights of man rooted in the 'natural' structure of the emergent bourgeois civil society.

Habermas is clearly conscious of the two opposing aspects of public opinion: it can be a device enabling more efficient domination or it can be a critical expression of the practical consciousness of the mass. He illustrates this by showing how modern natural law meant different things for the Americans and the French. The American Bill of Rights was conservative in that it was a mere inventory of the existing rights of a society of proprietors, an expression of 'common sense' or public opinion. As such, it was an expression of something which would eventually remove the need for law and state (Jefferson). The French declaration however was revolutionary in asserting a new system of rights which liberated commodity exchange and 'social labour' from state intervention within a fully social constitution. As such, the positivization of natural law in France was not the prudent application of norms to a given situation to enable it to flourish but, says Habermas, the installation of "a technically correct system of institutions with the aid of laws" (1974, p. 91). This was revolutionary because it did not simply ratify existing self-interest but enlightened public opinion to the point where it recognized the naturalness of the order being organized by the state. Thus to preserve this 'natural' constitution, the sovereignty of the people (the General Will) was required to prevent any slippage back into the previously depraved state of social intercourse. As the physiocrats argued, the natural order now required a distinctly political order to enable it to dominate: "the political society is a creation of the state, dictated by insight into the natural laws of motion of material life" (Habermas, 1974, p. 100). In France, public opinion was very much a device for a technically improved system of domination; but its mobilization inevitably stirred its other side, the critical-practical consciousness of the mass.

This, argues Habermas, is where Marx missed the point. Marx, he says, stood within the European bourgeois revolution's self-understanding when he criticized natural law. Naturally, therefore, he understood that it was a "merely political" revolution, which constructed a state ideally suited to the self-interests of the bourgeois class. A political society, "embracing both state and society" (Habermas), had been created which could never serve the interests of all classes. Marx went on to show that the 'natural' laws of capitalist society could never ensure real equality for all, and to denounce formal justice as a mask concealing class domination and exploitation. The critique of ideology applied by Marx to the bourgeois constitutional state consequently discredited legality and the revolutionary quality of Natural Law for ever (for Marxism). The critique of justice became a merely sociological exposé leaving nothing but a faith in a proletarian revolution based on the power acquired in the merely political, bourgeois revolution. What Marx had missed, says Habermas, because he stood inside the revolutionary natural law tradition, was that he had in fact merely criticized the 'liberal' natural law tradition of the Anglo-Saxon world. Without realizing it, Marx had failed to acknowledge the difference between the interpretation of Rousseau and the physiocrats, which "recognised no separation in principle of human rights from citizens' rights, of fundamental rights prior to the state from those conferred by the state" (Habermas, 1974, p. 112), and the Anglo-Saxon interpretation (Locke, Paine, Jefferson etc.) which argued that "the natural laws of society were to fulfill the promise of the natural rights of man" (p. 110). This latter liberal doctrine could never have served as the self-understanding of the French revolution. Marx had left the radical version intact.

The consequences of this error, argues Habermas, have been disastrous. The Marxist critique of law is only fully suited to "liberal", laissez-faire capitalism. The critique of law as an ideological mask is only partially appropriate for the critique of state-conferred rights in the advanced capitalist states.[7] In leaving the radical natural law tradition intact, Marxism never developed a critique of modern formal democracy, its failures and illusions; nor did it mobilize, in theory or in politics, the radical component of public opinion. Instead, all faith was put into the dialectical emergence of social justice from the proletarian revolution. Questions of justice and democracy submerged into a reliance on an 'objectivist' history. Habermas suggests that the revolutionary component of rationalist natural law, emphasizing democracy and free public discourse, must be reconnected to the ideal of legality (see 1974, p. 113). The critique of the technical, secretive, bureaucratic states of advanced capitalist and socialist societies requires a normative component to deal with the threat to democracy now posed in these states. This component in Habermas's view must involve the reinstatement of the reason and will of an enlightened public to its proper role in Marxist theory and practice. Jurisprudentially, Marxism is antiquated and destructive. Therefore, argues Habermas, it needs reconstructing to justify historically the values of public reason and political democracy which should form the core of its critique of the modern state.

For, in welfare states of the 'mass democracies', it is precisely the radical interpretation of natural law which has materialized. The laws of the capitalist mode of production no longer work autonomously in that sphere of private property and moral neutrality out of which 'human rights' emerged. The state is an active agent within the economy and the base-superstructure model is now inadequate. Ideology and law are not simply secondary phenomena, but first order determinants (via the state) of the modern social order.

The old "liberal" capitalism, in Habermas's conception, centred on the institution of the market, which "promises that exchange relations will be and are just owing to equivalence" (1971a, p. 97). "This bourgeois ideology of justice" depended on the category of "reciprocity", or consensual contract. Hence, given "the market economy", political domination in liberal capitalism was legitimated "from below" (in the infrastructure) rather than "from above" (in the superstructure). This constituted a major break with all social formations hitherto; previously the economic class structure had been based on and legitimated within institutionalized power relations. With the emergence of the capitalist mode of production, the legitimation of the class structure moved its site from the political to the economic:

> Only then can the property order change from a *political relation* to a *production relation*, because it legitimates itself through the rationality of the market, the ideology of exchange society, and no longer through a legitimate power structure. It is now the political system which is justified in terms of the legitimate relations of production: this is the real meaning and function of rationalist natural law from Locke to Kant. The institutional framework of society is only mediately political and immediately economic (the bourgeois constitutional state as 'superstructure'). (Habermas, 1971a, p. 97)

Traditional legitimations, "the older mythic, religious and metaphysical worldviews" rooted in "communicative action" or the "logic of interaction contexts", gave way as the development of the productive forces "makes permanent the extension of subsystems of purposive-rational action" (1971a, p. 96). In other words, "modernisation" (Habermas's term) was primarily characterized by the breakdown of cultural traditions which legitimated the limited, prior forms of purposive-rational action (work). With capitalism, such systems of action became unlimited and have self-sustaining growth.

"Traditional" legitimations thus broke down and gave way to the economic conditions of "instrumental rationality": organizations of trade and of workers, networks of transportation and communication, the institutions of private law, and the state bureaucracy (centred on financial administration). Rationalist natural law therefore played the role of criticizing tradition and reorganizing "the released material of tradition according to the principles of formal law and the exchange of equivalents" (1971a, p. 99). Along with "modern value-orientations" (such as the Protestant ethic), this form of law was part of the secularization process (Habermas thus extends Weber's concept). In passing, we should note that Habermas has thereby moved beyond Weber's concept of rationalization (and Marcuse's critique of that concept as a mere apology for modern political domination). What Weber saw as rationalization, Habermas views as (1) the economic legitimation which permitted the political system to adapt to "the new requisites of rationality" created in the "developing sub-systems of purposive-rational action" and (2) the establishment of the economic mechanism which made the expansion of purposive-rational action systems permanent. The new legitimations (whether scientific or legal in form) were the first ideologies because they actually concealed power relations:

> They replace traditional legitimations of power by appearing in the mantle of modern science and by deriving their justification from the critique of ideology. Ideologies are coeval with the critique of ideology. In this sense there can be no pre-bourgeois ideologies. (Habermas, 1971a, p. 99)

Weber's theory of rationalization failed to penetrate the veil of bourgeois justice ideology, to reach the unequal class relations concealed by that ideology, and is itself therefore (I would suggest) merely an articulate form of one fundamental bourgeois ideology (that of the progressive universalism aspired to by the bourgeois class).

The "principle of organisation" of the liberal-capitalist social formation, for Habermas, was the capital-labour relation "anchored" in bourgeois civil law (1976, p. 20). The emergence of this relation as the principle of social organization, along with its uncoupling from feudal political authority, meant that class relationships became depoliticized and class domination became anonymous. "Economic exchange becomes the dominant steering medium" and "the modern rational state becomes the complementary arrangement to self-regulative market commerce" (1976, p. 21). That state then proceeded to secure the structurally necessary institutions and processes for capital reproduction (e.g. penal law to protect property and commerce, labour law to protect labour from the "self-destructive side-effects of the market mechanism", laws to provide education, communication, transport, etc. and laws to adapt civil law to the needs of capital accumulation). The state performed these merely reactive, service functions; finding its justification in legitimate relations of production, "the justice inherent in the exchange of equivalents". Because in liberal capitalism, the economic system was not only the steering system but also the legitimation of the whole society, the social system was susceptible to profound crises of identity—given the opposition of class interests:

> Economic crisis is immediately transformed into social crisis; for, in unmasking the opposition of social classes it provides a practical critique of ideology, of the market's pretension to be free of power. The economic crisis results from contradictory system imperatives and threatens social integration. (Habermas, 1976, p. 29)

Economic instability therefore produced societal instability. Clearly, Habermas rejects a theory of crisis founded exclusively on Marxian political economy. (For fuller details of this rejection, see Habermas, 1974, pp. 219-235.) Political and ideological contradictions are vital components of capitalist crises.

Out of this chaos emerges 'state-regulated capitalism'. This social system involves economic concentration (i.e., multinationals, big trade unions) and state intervention in the market. Private, autonomous, small-scale commerce recedes in the face of huge armaments companies, and the like, which live on state contracts or are controlled by the state (for Habermas, these companies do not control the state). The state begins to engage in global planning to limit private enterprise in order to prevent 'dysfunctional secondary effects'. More radically, it actually replaces the 'market mechanism' at many points; for example, by unproductive state consumption, by redirecting capital investment into neglected sectors, by improving the material infrastructure of production, by heightening productivity through research, education and training, and by relieving capital of the need to amend certain social costs of production (e.g. unemployment compensation, welfare, ecological damage). By doing these things, Habermas says, the state recouples the economy to the superstructure and therefore "re-politicises" class relations (i.e. displaces them into the political system in a socially anonymous form). This movement provides the basis of the modern legitimation crisis.

Combined with a growing dependence on science ('the scientisation of politics'), the increasingly interventionist state makes the application of Marxian political economy to twentieth century conditions of dubious relevance for Habermas. "The root ideology of just exchange, which Marx unmasked in theory, collapsed in practice" (Habermas, 1971a, p. 101). State correctives and controls mean that politics is no longer merely superstructural and that the base-superstructure metaphor is no longer appropriate:

> If, however, the ideology of just exchange disintegrates, then the power structure can no longer be criticised *immediately* at the level of the relations of production. (Habermas, 1971a, p. 101)

The critique must begin with the state and therefore with the need for democracy (in participation and information). State capitalism cannot ignore bourgeois democratic gains and permanently revert to some kind of cosmological or patriarchal mode of legitimation:

> . . . through the universalistic value-systems of bourgeois ideology, civil rights — have become established; and legitimation can be dissociated from the mechanism of elections only temporarily and under extraordinary conditions. This problem is resolved through a system of formal democracy. Genuine participation of citizens in the processes of political will-formation, that is, substantive democracy, would bring to consciousness the contradiction between administratively socialised production and the continued private appropriation and use of surplus value. In order to keep this contradiction from being thematized, then, the administrative system must be sufficiently independent of legitimating will-formation. (Habermas, 1976, p. 36)

Thus, very generalized and very diffuse mass loyalty is obtained and participation excluded. Formally democratic procedures predominate and the passive citizenry is left with only the right to withhold acclamation.

This "civil privatism" ("political abstinence combined with an orientation to career, leisure and consumption" (Habermas, 1976, p. 37)), is of course, the complement to the "substitute programme" of the modern 'welfare state' with its extensive bureaucracy, secrecy and technology. Whilst the economy is reasonably stable, growth continues, individual upward mobility is possible and welfare services are maintained, then the substitute programme will secure private capital utilization and obtain a generalized mass loyalty.

Under these conditions, politics becomes negative, orientated toward the elimination of 'dysfunction' (the technocratic, elitist, system theorists' understanding of resistance to the new order). 'Deviance' hits the headlines and the sociology industry as a parade of "nuts, sluts and perverts" (Liazos, 1972), the ultimately political character of that demonstration being concealed: "the depoliticised public realm is dominated by the imposed privatism of mass culture" (Habermas, 1971a, p. 42). Social work, psychotherapy, the medicalization of social problems and prisons enter a boom period:

> The personalisation of what is public is thus the cement in the cracks of a well-integrated society, which forces suspended conflicts into areas of social psychology. There they are absorbed in categories of deviant behavior: as private conflicts, illness and crime. These containers now appear to be overflowing. (Habermas, 1971a, pp. 42, 43)

Routine interactions now become fair game for the head-hunting professions: purposive-rational action and technical reason invade even the most personal recesses of the private world of interaction and communication. The obverse effect of this was that eventually, by the late sixties, deviance and deviants became politicized, Habermas's writings gained recognition, and the welfare state-civic privatism couplet began to fall apart (see Horowitz and Leibowitz, 1968; Taylor *et al.*, 1973; Pearson, 1975). The ideological mask of technocratic welfarism (the techniques of 'behaviour modification') slipped away to reveal the ugly face of the authoritarian state, concerned less with 'treating deviance' than with punishing overt critique.

What Weber had not understood was that rationalization had entered a second phase (see Habermas, 1971a, Ch. 5). During the first phase, the modern state, based on the financial administration of the emergent national and territorial economy, articulated its legitimacy in legal terms. Today, however, the bureaucrats, the military and politicians rationalize their exercise of power more with science and technology than with law. What is significant about this is that decision-making has become separated from instituted and generalizable social norms. For Weber, the division of labour between politicians and experts meant that ultimately there were competing values and perspectives which were decided upon by values and power more than by reason. Today, however, "the objective necessity disclosed by the specialists seems to assert itself over the leaders' decisions" (Habermas, 1971a, p. 63). On Weber's view, democracy was reduced to the election, appointment and acclamation of elites whose exercise of power could be legitimated as procedurally correct but not rationalized (logic could not arbitrate between competing value-sytems). For Habermas, the modern technocrats of political science who justify political decision-making as rational administration based on technical necessity abandon democracy to some vague notion of the historical flow of an independent, self-regulating, asocial, technical reason, and thus provide in their systems theories an apologetic, ideological justification for structural depoliticization (see Habermas, 1976, p. 37). The substitute programme of advanced state-regulated capitalism occurs, therefore, at the expense of democracy and the Anglo-Saxon notion of civil rights. It is not really a rationalized state (if one takes a broader view of rationality than Weber's) since true political rationalization, says Habermas,

> . . . occurs through the enlightenment of political will, correlated with the instruction about its technical potential. This dimension is evaded when such enlightenment is considered either impossible because of the need for authoritative decisions or superfluous because of technocracy. (1971a, p. 80)

The depoliticization and substantive disenfranchisement of the public realm is the price we pay for the state's reconstruction of the private sector and civil law. Divorced from intersubjectively grounded ethics and undistorted public discourse, politics has become the solution of technical problems. The substitute programme is an attempt to manipulate the social system of class society whilst avoiding the public debates which would question the framework by which the state defined its tasks as technical ones.

Although the rise of the welfare state partially repoliticizes class conflict in the relations of production, it only replaces the political anonymity of domination in the liberal capitalist state (formal democracy) with social anonymity (social democracy). That is, the steering mechanism, the device for social integration, is now the interventionist corporate state which, by incorporating "reformist labour parties", manages the crisis and keeps class conflict latent. The "original conflict zone" is thus "immunised" (Habermas, 1976, p. 38). This has had several major effects: (i) the growth of wage differentials and disputes in the public sector, (ii) permanent inflation, (iii) permanent crisis in government finances, and (iv) disproportionate (sectoral and regional) economic development. Class conflict has been kept latent by extending the business cycle to produce a permanent inflationary crisis with minimized periodic crises and by scattering the effects of this 'stabilized crisis' over weak social groups (e.g. weak unions, consumers, schoolchildren, the sick, the elderly, etc.). In fact, this strategy functions, says Habermas, to break down class identity and fragment class consciousness.

Orthodox Marxist analysis regarded the state in liberal capitalism as the "collective-capitalist will" confronting individual capitalists as a non-capitalist in order to reproduce the general conditions of surplus value production. This view, comments Habermas, was then extended to the advanced capitalist state to argue that intervention in the market does not alter the overall economic process (1976, p. 51). It holds (he thinks) (a) that state interventions do not transform the dynamics of capital investment and cyclical accumulation crises, or control budget deficits and public expenditure inflation, (b) that the mental labour of scientists, engineers, teachers etc. is unproductive of surplus value, (c) that the average wage is still equatable with the costs of reproduction of labour power, (d) that democracy is only a superstructure of capitalist class domination and is therefore no obstacle to capital realization, and (e) that in fact some industries can privatize parts of the public administration, owing to the dependency of the state on its clients and thus displace private competition into the state itself. In other words, Marxist orthodoxy believes that the essential matter is still class opposition at the point of production:

> . . . the ability of capital to reproduce itself can basically never be a question of administrative efficiency, but always depends on concrete class relations and the character of class struggles . . . State measures 'to manage the economy' and their success can only be really evaluated in such a context and not as detached strategies of a political instance understood finally as being 'autonomous', i.e., as obeying independent laws of motion and as thus subjected to specific capitalist 'restrictions'. (Hirsch, 1978, p. 99)

Habermas, relying partly on Offe's work, modifies this position substantially. Because social integration in the advanced capitalist state is not a function of class domination's "unpolitical form" (the exchange of labour-power for capital) but a function of the political system, the class structure and the production of surplus value are directly affected by "political disputes". The economic process is therefore no longer self-regulating and the state must act in ways inexplicable by the immanent logic of capital. This displacement of the relations of production takes four forms, according to Habermas (1976, pp. 53, 54). The first two amount to the role of the state in liberal capitalism (see *supra* p. 129). The third form involves market replacement (e.g. state demand for unproductive commodities and state organization of scientific production). The fourth amounts to bailing out 'lame ducks', remedying ecological damage and improving working class living conditions (admittedly on the demand of the unions and labour parties). These forms of course all involve legislation. So, says Habermas, Marxian theory is violated: surplus value is indirectly produced by state policies and institutions (e.g. by recognized scientific work), some forms of labour obtain wages well above their reproduction cost, and capital realization is now limited by the state's need to legitimate itself through an appropriate (re-)distribution of use-values. Similarly the Marxian theory of crisis is considerably weakened. Capitalist contradictions are now expressed as much by irrational administrative decisions and consequent sectoral disorganization, as by bankruptcy and unemployment. Conflict resolution now involves state compromises which may not maximize capitalist gain, although some private interests are more compromisable than others. Indeed, crisis avoidance is consciously thematized by the state, thus enabling strategies impossible in laissez-faire capitalism.

Given this conception of the development of the capitalist state, it is easy to see why Habermas argues that modern social conditions have seen the realization of the continental, radical interpretation of classical natural law philosophy. Fundamental rights (albeit of a technical, highly specific, sometimes quasi-legal character) conferred by a bourgeois constitutional state, needing to legitimate its actions to the public, are the foundation of the modern, political-juridical order. Natural law philosophy of any other kind has no intellectual credibility. The question now at the heart of modern, contract theories of justice (e.g. that of Rawls) is procedural: which procedures and presuppositions have to be fulfilled before a justification (or legitimation) is entitled to produce a consensus? (See Habermas, 1979, pp. 184-205.)

Because of state interventionism and the disappearance of 'liberal' capitalism, the liberal distinction between private and public rights is now baseless. There is now only state licence and compulsion. And because state social engineering depends on scientific experts, positivistically unconcerned to recommend normative and practical contexts of use for their products, we witness a separation of the scientific methods for the technical control of social processes from the public norms of political action. This last connection was basic to all natural law philosophy right up to and including its key critic, Marx. No modern theory can grasp this separation—Marxism deposited concern with the normative content of political praxis as the unnecessary, fictive baggage of the bourgeois hypocrites—and we are left with the positivists' adaptation to dirigisme ("of pure control and manipulation").

In the modern welfare state, the fiction of the pre-political rights of the individual subject is untenable:

> . . . the fundamental rights were once, in the liberal manner, understood as the recognition and not as the conferring of natural freedom belonging to an autonomous private domain, external to the state, but now they can derive their specific meaning only from the context of objective principles constituting a total legal order which encompasses both state and society. (Habermas, 1974, p. 116)

So even the inalienable right to enjoy and dispose of private property is now considerably hemmed in by legislation of various kinds (e.g. planning, labour and conservation law), not to mention the fundamental social rights and provisions provided by the welfare state. The distinction between human and citizens' rights also folds for "the human rights themselves can no longer be interpreted in any other way than as political rights" (1974, p. 116).

Contrary to Pashukanis' (see Warrington, *infra*) and Poulantzas' view of the juridical subject (expressing commodity-exchange relations) as the centre-piece of bourgeois jurisprudence, Habermas states that:

> The rights to freedom, property and security, when they have been transformed in function socially or in the context of the welfare state, are no longer based on legal relations naturally stabilised by the interests of free commodity exchange; instead they are based on an integration of the interests of all the organisations acting in relation to the state, and in turn controlled by an internal as well as external public sphere. This integration has to be continually reconstituted in a democratic manner. (1974, p. 117)

Sociological critique, especially Marxist, forgets this last clause and merely insists that we cannot isolate formal, abstract rights from the concrete social and historical context. But, argues Habermas, the praxis of the welfare state cannot forget bourgeois democracy and is obligated to the Natural Law-related norms underlying modern legality. Therefore we must not forget it either and allow sociology to become scientistic, divorced from the norms of political action. Such a result would produce a devaluation of fundamental rights as mere ideology and blind us to the need to prevent these legal concepts from losing their radical historical meaning as a restriction on economic and political power (see also Thompson, 1977, 1980). The problem for a liberative, Marxist jurisprudence is this:

> . . . the revolutionary significance of modern Natural Law cannot simply be reduced to the social interrelationship of interests, and, on the other hand, the idea of Natural Law which points beyond the bourgeois ideology, though it cannot be salvaged by these means, can only be realised seriously by an interpretation in terms of the concrete social relations. (Habermas, 1974, p. 118)

But let there be no mistake: Habermas is under no illusions about Rousseau and the Enlightenment. He clearly recognizes that the revolutionary natural law tradition demanded extensive legal regulation and "despotic revolutionary enforcement" to sustain the 'natural laws' of bourgeois society, "because the natural laws of society do not operate with the absolute inviolability of the laws of physics, but rather are laws which must be made to rule by political means in the face of the corruption of human nature" (1974, pp. 118, 119). Conversely, the liberal natural law tradition was not as conservative as it looked, he says, because its proponents soon recognized that emancipated market society could only form a total, political society if private citizens bothered to influence the politics of reproducing their life-world. This recognition brought it nearer to the radical tradition with its emphasis on the General Will and the political constitution of the natural society. This convergence of the two traditions and charges in society itself worked to permit the realization of the political society, in the form of the transformation of the liberal constitutional state into the welfare state:

> ... the revolutionary element contained in the positivisation of Natural law has been resolved into a long-range process of democratically integrating the fundamental rights. (Habermas, 1974, p. 119)

The Legitimation Crises of Advanced Capitalism

Habermas's theory of crisis in advanced capitalist social formations posits crisis possibilities in all three main areas of social practice—the economic, the political and the cultural. As already indicated, he believes that the economic crisis (industrial warfare, cyclical business crises, etc.) has been displaced, at least temporarily, into the political system (Habermas, 1976, p. 61).[8] Two types of political crisis are possible—in rationality and in legitimation. 'Rationality deficits' in public administration occur where the state cannot adequately perform its role of steering the economic system. In a nutshell, Habermas believes that state-accelerated accumulation creates tensions ("contradictory steering imperatives" in administrators' actions) due to the unavoidable parameters of capitalist production and the emergence of "foreign bodies" in the capitalist employment system such as workerist orientations in unproductive labour (e.g. welfare recipients, housewives) and radical professionalism in the public sector. Increasing public participation is no solution because it thematizes the parameters of decision-making. Failure to command obedience is not disastrous, but loss of control over "planning-related areas of behaviour" is. In short, state administration in advanced capitalism must always be plagued with "rationality deficits" but these only really produce social crisis inasmuch as they reduce the motivation and co-operation of the citizenry.

Because class domination no longer takes the politically anonymous form of the law of value, "it now depends on factual constellations of power whether, and how, production of surplus value can be guaranteed through the public sector, and how the terms of the class compromise look" (Habermas, 1976, p. 68). It also depends on the fact that motivation in normal social interaction patterns still remains tied to norms requiring justification; the legitimation of the political order has become the lynchpin of social integration. But, because social conflicts therefore undermine the legitimacy of the governors, it becomes necessary to distance the administration from the legitimating system. To this end, says Habermas enigmatically, instrumental functions become distanced from fundamental, expressive symbols. These generalizable symbols which release "an unspecified readiness to follow", are found in "strategies" such as "the personalisation of substantive issues, the symbolic use of hearings, expert judgments, juridical incantations, and also the advertising techniques (copied from oligopolistic competition)" (Habermas, 1976, p. 70). In Habermas's analysis the mass media are crucial in publicizing and withdrawing attention from legitimation themes, and therefore in guiding opinion formation. Like Kirchheimer (1961) and Hall et al. (1978), Habermas draws a strong link between the symbolic/ideological content of law (procedure and pronouncement) and its selective transmission in accentuated forms by the mass media. However, this separation of administrative and legitimation functions leaves the "cultural system" free from admistrative control: "there is no administrative production of meaning". As Habermas says:

> Commercial production and administrative planning of symbols exhausts the normative force of counter-factual validity claims. The procurement of legitimation is self-defeating as soon as the mode of procurement is seen through. (1976, p. 70)

Moreover, once old traditions and standards are eroded by administrative action or advertising they are no longer available for legitimation purposes, and the state cannot guarantee the content of their replacement. Therefore, he argues, the expansion of state activity increases disproportionately the need for legitimation. Its encroachment into all areas of life inevitably thematizes for public discourse areas of practice which were previously totally self-legitimating and private (e.g. school curricula, family planning, marriage laws). Once the unquestionable, taken-for-granted, 'traditional' nature of certain beliefs, practices and institutions is destroyed, then their "validity claims" can only be stabilized "through discourse" (Habermas, 1976, p. 72). This means that civil privatism is threatened through the politicization of private/personal issues, yet as we have seen, civil privatism is a vital functional complement to the depoliticized public realm. Implicitly Habermas offers us clear reasons for the recent impact and general significance of political issues surrounding women and the family.

In sum, the interventionist welfare state demands much legitimation, but also creates substantial legitimation difficulties. These difficulties, however, would not lead to a legitimation crisis in themselves. People can be bought off in a social democracy through growth and redistribution. But, in the long run, this strategy cannot work because such growth can ultimately only be achieved within the priorities of profit maximization which clash with welfarism. "In the final analysis, *this class structure* is the source of the legitimation deficit" (Habermas, 1976, p. 73). Or, as he said more recently: ". . . class societies are structurally unable to satisfy the need for legitimation that they themselves generate" (1979, p. 163).

Legitimation difficulties would only become a legitimation crisis, in Habermas's view, if they combined with a motivation crisis, to the concept of which we now turn. Since 1945, expectations of affluence have increased and the state has been forced to the limits of its manoeuvrability and learning capacity within a capitalist mode of production.

> As long as the welfare-state program, in conjunction with a widespread, technocratic common consciousness (which, in case of doubt, makes inalterable system restraints responsible for bottlenecks), can maintain a sufficient degree of civil privatism, legitimation needs *do not have to* culminate in a crisis. (Habermas, 1976, p. 74)

From a technical systems-theory point of view, says Habermas, democratic modes of legitimation could equally be replaced with "a conservative authoritarian welfare state" or "a fascist authoritarian state". But, he says, both variants are "obviously" at odds with developed capitalist culture. The "socio-cultural system" produces demands unmeetable by authoritarian systems and only negotiable within a multi-party, mass democracy. Only if the "socio-cultural system" became rigid and required rewards that the system could not deliver would a legitimation crisis occur for certain. In short, it needs a motivation crisis emerging from a discrepancy between attitudes demanded by the state and the motivations supplied by the socio-cultural system. Logically, however, as we have learnt in the UK over the last 10 years, it could also arise in a situation where the state's negotiation positions became tougher and less flexible despite the relative constancy of mass demands; Habermas did not consider this alternative.

'Tradition' is important for Habermas. The interventionist state erodes and supports it. Modern formal democracies require a political culture which 'screens out' expectations of participation. This is achieved via the continuation of pre-bourgeois authoritarian culture emphasizing particularism and subordination. However the socio-cultural system, says Habermas, cannot sustain the civil privatism necessary for effective social integration. One reason for this is that the erosion of tradition permits conditions to appear which contradict civil privatism. We have already mentioned the politicization of private troubles; another important aspect of it is the divorce of law and morality which comes with 'modernisation'. 'Positivised legal norms' have been separated from privatized moral norms. The umbrella of bourgeois law in the 'liberal' capitalist state was put up over a realm of autonomous private action, criminal prohibitions notwithstanding, thus releasing "norm-contents from the dogmatism of mere tradition". But as long as the present mode of socialization continues, founding action on justifiable norms not on conditioned responses, the only way that the authorities can ensure conformity between their laws and our morality is to subject all the norms to a system of "discursive will-formation".[9] That, of course, is impossible because it would threaten the state structure and the whole social order. Whether it will ever occur is an interesting debating point.

Capitalism, in the meantime, has freed people from traditional, non-rational modes of justification and thus created its own legitimation problems. Morality has endured to a point today where it is dependent merely (but vitally) on discursive justice, that is, the abilty to redeem normative claims in a rational public discourse. Habermas hopes that the motivational crisis will be resolved this way, but seriously fears that social action could enter the evolutionary cul-de-sac of conditioned response behaviour, and that behaviour will become divorced from rationally justifiable motivations. The latter would be one precondition for a fascist mode of domination—one perfectly possible resolution of the pending legitimation crisis:

> . . . a legitimation crisis can be avoided in the long run only if the latent class structures of advanced capitalist societies are transformed or if the pressure for legitimation to which the administrative system is subject can be removed. The latter, in turn, could be achieved by transposing the integration of inner nature *in toto* to another mode of socialisation, that is, by uncoupling it from norms that need justification. (Habermas, 1976, pp. 93, 94)

From a jurisprudential angle, the danger is that rational-legal authority will become a mode of legitimation which is entirely procedural and divorced from "communicative ethics".[10] Once procedural legitimacy is totally supreme, politics, and therefore legislation and adjudication, can begin to divorce themselves from public morality without fear of critique: another basis for fascism. Habermas criticizes Weber's conception of "rational authority" as a technical, sociological one resting entirely on the empirical presence of mass acceptance of the dominant justificatory system. He insists that every effective belief in legitimacy must have an immanent relation to truth, and therefore contains rational validity claims which are testable and criticizable in rational discourse. That is, the belief in legitimacy is (still) more than a belief in procedural legality: legality does not (and must never) equal legitimacy. Yet, says Habermas, modern philosophical attempts to resurrect Aristotelian natural law have failed and Marxist analysis of legitimacy has been subject to Weber's terms of reference. Somehow there must be a universally acceptable procedure for deciding between normative validity claims. Why that is so and what it is forms the basis of the next section, but let me just round off this discussion by explaining Habermas's most recent ideas on the legitimation problems of the modern state.

Developing the theme that legitimation problems of the modern state cannot be solved outside the inherited normative restrictions, Habermas argues that we need to look further into the origin of the modern state to understand the depth and range of its normative identity.

To begin with, he contends that only states need legitimating. Stateless societies organized power communally within reciprocal kinship relations and therefore its exercise needed no legitimation. Multinational corporations or the world market are also not justifiable (or legitimable); again because they are not founded upon rationally contestable validity claims (Habermas, 1979, pp. 178, 179). However, states *are* founded in this way, via the "successful stabilisation of a judicial position that permitted consensual regulation of action conflicts at the level of conventional morality" (Habermas, 1979, p. 161). Legitimate power crystallized around the administration of justice by judges who applied laws which were "intersubjectively recognised legal norms sanctified by tradition". When judges were no longer referees pragmatically deciding between competing constellations of power, and when they employed penal sanction rather than restitution, then the state had arrived. Once political domination through this elevated procedure of law had been established, says Habermas, the material production process could be uncoupled from kinship relations and reorganized via relations of domination (1979, p. 162). On the basis of political domination, class exploitation in production could begin. Thus, turning Marx on his head, the state becomes the basis of class society in Habermasian social theory.

Around the nucleus of this judicial power, the state emerges as the mechanism of social integration. Threats to its legitimacy are posed by class confrontations, but that is natural because the existence of the state is the fundamental precondition for "a class structure in the Marxian sense" (Habermas, 1979, p. 182). Class struggle only becomes the motor of social development, or the steering device of society, with the advent of capitalism and that system of exploitation can only develop when political domination through a state, or legitimate political inequality, has been established. This is why, says Habermas, class societies can never satisfy their own legitimation needs—their very origins in the state presuppose normative consensus—and this fact itself is "the key to the social dynamic of class struggle".

But the legitimation problems of the 'liberal' capitalist state were not limited to class inequalities, others were acquired owing to the historical logic of state development. Problems relating to secularization (requiring state power to be justified in political not religious terms), changing legal philosophy (requiring law to be legitimated procedurally not in terms of a religious or cosmological world-view), the conflict between the civil law based on universalistic principles and the particularistic needs of social classes, the nature of sovereignty (requiring legitimation in terms of the sovereignty of the people or 'the nation'), and nationalism (demanding political realisation and egalitarian expression).

The laws of the free market and the new ideology of national consciousness, or nation-building, could not stem the tide and conflicts were diverted into the political system of the welfare state, "as an institutionalised struggle over distribution". On this Habermas adds a topical comment to his earlier formulation. He says that the state's legitimation problem today is not how to conceal the relation between capitalism and state praxis through welfare ideology. This is now impossible: Marxism need not expose what is already exposed. What the state has to do is to present capitalism as the only alternative. This is difficult because of the increasingly high costs of welfare, rising Third World commodity prices, devolutionary movements, internal subversion and the increasingly obvious biases in the mass media. Legitimation must therefore become more and more difficult.

The Development of Normative Structures and The Critique of Legitimations

Habermas has always insisted that the great achievements of purposive-rational action (such as science) could only work for emancipation if "enlightenment permeated existing political will". That event could only be guaranteed by "ideal conditions of general communication extending to the entire public and free from domination" (Habermas, 1971a, p. 75). The singular achievement of technology as ideology is that society's self-understanding has become detached from communicative action, and replaced by "a self-reification of man under categories of purposive-national action and adaptive behaviour" (1971a, p. 106). The work/interaction distinction is fundamental to Habermas's position (see 1971a, pp. 91, 92). Interaction or communicative action is governed by binding consensual norms, objectified in ordinary language and grounded in the inter-subjectivity of actual understanding. Work is simply strategic action dependent on rational calculation of means–ends contexts. There is no doubt that Habermas sees positivist styles of thought as severing legitimations from the normative regulation of routine communicative interaction (see 1971a, pp. 112, 113). The restoration of unrestricted, public–political discussion is the key plank in his critique of bourgeois legitimacy. The closer we get to his recent work, however, it seems that his call for a revived public opinion does not involve *actual* public opinion, but that ideal public opinion which would arise out of enlightenment in an ideal speech situation. Existing public opinion is formed in conditions of systematically distorted communication. Against hermeneutics, he argues that we cannot just accept public beliefs about legitimacy, because then we could not distinguish between legitimate and illegitimate domination (see Habermas, 1979, pp. 202, 203). If true, our theoretical knowledge of social systems should enable us to identify distorted communications for the public, elucidate them, and thus enlighten that public about the state.

Habermas has all along wanted to move beyond both empirical-analytic and hermeneutic knowledge to establish a critical theory (a reconstructive analysis) which would sustain the precision of the former and the understanding of the latter whilst involving the attainment of theoretical knowledge (i.e. of underlying mechanisms) (for detailed analysis of positivism and hermeneutics, see Habermas, 1971b). Such a theory would thus be orientated toward truth and emancipation.[11] It could not be bogged down in relativism, yet had to avoid a detached, elitist scientism which made no connection with practical discourse. Psychoanalysis provided a good model, for it not only interprets and elucidates the incomprehensibility of systematically distorted communication but also gives causal explanation of it (see Habermas, 1970, 1971b). Depending on its truth-value, this explanation can enlighten the patient, remove the symptoms and restore normal communication. But to move beyond purely relativist or descriptive hermeneutics, it is clearly necessary for Habermas to develop a model of normal communication. This he did by generalizing from the psychoanalytic setting.

Based on the psychoanalysts' certainty as to what psychopathology and therefore abnormal communication look like, Habermas (1974, pp. 17, 18) argues that normal speech acts, in "functioning language games" (oriented to reaching understanding), are "exchanged" on the basis of an underlying consensus (which constitutes their accountability when challenged). All speech acts assume four things: (a) comprehensibility, (b) truth of content, (c) appropriateness of performance and (d) authenticity of speaker. Now, of course, these assumptions are often contradicted by reality but they are nevertheless made, and unavoidably so (logically) if communication is to occur. The truth of assumptions (or validity claims) (a) and (d) is only provable (for the speakers) in action. Validity claims (b) and (c) however are only redeemable in, and referrable to "discourse" (see Habermas, 1976, pp. 107-108), and are routinely made with this knowledge. In action, we naively assume the validity of all four claims, but in discourse we can assess (b) and (c) because discourse, a search for arguments or justifications, is based on *anticipated* ideal speech conditions. It involves the assumption that argument and justification will be free from constraint and privilege. All motives except "co-operative readiness to arrive at an understanding" are inoperative and the validity of the facts and norms under discussion is reserved. Within this "peculiarly unreal form of communication", a consensus can be reached about truth and appropriateness. In short, discourse, or argumentative speech, always unavoidably contains certain validity claims within its structure. This is not Kantian transcendentalism, says Habermas, but an assertion of the universal structure of speech geared to understanding from the standpoint of reconstructive analysis (see Habermas, 1979, pp. 21-25; also Habermas, 1971b and Giddens, 1979, Ch. 3). The radical implication of which is that truth cannot be separated from freedom and justice (for further details of these arguments, see Habermas, 1974, pp. 1-40; 1976, pp. 102-110; 1979, Ch. 1; Held, 1980, Ch. 12; and the translator's introductions in Habermas, 1976 and 1979).

Because, in the course of evolution, domains of discourse have been institutionalized, discursive conversations have "become a systematically relevant mechanism of learning for a given society" (Habermas, 1974, p. 25). And that is their importance. Habermas clearly wants to criticize the Weberian theory of legitimacy and yet avoid abstract/transcendental moral philosophy by rooting his evaluative criteria in historical evolution.

Declining to return to natural law philosophy to criticize the empiricist conception of legitimacy, Habermas says recourse to the fundamental norms of rational speech is sufficient, the norms which we presuppose in every discourse. Legal decisions cannot be legitimated by procedural propriety because the implicit validity claims of all action (including the legal variety) specify the possibility of their redemption in discourse. Therefore if legal decisions are made without coercion and implemented regularly they "must be considered as the fulfilment of recognised norms" (Habermas, 1976, p. 101). Legitimacy, then, must be founded on justifiable or discursively redeemable norms. Weber's approach, resting on a fact-value distinction, can say nothing in the face of a pluralism of value-orientations in legislative discourse. For Habermas, however, rational discourse *can* separate generalizable interests from particular ones and therefore affirm their validity. (This is a tautology, of course, since he defines generalizability in the first place as the capacity to earn a consensual affirmation in rational discourse.)

The legitimation devices of modern capitalist societies contain ideological modes of justification, which for Habermas suppress generalizable interests and present sectional interests as generalizable. Their distorted communications systematically avoid the "thematization and testing of discursive-validity claims". The "normative power" of the state can be judged by the degree to which legalized norms correspond with the hypothetical norms of the mass of society which would have been affirmed if they could have decided (through rational discourse) on the basis of full information. Habermas goes so far as to say that it is meaningful and possible for the social scientist to reconstruct the "hidden interest positions" of parties in a conflict where they would be forced to become conscious of their interests and assert them (he says Marx did this). But if the modern state's problem is to suppress non-generalizable interests built into its actual norms and policies, then the problem of modern Marxists is to find "strata within the industrial working class . . . which, for structural reasons, are accessible to political enlightenment and which could be won over for non-economic goals" (Habermas, 1974, p. 7). Again the process of enlightenment is pivotal to the political dynamic, but it is not quite as elitist as it sounds. Habermas permits revolutionaries no truth prior to discourse with workers, truth is only confirmed if enlightenment occurs. Moreover, successful enlightenment does not entitle the activist to dictate strategic action on the basis of pure theory, that action has to be arrived at by consensus amongst all the participants to the discourse.[12]

We all know the passage in the *1859 Preface* ending in the conclusion that "mankind always sets itself only such tasks as it can solve". That *has* to be the axiom behind Habermas's recent attempt to give universal validity to his reliance on rational discourse for the critique of procedural legitimacy. The notion of rational discourse is the centre of Habermas's work. He arrives at it through epistemology, political philosophy, social theory, jurisprudence and psychology. His ideas in all those areas are held together by the concept of reason, which left him liable to criticisms such as those of Connerton:

> . . . to call the political reality of the present capitalist and socialist worlds before the tribunal of discourse is simply to bring the Judgement-Seat of Reason up to date: it repeats a bourgeois, pre-revolutionary abstraction. (1980, p. 107)

To overcome such objections of "political triviality" (Connerton), Habermas tried to ground this approach in the history of legitimations and the ontogenesis of moral consciousness, basically arguing that the learning capacity of a society was decisive in transcending crises and bringing a higher stage of development.

Relying on his distinction between work and communication, Habermas asserts that Marx limited the learning processes vital for evolution to the sphere of the productive forces, whereas the structures of reason and consciousness are of equal importance, e.g. in making possible new productive forces, new political institutions and new forms of moral action. The development of normative structures is of special importance (Habermas, 1979, p. 98). Culture remains superstructural, but for Habermas it is more crucial to social evolution than Marxists have conceded. Ultimately, changes in normative structures are conditioned by the problems posed for social systems by their modes of production, but the development of the production forces does not of itself bring about the overthrow of social relations of production (Habermas, 1979, p. 146). The resolution of social crises depends on changes in "moral-practical consciousness" which has its own developmental logic, not reducible to that of a mode of production.[13] Consequently, law and morality are now right at the centre of Habermas's theoretical stage, for they "mark the core domain of interaction" in that they maintain the "intersubjectivity of understanding" in moments of conflict: they regulate action conflicts consensually (Habermas, 1979, p. 116).

Carefully and tentatively proceeding, Habermas draws homologies between ego development and the evolution of world-views. Relying heavily on Piaget and Kohlberg for a theory of the stages of moral consciousness in the individual, Habermas distinguishes between preconventional, conventional and postconventional patterns of problem-solving by the individual and by the society. Moral and legal representations therefore move through these stages. The formation of states, via the structural elevation and separation of an adjudicative institution relying on conventional problem-solving, is a decisive step. It marks the move of the human species away from preconventional legal regulation based on an egocentric and pragmatic reciprocity (expressing itself in restitution and feud), and contains the recognition of social rules necessary for a territorial organization; albeit a recognition tied to the figure of the ruler and legitimated by mythological world views. Gradually, these necessary rules become detached from the ruler himself and legitimated by rationalized world-views. The intrinsic universalism within legal doctrine of this kind could not however be released while domination remained particularistic and status-based: it needed capitalism with its depoliticized, market-regulated economy. Conventional role identity shattered, and ego identity developed, in a world organized on the universalistic principles of bourgeois civil law. Expressed in modern natural law and formalistic ethics, "the collective identity of bourgeois society developed under the highly abstract viewpoints of legality, morality and sovereignty" (Habermas, 1979, p. 114). Eventually, the modern age saw the emergence of the postconventional stage of legal regulation with universalistic premises, separated from private morality, requiring legitimation by people with self-chosen abstract, ethical principles sustained by criteria of logical comprehensiveness, universality and consistency.

The critique of bourgeois legitimation according to communicative ethics needs this theory of the development of morality and modes of social integration (conflict resolution) since it cannot rely on a theory of the development of the productive forces and the class struggle. Communicative action, the other half of human existence, has its own developmental logic and, argues Habermas, cannot be explained by economic development in the same way as purposive-rational action. Communication depends on the background consensus of universal validity claims (truth, rightness, truthfulness) implicitly assumed in all speech. Not only is this consensus a natural part of modern adult interaction but it has also been institutionalized via bourgeois revolutionary ideology, in political and legal forms. On the other hand, strategic action is indifferent to supportive motivations, is egocentric, monologic and instrumental in content, and also requires institutionalization. However, Habermas observes, further rationalization within cultural/legal institutions would have to overcome systematically distorted communication because the "rationalisation" of communicative action means heightening its assumed capacity for understanding not for technical knowledge. Habermas therefore posits an internal contradiction within capitalist rationalization that is important for us because it amounts to the inadequacy of modern formal democracy and rational-legal authority for the institutionalization of bourgeois strategic actions. Normative consciousness and its correspondent superstructural institutions are based on an evolution that presents obstacles for autocratic and technocratic forms of bourgeois domination. Neither Weber's conception of rationalization nor Marx's theory of class struggle could grasp this.

This is not to replace either approach, says Habermas, with a species history amounting to the long march of reason or the history of the spirit. He claims that he has not dropped his materialist assumptions. He intends merely to supplement an analysis of modes of production with an analysis of the role of political, legal and moral structures in preventing or accelerating resolutions of social crises. Such a supplement is necessary, he thinks, because social crises are not generated in other social formations in the same way as in capitalism. The 'capital-logic' perspective cannot be transposed to the theory of historical evolution as a whole because the "principle of social organisation" in other societies does not reside in the economy (Habermas, 1979, pp. 124, 144). In "primitive societies" the regulation of the distribution of social wealth was performed by kinship systems and in the early civilizations by systems of political domination; and in postindustrial societies it might occur through the "educational and scientific systems". Moreover, capital-logic does not dictate that socialism will be the necessary or adequate response to modern crises.

In fact, however, Habermas does virtually abandon the Marxist theory of history in his "reconstruction" of historical materialism. Apart from regarding Marx's formulation of the mechanism of social crises as too technologistic and economistic, and regarding class societies as founded upon the growth of the state—points already mentioned, Habermas makes five other major criticisms of the Marxist theory of history:

(a)   Social or human reproduction is insufficiently captured by the Marxian concept of labour, which only sees it as a continuation of the mode of production. 'Labour', however, only delimits the basis of the reproduction of hominids. Once the economy of the hunt is supplemented by a family system, we must talk of modes of instrumental action *and* modes of communicative action based on normative action (see 1979, pp. 131-138).

(b)   The evolution of the modes of production need not be regarded as the evolution of the species-subject, as unilinear, as irreversible, necessary or progressive in every sense (pp. 138-142).

(c)   The superstructure is only dependent on the base at the critical (i.e. transitional) phases of social development. The economy is not ontologically basic but developmentally directive (pp. 142-144). I have outlined the ramifications of this already (*supra*, p. 137).

(d) There are all sorts of difficulties with the six modes of production and their
     sequence (pp. 151, 152).

(e) The concept of the mode of production is not broad enough to capture the
     universal dynamics of social development. Its weaknesses suggest the need
     for a more general concept of "the principles of social organisation" to
     supplement it. These principles seem to be the basic rules governing social
     action and determining a society's learning capacity. They are characterized
     by the normative/interaction structures which determine the dominant
     mode of social integration. Thus modes of legality are crystallizations of the
     most general, but most decisive, features of any social formation (pp. 152,
     154).

At the end of the argument, Habermas's programme of investigation is specified
as follows:

> But the historical sequence of modes of production can be analysed in terms
> of abstract principles of social organisation only if we can specify which
> structures of world views correspond to individual forms of social
> integration and how these structures limit the development of secular
> knowledge . . . The evolution of world views mediates between the stages of
> development of interaction structures and advances in technically useful
> knowledge. In the concepts of historical materialism this means that the
> dialectic of forces and relations of production takes place through ideologies.
> (1979, p. 169)

In the last analysis, his project is to understand the history of world-views in
order to determine which modes of social integration they will support and for
how long. Tying the analysis of legitimation to a communication theory has thus
taken him to the world views which support law and give it a pivotal role in the
current legitimation crisis of the advanced capitalist states.

A Critique

I hope that the exposition above has accurately and fairly conveyed the essence of
Habermas's brilliant and exhilarating analysis. There is far more in his work
than I can describe here. The significance of his theories for contemporary
debates on the form of law, the value of the rule of law, the modern strong state's
erosion of classical civil liberties, and on the relationship between the state and
ideology should be obvious (see Thompson, 1977, 1980; Hirst, 1979).

For me, Habermas's analysis illuminates the way in which the increasing
distance between legitimate political process and technically effective administration involves an increasing sacrifice of democracy to the unthematized,
concealed, sectional interests of international capital. Along that trail, some of

the classical themes of bourgeois law (procedural fairness, public declaration and civil liberty) are falling by the wayside. However, the element of public opinion and debate, always essential to bourgeois rational-legal domination albeit in restricted forms, has not yet fallen into decay. Given the rise of post-conventional forms of moral consciousness, a solution to the crisis of advanced capitalism must appeal to a generalizable interest. That is the problem as Habermas portrays it: advanced capitalism has generated political and cultural needs which it cannot appease economically. The implication of this is, in my view, that these needs can expect little satisfaction in the future and will run up against increasing closure, repression and evasion within the legal and regulatory institutions of the state. Since, therefore, the crisis in the modern capitalist economy is also a crisis in its steering device, the state, it must produce a crisis in justice. This must be especially so today, I think, because justice rarely takes the form of a neutral abstraction, more frequently being a clear expression of social policy. So there is not so much a crisis in pure law as a crisis in social justice. Law is rapidly being politicized in the popular consciousness. The failure of the state to deliver the goods must commonly take the form of a legal contraction: a closure in the possibility of law as an agency of legitimation.

The contribution of Habermas to modern theories of law, whatever the strength of my criticism (to follow), has been to sustain a systematic theoretical analysis which confronts many of the key issues concerning legality in the modern state. He has posed a substantial challenge or alternative to 'Dia-Mat' orthodoxies in Marxism which dismiss law because of its class content or bourgeois form. He has considerably undermined the view of law as a merely superstructural and uncontradictory component of social formations. He has given law a major role in social development and in the growth of capitalism in particular. In short, he has provided strong reasons why legal struggles and law-work might be central to the fight against the drift to fascism.

My commission has primarily demanded elucidation and exposition: not many people are familiar with Habermas's ideas about law. However, I would now like to air some criticisms.

His conception of 'liberal' capitalism seems somewhat Weberian, or even Friedmanite. What on earth was 'liberal' about it? Marx destroyed the notion that free exchange produced the free society, and the notion that capitalism could be understood as mere exchange. Habermas has it that the market regulated production ("in a decentralised and unpolitical manner") (1979, p. 189) and that this market is "anchored" in bourgeois civil law. But the essence of the capitalist economy is the exchange of labour-power for capital at the point of production; production therefore regulates the market as much as vice versa. Habermas neglects the relations of production in his analysis and hence underscores the role of class conflict and struggle in the construction of the necessary forms of law in this period and in the emergence of the later welfare legislation. For example, labour law is partly a state service to the economy, as he says, but it is also a reflection of class struggles at the centres of production. Hence it is nonsense to regard the steering mechanism of nineteenth century capitalism as 'depoliticized'. The economic realm positively bred politics, because of the palpably unequal exchange in the factory and the miserable surroundings and health conditions that it produced. Nor was this realm 'anchored' in civil law. Civil law, in fact, was anchored in the petty commodity exchange relations of pre-capitalist societies and had to be hastily expanded, reformulated and considerably developed to match the needs of industrial capitalism. The bourgeois ideology of justice rooted in the exchange of equivalents legitimated precious little. Indeed, it required the formation of the police, extensive criminal law legislation, more prisons and reformatories, mental hospitals, considerable softening of bourgeois attitudes, Methodism, the legalization of the unions, football, cricket and an awful lot of ale, before anything remotely like stability occurred. It is arguable that forms of working class self-help and direct industrial struggle were more important still. Detailed studies of proletarianization are of more use than simplistic and artificially neat legitimation theses. Class analysis is pivotal to Marxism: in Habermas it is too little and too marginal. He fails to capture the multitude of social conflicts and modes of pacifying them that abound in early industrial capitalism. Consequently, he completely neglects the role of coercion (economic and political) in stabilizing such societies. This leaves him without an analysis of the coercive role of criminal law in ensuring the development of capitalism: it did not just serve to maintain but was vital to the establishment of this mode of production. Like the feudal state, the capitalist state did not rest on normative validity claims redeemable in discourse but on dominant class power. On the basis of that power, and in the course of maintaining it, ideological legitimations developed in bourgeois society which were to some extent effective; but even then, they were of a much broader range than the political-juridical ones discussed by Habermas. Indeed, that latter discussion is crucially flawed by its insistence that, in capitalism, law and morality grow apart. That is too generalized a formulation. The broad divergence surely lies between *bourgeois* law and the morality of *the mass*, and even then there have been many convergences since the growth of industrial capitalism.

Regarding the advanced capitalist state, it is unclear why Habermas thinks that the legitimating ideology of "liberal" capitalism "collapses" (1976, p. 87). Somehow it just does, and is replaced by the "substitute programme" of the welfare state. The conflicts, tensions and struggles between the social classes involved in the process are not mentioned and one simply gets the impression that the cunning state lords it over the dumb workers. The role of the labour parties cannot be separated from class conflict/struggle and completely downgraded as 'the incorporation of the reformist party'. Moreover, the gains of the working people under the welfare state cannot be separated from the 150 years of struggle against the inertia, paternalism and self-interests of the bourgeois class and its political representatives. Also it is difficult to agree with Habermas that the class struggle became totally or permanently latent and that hope rests with the student movement (Habermas, 1971, pp. 120-122) or the deviant politics/political deviants of the 1970s (1976, pp. 91, 92). As the welfare state recedes, sharp class conflict returns.

Apart from the origins and effects of the "substitute programme", Habermas is theoretically wrong in his critique of the capital-logic theory of the modern state. Taking the points he makes one by one (see *supra* p. 132):

(a) It is difficult to see how any of the state's economic roles alter the fact that the state's overall task is prescribed and structured by the logic of capital.

(b) Any direct production of surplus value through state research agencies and funding would not constitute a breach of the laws of value. Indeed since the state now runs several industries, state capitalism is even further advanced than Habermas suggests. Following Marxian theory, what else would one expect?

(c) The existence of wage differentials contradicts the Marxian theory of reproduction costs as little as does profit differentials threaten the theory of the average rate of profit. It is the average rate that matters since Marx's analysis was an overall or class analysis.

(d) Capital realization is not limited by the costs of public welfare: the funds available for welfare, education etc., are limited by the needs of capital realization, as we now see.

(e) Crisis avoidance has always been the job of the capitalist state, the present situation is not new. Also, Marxist theory has always stressed the possibility of multiple crises within a social formation.

Clearly, then, Habermas has given us no adequate grounds for saying that the key contradictions of capitalism have been displaced into the state; and therefore for focussing his whole analysis on the state. I must agree with Hirsch when he states that the reproduction of capital depends first and foremost on the class struggle, that the state is a heterogeneous and chaotic structure closely tied to monopol capital, and that its legitimation difficulties are directly (although not exclusively) linked to valorization problems (Hirsch, 1978).[14] Therefore, legitimation problems are not the centre of the modern social crisis. Economic problems are central and give rise to legitimation difficulties.

The idealism apparent in Habermas's theoretical method and beliefs culminates in his recent work where he suggests that the development of normative structures is "the pacemaker of social evolution" (1979, p. 120). As we have seen, he sees a society's learning capacity as the basis of its ability to resolve crises. However, this position is, I believe, founded on a fundamental theoretical error: the distinction between purposive-rational action and communicative action, between work and symbolic interaction or, as he recently put it, between the modes of production and the rules of interaction. A distinction between economic and cultural practice is workable (see Sumner, 1979, Ch. 7), but the distinction Habermas makes is not of that type, what he does is to distinguish types of social action in a Weberian/Parsonian way according to their subjective component. Such a distinction does not run parallel to the economic/cultural distinction as Habermas seems to think: it cuts across it. The effect of this error is to reduce the Marxian concept of economic practice to a technical notion of work and to hive off its subjective/ideological component to communicative action (see also Therborn, 1970). Consequently, his attempt to supplement a developmental logic of technological growth with a developmental logic of communicative action is entirely misconceived. He reduces Marxism so as to supplement it and eventually to revise it entirely.

Habermas's idealist revision of Marx logically leads him to tie his legal analysis to a theory of communication. Having declared that traditional legitimations were rooted in communicative action and argued that these break down in the face of the modernizing influence of purposive-rational action (1971, p. 96), he naturally looks for the problems of legitimacy in bourgeois society in the lack of genuine communication and, therefore, democratic consensus. This approach colours his whole theory of law in modern society, yet it is fundamentally mistaken. Basically, the error lies, as it does in any 'modernization' theory, with the notion that traditional legitimations were rooted in reciprocal, consensual personal social relations. This is the concept of 'pre-colonial bliss', familiar to development theorists. In a nutshell, it is inadequate because pre-bourgeois legitimations were often rooted in forms of economic exploitation and political domination: class conflict does not begin, as Habermas argues, with the capitalist relations breeding in advanced feudalism. Communal reciprocity, in Europe at least, had disappeared well before advanced feudalism.[15] In my view, Habermas does not provide good historical grounds for his predisposition to search for the legitimation problems of capitalism in the failure of democracy and the demise of normal communication. Nor can we be satisfied with his theoretical tendency to give primacy to the political, both in feudalism and advanced capitalism; again the position is not sufficiently advanced or argued through.

What of the legal theory itself? To begin with, Habermas effectively turns Marxism on its head in favour of a Parsonian systems theory when he declares normative structures to be the key to social evolution and law and morality to be the key mechanisms of normative integration. This is a pure American structural functionalist view of the social function of law. Not a word is mentioned of class conflict or different class cultures, the key problem areas in this perspective, until we find him arguing that the problem in capitalism is to legalize the imperatives of "strategic action" within an institutionalized mode of communicative action or discourse. But how can law ever be a successful integrative mechanism in a class-divided society with a class state? How can laws be said to resolve *social* crises in a class society? In short, it's all topsy-turvy: a result of mixing American systems theory with Marxian political economy. How can he say he is merely supplementing Marxism when he argues that law is a mechanism for maintaining the intersubjective, normative consensus essential for "understanding"? How can he reconcile his two levels of social action—one, the economy based on *class exploitation*; two, the system of communicative action based on a *consensus* regulated through law? He would probably reply that the establishment of a separate, politically impartial adjudication system based on shared conventions was the basis of the state which, in turn, was the basis of class society, and therefore that normative regulation preceded class exploitation. But I would suggest that the rise of a state judiciary was based on established class power rooted in economic exploitation, not on shared conventions.

His arguments about Marx's misreading of natural law theory are persuasive at first glance. The difficulties Marxists have with the critique of law in advanced capitalist states can be seen in the recent recovery of Pashukanis' work. His ideas, based on commodity-exchange theory, are entirely unsuitable for the purpose and must lead to politically irrelevant positions. Commodity-form theories of law cannot handle the weight and variety of law in the modern interventionist state. Also they reject natural law theory and are only concerned with the normative content of law to expose it through their sociological nihilism. The state becomes merely an articulator of norms rooted in commodity exchange. This position is inadequate for many reasons and has been widely criticized (see Hirst, 1979; Warrington, 1980 and *infra*; Sumner, 1981).

But I do not accept that Marxism requires a normative critique of the modern state and its law separate from its sociological, analytic exposé of the weaknesses of bourgeois democracy and legality. Habermas does seem to persist with Weber's fact-value distinction despite his criticisms of it. He is so concerned to justify his preference for democracy over other values (in order to establish the illegitimacy of the present mode of political rule) that he seems to end up arguing that we must preserve democracy by preserving democracy. His hopes are pinned on the preservation of rational discourse, public opinion, public participation and the tie between norm and reason, yet these institutions are not just methods of progress for Habermas but forms of its realization. Public reason thus appears to be the major force in his social dynamics. But to posit the possibility of a tribunal of Reason begs the whole question of democracy in a class state. In any case, as I indicated earlier, Habermas's thesis that the generalizability of interests can be settled in discourse is entirely tautologous. Inevitably, we are back to class and other social divisions. If the analytic exposé of law depends on a class analysis, how can it be supplemented with a normative critique resting on a consensus theory of truth? It is quite contradictory. Habermas has not done enough, in my opinion, to show how the constraining features and consequences of class, race and gender divisions might be overcome in a functional democracy in order to restimulate the progressive role of public-political debate. The facts of modern life and the values of Habermas seem quite separate; the missing bridge between them is a practical political programme founded on an analysis of Western history.

Despite this, Habermas still has a point. Although we do not need a normative critique of law separate from our sociological analysis of law, the values underlying our work on law and state are very rarely discussed at length. Moreover, the concept of public opinion has disappeared from Marxist work entirely. Like law and democracy, it has often been regarded as an empty shell or a myth, never to be taken seriously. But if we want the rule of law and democracy for a socialist society, then we should also develop the concept of public opinion. We cannot assume a consensus on the matter: some Marxists would argue that public opinion needs enlightenment from the vanguard party and the apparatuses of the proletarian state, others would argue for the complete subjection of the state machine to the tribunals of public opinion. I think that there is a tremendous ambivalence within Marxism about public opinion. There is not a little elitism about working class consciousness, not a little reluctance to permit 'reactionary' opinions to have their full hearing, and not a little eagerness to define anything other than 'the correct line' as deficient. Such attitudes are hardly defensible as the ideals of political life in a socialist state; indeed, they look like the working principles of the Soviet state—and it is precisely Stalinism that Habermas is attacking.

Despite the fact that I would call for a development of Marxism's distinctively political values and concepts, and for their full insertion into the critique of the modern state, this critique cannot be divorced from economic analysis. The basis for political democracy is economic democracy. Habermas has dangerously separated his analysis of the political from his analysis of the economic. This cannot be justified by his assertion that the fundamental contradictions of our society have been displaced into the political sphere, because he needs to analyse the economy more closely to understand the form and effectiveness of such displacement. That being said, his emphasis on public opinion, rational discourse and democracy is worth retaining and combining with our analysis of the economy, for two reasons: (1) building these concepts into the theory and practice of the revolutionary movement itself would make it more legitimate as a potential instrument of leadership, and (2) democratization of the legal order (and other political institutions) is not an addendum to the class struggle (and other struggles) but part of it. Unless we define class struggle as an idealized clash between two classes fully conscious of their own "true" interests, continued pressure for the full democratization of the legal order (removing *all* the social discriminations it contains) must be part of the earthly class struggle. As we have seen, expropriation of the bourgeoisie does not of itself provide for democratic legality. Marxists must, as Thompson repeatedly suggests, start trusting public opinion now, not tomorrow. Habermas's writings, however flawed, do support our recent inclination to politicize legal issues. They do not however provide us with an adequate model of the relation between political action, science and public opinion, as I shall argue shortly. What they do is to correct the illusion that the mystificatory form and oppressive content of law amount to a nasty odour floating up from the economy and that the socialist economic revolution will disinfect the superstructure automatically.[16] That illusion is based on an analysis of laissez-faire capitalism, and is therefore out of date. Democracy must now be on the agenda as an end in itself, applicable both to the current defensive struggles against the aggressive capitalist state and to the future construction of a socialist society. Civil rights are not an eighteenth century illusion, but a claim by the subordinate classes and groups for a limit to the power of the state and the dominant class.[17]

However, Habermas's attempt to root his positive evaluation of democracy in a communication theory and the history of normative structures fails. Taking the historical perspective first, I cannot see how models of adolescent moral development can be translated into a model of moral evolution. Despite Habermas's sophistication, in his analysis, the law and morality of modern societies become the height of maturity or civilization, and those of older societies the expression of infantility or instinct. This is the Western nonsense of every modernization theorist. Also, I am not convinced that all Kohlberg's levels of individual moral development cannot develop within every mode of production. Nor is it obvious that our rulers' legal codes match Kohlberg's criteria of mature moral development; indeed, they often seem to express a preconventional selfish moral attitude.

Ultimately, his critique of the empiricist and relativist concepts of legitimacy depends on his theory of normal communication and his consensus theory of truth. However, I would argue that the transcendental qualities of speech which he posits are not logically necessary. They are patently "counterfactual", as he readily admits (see 1976, pp. xvii, xviii). In a society ridden with conflicts and tensions, it is common to lie, to deny others their right or turn to speak, to mumble out a sense of inferiority, to avoid reason in favour of prejudice and to lack the capacity or will to comprehend certain others. It is therefore hard to see how speech performances "unavoidably" assume validity claims of truth, appropriateness, comprehensibility and truthfulness. He surely cannot assume that people 'norm' their speech without regard to the typical features of discourse in specific interaction contexts. Moreover, speech is clearly not impossible without his nice assumptions. Even more crucial for his theory, it is not obvious why speech is aimed at understanding. Nor is he entitled, in the last analysis, to claim that his model is merely a normative yardstick to judge the quality of communication because if it is merely normative then it has no

obvious universality or claims to superiority. All these weaknesses in his theory
of the universal structure of speech must render his critique of proceduralist
views of legitimacy merely thought-provoking.

Critics of Habermas have already pointed out that the problems of basing a
theory of normal communication on the evidence of psychoanalysis (Giddens,
1979; Connerton, 1980 and see Habermas, 1974, Introduction). In psychoanalysis, the patient is voluntary: Habermas needs that assumption of consensus
to build a model of communication geared to reaching it. In social conflict, the
situation is different, and if that had been his base assumption his theory would
have been different. Habermas posits an exchange theory of speech (see 1974,
p. 17). This must be a very doubtful assumption for understanding modern
communication. Just as the lack of sustained, historical, class analysis under-
mines his theory of modern social crisis, so his lack of concrete, conflict analysis
weakens his theory of speech acts. Speech, discourse, reason, norms and values:
none of these aspects of culture can be abstracted without regard for their
contextualized, historical meaning in the structure of social relationships.
Habermas's reverence for the tribunal of rational discourse might look to the
enlightened worker like an academic's professional ideology. Ultimately, the
critique of bourgeois legitimacy cannot rest on Habermas's theory of the
universal discursive justifiability of democracy but on the meaning given to
democracy by the working class.

Acknowledgements

My thanks go to David Sugarman and Ian Taylor for encouraging me to write
this piece. Jane Kenrick, Bill Chambliss, Dennis Davis, Maggie Sumner,
Maureen Cain, David Sugarman and several anonymous commentators provided
much encouragement and some useful advice.

Notes

1. "However, Weber's formal rationality, so far from resting upon 'value-free'
    auspices, is in fact an historical constellation whose precondition is the separation of
    the orders of knowledge, work and politics. In the period of the bourgeois
    ascendancy, the value-free conception of rationality furnishes a critical concept of the
    development of human potential locked in the feudal world of 'traditional' values.
    Weber makes a fatality of technical rationality thereby identifying its historical role
    with political domination as such, whereas Marx's critique of class political economy
    showed the critical limits of economic rationality." (O'Neill, 1972, p. 224)
2. The state of neglect is presumably a reflection of what both Giddens (1979) and
    Sensat (1970) see as an abrupt dismissal of Habermas's work by Marxists as idealist

revisionism. Ultimately, I think that the critics have a point; but since Habermas willingly concedes the idealist charge and is openly revisionistic, their critical distance seems insular and dogmatic.

3. Although Connerton argues that critical theorists (Horkheimer, Adorno, Marcuse and Habermas) never severed their roots in the enlightenment philosophy of history as an "all-embracing process in which a historical subject attains its essence". (Connerton, 1980, p. 111)

4. "The rigidity, devoid of any experience, of the thinking that predominates in mass society, is hardened still further, if possible, while at the same time a sharpened pseudorealism which in all its externals furnishes the precise reproduction of empirical reality, prevents any insight into the character of preformation, in accord with the social control, of that which is offered." (Frankfurt Institute of Social Research, 1973, p. 201)

5. In a reflexive section at the end of his last (translated) book (1979, pp. 199-205), Habermas finally recognizes this and admits his close relation to the neo-Aristotelianism of writers such as Arendt, Ritter and Hennis, writers who have recently been concerned to ground a normative critique of justificatory (or legitimation) systems.

6. ". . . social philosophy was deprived ultimately of its really meaningful achievement, the certainty of universally valid statements, even by its own criteria, because it was only able to make reassuring claims about the practical consequences of its own teachings, without being able to attain theoretical certainty in the most important point: how the 'furthering of human life' could actually be brought about by putting theory into praxis." (Habermas, 1974, pp. 80, 81)

7. Elsewhere, I have argued for the full recognition of the complexity of modern law (see Sumner, 1979, Ch. 8). It is a form of ideology which expresses social relations and conflicts of many kinds (i.e. political and cultural as well as economic). It no longer centres on the ideological notion of the juridical subject—any law graduate knows that—only Marxists with their nineteenth century jurisprudence think otherwise. It mediates, expresses, defuses and conceals complex political relations, conditions and technicalities; more than ever, law is a *political* phenomenon.

8. "In the final analysis, the answer depends on whether capital expended so as to be only indirectly productive does attain an increase in the productivity of labour, and on whether the distribution of the growth in productivity in line with functional requirements of the system is sufficient to guarantee mass loyalty and, simultaneously, keep the accumulation process moving." (Habermas, 1976, p. 61)

9. Raising the vision of a society where there would be no need to criminalize deviance (see also Taylor, Walton and Young, 1973). Habermas proceeds to face the obvious rejoiners by arguing that the removal of the law-morality split is not feasible until we can know "the degree to which aggressiveness can be curtailed and the voluntary recognition of discursive principles attained" (1976, p. 87). Only when there is a universal "readiness to engage in discursive clarification of practical questions" could we count on widespread internalization of agreed norms; only then would morality be universal.

10. "Communicative ethics" does not root the morality of conduct in procedurally correct action but in action conducted according to norms which are discursively redeemable in an ideal speech situation of rational discourse.

11. See Scott (1978) for a brief comparison of the difference between Habermas's attempt to counter relativism and that of realist philosophy.

12. Habermas clearly sees this as a radical understanding of political activism, since he believes that people have become cynical about bourgeois ideas of freedom and

self-determination; public political discourse now seems to many a mere sham.

13. These stages of moral development are not mechanisms but phases. The mechanism behind the movement from one stage to another seems to be the demands put on "moral-practical consciousness" by the whole social system, dominated of course by the mode of production, in the form of interactional pressures.

14. Habermas himself has admitted twice in passing that class conflict and profit maximization are the fundamental causes of modern legitimation difficulties.

15. No more than this need be said because there is little to refute. Habermas's notion of development is not specified in detail, nor illustrated much, and using terms like 'traditional' or 'stateless' societies does not help.

16. This, in my view, is very much a late sixties early seventies criticism of Stalinism. Today I think to most Marxists, in Britain at least, it would seem old hat. Transformation of the very form of state power in a socialist society has been on the agenda for some years now. Nobody thinks it will happen automatically and needs no thought.

17. And therefore applicable in socialist society!? Understood as an important political form, albeit with some change of content (the right to capital?), it would seem that they should be. Such a heretical suggestion does of course raise issue with the traditional Marxist conception of revolution by force (against the bourgeoisie, the petit bourgeoisie, 'backward sectors', deviants and Uncle Tom Cobley).

References

(i) Jurgen Habermas:
(1970). "Towards a Theory of Communicative Competence". *Inquiry* **13**, 360-375.
(1971a). *Toward a Rational Society*. Heinemann, London.
(1971b). *Knowledge and Human Interests*. Beacon Press, Boston.
(1974). *Theory and Practice*. Heinemann, London.
(1976). *Legitimation Crisis*. Heinemann, London.
(1979). *Communication and the Evolution of Society*. Heinemann, London.

(ii) Others:
Connerton, P. (1980). *The Tragedy of Enlightenment*. Cambridge U.P., Cambridge.
Frankfurt Institute of Social Research. (1973). *Aspect of Sociology*. Heinemann, London.
Giddens, A. (1979). *Studies in Social and Political Theory*. Hutchinson, London.
Hall, S., Critcher, D., Jefferson, T., Clarke, J. and Roberts, B. (1978). *Policing the Crisis*. MacMillan, London.
Held, D. (1980). *Introduction to Critical Theory*. Hutchinson, London.
Hirsch, J. (1978). "The State Apparatus and Social Reproduction; Elements of a Theory of the Bourgeois State". In *State and Capital* (Holloway, J. and Picciotto, S., Eds). Arnold, London.
Hirst, P. Q. (1979). *On Law and Ideology*. MacMillan, London.
Hirst, P. Q. (1980). "Law, Socialism and Rights". In Carlen, P. and Collison, M. (Eds). *Radical Issues in Criminology*. Martin Robertson, London.
Horowitz, I. L. and Liebowitz, M. L. (1968). "Social Deviance and Political Marginality". *Social Problems* **15** (3), 280-296.
Kirchheimer, O. (1961). *Political Justice*. Princeton U.P., Princeton.
Liazos, A. (1972). "The Poverty of the Sociology of Deviance: Nuts, Sluts and Perverts". *Social Deviance* **20**(1), 103-120.

Lloyd, Lord (1979). *Introduction to Jurisprudence*. Stevens, London.

O'Neill, J. (1972). *Sociology as a Skin Trade*. Heinemann, London.

Pearson, G. (1975). *The Deviant Imagination*. MacMillan, London.

Scott, J. P. (1978). "Critical Social Theory: an Introduction and Critique". *Brit. Jo. Sociol.* **29**(1), 1-21.

Slater, P. (1977). *Origin and Significance of the Frankfurt School*. Routledge and Kegan Paul, London.

Sumner, C. S. (1979). *Reading Ideologies*. Academic Press, London.

Sumner, C. S. (1981). "Pashukanis and the jurisprudence of terror". *Insurgent Sociologist*, **X**(4), 99-106.

Taylor, I. R., Walton, P. and Young, J. (1973). *The New Criminology*. Routledge and Kegan Paul, London.

Therborn, G. (1970). "The Frankfurt School". In *Western Marxism* (New Left Review Ed.), pp. 83-139. New Left Books, London.

Thompson, E. P. (1977). *Whigs and Hunters*. Peregrine, Harmondsworth.

Thompson, E. P. (1980). *Writing by Candlelight*. Merlin, London.

Warrington R. (1980). Review of Beirne, P. and Sharlet, R. (Eds), (1980) *Pashukanis*, *Int. Jo. of Sociol. of Law* **8**(3), pp. 325-330.

Further Reading

There is rarely a substitute for the original texts. Habermas's works are loaded throughout with references to law, state, democracy and ideology, so there is no one outstanding reference. The first three chapters of *Theory and Practice* are probably the most instructive and the most jurisprudential. Chapters 3 and 5 of *Communication and the Evolution of Society* are important in linking rational, legal authority to the development of normative consciousness, and Part 3 of *Legitimation Crisis* contains a sharp discussion of the logic of legitimation problems (with special reference to Weber). However, since Habermas's work is interconnected and cumulative it is difficult to read any section of it without reading the whole corpus. The fact that Habermas has a language of his own perhaps explains why many find a total reading daunting. However, he is very consistent and very precise, so that once the reader has cracked his codes the experience is not that difficult and well worthwhile. Therefore, to read the whole I recommend beginning with *Toward a Rational Society* and moving on chronologically.

Unfortunately, there are not many complete summaries around. Apart from the excellent 'translators' introductions to Habermas's books, I found Giddens (1979, Ch. 3) very useful on some of the key concepts, although his is a critical commentary on Habermas's hermeneutics only. The critiques by Therborn (1970), O'Neill (1972), Slater (1977) and Hirsch (1978) were also very instructive, although not focussed solely on Habermas. But most valuable to me was Connerton's critical reconstruction of Critical Theory which, although again not focussed on Habermas, provided many insights. However, the new *Introduction to Critical Theory* by David Held, published just after my essay was written, will probably prove to contain the most valuable introduction to Habermas (Chs 9 to 12). These chapters look like an extensive and sympathetic summary. Held's defence of Habermas against his Marxist critics in Chapter 13 is especially useful in highlighting the issues of that debate. For my money, Held's defence is unconvincing and, indeed, he himself presents many strong criticisms of key Habermasian arguments. But, from what I can see of the popularity of Habermas in Cambridge, this will not be the last exposition or defence.

Of the works not referenced in the list above, the following came to my attention:

Sensat, Jr, J. (1979). *Habermas and Marxism*. Sage Publications, London.
This contains quite a clear exposition of Habermas's theories, but not much in the way of critique.
Anderson, P. (1976). *Considerations on Western Marxism*. New Left Books, London.
No mention is made of Habermas at all, but there are scattered cryptic comments on the Frankfurt School throughout.
Connerton, P. (Ed.) (1976). *Critical Sociology*. Penguin Books, Harmondsworth.
A very useful collection, containing two critical commentaries of Habermas's communication theory.
Smart, B. (1976). *Sociology, Phenomenology and Marxian Analysis*. Routledge and Kegan Paul, London.
I found Chapter 5 to be very clear and helpful on the key issue of the relation between sociological science and social emancipation.

I am sure that there are many more references that I have not had time to read and that there will be many more published in the next few years. My own thoughts will be developed a little further in:

Sumner, C. S. (1981). "The rule of law and civil rights in contemporary Marxist theory", *Kapitalistate* **9**, pp. 63-91.

7 Law, Plurality and Underdevelopment[1]

Peter Fitzpatrick

Introduction

The life of the Chagga people in Tanzania and the garment trade in New York have been analysed by Moore as "semi-autonomous social fields" (Moore, 1978). Such a social field "can generate rules and customs and symbols internally"; it has "rule-making capacities, and the means to induce or coerce compliance" (ibis., pp. 55-56). Yet the semi-autonomous social field is "also vulnerable to rules and decisions and other forces emanating from the larger world by which it is surrounded"; "it is . . . set in a larger social matrix which can, and does, affect and invade it" (ibid., pp. 55-56). The present essay develops these ideas in moving towards a radical theory of legal pluralism.

Theories of legal pluralism see the semi-autonomous social field as having its discrete legal order which is yet subordinate ultimately to the overarching state legal order. What is distinctive about the present analysis is that law—whether state law or the law of the semi-autonomous social field—is seen as constituted in significant part by the interaction of legal orders and their social fields. To take an example that will be elaborated on shortly, the family and its legal order are profoundly affected by the state legal order which is, in turn, set in its own social field. But what illustrates the main concern of this essay is that the state legal order itself is profoundly affected by the family and its legal order. There is a constituent interaction of legal orders and of their framing social fields. One side of the interaction cannot be reduced to the other. Nor can both sides be reduced to some third element such as the capitalist mode of production. In this, the present analysis seeks to counter monocausal descriptions or explanations of law.

Law, State and Society Series: "Legality, Ideology and the State", edited by D. Sugarman, 1983. Academic Press, London and New York.

Law, thence, takes on a greater diversity and richness than is usually afforded it academically.

A point of terminology and artifice: the radical pluralism advocated here is described in terms of 'plurality' to distance it from conventional pluralism. Also on terminology, 'legal order' is used as an analytical term to accommodate the distinctiveness of the law of the social field in question. 'Law' refers to the operative legal element and the term extends to law as constituted by the interaction of social fields and legal orders. Both 'legal order' and 'law' are used to encompass a degree of normative informality that some would see as falling outside of the legal sphere. With state law the legal sphere may appear more formal than with, say, the familial or the lineage group. But the contrast is usually overdrawn. State law integrally entails informal normative conventions, customs and principles. Assertions about the absence of law in, for example, lineage societies tend to reify law, granting it a reality only if it manifests a distinct identity. Law can be fused into wider social relations and have a distinct efficacy nonetheless (cf., Fitzpatrick, 1981).

The bulk of the essay develops this idea of legal plurality in the context of those parts of the Third World where the capitalist mode of production is established. (And I will use the term 'Third World' as confined to those parts.) Before doing this, an indicative account is given of why legal scholarship, critical or otherwise, has tended to ignore legal plurality and to espouse monocausal descriptions and explanations of law. Some contrary tendencies founded in legal pluralism and in work on the family and on 'informal communal ordering' are then sketched in. This serves as an introduction to the major part of the essay dealing with the Third World. This part starts with a critical overview of theories of underdevelopment. The main concern in this is to assert and defend a controversial perspective usually described as 'the articulation of modes of production'. This perspective sees social formations of the Third World as based on an interaction between the capitalist mode of production and pre-capitalist modes.[2] Law and its plurality are then explained both as they create and maintain this interaction of modes and as the interaction creates and maintains law and its plurality. That finishes the part dealing with the Third World. A final section, moving 'towards a conclusion', draws out implications of the analysis for law and legal plurality in the 'First World' of advanced capitalist development.

Some General Theoretical Perspectives on Legal Plurality

The dominant concerns of legal scholarship, whether Marxist, sociological or analytical/positivist, have not been responsive to legal plurality. Marxist scholarship has tended to be confined by Marx's overwhelmingly predominant concern with the capitalist mode of production (compare Gregory, 1982). Further, the causal dynamic of the mode of production in Marx's work and his schema of stages in which a mode successively replaces another involve the law characteristic of the prior mode being replaced by the law characteristic of the latter. In this general tendency of his work Marx was, of course, in very good company. Broadly, Marx, Weber and Durkheim were all primarily concerned with the emergence and existence of modern society—with capitalism, rationality, bureaucratic domination, an anticipated organic solidarity (Roxborough, 1979, Ch. 1). Traditional orders and the family were being swept aside or rendered marginal—"the woof of time is every instant broken, the track of generations effaced" (Tocqueville, 1862, p. 119). It was a new-created world. In this world it is not just the case that a new type of law displaces earlier types. Rather, the essential 'law' is not only defined by the new world but is definitive of it. Law is the epitome of a new rationality. A 'moral' order contrasts starkly with and gives way to a 'technical' or 'legal' order (Redfield, 1968, pp. 32-34 *et passim*; Black, 1976, pp. 39-41). The 'legal' order is, as well, intimately instrumental in the creation of the new world and the displacement of the old. With the emergence of law, Dumont observes, "there is no longer anything ontologically real behind the particular being, [and] . . . the notion of 'right' is attached not to a natural and social order, but to the particular human being" (Dumont, 1965, p. 22). For von Jhering "the progress of law consists in the destruction of every natural tie, in a continued process of separation and isolation" (as quoted in Diamond, 1973, p. 326). "In the midst of strangers, law reaches its highest level" (Black, 1976, p. 41). Césaire says of colonialism that the rule of the European bourgeoisie has torn up "the root of diversity" (Césaire, 1955, pp. 69-70). In the colonial situation law and legal rationality were relied on to order social fields perceived by the colonist as dangerously exotic and bizarre (Pye, 1966, p. 115).

There soon emerged a subordinate academic strand emphasizing the salience, even primacy, of such as "folkways" and "customary law" (Ball *et al.*, 1962; Stone, 1966, Ch. 2). Ehrlich provided the most developed view. For him the very basis of state law was a prior "social law" or "living law" which was the "inner ordering of associations" and the effectiveness of state law depended on its being in accord with this living law (see Partridge, 1961). Until recently it has been left to anthropology to sustain this tradition (see generally Pospisil, 1971, Ch. 4). Bohannan, like Ehrlich, sees state law as secondary or derivative: for him state law results from a "double institutionalization of norms" in which some "customs" operative within "social institutions" are "reinstitutionalized at another level" as state law (Bohannan, 1967, pp. 47-48). Pospisil contests the adequacy of seeing law and society in terms of interacting individuals and the state. He argues that society is made up of a collection of "subgroups" with their own legal systems and law is not just the property of society or the nation as a whole (Pospisil, 1971, Ch. 4; see also Smith, 1974, Ch. 4). There are several shortcomings with these theories. They assert or describe a static legal pluralism but do not explain it or account for the dynamic interaction between legal orders. Also, the emphasis on the derivative nature of state law denies an original effectiveness to state law and the effect of the state legal order on other legal orders.

Recent work dealing with plurality in the First World starts to address these shortcomings. Acute analyses by Abel and Galanter discern a current tendency for state law both to give way to "informal communal ordering" and yet for state law to extend in a supervisory way over such ordering (Abel, 1980; Galanter, 1980). Indeed this communal ordering often facilitates state intervention into people's lives. The aspect of such ordering usually focussed on is informal dispute settlement. In an innovatory analysis, Santos relates this tendency to "the changing nature of state power in late capitalism" (Santos, 1980). He too sees state law as expanding despite appearances of retraction in favour of community organization. Specifically, apart from increasing in its own right, as it were, state law sponsors and interacts with community organization as a way of disarming and neutralizing opposition to the dominant order. There are parallels here with the later analysis of underdevelopment and legal plurality.

The reliance on community, in terms of Santos's piece, would often involve reliance on the family and, in particular, on women's domestic labour provided in a household gift economy. Recent feminist scholarship indicates an element of specificity in the oppression of women. Such oppression cannot be reduced to a cause shared with other oppressions, such as the capitalist mode of production. Hence the exploration of patriarchy and the positing of a "family mode of production" (see, for example, Delphy, 1977). This is not to deny the profound effect of the capitalist mode on patriarchal relations. Rather, there is an integral interaction between the two. One cannot be reduced to the other (Foucault, 1979, pp. 99-100). The necessity of some such idea of interaction has, rather paradoxically, been underlined by the oft-noted "privatization" of the family and the decline in the authority of the family head (see Sennett, 1977). There is now less of an "implicit homology", in Donzelot's terms, between public power and the power of the family head and less explicitness and less hierarchical structuring of the family legal order (Donzelot, 1980, p. xx). Being unable to rely so much on indirect rule through the family head, the state now intervenes more directly in bolstering and organizing the family and in constituting and defining it. But this is only one side of the interaction. What is less remarked is the interactive effect the family has on state law. In maintaining its legal order the state often operatively incorporates and relies on the family legal order. In a more oblique but even more important way, state law relies for its identity on the family legal order. 'The rule of law' is constituted and legitimated in the universal equality of its application and in the element of voluntary involvement of the individual effected through such forms as the contract. These characteristics can only be sustained because more particularistic and more explicitly coercive controls are left or delegated to other legal orders, such as those of the family or the firm. In short, the conditions for state law being what it is include its not having to be something else. These themes will be returned to in the conclusion. Enough, hopefully, has been said to illustrate the significance of legal plurality and the connections between its First World manifestations and the more comprehensive analysis of the Third World situation that now follows.

Plurality and Underdevelopment

In an immediate sense, underdevelopment theory can be seen as a reaction against mainstream modernization theory in sociology and in economics and against classical Marxist theories of imperialism. Whilst they had little else in common, modernization and Marxist theories shared the view that the cause of underdevelopment lay in the pre-capitalist or 'backward' social formations of the Third World. The penetration of capitalism into these social formations would undermine them and eventually result in a capitalist development similar to that of the First World. Relying on the perspective of the chief originator of underdevelopment theory, André Gunder Frank, this penetration can be said to have indeed rendered the Third World capitalist but a special kind of capitalism was involved, one that itself was the cause of underdevelopment (see, for example, Frank, 1971a). For this was a 'dependent' capitalism, one integrated into the needs of the First World or metropolitan economies that exported it and one that preserved the competitive dominance of these economies. It was a constrained and stunted capitalism that did not generate development within Third World social formations. It did bring with it manufacturing and extractive industries and trading outlets all run on capitalist lines but these were restricted to particular purposes and confined to enclaves, leaving a hinterland where pre-capitalist economic forms persisted but now found their *raison d'être* in the generation of surplus realized ultimately within the metropolitan economies. Thus, although these pre-capitalist forms served the metropolitan economies, there is not that duality in Third World countries between 'modern' and 'traditional' sectors that mainstream theorists have tended to discern. There is rather a unity which is capitalist.

There have been two main and somewhat opposed lines of criticism of underdevelopment theory as recounted here. One involves a resurrection of the argument of classical Marxist theories of imperialism and sees capitalist penetration as leading to capitalist development. The other is more a refinement of underdevelopment theory and argues that the structure and operation of Third World social formations cannot be fully explained by focussing on the intervention of capitalism and the transfer of surplus but must be seen in terms of an interaction of resident pre-capitalist modes of production and the intervening capitalist mode.

The argument that capitalist penetration is leading to capitalist development, most notably propounded by Warren (1980), points to the large increase in capitalist investment in the Third World since the Second World War and to the substantial rates of economic growth that have resulted in some countries. Brazil is a much-cited example. However, it can be argued that this growth amounts to an intensified dependency or an intensified underdevelopment, that it is confined to enclaves leaving the great bulk of the population at least as badly off as they were before (see, for example, Taylor, 1979, pp. 54-59). This counter-argument fits the Brazilian case but it cannot apply fully to such countries as Singapore, South Korea and Taiwan where considerable benefits of export-led growth have 'trickled down' to the mass of the population. But still the argument for capitalist development, even in its most optimistic range, applies at present to only a few countries and, since these improvements are tied to recent, dramatic and uncertain changes in an increasingly precarious world economy, the case cannot yet be considered securely established (Bienefeld, 1980).

The second line of criticism of underdevelopment theory—the one stressing the interaction of modes of production—can be introduced *via* Laclau's seminal critique of Frank (Laclau, 1971). Frank, like many theorists of underdevelopment, sees capitalism in terms of exchange relations. Third World social formations are designated pervasively capitalist once they are even slightly infected by certain types of exchange. This is wrong, says Laclau. Capitalism, in Marxist terms, is or is based on a mode of production. Many 'economic systems' cannot be comprehensively described as capitalist or they contain relations of production that are pre-capitalist. These economic systems are constituted by different modes of production. This debate over whether Third World formations are capitalist or whether they encompass a plurality of modes of production has remained central to underdevelopment theory. It is also central to this essay and will now be elaborated on.

The debate has been refined in theories of the interaction or "articulation" of modes of production developed mainly by Marxist anthropologists (see, for example, Seddon, Ed., 1978). They draw basically on those strands in Marxist thought usually associated with Althusser. Although the diversity of views is enormous, the main thrust is that the mode of production is given effect in a social formation and a social formation contains more than one mode of production, although one of these will usually be the dominant mode (O'Laughlin, 1975, pp. 364-365; Wolpe, 1980, p. 9). The idea of the social formation is the frame of analysis. The social formation is constituted by the interaction of the modes of production—the economic level—and of the related legal-political and ideological levels, all concretely combined in a totality that is often, but not always, rendered in terms of a geographically located "society" or a country (Brewster, 1970, p. 313; O'Laughlin, 1975, p. 367).

Theories of the articulation of modes of production are developing an explanatory strength in relation to social formations of the Third World. This is probably best illustrated in the work of Rey and in recent British anthropological work (see Brewer, 1980, Ch. 8 and Clammer, Ed., 1978). With these theories, the capitalist mode of production is not seen as transforming pre-capitalist modes into its own likeness. True, it has had powerful solvent effects and has deeply disrupted the operation of these pre-capitalist modes but, to an extent that is central, these modes persist in interaction with the capitalist mode. This is partly because of their resilience and partly because of the nature of capitalist intervention. Negatively, the penetration of the capitalist mode is limited and leaves space for the persistence of pre-capitalist modes. Positively, the pre-capitalist mode serves as a basis for subsidizing capitalist production, reproducing labour power for example, and so pre-capitalist modes are often conserved. The resulting persistence and reinforcing of ascribed divisions based in pre-capitalist relations counters the consolidation of class elements introduced with the capitalist mode. Such consolidations would be threatening to a capitalist domination that is limited and insecurely based. Of course all these factors interact in complex ways but this should serve as a preliminary case for articulation theory.

I will now try to advance the analysis by considering what can be called post-articulation theory in its arguments against articulation theory and for a monocausal emphasis on the capitalist mode of production. The most cited and the most general argument would seem to be that advanced by Banaji (1977a). For him, assertions about the necessity for an articulation of modes of production result from narrow and erroneous views of what constitutes a mode of production. Only if one equates a mode of production with a form of labour process, such as wage labour in the capitalist mode, does it appear necessary to talk about articulation with another form of labour process such as communal labour or slave labour. Instead, Banaji widens the idea of a mode of production to cover what others see as an articulation of modes. Thus, he sees the capitalist mode as constituted in the expansive vagueness of an epoch of production fuelled by a collection of elusive laws of motion which seem to be derived from many strands of Marx's account of the capitalist mode of production. A capitalist mode conceived in this broad way can supposedly accommodate pre-capitalist forms within it. So, although the overall laws of motion may be capitalist, communal and slave (and other) forms of production or labour processes can operate within them. These are only 'forms' of production because they are not reproduced under their own laws of motion. Their reproduction, their continued existence depends on their relation with the capitalist mode (see also Banaji, 1977b). In the more concrete setting of the so-called African peasantry, Bernstein has provided an analysis along broadly similar lines but without the benefit of any elaborated constitution of the capitalist mode of production (Bernstein, 1977). For Bernstein, as for Banaji (1977a, pp. 34-35), the "peasant" does not operate even partly within a pre-capitalist mode. This mode has been destroyed. The conditions of the peasant's production are so comprehensively set from within this unspecific capitalist mode that the peasant is wholly subordinated to the capitalist mode. However, there is some hedging here since this subordination "stops short of full proletarianization" and "capitalist relations of production [are] mediated through forms of household production" (Bernstein, 1977, p. 73). Following this line of analysis is a final illustration of post-articulation theory, Snyder's incisive account of the "transformation" of a legal concept within a social formation in Senegal (Snyder, 1981a).[3] He charts the changes in the functions of this formerly pre-capitalist concept resulting from the dissolution of the pre-capitalist mode—a dissolution at times qualified as partial—with the introduction of capitalist commodity production. Although the pre-capitalist "form" of the concept persists, this is a "mere appearance" of continuity concealing a "transformation" in its operation.

These are potent analyses which are particularly valuable because they illustrate and help explain the profound influence and apparent dominance of the capitalist mode of production. But there are things they do not seem to explain. The literature on development and underdevelopment abounds with what resemble persistent elements of pre-capitalist modes (Fitzpatrick, 1980b, pp. 163-164, 168-169). If they are compatible with the capitalist mode it would entail a strange capitalism, one that could accommodate pervasive, often expanding production for use, much communal control of property and a very limited separation of direct producers from the means of production. Even the analyses of Banaji, Bernstein and Snyder assert the persistence of "forms" and "appearances". Where do these forms and appearances come from? Clearly they are not mere irrational survivals at most only marginally modifying capitalist relations. An immediate answer that these analyses would provide is that the forms are based in their relation to the capitalist mode of production. In this relation the pre-capitalist elements depend for their reproduction on the capitalist mode and even partial dependence in this is seen as sufficient to subsume them to capital. Doubtless the nature of these forms and the changes in them will owe much to this relation. Yet it is also a part of this integral relation that the persisting pre-capitalist elements through use-value production subsidize the operation of the capitalist mode of production (Banaji, 1977a, p. 34; Bernstein, 1977, p. 72). It is difficult to see how pre-capitalist elements can so subsidize the operation of the capitalist mode if they are totally of that mode. These elements must, it would seem, retain some independent identity and dynamic capable of sustaining the systematic production of use-value—subordination "stops short of full proletarianization", dissolution is "partial".

If so these elements could not be reduced to mere "form" or "appearance". Nor could a reduction in terms of the capitalist mode encompass the specificity and great diversity of pre-capitalist elements in the third world and the variety of their interactive effects with the capitalist mode. So, what even a largely 'immament critique' of post-articulation theory suggests is that these pre-capitalist elements cannot be entirely contained in their relation to the capitalist mode, taking even the broadest conception of that mode (cf. Wolpe, 1980). Rather it suggests that there is an interaction and interdependence between such elements and the capitalist mode with each having a degree of autonomy.

It could be said that these forms are still partly based in pre-capitalist modes yet are in the process of being eliminated through the intervention of the capitalist mode. That is, post-articulation theory could be seen as indicating a transitional tendency rather than being founded on something that has already happened. This is to recast the argument of the theory's proponents since they have it that the transition has taken place, even if forms or appearances of previous modes persist. But their argument could come close to a theory of existent transition if it were said that the capitalist mode has a solitary efficacy in the transition and the pre-capitalist modes are utterly contingent. This would be a time-honoured perspective. Marx and classical Marxist theories of imperialism saw the expansionary dynamic of the capitalist mode as inherently and inexorably removing pre-capitalist modes from the agenda of history no matter what, specifically, these modes were (Brewer, 1980, Chs. 2-5). This perspective can be related to the modernizing emphasis of Marx's work and its overwhelming concern with the capitalist mode of production, a mode that was the latest in a dubiously formulated succession of modes of production. Unless one accepts an overall schema of successive stages, an analysis of the transition from one specific mode of production to another has to take account of both and of their interaction (cf. *ibid.*, p. 184). A dynamic based solely in the capitalist mode cannot account for the dissolution, or for the persistence, of other modes. Hence the answer cannot be sought elsewhere in a general theory of transition since each transition will be different (O'Laughlin, 1975, p. 359). So, some would see the feudal mode as conducive to transition to the capitalist mode whereas other pre-capitalist modes are seen as not conducive to this transition (see Brewer, 1980, p. 185). It must, however, be quickly added that, as a general theory, the theory of articulation itself cannot lead to specific and comprehensive answers. Nor does it contribute any independent dynamic. It does indicate limits to theories focussed on the capitalist mode of production and it does open out analysis by providing a framework that accommodates other dynamic elements besides those that can be called capitalist. Also, with a theory of articulation one can move beyond the idea that to qualify as a mode of production the mode must be self-sufficient and not dependent for its reproduction on another mode (see, for example, Banaji, 1977a, pp. 33-35). Marxist analyses tend to see the capitalist mode as solely integral and effective with remnants and forms of pre-capitalist modes being functional to yet dependent on it. But, as this functionality suggests, the capitalist mode may be dependent on other modes for its reproduction. What may be involved, and what articulation theory enables one to explore, is an interdependence and synthesis of modes (cf. Marx, 1973, p. 97).

This interactive perspective becomes clearer when we move beyond considering the isolated peasant production unit and the beleaguered, fragmenting communal group. The effect of "subordinate modes" on "dominant modes" has received little attention (Long and Richardson, 1978, p. 204; see also Greenberg, 1980, p. 13). To take some examples indicating that effect, even with the intervention of the capitalist mode some forms of national economic organization resemble nothing so much as an Asiatic mode of production (Lev, 1978, p. 41). Many national economies and political systems are largely founded on networks of ethnically based patron–client relations (see, for example, O'Brien, 1975). There is a strong reliance on pre-capitalist elements in ideologies of liberation and nationalism and in constitutional organization (see, for example, Bozeman, 1971, pp. 21-22, 53-55 and 113-114). The functioning and structure of many state systems are shot through with and depend on "primordial" ties (see generally, Riggs, 1964).

This is not to argue for a duality of only marginally connected social fields. It is an argument for articulation, for an interaction of modes and of the related legal–political and ideological levels, an argument for a resultant yet for a dynamic process. As the analyses of Bernstein and Snyder vividly show, the capitalist mode penetrates integrally into the very reproduction of the pre-capitalist modes. But this penetration does not eliminate the pre-capitalist modes. It is a limited penetration and one that has conserving effects. The process is one of "conservation/dissolution", of "undermining and perpetuating" (see Foster-Carter, 1978, p. 213). At the same time the pre-capitalist modes influence the capitalist mode. The overall interaction of modes gives rise to forms of economic, political and legal organization that cannot be reduced to either the capitalist mode or a pre-capitalist mode (see, for example, Lindqvist, 1979, pp. 235-241; Taylor, 1979, pp. 187-193). In this light, many 'ethnic' and 'traditional' groupings can be seen as a product of both modes (see, for example, Cohen, 1969). In this light also and more generally, underdevelopment may not be caused by either capitalism or 'traditional society' but by their interaction. Some have discerned new modes of production arising from the interaction, such as a peasant mode and a colonial mode (see, for example, Alavi, 1975). But, again, articulation is a dynamic process; some elements of it make for sameness, some make for difference. To say a particular reality is not one thing or another does not mean it has to be a third. The term 'combined' will be used in the rest of this essay to describe the forms and relations that result from the interaction of articulation of modes of production.

The significance of this interaction of modes can be further elaborated by looking at its effect on capitalist class formation in the Third World. The capitalist mode brings with it its characteristic class positions. These, as is often noted, are "incomplete", "inchoate" and "emerging" (see, for example, Gutkind and Wallerstein, 1976, p. 13). These class positions are profoundly modified and their emergence inhibited by pre-capitalist relations. Much of the proletariat, including the 'sub-proletariat' of urban petty commodity producers and the occasionally employed, retains integral links with pre-capitalist social formations which continue to be the prime locus of loyalty. Even where these links are broken, people establish neo-traditional communities in urban areas. The national bourgeoise is often deeply divided between those members who retain a base in pre-capitalist and combined relations and those who more fit the pure capitalist mould. Senior state operatives—the so-called bureaucratic bourgeoisie—will frequently be tied to pre-capitalist and combined relations that pervade the state system. The peasantry, producing in the context of pre-capitalist and combined relations, appears to expand rather than become the declining, marginal class it is supposed to be under capitalism (Mortimer, 1975). To describe the peasant as a disguised proletarian obscures what is central to her/his class position—the divisive effect of pre-capitalist and combined relations.

As indicated earlier, the interaction of modes has also a profound effect on the state. Here the point will be developed briefly as a prelude to the analysis of law. The interaction of modes confronts the state with particular and enduring difficulties. The limited penetration of the capitalist mode restricts its ability to sustain a nation-state. The economically dominant class element of the metropolitan bourgeoisie—that "great absent member" (Amin, 1974, p. 393)—lacks internal political legitimacy and relies on the state, as supported by dominant national class elements, to secure its interests. Yet these dominant national elements tend to be but weakly established at the national level and they are divided between different capitals and different bases in pre-capitalist and combined relations. The resulting weakness of the state stands in stark contrast to the strong state called for by several social forces. There are four main aspects to these social forces. First there is the maintenance of some operative unity among a great diversity of pre-capitalist, combined and capitalist elements. Second, the capitalist mode makes for the emergence of a proletariat. Even a small proletariat could significantly challenge the insecure class elements dominant at the national level. The third entails the state's being "the primary mechanism of articulation between modes of production" (Lamb, 1975, p. 132). The state has to secure some integration between the modes so that the pre-capitalist modes can function in support of the capitalist mode. Yet the state also has to intervene to protect the pre-capitalist modes from some solvent effects of the interaction with the capitalist mode. Fourth, and finally, the persistence of production based in pre-capitalist modes means that the producers are not separated from the means of production and so legal-political compulsion is frequently needed to extract surplus (cf. Anderson, 1974, p. 403). For all these reasons, as will be seen in more concrete detail when analysing law, the state is directly and closely involved in production, in the extraction and redistribution of surplus and in class and inter-group struggles. Hence there is not that distancing between the state and these struggles and not that distancing between the economic and political spheres held necessary to constitute a "relative autonomy" of the state and a base for universalistic ordering (cf. Poulantzas, 1973, p. 257). Given this and its weakness, the state cannot secure a general legitimacy nor secure the deficit through coercion. Thus, division based in pre-capitalist and combined relations is central to the maintenance of some overall domination by the state, not only because it is division but also because it can serve to counter potentially threatening class consolidations. This acts to set structurally that tendency noted earlier for the effects of pre-capitalist and combined relations to penetrate and shape the very institutions of the state. The result is something close to a patrimonial state divided within itself in the service of a diversity of particularistic interests (see, for example, Turner, 1976). In short, the state palpably reflects conflicts and divisions within the national social formation and provides no universally accepted, overarching means of resolving or successfully mediating them.

Legal Plurality and The Third World

Everything said so far about the Third World can be read as integral to the analysis of law that now follows. This analysis will focus on the class elements just considered. With the intervention of the metropolitan bourgeoisie in the colonial period—using the term 'colonial' to cover comparable social formations not formally colonized—state law was central to that integration yet separation of the capitalist and pre-capitalist modes and central to that direct involvement in production and the extraction of surplus described earlier. Law served to incorporate pre-capitalist types of surplus extraction into the colonial state. It enforced and regulated cash-crop production and the monopoly dominance of metropolitan marketing enterprises. It destroyed or drastically reshaped pre-capitalist production systems. It effected the seizure of land. It provided labour for such as plantations and mines through systems of forced and indentured labour. In all these disruptive effects, state law operated in the cause of 'the civilizing mission'. Yet, in apparent contradiction, state law was also central in the conservation of pre-capitalist modes of production, claiming legitimation here in terms of 'trusteeship' and 'protection'. It restricted and controlled the extraction of factors of production from pre-capitalist modes. It limited and regulated the economic activities that people could undertake outside of the pre-capitalist modes. In performing these functions and in holding their contradictory elements in some equilibrium, law had to be of an authoritarian cast. "Despotism is a legitimate mode of government in dealing with barbarians, provided the end be their improvement . . ." (Mill, 1962, p. 136). This authoritarianism was reinforced where, as was common, metropolitan enterprises occupied monopoly positions in the colonial economy. In any case, the state and state law secured or attempted to secure the dominance of the metropolitan bourgeoisie in the colonial social formation. The state and state law were manifestly the preserve of a particular class element.

There are two qualifications to the account so far of colonial state law. First, legal systems based largely on bourgeois legality were introduced by the metropolitan bourgeoise to regulate relations between its enterprises and its resident colonists. I will return to this type of legal system shortly. The second qualification will be developed here. The conclusion that the state and state law were manifestly the preserve of the metropolitan bourgeoisie is qualified by the incorporation of pre-capitalist legal–political levels into the colonial state system. The limited penetration of the capitalist mode of production and the weakness of the colonial state provide a strong element of necessity here. These legal-political levels were incorporated, supported and preserved by the colonial state. This involvement in the state and the impact of capitalist penetration on pre-capitalist legal orders created combined types of law—types resulting from the interaction or articulation of modes of production. Thus, for example, "customary law" in Africa can be a combined type of law (Burman, n.d.; Chanock, 1978; Snyder, 1981c). In both the colonial and the current situations, and in formal terms, state law will usually encompass the combined type of law. So state law provided for 'indirect rule', 'chiefs' courts' and the like, the addition to state courts of assessors knowledgeable in pre-capitalist law, the 'recognition' of custom in state legal proceedings, the recognition of a plurality of systems of 'personal law' and the codification of 'customary law'. These accommodations can mean the extinction of the pre-capitalist legal order. But, on the other hand, the pre-capitalist legal order combines with the state legal order in ways that affect basically the operation of state law (see, for example, Hunt and Hunt, 1969). Indeed, state law is not the only dynamic legal factor. Pre-capitalist law operates often in opposition to state law and often despite efforts in state law to prohibit or supercede it (see Bryde, 1976, pp. 111 and 116; Fitzpatrick, 1980b, pp. 163-164). Further, pre-capitalist law develops innovatively to accommodate the effects of capitalist penetration (Bryde, 1976, pp. 120-121; Colson, 1975, pp. 76-78). Santos describes the operation of a "folk system", an "integral legality" in a Brazilian urban settlement innovatively combining basic communal legal relations with aspects of state law (Santos, 1977). Even when it appears state law is operating in an effective and straightforward way, it can be the case that it is being utterly subordinated to strategies and purposes located in pre-capitalist relations (see Cohn, 1967 and Abel, 1979, p. 247). Rosenn's account of the *jeito* in Brazil shows how this trick or 'fix' or fiction is used to subject the apparently straightforward operation of state law to particularistic relations (Rosenn, 1971).

The post-colonial period sees a greater intrusion of pre-capitalist and combined relations into the state system. The metropolitan bourgeoisie becomes the 'great absent member'. It can no longer regulate or contain or shield the state from this intrusion. The new and emergent 'ruling class' of the national bourgeoisie, including the so-called bureaucratic bourgeoisie, is tied materially to particularistic relations whilst claiming legitimation in terms of 'development' and 'modernization'. These reactions are not confined to the traditional but extend to a diversity of combined relations in such as regional ethnic organizations, political parties, trade unions and urban communal settlements. The national bourgeoisie is also divided between the divergent interests of different types of capital and between the bureaucratic bourgeoisie and the national bourgeoisie proper. These and particularistic ties obviate any consolidation of the national bourgeoisie in opposition to the metropolitan bourgeoisie. State law serves the continued dominance of the metropolitan bourgeoisie through legal standards and fiscal obligations attached to production which favour the metropolitan bourgeoisie (see, for example, Langdon, 1977 and Fitzpatrick and Blaxter, 1979). The national bourgeoisie is inhibited also in laws protecting and promoting small-scale peasant enterprises at the expense of national capitalist development in the countryside; many land reform laws, for example, are of this type. Bourgeois legality received further support in the post-colonial period in the maintenance of standards which, although formally applying to all equally, serve to favour the economically dominant, especially the 'absent' metropolitan bourgeoisie. Some relations within the national bourgeoisie will be regulated by state laws founded in bourgeoisie legality. An aspirant bourgeois can seek to use such state laws, with their protection of a sphere of autonomous individual action, to counter legal and moral obligations based in pre-capitalist and combined relations.

But these are limited supports for bourgeois legality and the authoritarian cast of state law continues from the colonial period. The post-colonial state does derive some strength and some potentiality for universalistic ordering from the dependence on it of dominant national class elements, since the state is the prime locus for the extraction of surplus and the distribution of it to these class elements. Yet the distribution of this surplus and competition for it are largely based in pre-capitalist or combined relations, such as patron–client relations, and so this very reliance on the state reinforces division. The state and its institutions remain, as in the colonial period, something to be captured in the service of particular interests. Lev shows that in Indonesia patrimonial and particularistic relations prevail over bourgeois support for the rule of law and for related constitutional/legal forms of judicial independence, restraints on executive power and civil rights (Lev, 1978).[4] Examples of this effect could, of course, be enormously multiplied (see Karst and Rosenn, 1975). It is almost a proverbial legitimation that constitutional forms and protections have to be often set aside because strong (authoritarian) government is needed for 'development' (see Claude and Strouse, 1978). This continued authoritarian cast of law imports a convenient discretionary form which both obscures official accountability and provides a means for the insertion of pre-capitalist and combined relations into the state system. These relations sometimes shape the constitutional order in an explicit and legitimate way. The recent Nigerian constitution provides a striking example of accommodating pre-capitalist and combined relations yet building on these in an attempt to secure more widely representative state institutions (see Williams and Turner, 1978). A dramatic constitutional confirmation of the basic place of pre-capitalist and combined relations is contained in the Malaysian constitution. It provides for extraordinary state powers to deal with 'emergencies' and legislation made under these powers overrides any provision of the constitution except certain provisions which include those dealing with ethnic identity and pre-capitalist law.

The penetration of patron–client relations, and of comparable pre-capitalist and combined relations, into the state system means that the state and state law are more responsive to members of subordinate classes than in the colonial period. Here could be some wider basis for the development of a more universalistic ordering. But, as against this, the responsiveness of the state and of state law is mediated through particularistic relations. Also the emergence of the national bourgeoisie calls for a greater extraction of surplus from subordinate class elements. The state's involvement in production and in the extraction of surplus not only persists into the post-colonial period but increases. This involvement is of many legal types. There are numerous fiscal measures. There is the state enterprise, including joint ventures with the metropolitan bourgeoisie. The state undertakes the control of the proletarian workforce through industrial relations laws and wage control laws. Laws establishing co-operatives integrate peasant communities into state structures of surplus extraction. There are legal controls on what the peasant can produce, where, how, for what price and for what markets, all often contained in a legitimating way in 'development programmes' (see Bernstein, 1977, p. 64).

Subordinate class elements are far from quiescent in the face of these exactions and controls (see, for example, Williams, 1980). But the state's legal means for dealing with such opposition are very restricted. Attempts are made to secure a legitimacy for state law by presenting it as an instrument for national unity and for development and as an ally against particularistic oppressions. But state law is not very effective in these things (see, for example, Harrison, 1979, pp. 161-171 and 376–385). The relation of subordinate class elements to state law is mediated and shaped by particularistic relations. This strongly counters such universalistic pretentions. It also counters legitimating supports for the use of state law as coercion. The demands on coercive law, and its inability to meet them, constantly lead officials to abuse and go beyond their legal powers, thus further alienating subordinate class elements from state law (see, for example, Martin, 1974). The inadequacy of these ideological and coercive means in dealing with opposition from subordinated class elements underlines the continuing centrality of the state's maintaining and relying on pre-capitalist and combined relations that counter class consolidation and effective class action. So, numerous laws render provisional the urban existence of much of the proletariat requiring them to maintain pre-capitalist and combined relations. These laws would include pass and vagrancy laws, property, building and town planning laws and licensing and other laws restricting economic activity outside of wage labour. Legal measures are sometimes taken directly to maintain pre-capitalist and combined relations within the peasantry such as varieties of land reform. Here, however, the more significant part of state law lies in adjusting itself to these relations and in providing ways that can be used to uphold them. Thus the Hunts' dramatic study of state courts in an area of Mexico shows these courts to be primarily responsive to a diversity of pre-capitalist and combined legal orders and this at the expense or in breach of state law (Hunt and Hunt, 1969). If a judge stood out against the more influential beneficiaries of these legal orders he would be demoted by the state—the state being activated in this through patronage networks linking these beneficiaries to it (ibid., p. 124). State law acts legitimately, in the formal sense, to incorporate and support pre-capitalist and combined relations and legal orders by providing local-level courts and governmental institutions and by providing for the establishment of co-operatives and the legal recognition of communal groupings. These various legal types are often used to integrate the local-level leader into the state system and they thus become bases for patron–client relations.

Hence the analysis of law in the post-colonial period has come full-circle and it is apt now to move, over-optimistically, 'towards a conclusion'—a conclusion promised to contain indicative implications for law and legal plurality in the 'First World' of advanced capitalist development.

Towards A Conclusion

The general argument has been for a necessary plurality in the constitution of law. For this argument, the theory of the articulation of modes of production provided the basis of a specific application. Doubtless this is not the only or the enduringly correct theoretical frame (cf. Friedmann, 1980). Doubtless also, theoretical assertions according some primacy to the mode of production, either as a constitutive basis for law or as an original epistemological category, should accommodate the potent criticisms made of such stances (see, for example, Hindess and Hirst, 1977). The limited aim here, however, has been to present some significant theoretical work developed in the Third World setting and to present it as strongly indicative of the existence and centrality of a plurality of legal orders in Third World social formations. This plurality encompasses not just, or not so much, a discrete and persisting difference of legal orders but a complex, mutually defining interaction between them. In particular, the 'dominant' state law can be seen, in significant part, as constituted through 'subordinate' legal orders. This is not only a matter of isomorphic invasion— of 'subordinate' elements permeating the 'dominant' order and serving to make it more like themselves. There is also a contrary outcome in that the beleaguered element of universal and equal application of state law is maintainable because necessary elements of particularistic and unequal rule are accommodated by pre-capitalist legal orders.

Intimations of the significance of a comparable legal plurality in the First World are numerous. They will be more comprehensively built on in another essay (Fitzpatrick, in press). Here some indicative illustrations are extracted parasitically from the subjects covered in the present volume, although by no means all possible illustrations will be used. It could be politic to make a start on the editor's concern with socio-legal history (see also Sugarman, 1981). In this perspective, the transition from feudalism to capitalism can be seen as entailing a long-persistent plurality of legal orders. As well, popular movements and organizations in the defence of traditional rights and the assertion of new rights can be seen as having some autonomous efficacy and not being thoroughly subordinated to the domination of ruling elements. Cain's account of Gramsci's "expanded formulation" of the state brings out the heterogeneity and legal plurality involved in 'state' power. The state, in this formulation, fuses elements of 'political society' and 'civil society'. There is here an integral involvement of 'so-called private organizations', religious and educational organizations for example. Law, as state law, serves to produce some homogeneity in support of the ruling group. But because of the "intervention" of these "private organizations" the state is not just "an instrument" in the hands of this ruling group (Buci-Glucksmann, 1980, p. 99).

Sumner's chapter, focussed on "law, legitimation and the advanced capitalist state", enables several pertinent aspects of Habermas' work to be drawn on here. For Habermas, it seems, "capitalist societies" are dependent on "areas of [pre-capitalist] cultural tradition" (Habermas, 1976, pp. 76-77). Yet the expansion of state activity with advanced capitalism penetrates these areas of cultural tradition destroying their independent integrity. These areas cannot be taken over, manipulated and maintained by the state—there is a "structural dissimilarity between areas of administrative action and areas of cultural tradition" (ibid., p. 71)—and they cannot be reproduced within the area of capitalist society. As these areas of cultural tradition lose their own power of legitimation, the state has to take on an extra burden of legitimation thus heightening that 'legitimation crisis' within advanced capitalism that so centrally concerns Habermas. Whereas work in socio-legal history and the Gramscian corpus would seem to grant, if not highly theorize, an enduring plurality, Habermas seems to envisage the demise of these areas of cultural tradition with the increasing expansion of state activity. What specifically happens, then, to capitalist societies with their apparent dependence on these areas of cultural tradition seems to be left as an open question. Nor does Habermas seem to confront directly the issue of why the necessity of these areas for capitalist society cannot have some countervailing effect on the forces making for the expansion of state activity.

Ignatieff's chapter has its own parallels with this one and can serve as a pretext for mentioning Foucault. Foucault's ideas of power could provide a penetrating and protean formulation of legal plurality and, especially as these ideas are developed in *The History of Sexuality* (Foucault, 1979), they can fit closely the experience of the Third World as it is drawn in the present essay. Further, Foucault shows, in effect, that the post-feudal emergence and constitution of the putatively free individual and of the analogous legal subject in modern law are contingent upon the pre-shaping effects of co-emergent "disciplines", and modern law, in turn, masks the operation of these disciplines and makes them acceptable (see ibid., p. 144 and Sheridan, 1980, pp. 152-157 and 183-186). To a large extent, these disciplines encompass or maintain non-state legal orders. It is probably the work, and the tradition (cf. Donzelot, 1980), of Foucault which hold the greatest promise for exploring the centrality of legal plurality in the First World.

Notes

1. I deeply appreciate the more than a little help from Maureen Cain, Roger Cotterrell, Shelby Fitzpatrick, Frank Furedi, Yao Graham, Abdul Paliwala, Dave Reason, Boaventura de Sousa Santos, Bob Spjut, Francis Snyder and David Sugarman. That not quite all the penetrating points made are drawn on here is due less to my disagreeing than to my being unable to develop some of them in the setting of the present essay.
2. 'Pre-capitalist' is used in this essay because it is the most common usage. It does tend to import the idea of inevitable stages of development from one mode to another up to the capitalist mode. Here the term is used shorn of that idea.
3. See also Snyder (1981b).
4. Just to make it clear, the general argument here is contrary to the common assertion that these legal artefacts tend to be limited in function because they are incompatible with persisting "tradition" (see, for example, Bozeman, 1971, p. 97). What is

involved here is the effect of combined relations, not of tradition or of pre-capitalist relations.

References

Abel, R. L. (1979). The rise of Capitalism and the Transformation of Disputing: From Confrontation over Honor to Competition for Property. *UCLA (University of California at Los Angeles) Law Review* **27**, 223-255.

Abel, R. L. (1980). Delegalization: A Critical Review of Its Ideology, Manifestations and Social Consequences. In *Alternative Rechtsformen und Alternativen zum Recht, Jahrbuch für Rechtssoziologie und Rechtstheorie, Band VI*. (E. Blankenburg, E. Klausa and H. Rottleuthner, Eds). Westdeutscher Verlag, Opladen.

Alavi, H. (1975). India and the Colonial Mode of Production. In *The Socialist Register 1975* (R. Miliband and J. Saville, Eds). Merlin Press, London.

Amin, S. (1974). *Accumulation on a World Scale: A Critique of the Theory of Underdevelopment*. Monthly Review Press, New York.

Anderson, P. (1974). *Lineages of the Absolutist State*. New Left Books, London.

Ball, H. V., Simpson, G. E. and Ikeda, K. (1962). A Re-examination of William Graham Sumner on Law and Social Change. *Journal of Legal Education* **14**, 3, 299-316.

Banaji, J. (1977a). Modes of Production in a Materialist Conception of History. *Capital and Class* 1977, **3**, 1-44.

Banaji, J. (1977b). Capitalist Domination and the Small Peasantry: Deccan Districts in the Late Nineteenth Century. *Economic and Political Weekly* August 1977, 1375-1404.

Bernstein, H. (1977). Notes on Capital and Peasantry. *Review of African Political Economy* **10**, 60-73.

Bernstein, H. (1979). Concepts for the Analysis of Contemporary Peasantries. *The Journal of Peasant Studies* **6**, 4, 421-444.

Bienefeld, M. (1980). Dependency in the Eighties. *IDS Bulletin* **12**, 1, 5-10.

Black, D. (1976). *The Behaviour of Law*. Academic Press, London and New York.

Bohannan, P. (1967). The Differing Realms of Law. In *Law and Warfare: Studies in the Anthropology of Conflict* (P. Bohannen, Ed.). The Natural History Press, New York.

Bottomore, T. (1979). Marxism and Sociology. In *A History of Sociological Analysis* (T. Bottomore and R. Nisbet, Eds). Heinemann, London.

Bozeman, A. B. (1971). *The Future of Law in a Multicultural World*. Princeton University Press, Princeton.

Brewer, A. (1980). *Marxist Theories of Imperialism: A Critical Survey*. Routledge and Kegan Paul, London.

Brewster, B. (1970). "Glossary", In *Reading Capital* (L. Althusser and E. Balibar, Eds). New Left Books, London.

Broderick, A. (Ed. 1970). *The French Institutionalists*. Harvard University Press, Cambridge, Mass.

Bryde, Brun-Otto (1976). *The Politics and Sociology of African Legal Development*. Alfred Metzner Verlag, Frankfurt am Main.

Buci-Glucksman, C. (1980). *Gramsci and the State*. Lawrence and Wishart, London.

Burman, S. B. (n.d.). Use and Abuse of the "Modern" versus "Traditional" Law Dichotomy in South Africa, roneo. Centre for Socio-Legal Studies, Oxford.

Césaire, A. (1955). *Discours sur le Colonialisme*. Présence Africaine, Paris.

Chanock, M. (1978). Neo-traditionalism and Customary Law in Malawi. *African Law Studies* **16**, 80-91.

Clammer, J. (Ed. 1978). *The New Economic Anthropology*. Macmillan, London and Basingstoke.

Claude, R . P. and Strouse, J. C. (1978). Human Rights Development Theory. In *Research in Law and Sociology: An Annual Compilation of Research, Vol. 1* (R. Simon, Ed.). JAI Press, Greenwich.

Cohen, A. (1969). *Custom and Politics in Urban Africa*. Routledge and Kegan Paul, London.

Cohn, B. S. (1967). Some Notes on Law and Change in North India. In *Law and Warfare: Studies in the Anthropology of Conflict* (P. Bohannen, Ed.). The Natural History Press, New York.

Colson, E. (1975). *Tradition and Contract: The Problem of Order*. Heinemann, London.

Delphy, C. (1977). *The Main Enemy: A Materialist Analysis of Women's Oppression*. Women's Research and Resources Centre Publications, London.

Diamond, S. (1973). The Rule of Law Versus the Order of Custom. In *The Social Organization of Law* (D. Black and M. Mileski, Eds). Seminar Press, New York and London.

Donzelot, J. (1980). *The Policing of Families: Welfare versus the State*. Hutchinson, London.

Dumont, L. (1965). The Modern Conception of the Individual: Notes on its Genesis and that of Concomitant Institutions. *Contributions to Indian Sociology* **VIII**, 13-61.

Fitzpatrick, P. (1980a). *Law and State in Papua New Guinea*. Academic Press, London and New York.

Fitzpatrick, P. (1980b). Law, Modernization and Mystification. In *Research in Law and Sociology: A Research Annual, Vol. 3* (S. Spitzer, Ed.). JAI Press, Greenwich.

Fitzpatrick, P. (1981). The Political Economy of Dispute Settlement in Papua New Guinea. In *Crime, Justice and Underdevelopment* (C. Sumner, Ed.). Heinemann, London.

Fitzpatrick, P. (in press). Marxiam and Legal Pluralism. *Australian Journal of Law and Society*.

Fitzpatrick, P. and Blaxter, L. (1979). Imposed Law in the Containment of Papua New Guinea Economic Ventures. In *The Imposition of Law* (B. E. Harrell-Bond and S. B. Burman, Eds). Academic Press, London and New York.

Foster-Carter, A. (1978). Can we Articulate "Articulation"? *The New Economic Anthropology* (J. Clammer, Ed.). Macmillan, London and Basingstoke.

Foucault, M. (1979). *The History of Sexuality, Volume I: An Introduction*. Allen Lane, London.

Frank, A. G. (1971a). *Capitalism and Underdevelopment in Latin America*. Penguin, Harmondsworth.

Frank, A. G. (1971b). *Sociology of Development and Underdevelopment of Sociology*. Pluto Press, London.

Friedmann, H. (1980). Household Production and the National Economy: Concepts for the Analysis of Agrarian Formations. *The Journal of Peasant Studies* **7**, 2, 158-184.

Galanter, M. (1980). Legality and Its Discontents: A Preliminary Assessment of Current Theories of Legalisation and Delegalization. In *Alternative Rechtsformen und Alternativen Zum Recht, Jahrbuch für Rechtssoziologie und Rechtstheorie, Band VI* (E. Blankenburg, E. Klausa and H. Rottleuthner, Eds). Westdeutscher Verlag, Opladen.

Greenberg, S. B. (1980). *Race and State in Capitalist Development: Comparative Perspectives*. Yale University Press, New Haven and London.

Gregory, C. (1982). *Gifts and Commodities*. Academic Press, London and New York.

Gutkind, P. C. W. and Wallerstein, L. (1976). Editors' Introduction. In *The Political Economy of Contemporary Africa* (P. C. W. Gutkind and I. Wallerstein, Eds). Sage Publications, Beverley Hills and London.

Habermas, J. (1976). *Legitimation Crisis*. Heinemann, London.

Hallis, F. (1930). *Corporate Personality: A Study of Jurisprudence*. Oxford University Press, London.

Harrison, P. (1979). *Inside the Third World*. Penguin, Harmondsworth.

Hindess, B. and Hirst, P. Q. (1977). *Mode of Production and Social Formation*. Macmillan, London.

Hooker, M. B. (1975). *Legal Pluralism: An Introduction to Colonial and Neo-colonial Laws*. Clarendon Press, Oxford.

Hunt, E. and Hunt, R. (1969). The Role of Courts in Rural Mexico. In *Peasants in the Modern World* (P. Bock, Ed.). University of New Mexico Press, n.p.

Karst, K. L. and Rosenn, K. S. (1975). *Law and Development in Latin America: A Casebook*. University of California Press, Berkeley.

Laclau, E. (1971). Feudalism and Capitalism in Latin America. *New Left Review* **67**, 19-38.

Lamb, G. (1975). Marxism, Access and the State. *Development and Change* **6**, 2, 119-135.

Langdon, S. (1977). The State and Capitalism in Kenya. *Review of African Political Economy* **8**, 90-98.

Lev, D. S. (1978). Judicial Authority and the Struggle for an Indonesian Rechtsstaat. *Law and Society Review* **13**, 37-71.

Lindqvist, S. (1979). *Land and Power in South America*. Penguin, Harmondsworth.

Long, N. and Richardson, P. (1978). Informal Sector, Petty Commodity Production, and the Social Relations of Small-scale Enterprise. In *The New Economic Anthropology* (J. Clammer, Ed.). Macmillan, London and Basingstoke.

Martin, R. (1974). *Personal Freedom and the Law in Tanzania: A Study in Socialist State Administration*. Oxford University Press, Nairobi.

Marx, K. (1973). *Grundrisse: Foundations of the Critique of Political Economy*. Penguin, Harmondsworth.

Mill, J. S. (1962). *On Liberty*. In *Utilitarianism, On Liberty, Essay on Bentham*. Fontana.

Moore, S. F. (1978). *Law as Process: An Anthropological Approach*. Routledge and Kegan Paul, London, Henley and Boston.

Mortimer, R. (1975). Social Science and the Peasant: A case of Academic Genocide? University of Papua New Guinea.

O'Brien, D. B. C. (1975). *Saints and Politicians: Essays in the Organisation of a Senegalese Peasant Society*. Cambridge University Press, London.

O'Laughlin, B. (1975). Marxist Approaches in Anthropology. In *Annual Review of Anthropology Vol. 4 (1975)* (A. Siegal, R. Beals and S. Tyler, Eds). Annual Reviews, Palo Alto.

Partridge, P. H. (1961). Ehrlich's Sociology of Law. *The Australasian Journal of Philosophy* **39**, 201-222.

Pospisil, L. (1971). *Anthropology of Law: A Comparative Theory*. Harper and Row, New York.

Poulantzas, N. (1973). *Political Power and Social Classes*. New Left Books and Sheed and Ward, London.

Pye, L. W. (1966). *Aspects of Political Development*. Little Brown, Boston.

Redfield, R. (1968). *The Primitive World and its Transformations*. Penguin, Harmondsworth.

Riggs, F. W. (1964). *Administration in Developing Countries — The Theory of Prismatic Society*. Houghton Mifflin, Boston.

Rosenn, K. S. (1971). The Jeito: Brazil's Institutional Bypass of the Formal Legal System and its Developmental Implications. *American Journal of Comparative Law* **19**, 514-549.

Roxborough, I. (1979). *Theories of Underdevelopment*. Macmillan, London and Basingstoke.

Santos, B. S. (1977). The Law of the Oppressed: The Construction and Reproduction of Legality in Pasargada. *Law and Society Review* **12**, 1, 5-126.

Santos, B. S. (1980). Law and Community: The Changing Nature of State Power in Late Capitalism. *International Journal of the Sociology of Law* **8**, 4, 379-397.

Seddon, D. (Ed. 1978). *Relations of Production: Marxist Approaches to Economic Anthropology*. Frank Cass, London.

Sennett, R. (1977). Destructive Gemeinschaft. In *Beyond the Crisis* (N. Birnbaum, Ed.). Oxford University Press, New York.

Sheridan, A. (1980). *Michel Foucault: The Will to Truth*. Tavistock, London and New York.

Smith, M. G. (1974). *Corporations and Society*. Duckworth, London.

Snyder, F. G. (1980). Law and Development in the Light of Dependency Theory. *Law and Society Review* **14**, 3, 723-804.

Snyder, F. G. (1981a). Labour Power and Legal Transformation in Senegal. *Review of African Political Economy* **21**, 26-43.

Snyder, F. G. (1981b). *Capitalism and Legal Change: An African Transformation*. Academic Press, London and New York.

Snyder, F. G. (1981c). Colonialism and Legal Form: The Creation of 'Customary Law' in Senegal. In *Crime, Justice and Underdevelopment* (C. Sumner, Ed.). Heinemann, London.

Stone, J. (1966). *Social Dimensions of Law and Justice*. Stevens and Sons, London.

Sugarman, D. (1981). Theory and Practice in Law and History: a Prologue to the Study of the Relationship between Law and Economy from a Socio-historical Perspective. In *Law, State and Society* (B. Fryer *et al.*, Eds). Croom Helm, London.

Taylor, J. G. (1979). *From Modernization to Modes of Production: A Critique of the Sociologies of Development and Underdevelopment*. Macmillan, London and Basingstoke.

Tocqueville, A. (1862). *Democracy in America, vol. II*. Longman, Green, Longman and Roberts, London.

Turner, T. (1976). Multinational Corporations and the Instability of the Nigerian State. *Review of African Political Economy* **5**, 63-79.

Warren, B. (1980). *Imperialism: Pioneer of Capitalism*. Verso, London.

Williams, D. V. (1980). State Coercion Against Peasant Farmers: The Tanzanian Case. Paper delivered at the *Conference of the Australasian Universities Law Schools Association*, Dunedin, August, 1980.

Williams, G. and Turner, T. (1978). Nigeria. In *West African States: Failure and Promise: A Study in Comparative Politics* (J. Dunn, Ed.) Cambridge University Press, Cambridge.

Wolpe, H. (1975). The Theory of Internal Colonialism: the South African Case. In *Beyond the Sociology of Development: Economy and Society in Latin America and Africa*. (I. Oxaal, T. Barnett and D. Booth, Eds). Routledge and Kegan Paul, London and Boston.

Wolpe, H. (1980). Introduction. In *The Articulation of Modes of Production: Essays from Economy and Society*. (H. Wolpe, Ed.). Routledge and Kegan Paul, London.

Wolpe, H. (Ed., 1980). *The Articulation of Modes of Production: Essays from Economy and Society.* Routledge and Kegan Paul, London.
Ziemann, W. and Lanzendörfer, M. (1977). The State in Peripheral Societies. In *The Socialist Register 1977* (R. Miliband and J. Saville, Eds) Merlin Press, London.

Further Reading

Lineaments of an instant tradition in legal plurality can be found in Abel (1980), Galanter (1980) and Santos (1980). All these are, in varying ways, concerned with 'delegalization'. Abel's is an acute, wide-ranging and demystifying analysis of the issues involved in delegalization. Galanter incisively relates issues of legal plurality and delegalization to theories of modern law. In terms of his title, Santos' main concern is with "the changing nature of state power in late capitalism" and instances of delegalization are largely illustrative, but in his immensely suggestive account the plurality of law and the plurality of power are central. The notion of legal plurality developed in the present essay can be greatly illuminated in Foucault's ideas of power (see especially, Foucault, 1979).

As for the more matured traditions of legal pluralism, valuable general accounts and illustrations can be found in Hooker (1975) and Pospisil (1971, Ch. 4). More theoretically elaborated, if often 'idealist' variants of legal pluralism can be found in the 'institutionalism' of several French and Italian legal theorists and in 'realist' theories of 'corporate personality' (see Stone, 1966, Ch. 11; also Broderick, Ed., 1970 and Hallis, 1930). M. G. Smith argues that law is particularly central in plural societies (Smith, 1974, Ch. 4). Wolpe's critique of pluralism can serve also as an introduction to theories of the articulation of modes of production (Wolpe, 1975).

The navel-gazing propensity of Marxist legal scholarship in the First World may be momentarily disturbed by Bottomore's assessment that "in the past two decades . . . perhaps the most impressive contribution by Marxists is to be found . . . in that large and growing area of study which has come to be known as the 'sociology of development' " (Bottomore, 1979, p. 141). As well as "large and growing" it is also diverse. Fortunately, capable and acute overviews have now been provided by Brewer (1980) and Roxborough (1979). Brewer's account is the more synoptic. Snyder's analysis of underdevelopment theory in its relation to law is particularly valuable (Snyder, 1980). A wide-ranging yet remarkably condensed theory of the state in the Third World is offered by Ziemann and Lanzendörfer (1977); they draw considerably on recent Marxist theorizing about the stage in the First World.

Work on underdevelopment and critical accounts of law in the Third World often build on confrontations with mainstream theories of development and modernization. Taylor provides a penetrating analysis of this kind for development and underdevelopment generally (Taylor, 1979; see also Frank, 1971b). In the same vein, a critical overview of theories of 'law and development' and of 'law and modernization' can be found in Fitzpatrick (1980b).

As for general works dealing with articulation theory, Brewer provides some straightforward accounts of it (Brewer, 1980, Chs 8 and 11). The dedicated could refer to the collections put together by Clammer (Ed., 1978), Seddon (Ed., 1978) and Wolpe (Ed., 1980). The fanatical will persist onto Taylor (1979). Taylor may be no stylist but his is a powerful and highly elaborated analysis. A case study of articulation theory in its relation to law can be found in Fitzpatrick (1980a).

8 State, Civil Society and Total Institution: A Critique of Recent Social Histories of Punishment

Michael Ignatieff

Until recently, the history of prisons in most countries was written as a narrative of reform. According to this story, a band of philanthropic reformers in the second half of the eighteenth century, secular Enlightenment theorists like Beccaria and Bentham, and religious men and women of conscience like the Evangelicals and the Quakers set out to convince the political leadership of their societies that public punishments of the body, like hanging, branding, whipping and even, in some European countries, torture, were arbitrary, cruel and illegitimate and that a new range of penalties, chiefly imprisonment at hard labour, could be at once humane, reformative and punitive. This campaign in Europe and America was powered by revulsion at physical cruelty, by a new conception of social obligation to the confined and by impatience with the administrative inefficiency manifested in the squalid neglect of prisoners. The Enlightenment critique of legal arbitrariness and the vernacular of religious humanitarianism gradually created moral consensus for reform which after many delays and reversals, culminated by 1850 in the curtailment of hanging, the abolition of branding and the stocks, and the widespread adoption of the penitentiary as the punishment of first resort for major crime (Lewis, O., 1922; Teeters, 1935; Condon, 1962; Lewis, D., 1965; Cooper, R. A., 1976; Whiting, 1975; Stockdale, 1977).

All of these accounts emphasized conscience as the motor of institutional change and assumed that the reformative practice of punishment proposed by the reformers was both in intention and in result more humane than the retributive practices of the eighteenth century. A third common feature of these accounts was their administrative and institutional focus on change within the walls and within the political system which ratified or resisted these changes. With the exception of Rusche and Kirchheimer's work on the relation between prison routines and emerging patterns of labour market discipline after 1550, few studies of imprisonment ventured beyond the walls of the prison itself.

The history of prisons therefore was written as a sub-branch of the institutional history of the modern welfare state. As such it has had an implicitly teleological bias, treating the history as a progress from cruelty to enlightenment. In the early sixties, historians in a number of fields, not just prisons but also in the history of mental health, public welfare, juvenile care, hospitals and medicine, began to point up the political implications of this history of reform. To interpret contemporary institutions as the culmination of a story of progress was to justify them at least in relation to the past and to suggest that they could be improved by the same incremental process of philanthropic activism in the future. A reformist historiography thus served a liberalism of good intentions, which in turn seemed to legitimize dubious new initiatives—psychosurgery, chemotherapy and behaviour modification—as legitimate descendants of the reforming tradition. It was in part to question the legitimacy of these 'reforms' in the present, that a new group of revisionist historians set out to study the reforms of the past. Another broader motive was perhaps at work too—the libertarian, populist politics of the 1960's revised historians' attitudes to the size and intrusiveness of the modern state; the history of the prison, the school, the hospital, the asylum seemed more easily understood as the history of Leviathan than as the history of reform.

Some, if not all, of the new historiography was avowedly political. Moreover, it saw itself offering intellectual support for the welfare rights, mental patients' rights, and prisoners' rights campaigns of the time. These motives inspired an outpouring of new revisionist history on the modern urban school (Katz, 1968; Lazerson, 1971), the welfare system (Piven and Cloward, 1971), the asylum (Scull, 1979), the juvenile court (Platt, 1969) and the prison. The three works which best embody the revisionist current as far as prisons were concerned were David Rothman's *The Discovery of the Asylum* (1971), an ambitious and justly well-received attempt to relate the emergence of the penitentiary, the mental institution, the juvenile reformatory and the urban school to the transformation of American society from the late colonial to the Jacksonian period. The second major work, dealing with France, was Michel Foucault's *Discipline and Punish* (1978), which followed his studies of the origins of the mental institution (*Madness and Civilisation* 1965), the origins of the hospital (*Birth of the Clinic* 1973) and his work on the evolution of the social and natural sciences in the eighteenth and nineteenth centuries (*The Order of Things* 1970). *Discipline and Punish* was not only about imprisonment, but about the disciplinary ideology at work in education and the army, and in the new psychology and criminology which claimed to offer a scientific analysis of criminal behaviour and intention. The third major work of the revisionist current was my own *A Just Measure of Pain: The Penitentiary in the Industrial Revolution* (1978). It was narrower in scope than the others, concentrating only on the prison's emergence in England in the period from 1770 to 1840.

Despite these differences of scope and intention, all three agreed that the motives and programme of reform were more complicated than a simple revulsion at cruelty or impatience with administrative incompetence—the reformer's critique of eighteenth century punishment flowed from a more, not less, ambitious conception of power, aiming for the first time at altering the criminal personality. This strategy of power could not be understood unless the history of the prison was incorporated into a history of the philosophy of authority and the exercise of class power in general. The prison was thus studied not for itself, but for what its rituals of humiliation could reveal about a society's ruling conceptions of power, social obligation and human malleability.

Within the last 2 or 3 years, however, as the wider political climate has changed, these revisionist accounts have come under increasing attack for over-schematizing a complex story, and for reducing the intentions behind the new institution to conspiratorial class strategies of divide and rule. The critique has put into question the viability of both Marxist and structural–functionalist social theory and historical explanation, not only in the area of prisons, but by extension in other areas of historical research. These larger implications make the revisionist/anti-revisionist debate of interest to readers beyond the historians' parish.

What this review of the debate hopes to show is that revisionist arguments, my own included, contained three basic misconceptions: that the state enjoys a monopoly over punitive regulation of behaviour in society, that its moral authority and practical power are the major binding sources of social order, and that all social relations can be described in the language of subordination. This does not, by implication, make the counter-revisionist position correct. In so far as it is a position at all, it merely maintains that historical reality is more complex than the revisionists assumed, that reformers were more humanitarian than revisionists have made them out to be, and that there are no such things as classes. This position abdicates from the task of historical explanation altogether. The real challenge is to find a model of historical explanation which accounts for institutional change without imputing conspiratorial rationality to a ruling class, without reducing institutional development to a formless *ad hoc* adjustment to contingent crisis, and without assuming a hyperidealist, all triumphant humanitarian crusade. These are the pitfalls—the problem is to develop a model which avoids these while actually providing explanation. This paper is a step towards such a model, but only a step. Since I am a former, though unrepentant member of the revisionist school, this exercise is necessarily an exercise in self-criticism.

The focus on three books and on a narrow, if crucial period, is necessary because this is where debate has been most pointed and most useful. With the exception of David Rothman's *Conscience and Convenience* (1980), Steven Schlossman's *Love and the American Delinquent* (1977), James Jacobs' *Stateville* (1977) and Anthony Platt's *The Child Savers* (1969), the revisionist and counter revisionist debate has not extended itself into the terrain of the twentieth century. We are still awaiting a new historiography on the disintegration of the nineteenth century penitentiary routines of lock-step and silence; the rise of probation, parole and juvenile court; the ascendancy of the psychiatrist, social worker, doctor, and the decline of the chaplain within the penal system; the history of drug use as therapeutic and control devices; the impact of electric and TV surveillance systems on the nineteenth century institutional inheritance; the unionization of custodial personnel; the impact of rising standards of living upon levels of institutional amenity and inmate expectation; the long-term pattern of sentencing and the changing styles of judicial and administrative discretion; the history of ethnic and race relations within the walls; the social and institutional origins of the waves of prison rioting in the 1950's and late 1960's. This is the work which needs to be done if historians are to explain the contemporary crisis in prison order epitomized at Attica and more recently at Santa Fe (Wicker, 1975; Silberman, 1978; for England, see Fitzgerald, 1977). The classics of prison sociology in the forties and fifties described prisons as communities, guaranteeing a measure of order and security through a division of power between captors and captives (Sykes, 1958; Clemmer, 1940). Why has this division of power broken down so often in the sixties and seventies? Thus far, only Jacobs' exemplary study of Stateville penitentiary in Illinois has offered a truly historical answer, integrating changes in institutional governance, inmate composition and expectation, and the racial politics of the outside world into a working explanation. His conclusions, that prisoners were often surer of their physical safety under the tighter and more self-confident authoritarian regimes of the Forties than they were under the well-meaning but confused reformist regimes of the sixties might appear to suggest that a return to authoritarianism is the best way to guarantee prisoners and guards' physical security, if nothing else. Unionized guards and the militant prisoners of today will not permit a return to the prisons of the forties. But if we cannot and ought not to repeat history, we can at least learn from history where we went wrong. In the market place of good ideas — decarceration, inmate self-management, due process grievance procedures, institutional re-design, token economies, behaviour modification — history offers a reliable guide to consumer choice and its invariable lesson is *caveat emptor.* Criminal justice activists may be disappointed by the literature I will review here because no answers are offered to the question 'What is to be done'? I do hope there is use, however, in learning some of the subtler errors which good intentions can entrain.

Let me begin by describing the revolution in punishment between 1780 and 1850. Rothman, Foucault and my own work may differ about explanation but we do agree about what happened. In each society the key developments seem to have been:

1. The decline of punishments involving the public infliction of physical pain to the body. Beccaria's campaign against the death penalty in the 1760's, the Pennsylvania statute of 1786, the reformed codes of the 'enlightened despots', the French revolutionary decrees against the capital penalty, Romilly and MacIntosh's capital statutes campaign in England culminated by the 1850's in the restricting of the death penalty to first degree murder and treason. The form of execution was also changed—in France the guillotine was adopted in 1792 as a scientific instrument of pain sparing the victim the possible incompetence of the hangman; the traditional Tyburn processional of the condemned through the streets of London was abolished in 1783 in order to curtail the public symbolism of the death spectacle (Linebaugh, 1975, pp. 65-119; Linebaugh, 1977, pp. 246-270; Foucault, 1978, p. 8); public executions in England ended in the 1860's; henceforth hanging took place behind prison walls (Cooper, D., 1974). The lesser physical penalties were also curtailed or abolished (abolition of branding in England, 1779; pillory in 1837; whipping of women, 1919; see also Perrot, 1980, pp. 59-60, for France). By 1860 the public ritual of physical punishment had been successfully re-defined as a cruel and politically illegitimate means of inflicting pain.

2. The emergence of imprisonment as the pre-eminent penalty for most serious offences. Imprisonment had been used as punishment on a selective but insubstantial scale prior to 1770. Places of confinement were generally used as waystations for persons awaiting trial, for convicted felons awaiting execution or transportation and crucially for debtors. Nearly 60% of the institutional population in Howard's census of 1777 were debtors (Pugh, 1968; Sheehan, 1977; Ignatieff, 1978, p. 28; Innes, 1980). Vagrants and disobedient servants convicted for a range of minor, work-related property offences punishable at summary jurisdiction were confined at hard labour in Houses of Correction (Beattie, 1974, 1977; De Lacy, 1980, Ch. 1; Innes, 1980). This use of imprisonment increased in the eighteenth century, for reasons we do not yet understand. In England it was not until the suspension of transportation in 1776 that English JPs and assize judges began to substitute sentences of imprisonment for sentences of transportation (Webb, 1963; Ignatieff, 1978, Ch. 4). At first criminal law reformers like

Beccaria showed no particular enthusiasm for imprisonment itself, preferring to replace hanging with a range of penalties ranging from hard labour in public to fines. It was only after 1776 in America and after 1789 in France that imprisonment began to replace hanging as 'the' penalty appropriate to modern, enlightened republics (Rothman, 1971, p. 59; Foucault, 1978, p. 115).

3. The penitentiary came to be the bearer of reformers' hopes for a punishment capable of reconciling deterrence and reform, terror and humanity. In England between 1780 and 1812, half a dozen counties built small penitentiaries mostly for the control of minor delinquency. The first national penitentiary, Millbank, was opened in 1816. An enormous warren of passages and cells built in the style of a turreted medieval fortress near the Houses of Parliament, it soon was condemned as a costly failure—the prisoners were in revolt against the discipline more or less continuously in the 1820's; a violent outbreak of scurvy closed the prison down for a year in 1824; but the lessons of failure were learned at Pentonville, opened in 1842. Its penitential regime of solitude, hard labour and religious indoctrination became the model for all national penal servitude prisons and most county prisons besides. In America the key developments of the penitentiary regime occurred between 1820 and 1830—Auburn, 1819-23; Ossining, 1825; Pittsburg, 1826; Philadelphia, 1829 (Rothman, 1971, pp. 80-81) and in France, la Petite Rocquette (1836) and the juvenile reformatory at Mettray (1844) (Perrot, 1980, pp. 60-61).

4. As systems of authority, the new prisons substituted the pain of intention for the pain of neglect (Ignatieff, 1978, p. 113). Reformers like Howard were appalled that the squalor in neglected institutions was justified for its deterrent value. Accordingly, regular diets replaced the fitful provision of food in eighteenth century institutions; uniforms replaced rags and personal clothing; prisoners received regular medical attention, and new hygienic rituals (head shaving, entrance examination and bath) did away with the typhus epidemics which were an intermittent feature of eighteenth century European prison life. These hygienic rituals in turn became a means of stripping inmates of their personal identity. This indicates the ambivalence of 'humanitarian' reform: the same measures which protected prisoners' health were explicitly justified as a salutary mortification of the spirit (Ignatieff, 1978, p. 100).

5. The new prisons substituted the rule of the rules for the rule of custom and put an end to the old division of power between the inmate community and the keepers. All accounts of eighteenth century prisons stress the autonomy and self-government of prisoner communities. Since common law forbade the imposition of coercive routines on prisoners awaiting trial and debtors, they were able to take over the internal government of their wards,

allocating cells, establishing their own rules, grievance procedures, and punishments (De Lacy, 1980, Ch. 2; Innes, 1980; Sheehan, 1977, p. 233). The implied authority model of the colonial American and British prison was the household. The keeper and his family often resided in the institution and the prisoners were called 'a family'. They did not wear uniforms, they were not kept to routines, and they defended an oral and common law tradition of rights, privileges and communities (Rothman, 1971, p. 55). By the 1840's in all three societies, a silent routine had been imposed to stamp out the association of the confined and to wipe out a sub-culture which was held to corrupt the novice and foster criminal behaviour. Under the silent associated system of discipline, prisoners were allowed to congregate together in workshops but were strictly forbidden to communicate. In the separate system at Pentonville and Philadelphia, prisoners were kept in complete cellular isolation and were forbidden any form of communication or association (Rothman, 1971, p. 81; Henriques, 1972; Ignatieff, 1978, Ch. I). While advocates of both systems argued fiercely over their respective merits, they both agreed in principle on the necessity of suppressing the prison sub-culture and ending the tacit division of authority between captors and captives which had prevailed in the *ancien régime*. From a positive point of view, solitude exposed the individual prisoner to the obedience training of routine and the religious exhortation of the chaplain. The chaplain, not the doctor or the governor, became the chief ideologist of the penitentiary, justifying its deprivations in the language of belief.

6. The new institutions enforced a markedly greater social distance between the confined and the outside world. High walls, sharply restricted visiting privileges, constant searches and patrols ended the interpenetration of outside and inside in the unreformed prison. Before reform, visitors enjoyed the run of the yards, women commonly brought their husbands meals, and debtors and outsiders drank together in the prison tap room. The aim of reform was to withdraw the prisoner from the corrupting influence of his former milieu, and at the same time, to inflict the pains of emotional and sexual isolation. Once again, the mixture of humane and coercive motivations becomes apparent. As an unintended consequence, however, the check to the power of institutional personnel offered by constant visitors was reduced. The new institutions, therefore, did not resolve the old question of Who guards the guards? Instead they posed the question in a new and thus far intractable way (Ignatieff, 1978, Conclusion; De Lacy, 1980, Conclusion).

7. All three versions agree that the emergence of the modern prison cannot be understood apart from the parallel history of the other total institutions created in this period—the lunatic asylum, the Union workhouse, the

juvenile reformatory and industrial school, and the monitorial school. Besides being the work of the same constituency of philanthropic and administrative reformers, these institutions enforced a similar economy of time and the same order of surveillance and control. They also expressed a common belief in the reformative powers of enforced asceticism, hard labour, religious instruction and routine.

These seven points provide a schematic summary of the revolution in discipline as the revisionist account would have it. Before considering the explanations offered for this revolution, we ought to pause to consider those objections which have been raised to the revisionist account as a description. A number of theses and monographs completed within the last couple of years have insisted that the descriptive picture is more complex, contradictory and inchoate than either Foucault, Rothman or I have suggested.

Margaret De Lacy's excellent Princeton dissertation on county prison administration in Lancashire, 1690-1850, argues that even a relatively dynamic county administration like Lancashire lacked the resources to impose the highly rationalized Pentonville model on all of the county institutions. Many of these remained much the same as they had been in the eighteenth century. Eighteenth century historians, particularly Joanna Innis, have argued that the pre-reform prison was neither as squalid nor as incompetently administered as the reformers made them out to be (Innes, 1980a). By implication therefore the revisionist account may have been taken in by their reformers' sources. It is less clear, therefore, that the history of the institution between 1780 and 1840 can be written as the passage from squalid neglect to hygienic order.

Michelle Perrot and Jacques Leonard have made the same case for France arguing that the highly rationalized institutions like La Rocquette and La Mettray cannot be taken as typical of the mass of local lock-ups, jails and hulks in mid-nineteenth century France. In these institutions, the persistence of disease and the continued use of whipping and chains would appear to suggest a melancholy continuity with the worst features of the *ancien régime* (Perrot, 1980).

It appears then that the revolution in punishment was not the generalized triumph of Weberian rationalization which the revisionist account suggested. Foucault's work (and my own as well) remained captive of that Weberian equation of the *ancien régime* with the customary, the traditional and the particularistic, and of the modern with the rational, the disciplined, the impersonal and the bureaucratic. The gulf between the reformers' rationalizing intentions and the institutionalized results of their work ought to make us rethink this equation of modernity and rationalization, or at least to give greater room for the idea that modernity is the site of a recurring battle between rationalizing intention and institutions, interests and communities which resist, often with persistent success.

Yet even if we admit that Pentonville and the Panopticon, Auburn and La Roquette were 'ideal types' rather than exemplary realities of their time, we still have to explain why it became possible between 1780 and 1840 and not before to conceive and construct them. However much else remained unchanged in the passage from the *ancien régime* to the industrial world of the nineteenth century, the penitentiary was something new and unprecedented and was understood as such by the great observers of the age, de Tocqueville, Dickens and Thomas Carlyle. A counter-revisionist account which considers only the local institutions which went on much the same as before will miss what contemporaries knew had to be explained about their own age.

Let us turn to this business of explanation and let us begin with the American case, with the work of David Rothman. In Rothman's account, the new total institutions of the Jacksonian period emerged in an overwhelmingly rural and agricultural society, growing beyond the boundaries of the colonial past yet still a generation away from the factory system, industrialism, European immigration and the big city. It is a fundamental mistake, he argues, to interpret the total institution as an "automatic and inevitable response of an industrial and urban society to crime and poverty" (Rothman, 1971, xvi). Americans were anxious about the passage of colonial society and the emergence of a restless, socially mobile population moving beyond the controls of family, farm, and town meeting, but there was nothing in this process which itself required the emergence of the new asylums and prisons. The catalyst for institutional construction was not social change itself but the way it was organized into an alarmist interpretation of disorder and dislocation by philanthropic reformers. Crime was read for the first time, not as the wickedness of individuals but as an indictment of a disordered society. This explains the emergence of new institutions aiming at the reformation and discipline of the deviant, disorderly, and deranged.

For a society which interpreted crime as the sign of the passing of the colonial order, the penitentiary symbolized an attempt to recreate the godly superintendence and moral discipline of the past within a modern setting. Rothman demonstrates brilliantly that the language developed in a society to explain disorder and deviance also defines the solutions it develops for these problems. An environmentalist theory of crime and faith in the reformative effects of isolation from the environment were linked together in a system of ideas, each legitimizing the other.

Rothman is better at recreating the reformers' systems of belief than in locating these beliefs in a believable social and economic context. We do need to know something about actual trends in crime during 1780-1820 if we are to understand the changing fit between reform, rhetoric and their social context. In the absence of such data, crime becomes a static and empty category in Rothman's analysis, and the reformers' alarmist discourse drifts away from any point of reference.

Why, we want to know, were the Jacksonians so specially anxious about change and disorder, and why did they look back with such nostalgia to colonial society? Rothman simply accepts the Jacksonian reformers' picture of the stable pre-revolutionary society they were leaving behind, but surely this was a questionable historical fable. Many eighteenth century Europeans regarded colonial America as a restless, rootless, dynamic and explosive society. Tom Paine's Philadelphia was no deferential idyll (Foner, 1976). Yet Rothman never questions the Jacksonian's rosy image of their own past, never asks how their account of it should have been so out of joint with what we know of colonial society.

One would have also liked Rothman to have explored the relationship between the rise of the total institution and the theory and practice of Jacksonian democracy. This was after all the period of the extension of universal manhood suffrage in the US. Tocqueville himself thought the relation was one of contradiction: "while society in the United States gives the example of the most extended liberty, the prisons of the same country offer the spectacle of the most complete despotism" (Beaumont and Tocqueville, 1964, p. 79). As Tocqueville suggested in the 'tyranny of the majority' sections of *Democracy in America*, democratic republics which represent law and order as the embodied will of all the people treat disobedient minorities more severely than monarchical societies which have no ideological commitment to the consensual attachment of their citizens. Rothman suggests but leaves unexplored the possibility of a connection between (a) Jacksonian popular sovereignty, (b) an environmentalist theory of crime as being the responsibility of society and (c) an interventionist social therapy taking the form of the 'total institution'.

If we turn to Foucault, we find that the relation between forms of sovereignty outside the walls and carceral regimes inside constitutes the main axis of his interpretation. Public executions which the reformers of the Enlightenment condemned as a carnal and irrational indulgence, can be read, Foucault argues, as symbolic displays of the highly personalized sovereignty of the king and of his alternatively vengeful, merciful relation towards his wicked subjects.

The execution suited a philosophy of order which ignored minor delinquency to concentrate instead on the ritualized despatch of selected miscreants. This exercise of sovereignty in turn implied a loosely articulated political nation in which

> each of the different social strata had its margin of tolerated illegality; the non-application of the rule, the non-observance of the innumerable edicts or ordinances were a condition of the political and economic functioning of society . . . the least favoured strata of the population did not have in principle any privileges, but they benefited within the margins of what was imposed on them by law of custom, from a space of tolerance, gained by force or obstinacy. (Foucault, 1978, pp. 84-85)

The illegalities of the poor, like the tax exemptions of the rich, were tolerated because of the persistent weakness of an under-financed, chronically indebted state, the tenacious survival of regional and local immunities, and the persistent countervailing power of the Parliaments (see Montesquieu, *The Spirit of the Laws*, 1748), the judiciary and the nobility. Above all, the margin of illegality enjoyed by the poor reflected a ruling conception of national power as the sovereign's will rather than the operation of a bureaucratic machine. The state, moreover, shared the punitive function with civil society, in the double sense that its public rituals (execution, pillory, whipping and branding) required completion by the opprobrium of the crowd if they were to have full symbolic effect, and in the sense that household heads, masters and employers punished directly without invoking the state's power.

Independently of Foucault, Edward Thompson, Douglas Hay and Peter Linebaugh seem to have reached a similar description of the exercise of sovereign power in eighteenth century England. They put the same emphasis on the symbolic centrality of the public hanging in reproducing awe and deference before the sovereign's mighty but merciful power, and they describe a philosophy of order essentially similar in its permissive approach to the small fish.

Permissive, however, is too nostalgic or sentimental a word for a tactics of order uneasily poised between an obvious and sometimes brutal concern to defend property rights (the Waltham Black Acts for example) and an equal distaste, moral, libertarian and economic, for the apparatus of state police (Hay, 1975, pp. 17-65; Thompson, 1975, Conclusion).

The Revolution Settlement and the common law tradition imposed limits on the discretionary power of eighteenth century magistrates, and the common people themselves were quite capable of forcibly reminding them of 'the rights of free born Englishmen' and of the protocol of customs guaranteeing free assembly (Thompson, 1971). It is possible that there was no corresponding corpus of rights in common law available to the French poor, but it is hard to believe that they did not hold to some customary beliefs and traditions about the proper bounds of monarchical 'police'.

Hay and Thompson's work shows up Foucault's tacit assumption that the only limits on public order policy were the mental assumptions of the authorities themselves and the structural weaknesses of the state apparatus. What is missing in his work is the idea that public order strategies were defined within limits marked out not only by the holders of power, but also by those they were trying, often vainly, to persuade, subdue, cajole or repress. Foucault's account consistently portrays authority as having a clear field, able to carry out its strategies without let or hindrance from its own legal principles or from popular opposition. Power is always seen as a strategy, as an instrumentality, never as a social relation between contending social forces. We need to know much more about the social process by which the margin of illegality enjoyed by the poor in the *ancien régime* was established before we conclude with Foucault that it owed its existence to the toleration of the authorities.

However we interpret the margin of popular illegality under the *ancien régime*, Foucault and I agree that the penitentiary formed part of a new strategy of power aiming at its circumscription between 1780 and 1850. This new strategy was the work of Burke's "sophisters, economists, and calculators"—the monarchical administrators like Turgot, Le Trosne and Baudeau, and gentry men of letters like Beccaria. In England, the new ideology found expression in Henry Fielding's proposals for reform of London police, in the 1760's, in Howard's penitentiary scheme of the 1770's, and in the hospital and asylum reforms led by the provincial Nonconformist professional classes in the 1790's (Ignatieff, 1978, Ch. 3). In the 1780's, too, Bentham and Romilly began their campaigns for the codification of law and for the curtailment of public execution.

The ideal of reforming through punishment and of apportioning just measures of pain to crimes previously tolerated or ignored was compatible with the democratic ideals of the French Revolution—equal rights, equal citizenship, equal punishment—but it proved no less compatible with Napoleonic centralism and the Bourbon Restoration. Beneath the whole surface play of debate about political rights and regimes between the 1770's and 1840's, Foucault argues, a new "carceral archipelago" of asylums, prisons, workhouses and reformatories slipped into place. The political divisions over regimes and rights hid a deeper, unstated consensus among the ruling orders over the exercise of power over the criminal, the insane and the pauper. This ideology forged in the 1760's by the Enlightenment reformers and opponents of the *ancien régime* was transmitted and reproduced by social interests in the Restoration and the July Monarchy often deeply hostile to the rationalist or egalitarian spirit of the philosophers themselves.

In England, the first bearers of the new disciplinary ideology were the reforming county magistrates and the Dissenting professional classes of the provinces—reformist in politics, scientific in mental outlook, rational and improving in their management of labour, county finance and personal estates. The new asylums, prisons, workhouses and schools which they built appealed to their residual religious asceticism, to their scientific and rationalist outlook, and to their impatience with the administrative incompetence and political corruption of the *ancien régime*. In the crisis years of early industrialization after 1815, the disciplinary ideology was taken up by the Evangelized professional, mercantile and industrial classes seeking to cope with the dissolution of a society of ranks and orders and the emergence of a society of strangers. The philanthropic campaigns to reform old institutions and to build new asylums, workhouses, prisons, and hospitals gave expression to a new strategy of class relations. In return for the humanity of minimal institutional provision, the disobedient poor were drawn into a circle of asceticism, industriousness and obedience. They would return to society convinced of the moral legitimacy of their rulers. The persistent ideal of prison reform was a form of punishment at once so humane and so just that it would convince the offender of the moral legitimacy of the law and its custodians. The penitentiary was designed to embody this reconciliation of the imperatives of discipline with the imperatives of humanity.

My own account places more stress than Foucault's on the religious and philanthropic impulses behind institutional reform. His version of the disciplinary ideology retains the secular rationalist tone of its initial Enlightenment formulation, while mine stresses the fusion of the secular rationalism embodied in Benthamism with the Quaker and Evangelical language of conscience epitomized by Elizabeth Fry. The penitentiary had at its core the religious discourse of the chaplain, just as the new Evangelical language of class relations had at its core the idea of rich and poor bound together in the common experience of sin and the common salvation of faith and industry.

My own account also places more stress than Foucault's upon the reformers' concern to legitimize institutional routines to the confined. As a consequence I have put more emphasis on the humanitarian intentions of the reformers. They were genuinely repelled by the chains, squalor and neglect they discovered in existing institutions, especially because these compromised the moral legitimacy of the social system in the eyes of the confined. In their theory of the reform of character, the crucial task was to persuade the poor to accept the benevolent intention behind institutional deprivations. Once convinced of the benevolence of the system, reformers argued, they would be unable to take refuge from their own guilt in attacking their confiners. Personal reformation thus meant succumbing to the benevolent logic of their captors. In Foucault's account on the other hand, reformers were not centrally concerned to legitimize new penal measures as humane. Reformers on his account simply took the humanity of their measures for granted and looked to the discipline to routinize the habits of the poor. My model of the reform of character is one of symbolic persuasion; Foucault's is of disciplinary routinization.

We both agree, however, on the relation between this new strategy of power and the social crisis of the post-1815 period, exemplified in recurrent surges of distress-related crime, pauperism and collective popular unrest. Foucault is sketchy in the extreme about the causation of this social crisis, but it is clearly implied as the backdrop of the institutional revolution in France. My account, likewise, does not purport to be a social history of crime and pauperism in the 1815-1848 period, but it does locate three major sites of crisis: the breakdown of social relations in the agricultural counties of the south-east between 1815 and 1831 as a result of the casualization of the agricultural proletariat. Rising rates of vagrancy, pauperism and petty crime through the 1820's and the explosion of the Swing Riots in 1831 are the symptoms of this crisis in rural social relations. The second site of crisis was in London. The Anti-Corn Law Riots of 1815, the Spa Field disturbances of 1816 and the riots attendant upon Queen Caroline's trial proved that the existing parish constabulary was hopelessly outdated in coping with urban crowd control while the soldiery brought in upon these occasions were a clumsy, brutal and therefore, alienating instrument of order (Silver, 1967). In addition there was growing anxiety among magistrates and philanthropists about the rising incidence of juvenile crime in the metropolis after 1815. Masterless apprentices, orphans, underemployed youths, child prostitutes all seemed to symbolize a breakdown in the order of the family, the parish and the workshop. The third site of crisis lay in the new northern industrial towns where regional labour markets tied to single industries like cotton proved extremely vulnerable to cycles of demand in the international economy. Mass unemployment in "bad years" like 1826 threw up the spectre of recurrent breakdown in labour market disciplines (Ignatieff, 1978, Ch. 6).

There cannot be much doubt that the new strategy of mass imprisonment, the creation of the Metropolitan police in 1829, and the diffusion of paid constabularies through the agricultural counties and the industrial towns in the 1830's, 40's and 50's must be seen as a 'response' to this crisis of public order. The creation of permanent police courts, the expansion of the scope of the vagrancy and trespass statutes, the formation of the Union workhouse system in 1834 represented additional attempts to 'grapple for control', to cope with a social order problem the size and magnitude of which clearly grew faster than any of the authorities anticipated (Silver, 1967; Radzinowicz, 1968, V; Phillips, 1977; De Lacy, 1980).

Yet there are dangers of social reductionism in this explanation. Institutional reformers did not justify their programme as a response to the labour discipline needs of employers. Indeed the reform discourse antedates the labour discipline crisis. Howard's penitentiary schemes, the police theory of the late Enlightenment, the hospital and asylum campaigns of the 1790's all anticipated the post-1815 crisis. Moreover, as Rothman pointed out in the American case, the facts of crisis itself would not explain why authorities chose the particular remedies they did, why they put such faith in institutional confinement when greater resort to hanging or to convict gang labour in public might have been equally eligible responses to the perceived breakdown of social controls.

Foucault's argument and mine nonetheless is that the massive investment in institutional solutions would have been inconceivable unless the authorities had believed that they were faced with the breakdown of a society of stable ranks and emergence of a society of hostile classes. This diagnosis of the malaise of their times in turn suggested an institutional solution. Mass imprisonment offered a new strategic possibility—isolating a criminal class from the working class, incarcerating the one so that it would not corrupt the industriousness of the other. The workhouse likewise would quarantine pauperism from honest poverty (Foucault, 1978, pp. 276-278). Beneath the surface debate over whether these institutions were capable of reforming or deterring their target populations, Foucault argues, lay a deeper consensus among the ruling orders about using institutionalization to manufacture and reproduce social divisions within the working classes between working and criminal, rough and respectable, poor and pauperized. Foucault claims that this strategy of division actually worked — that the institutional quarantine of the criminal did create a criminal class separate from the working class community. In this lay the secret 'success' of prison, beneath all its apparent failures as an institution of reform and deterrence.

The divide and rule argument works best in respect of the workhouse, where the creation of the Bastilles of 1834 does appear to have succeeded in making pauperism disgraceful to the poor. Before the Bastilles, the poor conceived of relief as a right and did not look upon it as a disgrace; afterwards, while many continued to insist on their rights, working class respectability came to insist on avoiding the degradation of appealing for relief and ending one's days in the public ward. The Bastilles do seem to have dug the gulf deeper between pauperism and poverty within the value system and the social behaviour of the poor themselves.

As regards imprisonment, however, the divide and rule argument seems to me now to have fallen prey unwittingly to the problem inherent in what criminologists call 'labelling theory'. The notorious difficulty with this approach is that it makes the state's sanctions the exclusive source of the boundary between the deviant and the respectable. This would seem to ignore the degree to which, in the nineteenth century as in the twentieth century, the moral sanctions condemning murder, rape, sexual and personal assault were prior to and independent of the punitive sanction, commanding assent across class lines. In punishing these offences, the state simply ratified a line of demarcation already indigenous to the poor. Even in the case of petty property crime, it is not clear that the criminal sanction was labelling acts which the poor excused as an inevitable response to distress or which they justified in the vernacular of natural justice. The poor, no less than the rich, were victims of property crime, and any study of London police courts in the nineteenth century shows they were prepared to go to law to punish members of their own class (Phillips, 1977; Davis, 1980). If a constant process of demarcation was underway between criminal and the working classes, it was a process in which the working classes themselves played a prominent part, both in their resort to law and in the informal sanctioning behaviour which enforced their own codes of respectability. Doubtless there was sympathy for first time offenders and juveniles convicted for minor property offences during hard times, doubtless there were offenders whom working people felt were unjustly convicted. Certainly repeated imprisonment did isolate the criminal from his own class — but it is a serious over-estimation of the role of the state to assume that its sanctioning powers were the exclusive source of the social division between criminal and respectable. The strategy of mass imprisonment is better understood in class terms as an attempt by the authorities to lend symbolic reinforcement to values of personal honour which they themselves knew were indigenous to the poor.

The behaviour of the politicized sections of the working classes leaves no doubt that they drew very strict demarcation between themselves and the criminal. Michelle Perrot's study of French prisons in 1848 shows that the revolutionary crowds who stormed the prisons reserved liberation for prostitutes, political offenders and conscripts, not for ordinary criminal offenders (Perrot, 1980, p. 241). In England, while political radicals often cited the criminal statistics as proof of the grinding pressure of distress on the poor, they never questioned the ultimate legitimacy of their convictions (Ignatieff, 1978, Ch. 4; De Lacy, 1980).

Thus, if fears by the ruling orders of a potential union of interest and action between the criminal and working classes are to be regarded as having had some influence in generating public support for mass imprisonment, it must be recognized that these fears were without actual sociological foundation. We are dealing with a form of social fantasy detached from observable reality. Moreover, it is not clear how general these fantasies of revolution were or even how influential they were in galvanizing public opinion in support for the total institution. The difficulty with arguments from class fear is that they are simply too vague, too global to account for the specific timing of institutional or legislative change. Class fear among educated public opinion in the 1820's and 1830's may have contributed something to the consensus that public order was too parlous and insecure to go on with the haphazard punishment and police strategies of the eighteenth century. But class fear cannot account for the specific idiosyncrasies of the institutional solution—the faith in silence, solitude, religious indoctrination and hard labour.

If we return to what reformers said they were doing, it becomes clearer to me now than it was when I wrote the book that the adoption of the penitentiary in particular and the institutional solution in general cannot be explained in terms of their supposed utility in manufacturing social divisions within the working class. This is because at bottom reformers like most of their own class understood deviance in irreducibly individual rather than collective terms, not ultimately as collective social disobedience, however much distress and collective alienation influenced individuals, but as a highly personal descent into sin and error. Given this individualist reading of deviance, the appeal of institutional solutions lay in the drama of guilt which they forced each offender to play out—the drama of suffering, repentance, reflection and amendment, watched over by the tutelary eye of the chaplain. Foucault's neglect of the religious vernacular of reform argument obscures the deep hold which this symbolic drama of guilt and repentance held for the Victorian imagination. To be sure, this hypothetical drama bore little if any relation to what actually happened in prisons, asylums and workhouses, and many Victorians, Charles Dickens among them, knew this full well. But nevertheless, even sceptics like Dickens and Mayhew were not immune to the appeal of a symbolic system of associations in which the reform of the guilty criminal was held to reveal the triumph of good or evil, conscience over desire, in all men and women. If there was a social message in the ideal of reform through institutional discipline it was that the institutional salvation of the deviant acted out the salvation of all men and women, rich and poor alike.

Where does all this leave the problem of agency? Whose interests did the new institutions serve? In whose name were the reformers speaking? Who directed the carceral archipelago?

On these questions of agency, Foucault's answers are notoriously cloudy. At some points, he refers to the "bourgeoisie" though this is hardly an adequate categorization of the shifting alignment of class fragments, aristocrats, financiers, professionals, industrialists, who competed for power in France between 1815 and 1848. At other points, Foucault slips into a use of the passive voice which makes it impossible to identify who, if anyone, was the historical agent of the tactics and strategies he describes. Yet before we condemn him out of hand it is worth noting that Foucault is trying to work free of what he regards as the vulgar Marxist conception of agency according to which the prison is a tool of a definable class with a clear-sighted conception of its strategic requirements. He also rejects the functionalist model according to which the prison is the designated punitive instrument within a social division of labour. In place of these accounts, he argues that punitive power is dispersed throughout the social system: it is literally everywhere, in the sense that disciplinary ideology, the *savoir* which directs and legitimized power, permeates all social groups (with the exception of the marginal and deviant), ordering the self-repression of the repressers themselves. The prison is only the most extreme site for an exercise of power which extends along the whole continuum of social relations from the family, to the market, to the workplace and to citizenship. If prisons and factories came to resemble each other in their rituals of time and discipline, therefore, it was not because the state acted in response to the labour discipline strategies initiated by employers, but because both public order authorities and employers shared the same universe of assumptions about the regulation of the body and the ordering of institutional time.

Given that all social relations were inscribed within relations of domination and subordination, ordered, so he says, by a continuous disciplinary discourse, it is impossible to identify the privileged sites/or actors which controlled all the others. The disciplinary ideology of modern society *can* be identified as the work of specific social actors but once such an ideology was institutionalized, once its rationality came to be taken for granted—a fully exterior challenge to its logic became impossible. The institutional system took on a life of its own. One cannot say, Foucault argues, that the political apparatus of modern states actually controls the prison system. There is a formal chain of delegation and responsibility from the legislature, to the bureaucracy, from the bureaucracy to the warden, and from the warden to guards and prisoners—but this does not take into account the way institutional systems develop their own inertial logic which each 'actor' feels powerless to change (even those at its very summit).

Since the appearance of *Discipline and Punish*, Foucault has reformulated this problem of agency as one of historical causation, putting a new stress on the way in which the new institutions emerged as the unintended consequence of levels of change, which in themselves were independent of each other—the new discourse on discipline in the Enlightenment, the search by the propertied for stricter legal and social protection, and the crisis in public order. The new discourse emerged prior to the social revolution of the nineteenth century and prior to the labour discipline needs of employers, but once in play ideologically, it provided the programme around which constituencies assembled their response to social turbulence and labour indiscipline. Once the disciplinary discourse's 'independence' of its social grounding is granted, then it becomes possible to work free of the various traps which the problem of agency has caused for historians—the conspiratorial all-seeing ruling classes of the Marxist account, the low rationality model of *ad hoc* 'responses' to social crisis, and the hyper-idealist version of reform as a humanitarian crusade (see Foucault's interview in Perrot, 1980).

But where does this leave the concept of a ruling class as the historical actor behind the making of the penitentiary? My own work has been criticized for using middle-class as a synonym for ruling class in a period in which it would be more accurate to speak of a bewilderingly complex competition for political power and social influence by different class fractions, professionals, industrialists and merchants, aristocratic magnates and small gentry farmers. While it is a convention of Marxist argument that such division of interest and jockeying for power were stilled whenever 'the class as a whole' felt threatened from below, my own work on the intense debates about social order policy suggests that choral unanimity was rare even in moments of universally recognized crisis. Unquestionably justices, MPs and philanthropists recognized each other as the rich and regarded vagrants, pickpockets and the clamouring political mob as the 'lower orders', but their sense of 'we' vs 'they' was not enough to make the ruling class into a collective social actor. One can speak of a ruling class in the sense that access to strategic levers of power was systematically restricted according to wealth and inheritance, but one cannot speak of 'it' acting or thinking as a collective historical subject. One can only ascribe historical effectivity to identifiable social constituencies of individuals who manage to secure political approval for penal change through a process of debate and argument in the society's sites of power. It would be wrong to think of these constituencies of institutional reformers as acting for their class or expressing the logic of its strategic imperatives. This would make them into ventriloquists for a clairvoyant and unanimous social consensus. In fact they managed to secure only the most grudging and limited kind of approval for their programme. The penitentiary continued to be criticized from multiple and contradictory points of view: it was inhumanly severe, it was too lenient; it was too expensive; it could not reconcile deterrence and reform; the reformation of criminals was a sentimental delusion, and so on.

In his most recent reflections, Foucault himself admits that the new carceral system was not the work of an overarching strategic consensus by a ruling class, but fell into place as a result of a conjuncture between transformations in the phenomena of social order, new policing needs by the propertied and a new discourse on the exercise of power.

Yet for all his disclaimers, Foucault's conception of the disciplinary world view, the *savoir* as he calls it, effectively forecloses on the possibility that the '*savoir*' itself was a site of contradiction, argument, and conflict. In England at least, for example, a pre-existing legal tradition of rights imposed specific limits to the elaboration of new powers of arrest, new summary jurisdiction procedures, just as *habeas corpus* limited carceral practice towards the unconvicted. At every point, new proposals for police, prisons and new statutory powers raised the question of how to balance the changing conceptions of security against pre-existing conceptions of the liberty of the subject. Foucault makes no mention of these legal limits.

These questions about the ruling class as a historical actor ought to be connected to earlier questions raised about the role of prisons in disciplining the working class. Given the frequency with which the popular classes themselves sought to invoke the penal sanction against members of their own social group, it would be difficult to maintain that they were simple objects of the punitive sanction. While the majority of punished offenders undoubtedly came from the popular classes, it would not follow from this that the function of imprisonment was to control these classes as such. Foucault's and my own work, I think, confused statements about the social fears motivating the construction of institutions, with statements about their actual function.

The 'social control' model of the prison's function which informed my own work assumed that capitalist society was systematically incapable of reproducing itself without the constant interposition of state agencies of control and repression. This model essentially appropriated the social control models of American Progressivist sociology according to which society was a functional equilibrium of institutional mechanisms in the family, the workplace and marketplace working together to ensure the co-operation of individuals in the interests of social order (Muraskin, 1976; Stedman Jones, 1977; Rothman,

1980). As Stedman Jones has pointed out, the Marxist version of this idea, and the structuralist version of it reproduced in Foucault, carries on the assumption of society as a functionally efficient totality of institutions. When applied to prison history, this model implies that institutions 'work' — whereas the prison is perhaps *the* classic example of an institution which works badly and which nonetheless survives in the face of recurrent scepticism as to its deterrent or reformative capacity. Instead of looking for some hidden function which prisons actually succeed in discharging, we ought to work free of such functionalist assumptions altogether and begin to think of society in much more dynamic and historical terms, as being ordered by institutions like the prisons which fail their constituencies and which limp along because no alternative can be found or because conflict over alternatives is too great to be mediated into compromise.

The second assumption in Marxist social control theory is that the use of the state penal sanction is essential to the reproduction of the unequal and exploitative social relations of the capitalist system. Marx himself qualified the centrality of state coercion, arguing while that the hangman and the house of correction were central in the 'primitive accumulation' process, that is, in the forcible establishment of wage relations, once such wage relations were in place, "the silent compulsions of economic relations" "set the seal on the domination of the capitalist over the worker". The extra-economic coercion of the state penal sanction was then invoked only in 'exceptional' cases (Marx, 1976, p. 899). My own work on the expansion of vagrancy, trespass and petty larceny statutes in the 1820's and 1830's suggested that state penal sanctions were required by employers, especially in the agricultural counties, to prevent their chronically underemployed casual labour force from passing out of the wage system into poverty and vagrancy (Ignatieff, 1978, pp. 180-183; also Linebaugh, forthcoming). Important as the penal sanction may have been in sustaining discipline in casualized, pauperized labour markets, or in constituting wage discipline itself in the face of worker resistance, we ought not to take these instances as typical of the role of state force once the wage bargain has been broadly accepted. We ought not to assume that exploitative social relations are impossible to reproduce without threat of force. Even in objectively exploitative, underpaid and unhealthy conditions of labour, one can conceive of men and women voluntarily coming to work not in the sense that they are free to choose wage labour but in the specific sense that they derive intrinsic satisfaction from the sociability of labour, from the activity itself, from the skill they manage to acquire, and from the pride they take in their work. Marxist theories of labour discipline consistently ignore these aspects of submission to the wage bargain, and consequently overstate the centrality of penal force in reproducing those relations. The fact that workers do submit to the wage bargain need not imply that they accept the terms of their subordination as legitimate; it is a cliché of labour history that those whose wage levels, skill and pride in craftsmanship gave them the most reasons for satisfaction with industrial labour were often the most militant in their political and moral challenge to it as a system. The point is simply that the punitive sanction of the state need not be regarded as decisive to the reproduction of exploitative and unequal social relations.

Going still further, it could be asked whether force itself, apart from its specific embodiment in state apparatuses of coercion, is decisive to the maintenance of social order. The tacit social theory of Foucault's *Discipline and Punish* describes all social relations in the language of power, domination and subordination. This would imply that individuals are naturally unsocial or asocial, requiring discipline and domination before they will submit to social rules.

Not surprisingly, therefore, Foucault sees the family as an authority system, linked to the carceral system of the state outside:

> We should show how intra-familial relations, essentially in the parent-children cell, have become 'disciplined', absorbing since the classical age external schemata first educational and military, then medical, psychiatric, psychological, which have made the family the privileged locus of emergence for the disciplinary question of the normal and the abnormal. (Foucault, 1978, p. 215)

Can a father or mother's social relations towards their children really be defined only in terms of Foucault's disciplinary question? Foucault would seem to be taking to the limits of parody a fashionable current of thought, nourishing itself in the Freudian analysis of oedipal conflict and in the feminist critique of patriarchal domination, which has, to my way of thinking, 'over-politicized' family social relations, neglecting the collaborative and sacrificial elements of family attachment and over-emphasizing the 'power' aspects of family interaction. This makes it easy to locate the family as an institution of domination on a continuum with prison, enforcing the same over-arching disciplinary rationality. This would ignore obvious distinctions between the basis of our obligations as family members and our obligations as citizens to the law. It would also neglect the extent to which loyalty to one's family or the desire to maintain one's authority as a family head could constitute the basis for refusal of state authority, for example, in resistance by families to the introduction of compulsory school attendance.

By describing all social relations as relations of domination, Foucault neglects the large aspects of human sociability, in the family and in civil society generally, which are conducted by the norms co-operation, reciprocity and the 'gift relationship'. He neglects that human capacity which Adam Smith called "sympathy", by which we voluntarily adjust our behaviour to norms of propriety in order to stand well in the eyes of our fellows (Smith, 1759). In Smith's social theory the order of civil society was reproduced, without state direction or class design, by an uncoordinated molecular process of individual self-regulation. Our obedience to legal norms could be understood both in terms of this largely unconcerted order-seeking behaviour, and also as an expression of conscious belief in the utility and the justice of such rules in themselves. In Smith's theory, the threat of penal sanction was not necessary to the reproduction of normal patterns of obedience. Punishment did not constitute the order of civil society; rather, it gave ritual and symbolic expression, in retributive form, to the moral value attached by individuals to rule-obedient behaviour (Smith, 1763).

This theory of social order may underestimate human being's mutual malignity, and it is justly criticized by Marxists for writing the facts of power, domination and subordination out of its account of the social process. But precisely because it tried to think of social order in terms that go beyond the language of power, it offers a more persuasive account of those social activities which we do experience as uncoerced subjects than one which conceives of order as the grid imposed by a carceral archipelago.

My point here is not to argue the virtues of Smithian social theory as against Foucault's structural functionalism or Marxist social control, but rather to use Smith to point to hidden features of both: their state-centred conception of social order, and their tendency to reduce all social relations to relations of domination.

How then are we to think through a theory of the reproduction of social life which would give relative weights to the compelled and the consensual, the bound and the free, the chosen and the determined dimensions of human action in given historical societies? Contemporary social theory is increasingly aware that it has been ill-served by the grand theoretical tradition in its approach to these questions — a Parsonian functionalism which restricts human action to the discharge of prescribed roles and the internalization of values; a Marxism which in its hostility to the idealist account of human subjectivity went a long way towards making the active human subject the determined object of ideological system and social formation; and a structuralism which likewise seems to make individual intellectual creativity and moral choice the determined result of cultural and discursive structure (Giddens, 1976). Work-a-day historians and sociologists in the field of criminal justice may well ask at this point what this high-flown theoretical debate has to do with them, or what they could possibly contribute to it. Its relevance is that any theory or history of punishment must make some ultimate judgement about what weight to attach to the state's penal sanction in the reproduction of obedient behaviour. What weight you give depends ultimately on how much importance you give to the consensual and voluntary aspects of human behaviour. The social control theory of the 1920's, as Rothman points out in an excellent review of that literature, placed so much stress on the consensual that they neglected the coercive; the social control literature of the seventies exaggerated the coercive at the expense of the consensual (Rothman, 1980). The first step back to a balance between these perspectives will require us to ask basically how crucial the state has been historically in the reproduction of the order of civil society. My suspicion is that the new social history of law and punishment in the seventies exaggerated the centrality of the state, the police, the prison, the workhouse and the asylum.

If we are going to get beyond our present almost exclusive focus on the state as the constitutive element of order, we will have to begin to reconstitute the whole complex of informal rituals and processes within civil society for the adjudication of grievances, the settling of disputes, and the compensation of injury. Historians have only just begun to study dispute and grievance procedures within civil society, in the same way as these are studied in the anthropology of law (Diamond, 1974; Roberts, 1980). Among such studies are Edward Thompson's discussion of the 'rough justice' rituals of sixteenth and seventeenth century English villages, by means of which wife-beaters, scolds, and couples who married out of their age cohort were subjected to the public scorn and humiliation of their neighbours (see also Thomas, 1971; Thompson, 1972; Davis, 1975). Because studies of such grievance procedures exist only for the early modern period, it would be easy to conclude that the state expropriated such functions in its courts and prisons in the course of consolidating its monopoly over the means of legitimate violence (Weber, 1947, pp. 324-337). The monopoly of the state of the means of violence is long overdue for challenge. The crimes which it visits with punishment ought to be interpreted as the tip of an iceberg, as the residue of those disputes, conflicts, thefts, assaults too damaging, too threatening, too morally outrageous to be handled within the family, the work unit, the neighbourhood, the street. It would be wrong, I think, to conclude that early modern English villages were the only communities capable of exercising these *de facto* judicial powers. Until recently, social histories of the working class family and the working class neighbourhood were too inscribed within the confines of their sub-disciplines to include discussion of the anthropology of dispute settlement and the social history of relations with the police, the courts and the prisons. But what is now opening up as an area of study is the social process by which crime was identified within these units of civil society, and how the decisions were taken to channel certain acts or disputes for adjudication or punishment by the state. The correlative process, from the state side, is how agents like the police worked out a tacit agreement with the local enforcers of norms, determining which offences were his to control, and which were to be left to the family, the employer or the neighbourhood (Fine *et al.*, 1979, pp. 118-137). Such research would indicate, I think, that powers of moral and punitive enforcement are distributed throughout civil society, and that the function of prison can only be understood once its position within a whole invisible framework of sanctioning and dispute regulation procedure in civil society has been determined. We have always known that prisons and the courts handled only a tiny fraction of delinquency known to the police—now we must begin, if we can, to uncover the network which handled the 'dark figure' which recovered stolen goods, visited retribution on known villains, demarcated the respectable and hid the innocent and delivered up the guilty. This new area of research will not open up by itself. Empirical fields of this sort become visible only if theory guides historians to new questions. This paper amounts to a plea to historians, criminologists and sociologists to engage seriously with texts they are apt to dismiss as abstract and ahistorical—the classical social theory tradition of Smith, Marx, Durkheim and Weber. The engagement ought to take the form of a self-criticism, for if I have argued correctly, these texts are the hidden source of some basic misconceptions—that the state enjoys a monopoly of the punitive sanction, that its moral authority and practical power are *the* binding sources of social order and that all social relations can be described in the language of power and domination. If we could at least subject these ideas to practical empirical examination, a new social history of order, authority, law and punishment would begin to emerge.

References

Babington, A. (1971). *The English Bastille*. MacDonald, London.
Bailey, V. (1975). "The Dangerous Classes in Late Victorian England" PhD. Dissertation, Warwick University.
Beattie, J. M. (1974). "The Pattern of Crime in England, 1660-1800" *Past and Present* **62**, 47-95.
Beattie, J. M. (1977). "Crime and the Courts in Surrey, 1736-53" in J. S. Cockburn (Ed.) *Crime in England, 1550-1800*. Methuen, London.
Beaumont, G. de and de Tocqueville, D. (1835). *On the Penitentiary System of the United States*. Carbondale: Illinois University Press, 1964 reprint edition.
Bellamy, J. (1973). *Crime and Public Order in England in the Later Middle Ages*. Routledge and Kegan Paul, London.
Bentham, J. (1791). *Panopticon; or the Inspection House*. T. Payne, London.
Branch, J. W. (1970). *The English Prison Hulks*. Phillimore, Chichester.
Canada. Standing Committee on Justice and Legal Affairs. 1977. Parliamentary Subcommittee on the Penitentiary System in Canada *Report to Parliament*. Queen's Printer, Ottawa.
Chill, E. (1962). "Religion and Mendicity in Seventeenth Century France". *International Review of Social History* **7**, 400-425.
Clemmer, D. (1940). *The Prison Community*. Holt, Rinehart and Winston, New York.
Cockburn, J. S. (Ed.) (1977). *Crime in England 1550-1800*. Methuen & Co., London.
Condon, R. (1962). "The Reform of English Prisons, 1773-1816" PhD. Dissertation, Brown University.
Cooper, D. D. (1974). *The Lesson of the Scaffold: The Public Execution Controversy in Victorian England*. Allen Lane, London.
Cooper, R. A. (1976). "Ideas and their Execution: English Prison Reform". *Eighteenth Century Studies*, **X**, 73-93.

Davis, N. (1975). "The Reasons of Misrule" in her *Society and Culture in Early Modern France*. Stanford University Press, Stanford.

Davis, J. (1980). "The London Garroting Panic of 1862: A Moral Panic and the Creation of a Criminal Class in Mid-Victorian England". In V. A. C. Gatrell, B. Lenman and G. Parker (Eds) *Crime and Law in Western Societies: Historical Essays*. Europa, London.

De Lacy, M. E. (1980). "County Prison Administration in Lancashire, 1690-1850". Ph.D. Dissertation, Princeton University.

Diamond, S. (1974). "The Rule of Law versus the Order of Custom" in his *In Search of the Primitive: A Critique of Civilisation*. Transaction Books, New Brunswick.

Donajgrodzki, A. P. (Ed.). (1977). *Social Control in Nineteenth Century Britain*. Croom Helm, London.

Durkheim, E. (1960). *The Division of Labour in Society*. Free Press, Glencoe.

Evans, R. (1975). "A Rational Plan for Softening the Mind: Prison Design, 1750-1842". Ph.D. Dissertation, University of Essex.

Fine, B., Kinsey, R., Lea, J., Picciotto, S. and Young, J. (Eds) (1979). *Capitalism and the Rule of Law: From Deviancy Theory to Marxism*. Hutchinson, London.

Fitzgerald, M. (1977). *Prisoners in Revolt*. Penguin, London.

Fitzgerald, M. and Sim, J. (1979). *British Prisons*. Basil Blackwell, Oxford.

Foner, E. (1976). *Tom Paine and Revolutionary America*. Oxford University Press, London.

Foucault, M. (1967). *Madness and Civilization*. Translated by Richard Howard. Tavistock, London.

Foucault, M. (Ed.). (1973). *Moi, Pierre Riviere . . . un cas de parricide au XIXe siècle*. Gallimard Julliard, Paris.

Foucault, M. (1976). *La Volonté de Savoir: Histoire de la Sexualité*. Gallimard, Paris.

Foucault, M. (1978). *Discipline and Punish*. Translated by Alan Sheridan. Pantheon, New York.

Gatrell, V. A. C. (1980). "The Decline of Theft and Violence in Victorian and Edwardian England" in V. A. C. Gatrell, B. Lenman and G. Parker, Eds. *Crime and Law in Western Societies: Historical Essays*. Europa, London.

Gatrell, V. A. C. and Hadden, T. B. (1972). "Criminal Statistics and their Interpretation" in *Nineteenth Century Society* (E. A. Wrigley, Ed.). Cambridge University Press, Cambridge.

Giddens, A. (1976). *New Rules of Sociological Method*. Basic Books, New York.

Goffman, E. (1961). *Asylums*. Doubleday Anchor, Garden City.

Gramsci, A. (1971). *Prison Notebooks*. Lawrence & Wishart, London.

Grob, G. N. (1973). "Welfare and Poverty in American History". *Reviews in American History* I, 43-52.

Hart, H. L. A. (1968). *Punishment and Responsibility*. Clarendon Press, Oxford.

Hart, J. (1955). "Reform of the Borough Police, 1835-1856" *English Historical Review* **70**, 411-427.

Hart, J. (1965). "Nineteenth Century Social Reform: A Tory Interpretation of History". *Past and Present* **31**, 39-61.

Hay, D. (1975). "Property, Authority and Criminal Law". In D. Hay, P. Linebaugh, J. Rule, E. P. Thompson and C. Winslow (Eds) *Albion's Fatal Tree*. Allen Lane, London.

Hay, D. (1979). "Crime and Justice in Eighteenth and Nineteenth Century England" *Crime and Justice*, **II**. University of Chicago Press, Chicago.

Henriques, U. (1972). "The Rise and Decline of the Separate System of Prison Discipline". *Past and Present* **54**, 61-93.

208 MICHAEL IGNATIEFF

Himmelfarb, G. (1968). *Victorian Minds*. Harper, New York.

Ignatieff, M. (1978). *A Just Measure of Pain: The Penitentiary in the Industrial Revolution, 1750-1850*. Pantheon, New York.

Innes, J. (1980). "The King's Bench Prison in the Later Eighteenth Century: Law, Authority and Order in a London Debtor's Prison". In John Brewer and John Styles (Eds) *An Ungovernable People: Englishmen and the Law in the 17th and 18th Centuries*. Hutchinson, London.

Innes, J. (Forthcoming). "English Prisons in the Eighteenth Century". Ph.D. Dissertation, Cambridge University.

Jacobs, J. (1977). *Stateville: The Penitentiary in Mass Society*. University of Chicago Press, Chicago.

Katz, M. (1968). *The Ironies of Early School Reform*. Harvard University Press, Cambridge, Mass.

Labour History Society, Great Britain. (1972). *Bulletin: Crime and Industrial Society Conference Report*.

Langbein, J. H. (1977). *Torture and the Law of Proof: Europe and England in the Ancien Regime*. University of Chicago Press, Chicago.

Lasch, C. (1973). "The Discovery of the Asylum". In his *The World of Nations*. Vintage, New York.

Lazerson, M. (1971). *The Origins of the Urban School*. Harvard University Press, Cambridge, Mass.

Leroy, L. E. (1973). "La décroissance du crime au XVIIIe siècle: bilan d'historiens": *Contrepoint* **9**, 227-233.

Lewis, W. D. (1965). *From Newgate to Dannemora: The Rise of the Penitentiary in New York, 1796-1848*. Cornell University Press, Ithaca.

Lewis, O. F. (1922). *The Development of American Prisons and Prison Customs. 1776-1845*. Montclair, N.J: Patterson Smith, 1967, reprint edition.

Linebaugh, P. (1975). "The Tyburn Riot Against the Surgeons". In D. Hay, P. Linebaugh, J. Rule, E. P. Thompson and C. Winslow (Eds). *Albion's Fatal Tree*. Allen Lane, London.

Linebaugh, P. (1976). "Karl Marx, The Theft of Wood and Working Class Composition: A Contribution to the Current Debate". In *Crime and Social Justice* **6**, 5-16.

Linebaugh, P. (1977). "The Ordinary of Newgate and his Account". In J. S. Cockburn (Ed.) *Crime in England 1550-1800*. Methuen, London.

Linebaugh, P. (Forthcoming). *Crime and the Wage in the Eighteenth Century*.

McConville, S. (1977). "Penal Ideas and Prison Management in England, 1700-1850", Ph.D. Dissertation. Cambridge University.

McKelvey, B. (1977). *American Prisons*. Patterson Smith, Montclair, N.J.

Marx, K. (1976). *Capital* Vol. I. Penguin, Harmondsworth.

Minchinton, W. E. (Ed.) (1972). *Wage Regulation in Pre-Industrial England*. David and Charles, Newton Abbot.

Mitford, J. (1973). *Kind and Usual Punishment: The Prison Business*. Knopf, New York.

Moir, E. (1969). *The Justice of the Peace*. Penguin, Harmondsworth.

Morris, N. (1974). *The Future of Imprisonment*. University of Chicago Press, Chicago.

Muraskin, W. A. (1976). "The Social Control Theory in American History: A Critique". *Journal of Social History* **11**, 559-568.

New York State Special Commission on Attica. (1972). *Official Report*. Bantam, New York.

Pashukanis, B. (1978). *Law and Marxism: A General Theory*, 3d. edition. Ink Links, London.

Perrot, M. (1976). "Délinquance et systèmes pénitentiaires en France au XIXe siècle". *Annales: économies, sociétés, civilisations.*

Perrot, M. (Ed.) (1980). *L'impossible prison, recherches sur le système pénitentiaire au XIXe siècle.* Seuil, Paris.

Phillips, D. (1977). *Crime and Authority in Victorian England.* Croom Helm, London.

Piven, F. F. and Cloward, R. (1971). *Regulating the Poor.* Vintage, New York.

Platt, A. M. (1969). *The Child Savers: The Invention of Delinquency.* University Press, Chicago.

Playfair, G. (1971). *The Punitive Obsession.* Victor Gollancz, London.

Pugh, R. B. (1968). *Imprisonment in Medieval England.* Cambridge University Press, Cambridge.

Radzinowicz, Sir Leon. (1948-1968). *A History of English Criminal Law* 5 Vols. Stevens and Sons, London.

Renner, K. (1949). *The Institutions of Private Law and their Social Functions.* Routledge and Kegan Paul, London.

Roberts, S. (1980). "Changing Modes of Dispute Settlement: An Anthropological Perspective". In *Law and Human Relations: A Past and Present Society Conference,* London, 2 July 1980.

Rothman, D. J. (1971). *The Discovery of the Asylum.* Little Brown, Boston.

Rothman, D. J. (1980). *Conscience and Convenience: The Asylum and its Alternatives in Progressive America.* Little Brown, Boston.

Rothman, D. J. (1980). "Social Control: The Uses and Abuses of the Concept in the History of Incarceration". Unpublished paper, 1980.

Rusche, G. and Kirchheimer, O. (1939). *Punishment and Social Structure.* Columbia University Press, New York.

Schlossman, S. L. (1977). *Love and the American Delinquent: The Theory and Practice of "Progressive" Juvenile Justice, 1825-1920.* University of Chicago Press, Chicago.

Scull, A. T. (1977). *Decarceration: Community Treatment and the Deviant — A Radical View.* Prentice Hall, Englewood Cliffs, N.J.

Scull, A. T. (1979). *Museums of Madness.* Allen Lane, London.

Sellin, J. T. (1944). *Pioneering in Penology: The Amsterdam House of Correction in the Sixteenth and Seventeenth Centuries.* University of Pennsylvania Press, Philadelphia.

Shaw, A. G. L. (1971). *Convicts and the Colonies.* Faber, London.

Sheehan, W. J. (1977). "Finding Solace in 18th Century Newgate". In J. S. Cockburn (Ed.) *Crime in England, 1550-1800.* Methuen, London.

Silberman, C. E. (1978). *Criminal Violence, Criminal Justice.* Random House, New York.

Silver, A. (1967). "The Demand for Order in Civil Society: A Review of Some Themes in the History of Urban Crime, Police and Riot". In D. Bordua (Ed.) *The Police: Six Sociological Essays.* Wiley, New York.

Smith, A. (1759). *The Theory of Moral Sentiments,* edited by D. D. Raphael. Clarendon Press, Oxford, 1976.

Smith, A. (1763). *Lectures on Jurisprudence,* edited by R. L. Meek, D. D. Raphael and P. G. Stein. Clarendon Press, Oxford, 1978.

Sparks, R. F. (1980). "A Critique of Marxist Criminology". *Crime and Justice* **II.** University of Chicago Press, Chicago.

Stedman Jones, G. (1971). *Outcast London.* Penguin, London.

Stedman Jones, G. (1977). "Class Expression versus Social Control?" *History Workshop Journal* **IV,** 163-171.

Stockdale, E. (1977). *A Study of Bedford Prison 1660-1877.* Phillimore, London.

Stone, L. (1979). *Family, Sex and Marriage in England, 1500-1800.* Penguin, Harmondsworth.

Storch, R. D. (1975). "The Plague of the Blue Locusts: Police Reform and Popular Resistance in Northern England, 1840-1857". *International Review of Social History* **XX**, 61-90.

Sykes, G. (1958). *The Society of Captives*. Princeton University Press, Princeton.

Taylor, I., Walton, P. and Young, J. (1975). *The New Criminology: For a Social Theory of Deviance*. Routledge and Kegan Paul, London.

Teeters, N. D. (1935). *The Cradle of the Penitentiary: The Walnut Street Jail at Philadelphia, 1773-1835*. Philadelphia.

Thomas, K. (1971). *Religion and the Decline of Magic*. Weidenfeld and Nicolson, London.

Thompson, E. P. (1963). *The Making of the English Working Class*. Pantheon, New York.

Thompson, E. P. (1971). "The Moral Economy of the English Crowd". *Past and Present* **50**, 76-136.

Thompson, E. P. (1972). "Rough Music! le charivari anglais" *Annales: économies, sociétés, civilisations* **XXVII**, 285-313.

Thompson, E. P. (1975). *Whigs and Hunters*. Allen Lane, London.

Thompson, E. P. (1980). *Writings by Candlelight*. Merlin, London.

Tobias, J. J. (1972). *Crime and Industrial Society in the Nineteenth Century*. Pelican, Harmondsworth.

Tocqueville, A. de (1969). *Democracy in America*, edited by J. P. Mayer. Doubleday Anchor, New York.

Tomlinson, M. H. (1975). "Victorian Prisons: Administration and Architecture". Ph.D. Dissertation, Bedford College, London University.

Trumbach, R. (1978). *The Rise of the Egalitarian Family: Aristocratic Kinship and Domestic Relations in 18th Century England*. Academic Press, London.

Webb, B. and Webb, S. (1922). *English Prisons Under Local Government*. Frank Cass, London. 1963.

Weber, M. (1947). *The Theory of Social and Economic Organisation*, edited by Talcott Parsons. Free Press, Glencoe.

Whiting, J. R. S. (1975). *Prison Reform in Gloucestershire, 1775-1820*. Phillimore, London, 1975.

Wicker, T. (1975). *A Time to Die*. Quadrangle, New York.

Further Reading

Three works embody the revisionist paradigm described and criticized in this essay: Foucault (1978); Ignatieff (1978); and Rothman (1971).

Objections (express or implied) to the revisionist account as an accurate description of the history of punishment can be found in: Delacy (1980); Innis (1980a); Perrott (Ed.) (1980); Tomlinson (1977).

For a scholarly study of the English prison published after this essay was written, see McConville, S. (1980). *A History of English Prison Administration Vol. I, 1750-1877*, (Routledge, London). See also the essays in Bailey, V. (Ed.), (1981). *Policing and Punishment in 19th Century Britain*, (Croom Helm, London). Roth, R. (1981). *Pratiques Pénitentiaires et Théorie Sociale*, (Librairie Droz, Geneva) is an excellent study of the local, philosophical, legal and social forces which grounded prison reform in Geneva, 1825-62.

Foucault, M. (1980). *Power/Knowledge*, (C. Gordon, Ed.), (Harvester, Brighton) contains several interviews and other writings by Foucault which reveal the ways Foucault has revised his views on the history of punishment. An important supplement is the fascinating collection of materials edited by Michelle Perrot (Perrot (Ed.), 1980). Here, Foucault's work is assessed by several leading French historians of nineteenth century punishment and is debated with Foucault. Perrot (Ed.) (1980) and Roth (1981) are reviewed by Ignatieff in (1982) *Social History*, pp. 227-229.

Two important aspects of this essay—the critique of 'social control' and the argument that law and ordering are *not* the exclusive property of the state—are also discussed in the essay by Sugarman in his collection.

9 Law, Economy and The State in England, 1750–1914: Some Major Issues

David Sugarman

Introduction

Until recently, the historical linkages between law, economy and the state in the period after 1700 had not been afforded much detailed attention by either lawyers, historians or sociologists. Traditional legal history has been primarily concerned with the earlier period, and generally it has been reluctant to investigate the connections between law, society and economy in any systematic fashion. Economic and social historians and sociologists have tended either to ignore the historical development of law, society and economy or treat that relationship as relatively unproblematic.

Part of the problem stems from the vast range of subject-matter and source materials such an enterprise would embrace. The artificial divisions separating legal, economic, social, intellectual and business history from one another, as well as history from sociology, have also inhibited the development of an inter-disciplinary, holistic, history of law and material society. Although much work has been done, it tends to be written in relative isolation within the confines or traditions of a particular specialism. Major pertinent literature in other disciplines or sub-areas tends to be overlooked. These reasons help to explain the absence of any synthetic overview of the historical relationship between law, economy and the state in modern England. Outside lawyers' legal history, most attention has been afforded to the criminal law and its institutions. Private law—such as the law governing property, contracts, families and companies—has tended to receive short shrift. Social and labour history emerged in opposition to a historical tradition which concentrated upon the 'great men' of

Law, State and Society Series: "Legality, Ideology and the State", edited by D. Sugarman, 1983.
Academic Press, London and New York.

history and sought to recover the history of 'the people', meaning the working-classes. Not surprisingly, perhaps, they have tended to ignore 'rich man's law' (i.e. private law) and the legal professions, save in the context of the rise of the modern labour movement—just as they have tended to neglect the middle and landed classes. It could be argued that the study of law, especially 'rich man's law', involves special theoretical or methodological difficulties. For example, that ". . . the hetrogeneity and pluralism of the English ruling class, its complex and contradictory network of social elements, its lack of a clear profile, all contribute to make analysis very difficult" (Seed, 1981, p. 176). Yet these acknowledged difficulties apply with equal force to the historical study of the working classes. They have not, apparently, impeded the emergence of a lively and fruitful 'history from below'. Moreover, 'rich man's law', may affect and be influenced by *all* social classes, directly or indirectly. Thus, the history of the working classes cannot be fully understood in isolation from dominant social groups and the legal orders those groups most utilized. Analogous restrictions on focus are evident in the sociology of law and 'law-in-context'. With important, but numerically small exceptions, these also have reflected a general absence of concern with 'rich man's law', let alone its historical antecedents (cf. Cain, 1975). As a result, the old specialisms and divisions have been largely reinforced in new ways. The possibility of understanding whole social formations and whole legal systems—the totality rather than a segment—and, therefore, the present conjuncture, has been thwarted (Seed, 1981, p. 178).

There are signs, however, that this state of affairs may be changing for the better. There seems to be an increasing acknowledgement within labour and social history that it has to give greater attention to the middle and landed classes. In recent years, there has been a remarkable growth of interest in the historical relation between law, society and economy, though most attention has continued to focus upon the history of crime and criminal justice. Business and social historians have begun to explore a wealth of legal and quasi-legal records which previously tended to be neglected, for example, bankruptcy records and statistics, company accounts, probate records etc. The development of social history and more recently, the history of gender divisions, has made exciting contributions to our knowledge of the linkages between law, power and sexual divisions in historical causation.

This essay attempts to provide an introductory synthesis or overview of some of the key issues pertaining to the historical relation between law, ideology, the state and economy in England in the period 1750-1914. I have concentrated largely upon the private law order given its relative neglect. It is hoped that this overview may stimulate further interest in, and work towards, a more avowedly inter-disciplinary economic and social history or historical sociology of law, society, and economy.[1] It should be stressed at the outset, however, that it is not intended to offer an exhaustive summary of the work done in the area, but merely to point to some of the issues and subject-matter which it is considered are central to an adequate consideration of law, economy and the state in England, during the period 1750-1914.

Law and Economy

Was law important in the economy?: on facilitative laws and self-regulation

Lawyers, historians and sociologists have too often treated the law's 'essential' role in securing certainty in commercial transactions as axiomatic. The truth is, however, considerably more complex. For example, in his groundbreaking history of American law, Lawrence Friedman has concluded that American commercial law was actually, ". . . too elegant (and too unknown except to lawyers) to have much effect on the actual working of the market" (Friedman, 1973, p. 233).

In fact, it is clear neither that industry and trade wanted or needed the law, nor that the law did, or could have provided, the predictability so often asserted. Given the devotion of business to self-regulation and given the potency of economic and financial might, why, it might be queried, should the law be necessary to such interests? Traders and entrepreneurs might, on occasions, actually have a stronger interest in a legal system characterized by confusion and complexity, which they could exploit, rather than the supposed certainty and calculability which lawyers often argued enterprise required of the legal order.

Yet many of the rich especially, either voluntarily or by virtue of mandatory enactments, committed to legal form the arrangements they wished to make, in order to regulate aspects of their social and economic affairs. Thus the strict settlement, the turnpike trust agreement, the partnership arrangement, the indentured apprenticeship contract, the constitution of the friendly society, agreements for the sale or purchase of innumerable items, were all enclosed in legal documents. In respect to some agreements, the guidance and expertise of lawyers were called upon to assist their clients to attain given ends where institutional or practical obstacles were encountered. How to ensure the preservation of the landed estate in the event of unforeseeable contingencies affecting intended inheritors; how to provide for the permanency of an economic enterprise with fluctuating membership; how best to guarantee the right of recovery against third parties and to avoid, if possible, personal or corporate liability? For these tasks, lawyers would invent courses of action or simplify older forms, resort to legal fictions, and adapt one mechanism of the law to a fundamentally different purpose from that for which it was originally created.

However, the use of legal formalities did not, of necessity, engulf the parties concerned in the paraphernalia of the legal system. The use of legal formalities such as a contract or trust deed might be utilized as tools to secure a good deal of autonomy *from* the legal order. This can be seen as part of a wider preference extending beyond the Stock Exchange and throughout the City, to the professions, trading and co-operative associations, trade unions and even individual contractors: namely, the desire to self-regulate one's own affairs unimpaired by the law or to utilize its coercive power only as a matter of last resort. In other words, the legal system might co-operate in its partial or complete supersession. Commerce and industry might value certainty and calculability. But often they *also* preferred their own adjudicators (thus, the wide use of arbitration or the demand for special 'commercial' juries); and they valued the ability to formulate their own private or 'home-made' legislation, as opposed to that laid down by Parliament or the courts. In short, the evidence indicates that the legal system was utilized in a pragmatic fashion. Some of the functions or institutions of the legal order were more valued than others. The legal system permitted the appropriation of those facets of the legal order deemed most useful, such as coercion and law enforcement in the final instance, whilst at the same time allowing the relevant actors considerable space for self-regulation (cf. Ferguson, 1980).

How did the law facilitate and legitimate this desire for self-regulation? Some jurists, like most lay persons, define the law exclusively in terms of something which we either obey or disobey, as requiring persons to act in certain ways whether they wish to or not; that is, as a directly coercive instrumentality analogous to orders backed by threats. The criminal law is the paradigm of laws of this kind. However, this model of law as coercive orders obscures the variety of laws to be found in legal systems. Co-existing alongside the criminal law is another type of law called facilitative or power-conferring laws (Hart, 1961, Chs II, III and V). Such laws do not impose duties or obligations. Instead, they provide individuals with *facilities* for realising their wishes, by conferring legal powers upon them to create, by certain specified procedures, and subject to certain conditions, structures of rights and duties within the coercive framework of the law. For example, the law confers on individuals the power to mould their legal relations with others, by marriages, contracts, wills, companies and trusts. The law provides a skeleton for individual choice. In varying degrees, this facilitative power affords the parties concerned the opportunity to make their own law (private law-making), and even the opportunity, on occasions, to bypass or attenuate the legal or equitable obligations established by Parliament or the courts, that otherwise would apply.

Facilitative laws are but one instance of a wider phenomenon, namely, the role of the law in the facilitation and legitimation of a plurality of semi-autonomous realms—a role which has yet to be fully chronicled. The law simultaneously exemplifies such a realm and defines and reproduces a mode of thought and practice which promotes a variety of semi-autonomous realms with powers that in some respects resembles those of the state. Here, for instance, one thinks of 'the village community', the estate, the guild, the city, the church, local government and local courts, the strict settlement, corporations, the state, the Crown, the law merchant, the trust and arbitration (Sugarman and Rubin, forthcoming). Thus, facilitative laws, such as the law of contract or land law, built upon as well as were imbricated within this long-standing tradition of semi-autonomous realms. Facilitative laws were also dependent upon the lawyers' drafting skills in utilizing, manipulating and expanding the delegations of authority permitted by law, custom, or indigenous practices. Moreover, the semi-autonomy or monopoly position that the law facilitated and legitimated was enforced by the continuous, low-key, "controlled interventionism" (Polanyi, 1944, p. 140) of the state.

Thus, the private law form of facilitative laws conceals their quasi-public law qualities. In other words, facilitative laws straddle private and public law; in so doing, they illustrate the inadequacy of the public/private law distinction, that is, its insensitivity to the hybrid and ultimately coercive nature of all law, public *and* private. Facilitative laws are agencies of *state* policy in that they define the range of permissible conduct, albeit through the self-directing actions of private individuals. They are *also* instruments through which individuals may expand or contract their autonomy, and, in so doing, promote, qualify or subvert official state policy.

How did this relative autonomy from the mainstream of formal rules and obligations of law develop? At one end of the spectrum, it was dependent upon the lawyers' drafting skills in constructing institutional arrangements beyond, or on the fringes of, the law. Taking one step back, this in turn was stimulated both by the professions' attempts to create and control a market for their talents and also by the eagerness of potential clients to secure the advantages of the various forms of self-regulation afforded by the law. The ingenious conveyancers such as Sir Orlando Bridgeman who devised the strict family settlement in order to assist the English landed classes to retain their estates in the family from generation to generation, or the advice of counsel such as Serjeant Pengally on the scope of the Bubble Act and its exceptions, or of Bellenden Ker on the law of partnership, created for counsel an important role in shaping the activities of the landed class and of business practice. Also vital was the often tacit support of the courts to such arrangements; and the ability of those who used them to head off litigation that might endanger such arrangements or, at least, limit them or render them uncertain. At the other end of the spectrum lay the political and economic power of the diverse interests that could secure through lawyers, the courts or Parliament, the necessary state sanction for self-regulation or other forms of assistance: the great trading companies of the sixteenth and seventeenth centuries, the great landed families, the City, the railways, manufacturers, the professions and other pressure groups (Sugarman and Rubin, forthcoming).

Freedom of contract

In the nineteenth century, the rise of freedom of contract as *the* pre-eminent doctrine of English private law encouraged Parliament and the courts to extend considerably the degree of legitimate autonomy afforded to the private sphere (Atiyah, 1979, esp. Pt II). This ideology embodied the fiction that equal bargaining power must normally be assumed to exist in all commercial transactions. It has been argued that the doctrine of freedom of contract warranted the incorporation of wide exemption clauses, the growth of one-sided 'standard form' contracts, and, in the context of employment contracts, led to drastically reduced limits being imposed on the employee's rights to sue their employer (for example, Dawson, 1947; Simon, 1954; Friedman, 1972, pp. 119-160; Horwitz, 1977, pp. 188-210; Stevens, 1979, pp. 138-143 and 160-164. Cf. Simpson, 1979).

> Thus, the contractarian ideology above all expressed a market conception of legal relations . . . Since the only measure of justice was the parties' own agreement, all pre-existing legal duties were inevitably subordinated to the contract relation . . . The circle was complete. The law had come simply to ratify those forms of inequality that the market system produced. (Horwitz, 1977, p. 210)

The ideology of freedom of contract was an important element in the liberalization of English company law in the nineteenth century. General incorporation by registration first became available in 1844 and limited liability was generally extended to shareholders in 1855. The statutory regime was extremely liberal. Initially, the courts' reaction to this regime was mixed. Some attempt to construct a regulatory system can be detected. However, as in other areas of private law, the power of freedom of contract, the rise of legal formalism and perhaps, an increasing sympathy towards these agencies of economic growth, encouraged the courts frequently to adopt the mantle of legal abstentionism, rather than that of a watch-dog. The separation of ownership from control was legitimated by characterizing the companies' internal relations (i.e. relations as between shareholders *inter se* and shareholders and management) as primarily contractual. The evolution of the holding company and the utilization of the corporate form by *de facto* partnerships or even one person was facilitated by a rigid adherence to the separate personality of the company. The wave of mergers and amalgamations at the end of the nineteenth century could occur unimpeded by the law. Indeed, the seeming willingness of the law to permit the concentration of capital, mirrored its refusal, by and large, to use the law as means for controlling cartels and monopolies in contrast with the United States. Cartel agreements, contracts in restraint of trade, distributive agreements and intellectual property (trade marks, patents etc.) enabled companies to expand the scale of their enterprises whilst conforming to the letter of the law. The ideologies of legal formalism, freedom of contract and free trade constituted a kind of intellectual buffer zone which drained legal interventionism of its legitimacy. But the power of these ideologies was seemingly selective. The tendency of English law to refuse to regulate trade competition and the growing use of the corporate form by trade and industry, starkly contrasts with ". . . the courts' readiness to impose liability on trade unionists in logically similar circumstances" (Cornish, 1979, p. 297).

Sanctions

A factor determining the use or non-use of law is the nature and effectiveness of an accompanying sanction. What type of sanction, if any, is employed, is often intimately associated with the character of the relationship between parties. Mutual economic interdependence will influence significantly whether any, and if so which, sanctions will be invoked. Not all employers sue their employees for breach of contract. Macaulay's well-known study of American businessmen which concluded that where the contracting parties are relatively equal and recurrently deal with each other, the law is fastidiously avoided, and that it is perceived as inimical both to that relationship and to the ability to govern one's own affairs, has received extensive comparative support (Macaulay, 1963; also Beale and Dugdale, 1975).

Legal enforceability, that is, lawful coercion, was probably the most important instrumental facility offered by the legal system.

> Legal enforceability lends point to adjudicative processes by supplying a motive for compliance with the decision reached. A decision whose concomitant is legal enforceability is a powerful resource for the winner confronted with the problem of extracting performance from a recalcitrant loser. The problem of the recalcitrant loser strongly suggests that few systems for the adjudication of commercial disputes could be viable without the ultimate sanction of legal enforcement. Nevertheless, legal enforceability is dispensable, albeit only in exceptional circumstances. (Ferguson, 1980, pp. 154-155)

For example, on the Stock Exchange, ostracism was the potent force preventing the widespread repudiation of sales agreements by contractors well aware that legal sanctions for such repudiation were non-existent because the relevant bargain was legally unenforceable (Ferguson, 1980, pp. 154-155). Thus, commerce's need for legal coercion, directly or indirectly, cannot be assumed as axiomatic. For instance, informal collective price and output controls within a market or industry may be unenforceable in law; however, the economic sanctions cartels can impose on existing firms may be as substantial as those of the legal order. On the other hand, it is probably unlikely that parties will be unconcerned about the absence of a legal guarantee in commercial transactions unless the relevant market is characterized by an unusually high degree of self-regulation or collective cohesion. Furthermore, in the context of trade debtors and other defaulters, some plaintiffs may have regarded litigation as essential, even where this might, in itself, prove uneconomic. For ". . . unpaid bills had to be 'chased' because if it got known that their company or agency did not take defaulters to court, then nobody would pay" (Cain, 1982, p. 13). In this way civil litigation may have a "general deterrence" function (Cain, 1982).

> If, as Foucault suggests, we rid ourselves of 'the illusion that penalty is above all (if not exclusively) a means of reducing crime', and assume that changes in the kind and degree of punishment (and other sanctions) reveal something about the structure of the societies in which they are found, then it makes sense to give careful attention to both changes in the kind and degree of punishment (and other sanctions, both public and private law) within a specific society over time and the differences in punitive controls (and other sanctions) that exist between different societies at a fixed point in time. (Spitzer, 1979, p. 208)

In other words, a new economic and social history of law may be able to illuminate the historical and comparative relationship between public and private law sanctions and the social organization and economic change within and as between different nation states.

It would be foolish to assert that doctrinal development had no perceptible effect on subsequent economic behaviour, or that, alternatively, economic behaviour itself inspired no changes in the common law, for the example of Lord Mansfield's creation of the law merchant testifies otherwise (Fifoot, 1936). What is asserted is that there is little value in adopting sweeping generalizations concerning the relationship between case law and economic development. The theme will most profitably be examined topic by topic and only once this kind of exercise has been accomplished over a sufficiently broad area, will we be in a position to point to, or to refute, the existence of a systematic pattern of development.

Courts and litigation

Were the courts preferred to other institutions as a forum for dispute settlements? The expensive and time-consuming character of the civil law courts especially Chancery, was infamous. "No man, as things now stand", said in 1839 George Spence, an authority on the Court of Chancery, "can enter into a Chancery suit with any reasonable hope of being alive at its termination, if he has a determined adversary" (cited, Bowen, 1907, p. 529). In addition, areas of the law important to business and industry, such as the law governing partnerships and companies were notoriously complex and ambiguous throughout the eighteenth and most of the nineteenth century, that is, throughout much of Britain's Industrial Revolution. Indeed, a large body of business people preferred to resort to *arbitration* to settle their disagreements rather than the civil law courts. Whilst the majority of the population were effectively deprived from utilizing the central civil courts of London, the same cannot be said of the criminal courts. David Philips' work has shown that Parliament had made provision for the expenses of prosecutors from the mid-eighteenth century and that this was widely utilized by a broad spectrum of social classes (Philips, 1977, Ch. 4).

What were the political and economic consequences of securing legal change through the courts rather than through Parliament? Morton Horwitz has argued that in nineteenth century America, the impact of substantial law-making by the courts was to mystify the underlying policy choices and deny the kinds of open debate and compromises more likely to ensue from the legislative process. (Horwitz, 1977, pp. xiv-xvi and 99–101). To what extent is this thesis applicable to England; and, if it is, can we measure the costs incurred, and if so, how? Horwitz rightly warns against the casual application of the concept of *laissez-faire* to the common law power of judges. He argues

> Strictly speaking there would never be a *laissez-faire* regime unless judges refused to enforce all contracts and refused to compensate all injuries . . . (Under) certain circumstances even judicial refusal to act could be motivated by developmental goals. In this sense, the contractarian ideology of 19th century judges was both instrumental (in the sense of promoting economic development) and *laissez-faire* (in the traditional sense of being hostile to legislative or administrative regulation). In short, when it comes to analysing the activities of private law judges deciding disputes concerning tort, contract and property, the category *laissez-faire* is often not useful primarily because it does not distinguish between developmental and distributional goals. It also ignores the political significance of leaving the task of government regulation primarily to judges. (Horwitz, 1977, p. xv. Cf. Sugarman, 1980)

The double-edged impact of law on economy

In this section and the next I consider two examples which illustrate the complexity of the relation between law and economy: firstly, patents and secondly, the absolute ownership of land.

The illustrative case of patents

The idea of granting a market monopoly was an old one, as the development of the guilds and boroughs exemplifies, and, until the modern period, it was intimately associated with the exercise of the royal prerogative. In its efforts to declare these exercises void, Parliament challenged the Crown and indicated its preference for competition in the Statute of Monopolies of 1624. Exceptionally, Section 6 permitted patent monopolies for 14 years upon "any manner of new manufacture within the realm to the true and first inventor". It was the rise of industrialization which led to a substantial increase in the number of patents. In the 1750's less than 10 patents a year were being granted; in the 1760's that number more than doubled. By the 1810's the average was 110 per annum and in the 1840's 458 per annum (Cornish, 1981, p. 81, n. 17). How important to the process of industrialization was the protection for inventors afforded by rights of patent?

> Among the famous, Boulton and Watt secured large sums from their steam engine patents, but these came partly from a special extending Act . . . (and after laborious litigation). Arkwright's main patent threatened the whole industry but proved to be too obscurely drawn to survive the attack on its validity. Crompton had to be given a parliamentary reward of £5000 since he had virtually no commercial return from his spinning-jenny. It is likely that patents provided equally sporadic encouragement for those with less celebrated improvements. (Cornish, 1981, p. 81 and n. 18)

In elucidating why this was the case, a significant factor was undoubtedly the slow, expensive and cumbersome system for obtaining and enforcing patents. Dickens satirized the obstacles the law placed in the way of inventors in *Little Dorrit*. As Cornish notes, "Separate patents had to be secured for England, Ireland and Scotland and a large number of officials had to give their approval" (Cornish, 1981, p. 82, n. 22). Only in 1852, *after* Britain's technological primacy had been established, was a straightforward and relatively inexpensive patent system inaugurated. Yet the advance was double-edged. The liberalization of patent registration brought with it the increased possibility of costly and interminable litigation.

> This might deter the genuine inventor from seeking protection, but it left the swashbuckler plenty of room to brandish dubious patents, hoping that competitors would find it simpler to treat shadow as if it were substance. (Cornish, 1981, p. 82)

Further, the courts often proved unsympathetic in their interpretation of the law when confronted with those seeking to enforce market monopolies (Cornish, 1981, p. 84).

Property

Property and property relations as symbiotic with law

Land was and still is a cardinal source of power and inequality. What was the relationship between, on the one hand, property and property relations and, on the other, law and lawyers? Who influenced who? How? Why?

" 'Property and law are born and must die together', wrote Bentham. 'Before the laws, there was no property: take away the laws, all property ceases. The organs of the law are symbiotic with property." (Offer, 1981, p. 11).

The identification of property and production relations with law is especially intense in England given that ordinary English language uses *legal* terms to describe property and production relations; and that no ready-made alternative to this usage exists (Cohen, 1978, pp. 224 and 240). The two-directional, inter-connection between law and property has recently been stressed in Edward Thompson's work on eighteenth century England. Thompson concludes that in the agrarian context of eighteenth century England the Marxian distinction between law as an element of superstructure, and the actualities of productive forces, is untenable. He argues

> For law was often a definition of actual agrarian *practice* . . . How can we distinguish between the activity of farming or of quarrying and the rights to this strip of land or to that quarry? The farmer or forester in his daily occupation was moving within visible and invisible structures of law . . . Hence, 'law' was deeply imbricated within the very basis of productive relations, which would have been inoperable without this law. (Thompson, 1975, p. 261)

The relationship between law, land and property relations is portrayed as one of reciprocal influence and reinforcement. Yet, we cannot stop there, for many questions remain unanswered. 'Imbrication' tells us how law, land and property relations engage with one another. But it tells us nothing about which of these constituents (if any) tend to predominate or endure in the short-run and the long-run. In other words, was the reciprocal relationship between law, land and property relations symmetrical or asymmetrical? Were changes in property law never explicable solely in terms of either changes in property relations or the autonomous, imminent drive of the legal order? If the relationship between law, land and property relations was functionally interdependent, as Thompson's use of 'imbrication' seems to imply, we must ask, functional for whom and for what?

Capitalism and the rise of absolute private property

Surprisingly, economic historians have tended to take for granted the relationship between law, property relations and the rise of capitalism. In effect, they have been inclined to treat that relationship as ". . . a 'given', to be held static in the background of analysis . . ." (Scheiber, 1981, p. 104). In so far as historians and sociologists have considered the relationship between law, property and property relations, the tendency has been to focus upon a key feature of the transformation from feudalism to capitalism: the rise of absolute private property. This concern with the rise of absolute private property is not surprising: it informs the work of influential writers such as Marx, Weber and Macpherson. Even here, however, the role of law rarely receives detailed attention. There has been a marked tendency to adopt a rather simple, functionalist, model of law and economy in the historical and sociological literature; and this is well illustrated in historical work on property and property relations. In what follows, I have tried to indicate some of the potential pitfalls of such a model.

Marx's analysis of the rise of absolute private property and the chronology he suggested has greatly influenced non-Marxist, as well as Marxist historians and sociologists. Thus, a brief explication of his views still constitutes an important starting point for discussion. For Marx, the great transformation from feudalism to capitalism occurred in England in the last third of the fifteenth century and in the sixteenth century. During this period an 'agricultural revolution' which forced the peasantry from the land on to a labour market, laid the foundation for the capitalist mode of production. Marx argued that the "economic structure of capitalistic society has grown out of the economic structure of feudal society. The dissolution of the latter set free the elements of the former" (Marx, 1954, p. 668). The rise of absolute private property was a fundamental constituent of the rise of capitalism; and that it did not develop until capitalist production predominated. Thus, ". . . the legal view . . . that the land-owner can do with the land what every owner of commodities can do with his commodities . . . this view . . . arises . . . in the modern world only with the development of capitalist production" (Marx, 1980, p. 616). The history of landed property and the metamorphosis of tenurial law provides a 'mirror' in which we can observe the rise of capitalism (Marx, 1973, p. 252). Marx's view of feudalism stressed its dynamic character. Feudalism was not a monolithic social formation. Alongside free peasant proprietors existed a relatively small number of wage labourers from at least the latter half of the fourteenth century. Engels reaffirmed Marx's view of a transformation in the nature of property relations and property law. Capitalist production, "by changing all things into commodities, (it) dissolved all inherited and traditional relations and replaced time hallowed custom and historical right by purchase and sale, by the free contract" (Engels, 1902, p. 96). Thus, Engels asserted that Marx had already foreseen Maine's dichotomy between status and contract and had located the shift from the former to the latter in the sixteenth century. Historians and sociologists, despite their diverse value-judgements, have tended to adopt this dichotomization and the model of transition and revolution it implies.

Recently, the conventional chronology has been challenged. The revisionists accept the conventional view that absolute private property and the security the law afforded it were crucial to modernization. Indeed, in some revisionist accounts, the rise of absolute private property and the central role of the law therein become *the* cornerstones of their explanation why capitalism first emerged in Western Europe. However, the revisionists, implicitly or explicitly, repudiate the idea that absolute property rights only began to predominate (at the earliest) from the late fifteenth and sixteenth centuries, and therefore, the conventional view of medieval England. The chronology of the transition is pushed backwards. 'Possessive individualism' and its legal underpinnings were, it is asserted, alive and well in thirteenth century England (see North and Thomas, 1973 and Macfarlane, 1978). Here, property law and other legal institutions are elevated to significant determinants of modernization in the quest for why and how the industrial revolution occurred first in England. The revisionist accounts, such as those of North and Thomas, and Macfarlane, are stimulating and provocative contributions to the wider debate about the transition from feudalism to capitalism (cf. Chaytor, 1980; Hilton, 1980; Corrigan, 1981). Too often, historians and sociologists have adopted a static one-dimensional model of transformation or transition—from pre-capitalist to capitalist society. The revisionist contribution usefully problematizes this often taken-for-granted dichotomy. In particular, Macfarlane's work re-emphasizes the importance of local studies of real people in the generation and refinement of general theories of law, property and economy. Whether Macfarlane's findings are typical, as opposed to being peculiar to the localities investigated, will only become clear once further reconstructions of the lives of villagers have been undertaken.

Absolute private property versus a plurality of legal forms

Interestingly, despite their political differences, there is a strong core of consensus shared by all the participants to the debates concerning the relationship between property, property relations and property law outlined above. They all appear to agree about the nature of the transition or transformation (captured in such phrases as 'the rise of absolute private property' and 'the shift from status to contract'). Indeed, for all their political differences, these studies ". . . have in common that their method posits law . . . (or 'property' or 'state') as a reified author of social change; i.e. they give legal form an active *functional* role in shaping the social order." They assume . . . "that law-and-society is a set of linked hierarchical structures in which legal rule induces social response (and vice versa), instead of separate social spheres connected to one another only in the loosest and most problematic ways" (Gordon, 1978, pp. 2 and 3). To accept the latter hypothesis does not necessarily entail the view that the legal order was irrelevant in economy and society. It does, however, have a number of virtues. It serves to question whether the particular regime of property, property relations and (in particular) property law that historians and sociologists have associated with the rise of modern society and the Western World in particular, was as indispensable or even the important precondition of economic growth that so many seem to assume. In other words, the relationship between the legal realm and social practice and within the realm of ordering and organization (state and non-state) may be more discontinuous and problematic than some overly-functionalist accounts of property, property relations and property law may imply.

To illustrate this argument, let us return to some of the accounts of the metamorphosis of property, property relations and property law outlined in this section. On further investigation the much vaunted rise of *absolute* private property turns out to be somewhat more complex and contradictory.

One respect with which property remained *qualified* in practice concerns the notion that property ownership gave rise to obligations as well as rights. Whilst this idea operated with special force within the family, it also extended to the public, at least until the end of the eighteenth century, and probably later (Atiyah, 1979, pp. 89–90; Offer, 1981, p. 401).

Property was also qualified in practice because it was ultimately a creature of state law; and what state law protected and enforced, state law might restrict or take away. For example, actions against the Crown in contract and tort for damage to the property or person of others were severely limited. Whilst in theory the Crown was subject to the law, in practice this was not the case as there was no institution to enforce the law against the Crown. The courts were those of the Crown, and thus, the Crown could not be sued in its own court. The Crown could be a plaintiff but not a defendant. The Crown might voluntarily abide by a decision of a court of law, and an elaborate system of petition of right was developed to facilitate this arrangement. However, liability in tort, such as the employers liability for the negligence of employees during the course of their employment, fell beyond the ambit of this arrangement. This doctrine remained intact until 1947 when the Crown Proceedings Act sought to simplify and extend the law. Other instances of the Crown's ability unilaterally to alter property rights include Charles II's successful struggle to control the personnel and thus the government of the borough and city corporations, notably the City of London, over which the Crown had, in 1682, slight legal control. This attack culminated in the Crown's forfeiture of the Charter of London and of other boroughs as well as bodies such as livery companies. These examples illustrate that the space afforded property rights by the Crown was neither absolute nor uncontested. Indeed, once the whole range of state activity and interventionism is considered, and not just the activities of the courts alone, the notion of a pure, unequivocal private property becomes much more problematic.

A further way property rights were limited in practice was in terms of the great expense, the length of time and the sheer difficulties of enforcement which might conspire to prevent property owners fully exercising their rights. Historians and sociologists have, for example, stressed the importance of the extension of the umbrella of 'property' to intangibles such as shares, copyrights and patents. However, the average shareholder, copyrightholder and patentee did not have the financial resources, the time and the contacts to enforce their rights. The success of the Watt and Boulton partnership in protecting their patent would appear to be the exception, rather than the rule. Here, again, we see historians and sociologists conflating the existence of a legal rule, right or duty with the separate questions of its operation, mediation and enforcement in practice.

But there are other reasons why property was more limited in law and practice in the seventeenth, eighteenth and nineteenth centuries, than the kind of accounts outlined above recognize. What these accounts tend to de-emphasize is the continued importance of the *institution* of property as a 'bundle of rights' i.e. a range or hierarchy of different rights vested perhaps in different people co-existing in the same piece of land or goods, which qualified the use and enjoyment of property.

The recent work of social historians testifies to the persistence, albeit in an increasingly bowdlerized form, of traditional use-rights such as the right to remove firewood and rights of pasture which in practice qualified the actualization of absolute conceptions of property. The prohibitions upon forestalling, regrating and engrossing survived Coke's attacks and, together with customary restrictions on the price of staples (especially during periods of dearth), were sporadically resuscitated. This "moral economy" with its blend of paternalism, common property, notions of just price, and political expediency in the face of the English crowd, like use-rights and perquisites, co-existed alongside the rise of the idea of absolute property and qualified that ideal in practice well into the nineteenth century (Thompson, 1971 and 1976).

Thus, the "restrictions on use and disposition", the "complications of title", the "thicket of conflicting rights" which Landes (1969, pp. 15-16) locates in a pre-industrial, pre-absolute propertied world, did not cease with the rise of industrialization and general absolute private property. Indeed, all the authors so far considered ignore the notorious and persistent technicality and obscurity of English land law. This survived at least until the reforms of 1925; and, thus, in turn, made all transactions in land extremely expensive in England.

This qualified notion of property, reaching back to the tenures of medieval feudalism, endured in practice despite the rise of an absolute conception of property. Indeed, in the very period when Marx, Macpherson (1978, pp. 3-11), Landes and others detect the growing ascendency of an absolute conception of property, R. S. Neale (1975) observes that the traditionally *qualified* institution of property was being evolved into a vital vehicle for industrialization. Neale contends that a ". . . flexible and functional, rather than absolute and categorical (institution of property) had developed in England by the second half of the 17th century . . ." (Neale, 1975, p. 95); and that this grew out of the changing needs of the *landed* rather than the demands of middle-class traders and industrialists or because of changes in ideology. Moreover, Neale asserts that this new flexible notion of property ". . . provides the legal and a good deal of the institutional framework which alone made possible the development of industrial capitalism in Britain" (Neale, 1979, p. 95). Because English land law recognized a wide and complex range of qualified property rights, private property rights were rarely absolute in practice.

> Thus, whatever the notion in regard to property held by economic and political theorists at the turn of the 17th and 18th centuries, society and law recognised divisibility of property titles and recognised legal titles to present and future income as property, now giving legal form to the notion that property was the product of labour and capital as well as the product of land and all three together . . . Law and society worked with a fee-simple tenure so spotted that the quantity of spots changed the quality of the beast. (Neale, 1979, p. 99)

He goes on to argue that although this flexible notion of property was originally created as a result of the needs and power of the landed, it was subsequently borrowed and exploited by the industrial sector for their own advantage—a phenomenon clearly exemplified in the gradual embourgeoisement of the trust.

Thus it seems that writers from diverse traditions have exaggerated the dominance of an absolute and exclusive conception of property since the seventeenth century; and correspondingly tend to ignore the role played by other conceptions of property ideologically, politically and economically.[2] Indeed, Neale rightly argues that an absolute conception of property, if put into practice, would ultimately constitute a brake upon the economic development of property and the ability to restrict the future alienation of that property. His work augments that of Macpherson (1978, pp. 3-11) by stressing the importance economically, of the traditional, flexible, qualified conception of private property in the seventeenth, eighteenth and nineteenth centuries. Thus, the legal conception of property became even more subtle and complex from the seventeenth century; and that whilst this more instrumental conception of property was no doubt originally shaped in the interests of the landed relative to those of trade, it was undoubtedly assisted by the fact that legal institutions such as the trust, the settlement and the mortgage had been refined by lawyers so as better to serve the need of the seventeenth century landed interest. In other words, changes *within* the law, as well as the power of the landed, brought about a more flexible and versatile conception of property in the seventeenth century.

Thus, the ideal of absolute ownership was qualified in practice by those very groups who, it is oft assumed, would benefit most from absolute ownership. Landowners sought legal restraints on ownership and use to ensure that property remained intact for the family over several generations. How was this qualification of property facilitated in law? There

> . . . was the traditional entail by which land was held by a tenant or holder without the power to sell, mortgage, or lease, the succession to the land being predetermined usually in favour of eldest sons, one after the other. The Whig aristocrats must have felt torn by their dynastic ambitions for their descendants, and on the other hand, by their own desires to be free from the restrictions imposed upon them by the dead hand of the past. The dynastic ideology was very important . . . (Atiyah, 1979, p. 88)

Now the principal medium through which the law served this ideology was the strict settlement of land, an elaborate legal device conceived by conveyancers at about the time of the Restoration. The strict settlement helped to perpetuate the great landed estates in the hands of eldest sons. It would also

> . . . provide for widows, younger sons, and daughters, and, above all, maintain the property intact—or preferably augmented—in the family. These competing family rights necessarily meant that the freedom of the land 'owner'—who was often no more than a tenant for life, or tenant in tail, legally speaking—was limited. The freedom of one generation was limited by that of earlier and later generations. (Atiyah, 1979, p. 88)

The strict settlement is one of the very few legal devices to which economic historians have afforded some attention. In particular, historians have scrutinized two interrelated features of the historical development of the strict settlement. First, there is an important debate concerning the role of strict settlement in the accumulation and preservation of the huge landed estates of England (Spring, 1964; Beckett, 1977; Bonfield, 1980). Second, the strict settlement and the political controversy surrounding the reform of land in nineteenth and twentieth century England have also interested historians (Offer, 1981). The former has raised important questions about the role of property law in the preservation and accumulation of private wealth, power and the patriarchal family. The latter has served to highlight the centrality of property, and the politics of property in nineteenth century life. Both have illuminated the role played by lawyers in economy and society, both as the ingenious inventors of forms of private ordering and organization designed to further certain interests and ends; and as the most powerful modern professional interest group—one which was able to play a leading role in the marginalization of land reform, and therefore the redistribution of wealth and power in the modern period.

The complex and contradictory relationship between the development of an absolute and a more qualified private property has yet to be adequately reconstructed. However, this section illustrates a number of issues raised by a history of law, economy and the state. For example, the loose fit between the idea of a legal concept such as 'property' and its operation in practice; the co-existence over long periods of competing conceptions and practices bearing the same name; and the manner in which a legal institution shaped with certain interests in mind, could be utilized to the benefit of different interests.

What is fairly clear is that by the late eighteenth century, property is increasingly becoming subsumed to contract, that is, taking on the qualities and functions of capital (Atiyah, 1979, pp. 102-111). All this is not to deny that the so-called rise of absolute private property did not occur; but merely to stress that both as an idea and as a practice, property and property law operated in more variegated fashion than has sometimes been recognized.

The plurality of law and legal institutions

What was or is meant by 'the law' and 'legal institutions' cannot be taken for granted. A legal system usually possesses a range of facilities which may be analytically distinguished and which need to be differentiated if the relation between law and economy is to be advanced beyond the level of simplistic hypothesis. Here, for example, one thinks of:

 (i) its procedures for establishing the facts and adjudication on the basis of those facts;
 (ii) general substantive rules which guide citizens, their legal advisors and adjudicators;
 (iii) appeal procedures, such as judicial review of the facts or law;
 (iv) the enforcement of judgements, that is, legal coercion;
 (v) its restitutive function;
 (vi) its capacity to act as an insurance against financial or physical loss, for instance, by way of contract;
 (vii) its provision for physical punishment signifying a 'public' wrong;

(viii) its ideological and symbolic dimensions, as distinct from its instru-
       mental concerns;
 (ix) its ability to provide a degree of private ordering and organization and,
       thus, a degree of autonomy from the legal order, for example, by
       resort to facilitative laws, such as the laws governing companies,
       families, land and contracts; and
  (x) its function of deterrence.

To emphasize the plurality of law and legal institutions sensitizes us to their
manifold dimensions thereby avoiding a monolithic usage. Moreover, attention
to legal pluralism assists us to escape from a definition of law that assumes that
the problems of ordering and organization are exclusively the domain of the
state. In other words, stress on legal pluralism is to recognize the complex
co-existence of state law regulation (such as statute law and court decisions) and
other systems of normative ordering such as custom and practice and indigenous
ordering such as the family, the company, the work place and business and social
networks (Cain, Fitzpatrick, Ignatieff and Sumner *infra* . . . Also, Thompson,
1971 and 1976; Moorhouse and Chamberlain, 1974; Mitchell, 1975; Foucault,
1979; Griffith, 1979; Joyce, 1980; Galanter, 1981). Sometimes these discrete but
intertwined systems complement one another; on other occasions they may
conflict or compete.

'The law' means different things to different individuals and groups. To the
small trader it may be a costly and inconvenient burden, to the lawyer it may be
the professional ideology of the legal profession; and to many lay persons, it may
be the stereotyped 'tough cop' of television fame. Similarly, the *form* of law, that
is, its general structure, its categories, methods and procedures must be
distinguished from its *content*, in the sense of particular case law or statutes,
facilitating or prohibiting certain behaviour. The latter, in turn, must be
distinguished from the *ideology* of the legal profession, by which is meant, for
example, that law is held out to be a science which lay persons cannot properly
understand (yet which is congruent with commonly held values), and that the
law is both apolitical and necessary. Additionally, form, content and ideology
must in turn be distinguished from the *structure* of the profession, for example,
that High Court judges must be barristers of 10 years standing and that there
exists a basic separation of solicitors from the bar (McBarnet and Moorhouse,
1977). One reason why these distinctions between form, content, ideology and
structure are important is that tensions may be generated within and between
one element and another. For example, at least in the modern period, the form of
law has defined relevant actors for legal purposes as individuals. Recovery is,
therefore, defined as recoupment by an individual for harm suffered by an
individual. Similarly, collectivities such as companies, trade unions and trusts
are also conceptualized as individuals. For legal purposes, this 'individuality' is
an abstraction, shorn of its particular context and its relative position and

power in society. As a result, substantial differences between relevant actors are obscured and ignored. Thus, the form of law may tend to narrowly define legal issues and, therefore, reinforce systematic inequalities. This is memorably conveyed in Anatole France's famous, ironic praise of "the majestic equality of the French law, which forbids both rich and poor from sleeping under the bridges of the Seine". Furthermore, the individuating, abstract form of law ". . . serves as an additional barrier to organisation of the under-dog to upset existing social arrangements . . ." (Tushnet, 1977, p. 102). In other words, because the legal form is inherently individualized, the expression of collective interests tends to be discouraged. Because the form of law adheres to a formal rather than a substantive conception of justice, the legal system may ratify itself merely by observing formal procedures or 'precedent'. Here is an instance of a wider phenomenon: namely, that the law participates ". . . in the construction of the social world, populating it with creatures of law's own devising, abstract self-determining individuals and artificial corporate persons, ascribing 'interests' to them and deciding when their sufferings are recognizable 'harms' " (Gordon, 1981b, p. 1035).

Given a conceptual awareness of the distinctions between form, content, ideology and structure, there exists additionally, a need for the historical study of law, economy and the state to give somewhat greater attention to the similarities and differences between the civil and criminal law at these levels. Especially fruitful will be those studies that examine the inter-face and inter-action between civil and criminal institutions, for example, in the context of indebtedness, bankruptcy, corporate liquidation and the regulation of trade unions. Similarly, the public law (administrative and constitutional law) interface with private law may prove especially insightful in a study of the formation of the modern state. Maitland has warned that,

> . . . there is hardly any department of law which does not, at one time or another, become of constitutional importance . . . If we are to learn anything about the constitution, it is necessary first and foremost that we should learn a good deal about the land law . . . (Indeed) our whole constitutional law seems at times to be but an appendix to the law of real property . . . (Do) not get into the way of thinking of law as consisting of a number of independent compartments . . . so that you can learn the contents of one compartment, and know nothing as to what is in the others. No, law is a body, a living body, every member of which is connected with and depends upon every other member. (Maitland, 1908, pp. 538-539)

In addition, a historical understanding of the relations between law, economy and society can only be advanced where a pluralistic conception of legal phenomena is acknowledged and differentiated. Thus, one cannot conceive of law as exclusively pertaining to the decisions of The Royal Courts in the Strand, or to the enactments of Parliament. For if we are to secure an accurate account of the impact and usage of law in economic affairs during the later eighteenth and nineteenth centuries, the role of local courts, legal literature ('academic' and 'practical'), the private law-making of lawyers, custom and practice among different and differing interest groups within the economy, the influence of or administration by quasi or non-legal personnel, the tensions between local and central regulation, indigenous vs state conceptions of legality, discretionary practices and enforcement, arbitration and other extra-legal mechanisms for dispute resolution, are just some of the other phenomena that must be considered. What links if any existed as between these different facets of ordering and organization? Were they mutually dependent and functionally related or was their inter-action problematic?

Ideological Dimensions of Law

Law's legitimation function

The ideological role of the law, especially its legitimation function, is of central importance in the historical study of law and economy. Thus, the law's role in justifying the world and existing power relations in civil society to both rulers and the ruled, thereby inducing willed obedience, cannot be neglected. Some of the major issues are the ideological role of commercial law in conceptualizing business practices; the relationship between legal and dominant ideology, or legal and indigenous ideologies; the diverse dimensions and functions of law as ideology; and the extent to which legal ideology is absorbed, modified or rejected by different classes or interest groups. For example, what role did private law play in facilitating and legitimating absolute private conceptions of property and also the moral ethos associated with mid-Victorian, middle-class England, for instance, self-responsibility, self-help, enlightened self-interest and the work ethic?

While recognizing that one function of ideology is to confer legitimacy on an institution, it nonetheless remains true that the empirical meaning of legitimacy in this context, that is, what individuals actually know or care about the legal system and how this influences, if at all, their conduct, has tended to be ignored or treated as self-evident both in the realm of history and in the sociology of law. If a gulf exists between the law in action and the (occasionally competing) values by which it claims legitimacy (for example, the values of equality, freedom of speech and expression, individuality and community), or if the law and an individual's economic self-interest are in conflict, to what extent is this perceived and if so, how? (Cf. Abel, 1977). Is the supposed legitimacy of the law eroded as a result? If so, with what consequences? A theoretically informed history of law, economy and the state might be able to provide some much needed data in respect of questions of this kind. In any such work, monolithic and question-begging conceptions of 'public opinion' and 'class interest' must give way to a recognition that individuals vary in their perceptions and experience of the legal system and of the gulf between, on the one hand, the ideals and rhetoric of the law, and, on the other hand, the reality of the law in practice. In part, this is to warn, as will be remarked later, against accepting at face-value, or generalizing from, the legal profession's own pronouncements as to the centrality, purity and legitimacy of 'the law', declarations that often are little more than self-serving. On the other hand, one must beware of engaging in crude economic reductionism which views the legal professions as wholly reflective of the aims of capital or the state. Instead, there is a need to reconstruct an individual's perhaps complex and contradictory perception and experience of the legal system and of the values which that system supposedly imbibes. It would seem that there may be a tension between belief about the law and experience of the law. Law may be experienced as a coercive instrument held *in terrorem* or as a liberating 'tool', or as something which confirms the individual's sense of helplessness and dependency. Is the law an arena wherein it was possible to advance certain political or social values (Thompson, 1975, pp. 258-269; Brewer, 1980)? The tactical use of the law as a tool in negotiation both by and with authority offers one specific perception which may not gel with more romanticized accounts of law as a preserver of liberty on the one hand or as a tool of class repression on the other. Another is the seemingly tenacious existence of behaviour inconsistent with the state law order (Hay *et al.*, 1975; Stevenson, 1979; Brewer and Styles, 1980; Jones, 1982). To what extent are status, class, sex, age, family relations and geographic location important variables in mediating between perception and experience of law in history? Until we know more about the answers to these kinds of questions as well as about the motives and mores grounding the use or non-use of the law in specific contexts by individuals (which may, in turn, be influenced by the nature of the wrong, the remedies available and the relation between the parties concerned), then the legitimacy or otherwise of the criminal and civil law will escape our understanding.

Law and social control

In the last decade, especially with the eruption of a sizeable body of social history, the regulation of *social* behaviour through the instrumentality of the law has been afforded special attention. Some of this work has been at pains to explore the law as a mode of organizing beliefs and values (influenced, in part, by Gramsci's notion of "hegemony") and as a means of "social control" — in addition to law as a directly coercive weapon (Sugarman, 1981, pp. 81-98). This body of work has the virtue of transcending the tendency to treat law exclusively as a directly coercive behavioural injunction. It recognizes that:

> Among other things it (the law) includes educational efforts, rewards and other incentives, symbolic deployment of legal forms, publicity (favourable or adverse), continuous supervision, public signs and signals, recognised statutes and entities, grants with strings attached, and on and on and on. (Summers, 1977, p. 126)

Thus, in terms of its non-directly coercive facets, the law has been viewed as an instrument (together with the school system, religions, the work place and other institutions and activities) by which certain attitudes tend to be eclipsed whilst others tend to be disseminated. It is the law's educational, disciplining, symbolic and related ideological facets which have in recent years been stressed in a number of historical and sociological studies touching on law and legal institutions. The strength and weakness of this approach are well illustrated in the recent development of a revisionist history of the prison and punishment (Ignatieff, *infra*).

Some uses of 'social control' and 'hegemony' have been consciously and unconsciously premised upon an extremely functionalist model of society and a simplistic conception of ideology as 'a trick' or 'false consciousness'. The nature and extent of ideological control has therefore been substantially overstated. Gareth Stedman Jones, in an early and important critique, pointed out that:

> It is not difficult to demonstrate that a casual usage of 'social control' metaphors leads to non-explanation and incoherence. There is no political or ideological institution which could not in some way be interpreted as an agency of social control . . . It is as if . . . the . . . masses . . . were simply a blank page upon which each successive stage of capitalism has successfully imposed its imprint. (Jones, 1977, p. 164)

It is also misconceived in so far as it assumes that the coercive and ideological weaponry of law and state are *the* cement of the social order; and that the state possess a *monopoly* power to discipline and punish. The potential for embourgeoisement by social control must be seen in the context of the co-existence of a plurality of orderings and organizations, state, non-state and anti-state, shaped from "below" as well as "above" (Ignatieff, *infra*; Thompson, 1981). This plurality of normative systems and the individuals and social groups that construct, apply and defend them, refract, mediate, obstruct or reinforce the state law order. In short, emphasis on the plurality of ordering and organization constitutes a vital step towards breaking loose of all-embracing conceptions of social control which minimize human agency. Indeed, in the light of our earlier discussions, the widespread existence and utilization of alternative forms of normative ordering, the patchy application and enforcement of state law norms, the selective, pragmatic use of the state legal order by its clientele[3] and the significance of regional variations, the role of 'ordering from above' as a fully-fledged agency of social control in eighteenth and nineteenth century England, increasingly looks double-edged and problematic. Increasingly the notion of 'social control' looks rather less like a solution than a short-cut both to some old intractable problems and to new modes of conceptualization. This does not, by implication, invalidate the critique mounted of conventional histories of crime, punishment and popular recreations; nor the revisionists' quest for 'connections' between law and the political, social and economic order.

The historical specificity of ideologies

Clearly, the way we conceptualize the historical specificity of ideologies is extremely important. A step towards a new way of theorizing capitalist societies, and the role of law as ideology therein, has been taken in recent work on theories of ideology (Althusser, 1977, pp. 141-159; Williams, 1977, esp. pp. 55-71; Foucault, 1979, pp. 91-102 and 1980, pp. 109-133; Hirst, 1979). This work has shown the inadequacy of thinking of ideology as existing within a separate domain of ideas, or as an unreal or illusory reflection of social relations. As John Urry explains,

> ... there is nothing unified about 'ideology' and that much of what is located under that category is properly to be seen simply as differentiated, diverse and hetrogeneous social practices. Certain of these are linked fairly directly to capitalist social relations, others most definitely are not. (Urry, 1981, p. 57)

In part, this work is but one instance of a wider movement: a movement which recognizes the need to develop a new history and theory of capitalist society ". . . which does not presume that such societies are functionally ordered and cohesive with an effective incorporation of the subordinate social forces through a dominant ideology" (Urry, 1981, pp. 6-7). Real advances will require that the new theories of ideologies are tested and refined in conjunction with historical studies of real people and real communities. In particular, just as the state has no monopoly over the power of coercion, so the 'ideological state apparatuses' or 'economy' are not the sole institutions which produce ideological effects, though clearly they may be very important. This is merely to recognize the multiplicity and diversity of social groups and practices within capitalist societies and that some of these may exert significant ideological effects. This recognition serves as a useful counter to those concepts of ideology which lead either to an over-extension of the capital-relation, or, an over-extension of the role of the state.

The problems raised by the historical study of law as ideology and social control are similar to those we encounter in the study of the relation between law, economic interests and the state—the subject matter of our next section. Our discussion of these general problems, and some possible ways of overcoming them, is continued there.

Law, State and Economic Interests

What was the relationship between law, legal change and the formation of the modern state? The political significance of the modern English state stems, in part, from the fact that the political 'shell' it inhabits is that of a representative democracy. What was the relation between the law, legal thought and lawyers and the adoption and preservation of a democratic form of state?

Inter- and intra-class conflict and the law

The view that law, state and the 'ruling class' are mutually reinforcing largely derives from much interesting work on the relation between 'authority' and the operation of the *criminal* law and its institutions in the early modern and modern periods (for example, Hay *et al.* (Eds), 1975; Thompson, 1975; Ignatieff, *infra*; Philips, 1977). This research has tended, in its neglect of private law, to focus attention upon the manner in which the strongest economic and political interests and/or the state dominated weaker groups in society. In other words, it has concentrated upon *inter-class* 'domination' and the consequences thereof for the interests of the 'dominated'. The study of *intra-class* conflicts *within* groups such as the working classes, the City, the landed, mercantile and industrial interests—and the role of the law in their resolution—has correspondingly been ignored. Often there is a tendency to treat the ideology and interests of the respective groups as self-evident and homogeneous. By exploring both the criminal *and* the civil law and their respective institutions as fora for intra-, as well as inter-class conflict resolution, a more complete and accurate picture of the relationship between law and industrialization, and its problematic qualities can be grasped. For example, in respect of intra-class disputes, how did Parliament and the courts balance the property rights of the landed to enjoy their land with the necessity of factory owners and railway contractors to develop their land in a manner likely to affect that enjoyment? What role did the law play in mediating and legitimizing disputes between, say, insurers and those requiring cover against risks; company directors and promoters as against shareholders and creditors; large firms at odds with small firms; or those Manchester industrialists who favoured free trade vs inventors who stressed that the monopoly conferred by patents was in the public interest? What were the outcomes of these conflicts: who won, how and why? What was the economic and social impact of legal dispute settlement of this kind within and as between classes?

The popular legitimacy of the law

The examples in intra-class disputes above could suggest that the primary fora for perhaps the bulk of intra-class dispute settlement at law lies within the province of the *civil*, rather than the criminal law; and that given the cost of going to law, and thus the relatively large sums involved, the main protagonists were likely to be middling to substantial property owners. However, it is too simplistic to treat the criminal law as merely that arena where, in the bulk of cases, the law was imposed upon the labouring class by an impersonal state or 'the bourgeois class'; that, in short, it was simply a locus of class conflict. The work of David Philips suggests that by the mid-nineteenth century a significant percentage of prosecutions (20% in the Black Country) were brought by unskilled workers against other members of their class (Philips, 1977). *Use* of the law, however, does not of itself denote a general belief in the legitimacy of the law or even of a particular law or institution. For instance, at the very same time as workers were bringing a significant proportion of prosecutions for theft, the new model police were encountering bitter (and sometimes violent) popular resistance; and poaching and other 'crimes' continued to enjoy popular legitimacy (Hay *et al.* (Eds), 1975; Jones, 1982; Sugarman *et al.*, 1982). This suggests a variegated, selective, pragmatic approach to the use and popular legitimacy of the criminal law by the working classes (Hay, 1980, pp. 72-75) not unlike that which we seem to have found in the context of the civil law and its use by the middle and landed classes. Thus, it is too simplistic to characterize the criminal and civil law wholly in terms of a locus of class conflict or consensus. As was indicated above, the sheer complexity of the questions surrounding the popular legitimacy of the law and attitudes thereto—as well as our lack of sufficient knowledge—is likely to make such generalization extremely misleading.

The heterogeneity of civil society

In this essay, it has been emphasized that law cannot be viewed as an un-differentiated unity. The different parts of the law, legal institutions and the legal professions and the manifold facilities they offer are ". . . differently integrated . . ." into the state and civil society (Urry, 1981, p. 115). This, amongst other things, makes it very difficult to conceive of the law as simply part of the capitalist base or of the superstructure. Equally, the objections to the view that law is coterminous with the state or directly derived from capital seem fundamental. Indeed, once the problems of ordering and organization become viewed pluralistically—that is, once it is recognized that certain aspects of ordering and organization are either outside the state proper, such as indigenous, customary or informal rights and practices, or connected to the state's coercive powers in complex and indirect ways, as with facilitative laws—these reductionist characterizations become untenable.

The best of the recent histories of crime, for example, have revealed the tentativeness, variability and complexity of developments in the procedures and institutions of eighteenth and nineteenth century justice. Changes in legal controls are seen as unplanned and highly contingent stopgaps as much as systematic and calculated efforts to contain the conflicts of the emerging market economy. Different social groups might vary in their responses to changes in policing. Further, the alignments were rarely clear-cut and predictable. For instance, Victor Bailey's fine study of the policing of "outcast London" in the 1880's, especially the Trafalgar Square riots of 1886-87, brings to light the disagreements over the proper methods of control between the Chief Commissioner, the judiciary and the Home Secretary. The gradual spread of national uniformity in policing co-existed alongside differing tempos and configurations of development in specific localities (Bailey, 1981). This kind of work constitutes a powerful counter to those who see the whole story in terms of escalating social control. However, different regional patterns do not necessarily mean that changes in policing and punishment were unrelated to the longer-term patterns discernable, for example, in prison building and in the criminal statistics (see Gatrell *et al.* (Eds), 1980, pp. 238-338).

The symbolic dimensions of the law

The problematic role of the state in relation to the law, especially during the period described as *laissez-faire*, is amply exposed when we consider the apparent contradiction of a 'legal abstentionist' state authorizing the enactment of such measures as the Factories Acts and the Companies Acts 1825-62 or, indeed, the other vast array of regulatory legislation. Whence did these statutes spring? Which interests were advanced by their passing? Did such measures have any significant instrumental impact on the economy? Perhaps the significance of much of the legislation of that era is to be found more in their symbolic appeal, or in satisfying the political or status demands of their sponsors or supporters. The complex and dynamic interaction between symbolic and instrumental concerns has been described in several valuable 'emergence studies' in which attention is focussed upon the origins and generation of specific legislative enactments and (though less frequently) the impact of the legislation in question (Anderson, 1971; Carson, 1974). Moreover, such an analysis is not limited to explaining how legislation comes about, but also seeks to explain why laws might remain unrepealed, despite their apparent ineffectiveness and the power of legal ritual (Hay *et al.*, (Eds) 1975, pp. 17-63; Roeber, 1980).

Law, state and the rise of capitalism

A leading business historian has argued that, "Historically, the most important way in which the state stimulated industrial growth in a capitalist setting was through its ability to restructure the institutions of society—i.e. through its ability to create a capitalist setting in the first instance" (Supple, 1973, p. 307). What role did the law (including legal institutions and the legal professions) play in sustaining, constituting, legitimating, or restraining the creation of this 'capitalist setting' by the state? This essay cannot hope to offer more than the briefest incursion into what is a vast and highly controversial area.

For Marx, "the expropriation of the agricultural producer, of the free peasant, from the soil" (Marx, 1976, pp. 899-900) and, thus, the rise of an absolute and exclusive private property were the basis for the emergence of capitalism. "The conditions in which the 'natural laws' of political economy could operate had to be forcibly *constructed*" (Corrigan and Sayer, 1981, p. 22). The role of the law in this process was undoubtedly multifaceted. It both confined and orchestrated the 'expropriation' of free peasant and common land. The Enclosure Acts, for instance, helped to destroy independent small-holdings and created a class of landless labourers whose livelihood depended entirely on employment by landowning farmers or (later) factory owners.

> Enclosure Acts are part of a wider, and centuries-long, transformation of communal and feudal into *private* property, within which not only who owned what but what it meant to be an owner were turned upside down. It is a far cry from feudal tenure to the *jus utendi et abutendi*, from the complicated network of personal lordship and servitude, substantial right and obligation, which enmeshed lord and serf, to the substantially rightless but formally free wage labourer voluntarily contracting with his or her chosen employer. Property did not have just to be seized, it had to be *constituted*. (Corrigan and Sayer, 1981, p. 23)

The wider transformation operated at a number of levels. Socially, it encouraged ". . . the kind of progress that meant the factory bell, the workhouse, and a loss of liberty however limited" (Richards, 1979, p. 113)—a kind of progress which some social groups rejected and tried to resist. Over the centuries, previously non-criminal activity became criminalized. They were, variously, civil offences that became criminalized; traditional perquisites of employment (such as the coal hewer's allowance of fuel, the shipwright's right to take for firewood the chips that fell from the axe and the cooper's established claim to the draining of molasses and spilt sugar on the floor of the warehouse); and legal rights associated with common land and common rights (such as the small animals and fish found on common land, which were a valuable source of food for people as well as animals); other widespread rights on the commons included pasturage for cattle and fowl, turfing and wood gathering. Legislation outlawed workers' combinations, enlarged the working day and fixed wages (Sugarman et al., 1982). The doctrine of freedom of contract was perhaps in part a response to the intrusiveness of the mercantilist state; that is, part of an attempt to bring the capricious, privileged and corrupt power of the eighteenth-century state within greater control than previously. For some people it may have encouraged self-responsibility and a degree of individual self-determination.[4] Like today's "authoritarian populism", it addressed ". . . real problems, real and lived experiences, real contradictions" (Hall, 1979, p. 5). But alongside these features, however, it underpinned a new conception of labour as a 'marketable commodity'. The freedom of contract doctrine also constituted a powerful intellectual and practical obstacle foreclosing state intervention on behalf of the casualties of the newly ascendent market economy. On the other hand, beginning in the 1840's, the English state also intervened to provide tighter and wider protection for workers. Does the latter indicate a shift in the character of the nineteenth century state, into a more neutral stance as between capital and labour; or, is it simply an instance of where sufficient political power forced major law reforms (Richards, 1979, p. 115)?

The mid-nineteenth century state was not simply the pliant instrument of capital nor, indeed, any other influential group. An increasing band of state administrators, officers and experts were interposed between the influenced nineteenth century policy-making (Corrigan, 1977 and Corrigan (Ed.), 1980; Finer, 1952; Parris, 1969). True, the elitist structure of the civil service and the old patronage persisted long after the Northcote-Trevelyan Report and the advent of open competition in 1870. Sometimes this state expertise was undoubtedly used as an ideological resources against working-class causes. On other occasions, however, it conflicted with the interests of employers who sought to evade or neutralize the newly-emerging protections for the health and safety of labour (Bartrip and Fenn, 1980, pp. 184-185). State servants and others may act as if the state has interests of its own (see Skocpol, 1979, pp. 24-33). In addition, although the influence of religious and humanitarian opinion has probably been exaggerated by some historians, and although their motivation was undoubtedly problematic, neither can their sway and prevalence be ignored. Residual paternalism, the need to prevent revolution and the influence of Benthamism (both its 'individualistic' and 'collectivistic' strands) have also been shown to have exercised influence upon and within the nineteenth century state. If, therefore, we cannot simply reduce the nineteenth century state to the needs

of capital, it should not be concluded that the state was unimportant to the requirements of capitalism. As our discussion above testifies. Supple is undoubtedly
correct when he warns that: "before we conclude that the first Industrial
Revolution owed everything to the market and nothing to government, it is worth
remembering that the very characteristics of the market environment which
distinguished Britain's position from that of other European countries were in
large part a function of *state* action" (Supple, 1973, pp. 314-315, my emphasis).

In fact, the evidence is clear that *laissez-faire* and state interventionism were
not polar opposites but rather, different sides of the same coin: both co-existed in
nineteenth century England. State action and, therefore, the law were essential to
the creation of *laissez-faire*—a paradox which few historians of nineteenth
century government have recognized (see Polanyi, 1944, pp. 135-150 and
Supple, 1973). Unfortunately, the historical debate as to whether there ever was
an age of *laissez-faire* has unwittingly served to narrow or exclude the kind of
questions, issues and concerns that require investigation if we are to decipher the
formation and changing nature of the modern state. As R. A. Lewis observed,
"Historians of 19th century government growth are still in the position of the
three blind men handling various parts of the elephant, and speculating from
limited data and much conjecture as to the exact nature of the beast" (Lewis,
1974).

Central state versus local state

The state in eighteenth and nineteenth century Britain was not a centralized,
rational monolith. The law (civil and criminal), ". . . along with many other
political and economic functions, continued in large part to be located at a local
level . . . This dichotomy (local/centre) within the state structure provides . . .
(a) principal axis along which" (Hogg, 1979, p. 7) conflicts over law, state,
society and economy are to be understood.

> Pivotal in the local/central struggle were the local justices of the peace who
> were (in the 18th and early 19th centuries at least) in most cases, tied very
> strongly to the landed gentry and the traditional pattern of social relations,
> and who fulfilled crucial administrative, as well as judicial, functions; in the
> transitional period they became the effective focus of local power and
> government. Justices . . . found themselves with responsibility for the bulk
> of the civil administration of the country—bridges, gaols, houses of correc-
> tion, wages, prices, markets, enclosures, licensing, turnpikes, administration of
> poor relief, etc. All key functions in a developing country. (Hogg, 1979, p. 7)

In the nineteenth century, the imperatives of local, political and financial
administration hindered, for instance, the creation of a national police force and

prison system (Philips, 1977, pp. 53-95; Ignatieff, 1978, pp. 95-109). The political struggles around this dichotomous state structure constitute an important, though oft overlooked, factor delimiting and mediating between law, state and material society, in the modern period.

One aspect of this struggle was the tension between, on the one hand, the tradition of local and special courts and, on the other hand, a formal state system of courts. By the mid-nineteenth century, the latter had eclipsed the former. To some extent, the economic self-interest of the legal profession and its ". . . ideological opposition to the underlying values and public policies served by . . ." local and special courts account for their suppression (Arthurs, forthcoming). However, in his pioneering work on the evolution of English administrative law, Harry Arthurs suggests that

> at the very moment when the common law courts seemed to be achieving an adjudicative monopoly, they were challenged by new manifestations of pluralism, principally commercial arbitration (which, in fact, was not new at all) and the administrative regimes which were established with increasing frequency from the 1830's onwards . . . Whether . . . (the task) involved the resolution of commercial disputes, or the implementation of new, inter-ventionist public policies, 'law' — in the formal sense — could not do what needed to be done. (Arthurs, forthcoming)

In public law, as in private law, the state legal order was a last resort rather than imbricated in the day-to-day activities of public administration.

The modern state, public law and regulatory agencies

But what of Dicey's famous remark that, "There exists in England no true *droit administratif*"? (Dicey, 1885, p. 390). It is now generally recognized that Dicey wholly misled lawyers and others to believe that England possessed no administrative law at all (Cosgrove, 1980, pp. 91-113). In fact, administrative law (as opposed to judicial review) grew rapidly in the nineteenth century; and that it was quite well developed by 1870 (Arthurs, forthcoming).

Alongside the growth of public law, at both a local and central level, we find the central courts generally averse to involvement in the day-to-day adminis-tration of the nineteenth-century state. The English judges of the latter half of the nineteenth century seem more afraid of intervention in the economy by the state or the overt politicization of their position in the public's eye than of the abuse of private power (Stevens, 1979, pp. 133-184). Their antagonism towards administrative law, fuelled by Dicey's edict that administrative law was both un-British and inconsistent with the Rule of Law, caused Parliament, from the turn of this century, deliberately to bypass the courts so that, for example, under the new social security legislation of 1908–11, appeals to the courts were strenuously avoided. "By 1920, therefore, the judges had been removed, had removed themselves or been restrained from entering large areas of competence in the modern state" (Abel-Smith and Stevens, 1967, p. 117).

If the courts were unenthusiastic about controlling the abuse of public power, how successful were the new regulators and regulatory agencies in the imposition, policing and enforcement of a plethora of minimum standards, in a variety of contexts? Indeed, there are a host of questions relating to the nature, scope and effectiveness of the new regulatory public law and its agencies (local and national) to which too little attention has been afforded. Yet clearly the historical development of modern public law (by which is meant administrative agencies and procedures of a quasi- or non-judicial kind) may have much to tell us about business–state relations, as well as about the changing nature and scope of the modern state.

For example, to what extent did the growth of regulatory agencies preserve the 'public interest' (an elastic mandate, to which all interests seek to identify themselves) as against the particular interests of those directly involved in and effected by regulation? Did a conception of the 'public interest' emerge from within the process of regulation; or, was it submerged by vying interests seeking to benefit from state regulation? To what extent did regulatory functions conflict within and as between different regulatory agencies?: who won, how and why? What did business want to obtain from regulation and what did they receive in practice? How did regulatory agencies and regulators choose between and balance up the competing interests of industrial and business competitors within a particular industry or sector?; or, the interests of labour and consumers as against those of the regulated? What was the impact of industrial pressure on the shape of regulatory legislation and the policies adopted by regulatory agencies? What have been the economic effects of regulation?

How did regulation and the attitudes of both regulators and those regulated change over time? Was regulation and the attitudes it engendered different as between different industries and sectors? Did regulators conceive of their roles as that of a watch-dog or as a neutral umpire, holding the balance between business and employees or consumers? In so far as administrative regulations departed from the procedural norms of the judicial process, have those regulated been treated more unfairly and prejudicially as a result? Has the machinery for making administrative regulatory decisions tended towards more political decision-making than that of the judicial process?

In answering some of these questions, we can draw, in part, on some of the excellent studies of nineteenth century state servants and more directly still, their reports, papers as well as several of the most famous Blue Books of the nineteenth century (Finer, 1952; Parris, 1969; Corrigan, 1977). In addition, some of the areas regulated, notably, the area of safety at work, have been the subject of illuminating historical studies (see Hutchins and Harrison, 1903; Thomas, 1948; Ward, 1970; Carson, 1974).

Towards an Intellectual History of Law, Economy and the State

Here we return to the debate over the alleged autonomy or relative autonomy of law from economic determinism. What were the major intellectual currents which helped to shape modern law and which law assisted in shaping? To what extent did the intellectual structure of the law ('legal consciousness') mediate, impede or facilitate the influence of economic interests and other desiderata on lawyers and law-making?

Recently, important advances have been made in attempting to relate the development of modern legal doctrine in England to economic, social and political ideas. Atiyah's work on the relation between contract law and the rise of classical political economy is probably the most important intellectual history of English law published this century (Atiyah, 1979. Cf. Mensch, 1981). Similar, though more modest, work in related areas include: Brenner's examination of nuisance law during the Industrial Revolution; and Danzig's examination of the leading damages case in contract, *Hadley* v. *Baxendale* (Brenner, 1974, Danzig, 1975).

Moreover, research has highlighted the rich variety of intellectual stimuli on nineteenth century legal science. For example, the influence of German legal and historical writings on legal jurists—in particular Savigny, Ihering and Gierke; the influence of social evolutionism and the comparativist method of Victorian anthropology and philology; the appropriation and incorporation of civil law ideas by judges and jurists; the influence of Roman Law on 'legal science'; the reciprocal influence of legal scholars associated with the Law Schools of Harvard, Oxford and (to a lesser extent) Cambridge; and the general and long-standing influence of the natural sciences methodology on the rhetoric and aspirations of legal scholarship (for example, Burrow, 1966; Simpson, 1975; Sugarman and Rubin, forthcoming). The links between the aspirations of university liberal law scholars such as Austin, Maine, Dicey and Bryce (who formed part of a new 'intellectual aristocracy'), national politics and the fears aroused by the extension of the franchise and democracy has also begun to be explored (Sugarman, 1983, pp. 106-110). From a very different perspective, Michel Foucault has uncovered the rise of similar social institutions designed for social control in law, medicine, education and the workplace (for example, Foucault, 1980).

The period *circa* 1860 to 1900 is of special interest. In a whole series of ways the relation between the individual and the state was being re-examined.

> The change from social contractarianism to legal positivism may not, at first, have carried much political significance. But these changing ways of thinking about the relation between the individual and the state were ultimately to be of profound importance . . . Inevitably, the command theory (of legal positivism) carried with it implications about majority rule. If the sovereign could command, he could coerce; indeed, the whole essence of a law was that it was a command backed by a sanction. There was no longer any question about assuming that the fundamental principles of the state could not be altered without the broad consent of the landowning, or any class. Every class was now at the mercy of a Parliamentary majority. (Atiyah, 1979, p. 342)

This, in turn, provoked a significant debate concerning the separation (or otherwise) of law and morality. The inability to confront the consequences of this 'legitimation crisis' encouraged the adoption of a new concept of social contract, that is, a new mode of reconciling law, state and the consent of the people: namely, 'public opinion'. 'Public opinion' was the conduit pipe through which the law, state and economy achieved a degree of moral and democratic legitimacy. In a period when the legitimacy of law and legal obedience was being questioned both externally, in terms of the legitimacy of Britain's imperial hegemony, especially in India and Ireland, and internally, in respect of the growing economic and political power of the working classes, this debate carried with it not inconsiderable political overtones too.

The growing power and autonomy of large companies, trades unions and an increasingly 'interventionist' state helped generate an important intellectual debate concerning the nature, scope and legitimacy of this legal, political and economic 'pluralism'. Did not the growth of corporations or quasi-corporations (i.e. of bodies autonomous or semi-autonomous of the state legal order) fundamentally challenge the traditional notion of society as composed of individuals whose collective embodiment is the state with whom (metaphorically speaking) they have individual contracts? Did it not require a new way of conceiving of the relation between individuals and state; and a new way, both sociologically and legally, of conceiving of corporate associations? For Maitland, this meant the acceptance of "the realities" of a plurality of overlapping social groups and ". . . the reversal of Maine's *laissez-faire* individualist version of progress from status to contracts . . ." (Burrow, 1974, p. 283):

> Nowadays it is difficult to get the corporation out of our heads. If we look at the doings of our law courts, we may feel inclined to revise a famous judgement and to say that while the individual is the unit of ancient, the corporation is the unit of modern law. (Maitland, 1898, p. 133, cited Burrow, 1974, p. 283)

In respect to the role of ideas in legal history, legal historians, in particular, have been prone to insist on the autonomy of the law. They tend to regard the ideas and doctrines formulated by judges and legal scholars as the exclusive determinant of legal development. Is the choice simply between those accounts which are reductionist, that is, generally assume that law, state and ideology are decisively shaped, albeit sometimes in a complex and mediated fashion, by the nature of economy; and, those accounts which are autonomist? In the United States, several recent legal histories argue for versions of the 'relative autonomy' thesis in new and challenging ways.

G. Edward White's history of American tort law, for instance, regards ideas as a principal, but not complete, explanation of legal causation (White, 1980. Cf. Gordon, 1981a). He is critical of those who have ascribed the emergence of an independent identity for torts, and, in particular, the tort of negligence in the late nineteenth century, to industrialization and to an accident problem of hitherto unprecedented dimensions. "The emergence of Torts as a distinct branch of law", claims White, "owed as much to changes in jurisprudential thought as to the spread of industrialisation" (White, 1980, p. 3). The fact that industrialization transformed the typical forms of tortious injury from that between individuals in a close relation to one another, to one between strangers, was undoubtedly important. But a new law of torts, characterized by broad principles, did not simply arise in response thereto. White stresses that the death of the writ system required both changes of a procedural kind and a profound restructuring of the intellectual foundations of law. Negligence provided a new conceptual basis with which to underpin the law of private wrongs. Further, this shift to broad principles was also stimulated by the intellectual preoccupations of the age. In an effort to construct order out of the increasingly fragmented world of nineteenth century society, systematization and the articulation of broad general principles became a major object of Victorian intellectuals. Legal scholars reflected this concern also. Two of America's leading legal conceptualizers, St John Green and Holmes, played a central role in the reconstruction of the intellectual foundations of tort law in a new, broad and unified scheme. Unlike his earlier work, the causal connections posited by White are much more complex; legal thought is no longer simply the reflection of a particular social and political *milieu*. Instead, the history of the intellectual form and structure of the law is treated as a discrete realm capable of analysis in its own terms, alongside more overtly 'economic' interpretations of legal evolution. In part, White conceives of this approach as a counter to excessively economistic histories of law.

Other American legal historians have also been concerned with the history of legal thought, specifically with the historical specificity of legal categorizing and reasoning (legal consciousness). Modern Anglo-American legal historiography has been largely devoted to explaining ". . . which, among various historical forces 'caused' a particular judicial decision" (Vandevelde, 1980, p. 326). Duncan Kennedy and others, however, adopt a focus wholly outside this approach to legal history.

> Rather than attempting to explain the cause of particular decisions, it attempts to describe the structure of legal thought. The difference lies both in using a purely descriptive rather than explanatory approach, and in examining the structure of an entire conceptual scheme rather than the outcomes of particular decisions. The effort is not to explain why a particular side won on a given day, but to describe the conceptual apparatus by which the court justified its decisions. (Vandevelde, 1980, p. 326)

This approach stems from the belief that a description of the form of legal thought over time is crucial in the study of legal history, regardless of whether one sees legal thought as a dependent or independent variable. By concentrating on the conceptual structure it is hoped to overcome a major drawback of that approach which focusses on the forces which caused particular decisions or doctrine, especially instrumentalist approaches: namely, ". . . that of attributing so much importance to particular outcomes within the (legal) framework that the framework itself becomes invisible" (Kennedy, 1979, p. 220). But what exactly is meant by legal thought or structure? In essence, it means ". . . the activity of categorizing, analysing, and explaining legal rules" (Kennedy, 1979, p. 210). As Vandevelde puts it,

> Legal thought is, in essence, the process of categorization. The lawyer is taught to place phenomena into categories such as fact or law, substance or process, public or private, contract or tort, and foreseeable and unforeseeable, to name but a few. Categorizing phenomena determines how they will be treated by the legal system . . . The task of the legal historian who examines . . . legal thought is to explore the origins and structures of the categories." (Vandevelde, 1980, p. 327)

This approach has grounded historical investigations of the concepts of form and substance in private law adjudication (Kennedy, 1975-6), the conceptual structure of Blackstone's *Commentaries* and their influence on and relation to liberal legalism (Kennedy, 1979), the City as a legal concept (Frug, 1980), the transformation of the concepts of property, contract and tort (Anonymous, 1980 and Vandevelde, 1980) and the structure of classical legal thought in America, 1850-1940 (Kennedy, 1980). It has the additional virtue of illuminating the ways conceptions of justice, legality, social needs and rights do not exist in a separate realm apart from law, but are constructed, in part, by the legal system itself (cf. Klare, 1979). Moreover, it has pointed to the way the ostensible values underpinning legal concepts and structures are often contradictory. The tensions this generates may partly or wholly explain certain changes in the form and content of law over time.

Another approach utilized in some intellectual histories of modern American law and scholarship is more directly concerned to relate law to the material world. Rather than relate legal change directly to, say, the distribution of property or the power of dominant economic interests, this work explores the striking intellectual parallels between law and other spheres such as history, politics and economics in terms of their common tasks, concerns and methods at a specific historic conjuncture (Gordon, 1978, p. 8 and 1981a, pp. 910-911). For instance, the revolt against legal formalism in America has been linked to a wider movement that embraced history, economics, philosophy and political science (White, 1957). In an excellent study, Edward Purcell has examined the ways in which the spread of pragmatism and scientific naturalism affected developments in philosophy, the social sciences and law in the years after 1910, and traces the effect of these developments on traditional assumptions of democratic theory (Purcell, 1973).

These three, albeit very different, analytic frameworks have the virtue of seeking to give due weight to *both* the power of economic interests in influencing the content of the law *and* the power of legal thought and consciousness as a distinct but important influence in the evolution of the law and legal institutions, thereby transcending the either-orism implied by the reductionism vs autonomism debate. They also serve to illuminate and provide a degree of specificity to our understanding of the relative autonomy of the law. Of course, it is essential to relate legal development to its economic, social and political context. But that context *also* includes language systems, patriarchy, ideas and beliefs as well as (say) the economic structure of society. These are often difficult to disentangle and in so far as they can be differentiated, relate to one another in highly complex ways. This is merely to warn against a reductionist interpretation that defines 'context' such that being artificially constricted to purely economic desiderata it therefore excludes a variety of other important social phenomena.

The Legal Professions

It will be clear from our discussion so far that to comprehend the relation between law, economy and the state, it will be necessary to understand the role of the legal professions. While it is hoped to explore aspects of this theme in more detail in a subsequent volume (Rubin and Sugarman (Eds.), forthcoming), some brief preliminary comments may be in order.

The work that does exist concerning the period since 1800, understandably perhaps, concentrates upon the relatively common background of bench and elite bar (public school, upper class etc.) and the very strong connections between Parliament and government, on the one hand, and members of the legal professions, on the other (Duman, 1982, 1983). In particular, it has been asserted that on occasions, the causal connections between the material or class self-interest of the courts and their actual decisions are extremely intense.

For example, Philips has shown that from the 1830's onwards, as the social composition of the Black Country magistracy changed from predominantly landed to predominantly industrialist, so the number of prosecutions for industrial theft increased markedly. Prosecutions were commonly brought by iron and coal masters—and it was they who were now dominating the Black Country bench (Philips, 1977). Bramwell's vigorous and unequivocal commitment to *laissez-faire* is notorious (Atiyah, 1979, pp. 374-380, 396-397); but how typical was Bramwell? And Halsbury's court-packing tactics so as to ensure that decisions were strongly adverse to the position of trade unions has been uncovered (Stevens, 1979, pp. 84-85 and 90-98).

Important though these data are, it does not, of itself, establish an *invariable* and *direct* relationship between, on the one hand, the class background of judges, legislators or winning litigants and, on the other hand, the outcome of particular cases or the enactment of specific legislation. The sometimes complex and contradictory nature of the relevant causal relations becomes apparent in the light of the historical specificity of the so-called relative autonomy of the law and legal professionalism. The characteristics usually associated with modern legal professionalism include: the supposed separation of the law from 'natural' reason (and, thus, the cognizance of lay persons)—as well as its separation from 'politics', 'economics', and 'morality'; its corresponding treatment as a neutral 'science'; its 'logical formal rational' form; and the asserted subjugation of society to the Rule of Law. Historically speaking, to what extent did these facets and other shared values of professionalism, mediate between and delimit, on the one hand, the economic and political needs of, say, economic dominant groups or the state—rather than simply mirror them,—and, on the other hand, the social and material self-interest of the legal professions and the judges (cf. Larson, 1977; Prest (Ed.), 1981)? In fact, the historical specificity of the relative autonomy of the law is only beginning to be explored by historians and sociologists. (For example, Miller, 1966, pp. 99-265; Tushnet, 1977, pp. 87-94; Klare, 1978.) Bouwsma has argued that lawyers were at the forefront of secularism throughout post-Reformation Europe in the sense of treating the claims of their craft as autonomous of and distinct from the edicts of politics, religious belief and the personal values of individual lawyers (Bouwsma, 1973). Wilfred Prest's recent study of the spiritual and material worlds of Sir Henry Finch illustrates the "segregation . . . of 'public' calling from 'private' belief", albeit a segregation which he recognizes was never absolute (Prest, 1978, p. 116). Prest contends that this separation ". . . helps to clarify the readiness of many lawyers to accept Crown office during the 1630's, despite the distaste they must have felt for the government's ecclesiastical policies" (Prest, 1978, p. 116). More striking still, Richard Cover has detailed the way some leading American judges felt constrained by the demands of professionalism, such as consistency, to uphold slavery despite their own personal abhorrence of black slavery (Cover, 1978).

The relative workload of the courts and its impact on judicial law-making, the form and structure of legal reasoning and the presentation of judgements has only begun to be systematically explored. Atiyah has pointed to ". . . the growing pressure on the courts arising from the vast increases in population and commercial activity" as a possible factor in the rise of extreme legalism ("legal formalism") in the latter half of the nineteenth century (Atiyah, 1979, p. 390). As Friedman puts it, "Judges were rushed, and dockets were crowded; there was less time to polish and re-word opinions" (Friedman, 1973, p. 540). Further, recent histories of crime have stressed that the law may simultaneously serve as a tool of dominant economic interest groups *and* actually check the power of dominant groups in society *vis à vis* less powerful ones. A commitment to the Rule of Law limits rulers as well as the ruled (Thompson, 1975, pp. 258-269). Other factors seemingly reinforce the autonomy of the legal professions. For example, the fact that cases come before the courts in a relatively random fashion — the so-called 'accident of litigation' — and the relatively unsystematic manner in which a minority of these are reported highlights the importance of chance and the unplanned in determining the actual content of the law.

These then are just some of the factors that appear to reinforce the autonomy of legal professionalism. And in so doing, they emphasize that the causal connections between lawyers, the law and economic self-interest are complex and contradictory. However, the empirical content and effect of the factors under-pinning legal autonomy enumerated above have scarcely been probed. Until this is undertaken, broad assertions about the effectivity or otherwise of legal autonomy must be treated with caution. Tested alongside these must be those factors which posit a strong and direct link between economic interest and power, on the one hand, and legal activity on the other. For instance, how far can lawyers not react to economic stimuli? Broadly speaking, lawyers are paid because economic agents find it profitable or necessary to do so. Did the general run of legal thinking not eventually conform to the economic forces of the age that were both shaping society and paying their fees? The fact this was or was not appreciated is not to the point. Nor would this be surprising. From their genesis as officers of the law courts at the beginning of the thirteenth century, the attorneys had always been the agents of other men. The private practice of the lawyer adopts a form substantially akin to that of an ordinary commercial under-taking. Moreover, in one very obvious respect at least, the legal professions were directly involved in capital accumulation. Thus, historians have stressed the vital role played by attorneys as conduits of capital in local capital markets (for example, Anderson, 1972).

A host of other factors further emphasize the closeness of the connections between economic power, wealth and legal practice that require empirical investigation. For example, the lack of legal aid in civil cases meant that perhaps in the past even more so than today only the economically stronger parties had the opportunity to select the best advice and advocates likely to win cases, the cases which might actually go before the courts, and thereby establish precedents which might, in turn, be reported in the law reports and thereby influence future courts and litigants and, thereby, in a real sense, determine the content of the law. The causal connections between economic power, the bringing of litigation, the use of certain counsel and the reporting of case law and thereby the construction of precedents requires our attention (McBarnet and Moorhouse, 1977). For instance, there may be a clear relationship between a socially and economically powerful lobby supportive of or opposed to specific laws, the amount of litigation surrounding the ambit of this law, and the range of defences and exceptions to liability under the law which are developed. Also important are the causal connections between the economic power of a party and the ability to cause a case to be settled out of court. This may adversely affect the weaker party in a series of ways. For example, if the case had gone to court, the weaker party may have secured higher compensation—a situation that is not infrequent in context of negligence claims against insurance companies, manufacturers and employers. It also permits the stronger party to prevent possible unfavourable precedents from being established. Credit companies and those using extensive exclusion or penalty clauses might fall into this category. Further, the power to 'impose' a settlement may be used to prevent the courts considering the cases likely to establish precedents inimicable to the interests of the stronger party. The stronger party will be able to use the law to wear down and even 'gag' the weaker party on occasions. The successful use made by Distillers of the law of contempt against the revelations of 'The Sunday Times'; or the unsuccessful use of 'gagging writs' for defamation by Dr William Wallersteiner are contemporary examples of this power. Moreover, since the weaker party has not argued his or her case before the court, the opportunity for a precedent which might have assisted others in the position of the weaker party will have been lost. It is illusory, therefore, to ignore such considerations in assessing the efficacy of legal rights and duties. Similarly, the legal and practical problems related to the actual enforcement of legal obligations must be considered in any historical assessment of the utility, economic efficiency and justice in respect of the role of the law and legal professionalism in the process of industrialization. It could be suggested, therefore, that the 'accident of litigation' and those cases that get reported and the establishment of precedents and, therefore, the future shape of the law, appears significantly less fortuitous but is ultimately locked into the material relations within society, albeit in a manner that, on occasions, may neither be intended nor immediate in the eyes of the actors themselves.

Thus, the historical specificity of the relative autonomy of the legal professions constitutes one of the most perplexing areas in a modern historical sociology of law. It is unlikely that the kind of questions enumerated above can be satis-factorily addressed at a very high level of abstraction.

Conclusion

I would not pretend to have offered a full examination of the issues posed in this essay nor a complete survey of the relevant literature. I have tried to show what an economic and social history of law can do as well as indicate (although not in any exhaustive fashion) what it is or is about. I hope that this essay presents a positive and encouraging survey of a truly fascinating field. Perhaps some readers will not have realized how much has already been achieved and the promise that lies ahead. Some readers may also have been made aware of additional significant literature pertaining to their work.

The historical study of law, economy and the state is one way, although not the only way, of extending our knowledge of the uses and limits of the law. But it is not only 'the law' that such a history may illuminate. Law is part of society and economy: it is a social, intellectual and economic as well as a legal institution. Moreover, a history of law, economy and the state traverses the boundaries separating the disciplines of anthropology, history and sociology. Despite the differences between these nominally discrete disciplines, they confront common issues which our subject might enlighten. For instance, all three are fundamentally preoccupied with

> . . . the puzzle of human agency . . . The problem of agency is the problem of finding a way of accounting for human experience which recognises simultaneously and in equal measure that history and society are made by constant and more or less purposeful individual action *and* that individual action, however purposeful, is made by history and society . . . People make their own history—but only under definite circumstances and conditions . . . The variations on the theme are innumerable; and the failure of human sciences to work the theme to a satisfactory conclusion is inscribed on page after page of the literature of each of those sciences . . . The estranged symbiosis of action and structure is both a commonplace of everyday life and the unbudgeable fulcrum of social analysis. (Abrams, 1982, pp. xii-xiv)

As this essay evidences, the historical study of law, economy and the state has proved fertile in enhancing our understanding of the central problems of agency and structuring.

Being truly historical, such a history serves as an important counter to static, Whiggish accounts which treat the law and economy of modern English society as an inevitable end-point, simply reflecting a solid consensus of almost *volksgeist* proportions. "Only the successful (in the sense of those whose aspirations anticipated subsequent evolution) are remembered" (Thompson, 1968, p. 13). In contrast, some of the best social history of law has served to remind us that legal intervention or abstention did not occur *in vacuo*. Sometimes it involved the marginalization, suppression, qualification or consolidation of pre-existing social and economic relations and, therefore, of specific historical alternatives (Corrigan, 1977). The recuperation of these alternatives must be a major task of the economic and social history of law. As Edward Thompson, in a justly celebrated passage argued, we must seek ". . . to rescue . . ." such alternatives and the individuals and groups who embodied them, ". . . from the enormous condescension of posterity . . . After all, we are not at the end of social evolution ourselves. In some of the lost causes of the people of the Industrial Revolution we may discover insights into social evils which we have yet to cure" (Thompson, 1968, p. 13).

Unlike much conventional legal history, our subject looks at law and legal institutions not just through the eyes of lawyers, but also through the eyes of individual users and non-users. Further, it is sensitive both to the political dimensions of law, lawyering and law-making; and to the connection between law and objective social and economic structures. This represents a conscious attempt to transcend the confines of lawyers' legal history—without, however, jettisoning its undoubted virtues. In short, the issues our subject poses and endeavours to illuminate are formidable, long-standing and fundamental.

Despite the potential our subject holds, and its intrinsic interest and relevance to a variety of disciplines and subject areas, I have tried to indicate some of the ways in which this promise has not been consistently realized in practice. The relevant literature, whether overtly concerned with law, economy and the state or not, has tended to regard 'law', 'state', 'economy', 'ideology' and 'social classes' as undifferentiated monoliths. For example, the nature and scope of law and legal institutions is often treated in an artificially circumspect manner which must inevitably generate a misconceived view of the interconnections or otherwise between law and material society. Thus, law and legal institutions tend to be equated *either* with the criminal law *or* the civil law; as either coercive *or* consensual in nature; as either case law or statute law. There is also a strong tendency to give undue attention to the royal (central) courts, and correspondingly to neglect local courts, legal and quasi-legal personnel, administrative jurisdictions, tribunals, the private law-making of the legal professions and legal literature. Once these relatively discrete levels of the state legal order are recognized it becomes much more difficult to view 'the law' as a coherent unity which people experience as such. In fact, one might hypothesize that the rich variety of different levels that constitute the state legal order are *not* yoked together in any simple, mutually dependent manner; but, instead, that their interaction and inter-penetration is problematic and indeterminate. Indeed, Weber recognized that formal rationality and justice may impede or conflict with the exercise of substantive rationality and justice (Weber, 1954, pp. 224-255). The tensions and contradictions *within* the state order as between its different spheres and functions and the pressures this generates towards changes in the content and form of the law, have tended to be neglected by historians, sociologists and lawyers.

It is also (and incorrectly) assumed that law, ordering, organization, coercion and social control are the exclusive property of the state. In other words, there is a tendency to confine our subject to the legal activities of the state. In contrast, this essay has stressed the importance of a pluralistic approach to law, ordering and organization. Since coercion, social control, ordering and organization are not the exclusive province of the state, a plural perspective requires a shift in emphasis towards all social arenas in which ordering and organization are maintained. Thus, in addition to the state legal order, we must investigate, on the one hand, those units or systems smaller than the state legal order and their interaction (or otherwise) with the state law order. On the other hand, we must consider the international legal order and its impact on national ordering, organization and economy (Griffith, 1979).

Another common pitfall we have stressed is an inclination to assume that the linkages between law and material society can wholly be explained in simple functionalist terms: that law was essential to certain social and economic ends; and/or that law mirrored either the needs of dominant classes or a general consensus. As we have tried to indicate, the connections between law and economy may be much more complex and contradictory than these generalizations allow. We have shown, for instance, that in at least three areas where it has often been assumed that the law reflected either the needs of an industrializing society or dominant economic interest groups—namely, the law relating to contract, land and patents—that their operation and supposed importance in practice was much less clear-cut and more variegated than functionalist interpretations tend to permit. As Robert Gordon observes, "There are simply too many variables in economic growth to support a hypothesis that any . . . (particular legal regime) is socially (and economically) 'necessary' . . ." For example,

> . . . it is actually very difficult to account for the emergence of negligence as a general organizing principle of tort liability as if it were a technological response of the law to the 'social needs of industrialisation', for one would then have to explain, for instance, why England and the United States seem to have undertaken the systematic generalization of the fault principle to include all tort liability at the same time (1870's and 1880's) despite England's much earlier industrialization as well as why Germany responded to industrialization by *imposing* strict liability on railroads and industrial concerns for accidents by way of exception to a pre-existing fault standard! (Gordon, 1981a, p. 907)

In a similar vein, A. W. B. Simpson has argued that, "If . . . the rule in *Hadley* v. *Baxendale*, (1854) is, as it has been argued, peculiarly appropriate to mid-nineteenth century industrial capitalism, what was it doing in Orleans in the 1760's?" (Simpson, 1979, p. 591). Although other nation states sought to import Britain's Industrial Revolution they did not on the whole adopt the policy most associated with the British state during Britain's industrial heyday, namely, *laissez-faire*. (Supple, 1973, p. 302). As Weber concluded: ". . . modern capitalism prospers equally . . . under legal systems containing rules and institutions which considerably differ from each other at least from the juridical point of view." (Weber, 1954, p. 315). Likewise, there was no single 'capitalist' form of law—whether we call it contractual, commodity form or absolute private property. It is more accurate to view each as one of several *forms* of capitalist law which co-existed over long periods, complementing and conflicting with one another.[5]

What of the law's latent functions or ideological dimensions? Another canon of much simple functionalist writing is the assumption that all people are more or less persuaded by the legitimacy of the law and legal institutions and of their ideological dimensions more or less all the time. Perhaps the most important variant of this view is the thesis that the law and legal institutions constitute important mechanisms of social control whose ideologies breed passivity and facilitate the embourgeoisement of the lower orders of society. However, as we have seen, legal ideologies are not static monoliths. Adherence to the legitimacy of the law may be extremely superficial for all social groups; and that traditional, semi-autonomous, indigenous norms and pragmatic considerations may influence adherence or non-adherence and the degree of adherence, as well as more immediate economic considerations and fear of the coercive might of the state. (Cf. Moorhouse and Chamberlain, 1974; Sarat, 1977; Hay, 1980, pp. 72-75.)

Part of the problem has been the assumption in some work that law and state are essentially related to the relations of production. This assumption ignores the character of civil society. Law and state may not only be related (albeit in a complex manner) to relations of production but are also related to civil society.

> It is within civil society that various limitations are placed on the state, that it is substantially impotent to act in various ways and that this stems from 'civil life' and the 'mutual plundering' that occurs between the various social groups . . . It is through the interposing of civil society that we can see that similar capitalist economies do not necessarily produce similar (legal and) state forms. (Urry, 1981, pp. 99 and 83)

Once we interpose civil society and the plethora of social groupings it contains; the complex of personal and impersonal relations that characterize everyday life; and the elaborate interaction between state and non-state ordering and organization, then it becomes much more difficult to talk of the relation between law and economy in terms of a close functional fit (Gordon, 1981b, pp. 1053-1054). Law, society and economy cannot, therefore, be analysed in Pavlovian terms, whereby legal norms and institutions condition social and economic behaviour or vice versa. Other false assumptions ground simple functionalist analyses.

For example, they tend not to differentiate as between discrete social actors and different levels of abstraction. Human individuals, social classes and groups, the legal professions, the courts and the state are implicitly or explicitly treated the same in respect of their links with law and the material world. However, from the standpoint of most citizens, for most of the time the law, instrumentally speaking, is a last resort, a costly, time-consuming, unfamiliar and unwelcome aberration which is utilized pragmatically and often is avoided if possible. It is not that anarchy in the sense of the absence of order or uniting principle prevails (though undoubtedly a degree of anarchy exists); but that *other* non-state or quasi-state systems of ordering and organization may carry greater weight and, therefore, wholly or partially supplant the formal state law order in particular situations. For most citizens at most times, the relation between the state legal order and social and economic practice is problematic and not ongoing. However, from a different perspective or at a higher level of abstraction we may be able to detect the existence of causal connections or what has been called "causally significant analogies between instances . . ." (Stinchcombe, 1978, p. 7). We cannot assume that all causes in history operate through intentional, conscious, individual or group behaviour. In addition, it is often necessary to embark upon an objective structural analysis at a higher level of abstraction in order to explain legal and economic change (or order). The quest for the most profitable level (or combination of levels) at which to investigate continuity and discontinuity is a major problem in historical-socio research. In part, it will depend upon the questions one is asking, what one is trying to describe and the hypotheses one wants to test. In other words, both micro and macro historical-socio explanations require attention.

A major problem, therefore, for the future development of our subject is the construction and testing of analytic frameworks which are sensitive to individual (agency) *and* society (structure), continuity *and* discontinuity, function *and* dysfunction (patent and latent) within and as between law (state *and* non-state) and material society. Such an enterprise will require a more theoretically informed practice of historical research and scholarship than has conventionally characterized the varieties of 'history'. Until the tradition of positivist-empiricist history is transcended and the historical enterprise is conceived in more holistic and inter-disciplinary terms, our knowledge of the historical relation between law and economy will not advance in real insight. Balkanization as between and within disciplines has to be overcome if relevant institutions and practices are to be understood in their entirety and connections thus far overlooked are to be perceived (cf. Jones, 1972).

To reject outright the positivist-empiricist method and insist upon a more inter-disciplinary and theoretically informed history of law and material society does not necessarily entail the renunciation of a continually close involvement with historical detail. Neither does it automatically involve an insensitivity to our often woeful lack of data, nor the need to rescue for posterity the wealth of pertinent historical data before it is lost for ever. Indeed, the sensitivity which, say, the best lawyer's legal history has shown in these matters is *also* a *sine qua non* of the historical sociology of law, economy and the state.

If the positivist-empiricist method is to be rejected so too is that strand of sociological history which ransacks secondary sources in order to 'theorize the facts'. Such work fails to produce new evidence or take old arguments further. Further, this tradition seems

> . . . unaware that many of the simplest facts about capitalist development and the emergence of . . . (new forms of law, ordering and organization) still await research. There is an almost touching positivism in . . . (their) belief that the 'facts' can simply be read off from . . . (one secondary source or another). High theorists . . . who descend from their eyries for quick swoops over the empirical terrain are unlikely to return to their nests with anything more than the musty grain of cliché unless they are willing to settle down among the stubble to peck away with the rest of us pigeons. (Ignatieff, 1981, p. 237)

Whilst the history of law and economy needs better theory, theories of law, society and economy are best developed, through continual and close involvement with empirical sources. As Arthur Stinchcombe puts it, the ". . . great theorists descend to the level of . . . detailed analogies in the course of their work. Further they become greater theorists down there among the details, for it is the details that theorists in history have to grasp if they are to be any good" (Stinchcombe, 1978, p. 124).

No one analytical framework or viewpoint is likely to provide all the answers, let alone the perfect model. This, in turn, means being sensitive to the weaknesses as well as to the strengths of one's own perspective—to what one's theories, hypotheses and methodologies leave out or obscure as well as to what they may illuminate. Multiple approaches are, therefore, essential for the realization of an undogmatic history of law and material society. They might enable us to re-interpret existing data and question the validity of more traditional analyses. Comparative histories of law and economy would also constitute a formidable resource for both constructive and contrastive purposes (cf. Skocpol, 1979).

The broader tasks and perspectives espoused in this essay inevitably have consequences for the kind of data that is the focus of study. A compass which recognizes the plurality of law (state and non-state), for example, must transcend the study of law reports and legislation and devote attention to those sources more familiar to business, economic and social historians. The resources of state papers, company records, contemporary literature, oral history, the myriad of legal, quasi-legal and extra-legal documents such as or touching upon, marriage, divorce, wills, bankruptcy, indictments and so on, the advices and private law-making housed within the offices of the legal professions or public registries and the records of village communities are just some of the more obvious source which require attention—and which in some cases have already begun to be utilized to great effect. Clearly, this is a colossal, not to say daunting, proposition; but it cannot be shirked. Historical writing, as one commentator has recently reminded us, is undoubtedly difficult work (Anderson, 1981). To achieve an inter-disciplinary history of law and material society, however, is especially demanding given its avowed concern with formidable problems of theory and method. To describe the kinds of continuity, discontinuity, refraction and mediation outlined in this essay greatly complicates the task of exposition and demands the formulation of new conceptual apparatuses and, therefore, of a more sensitive language than that currently at hand. Perhaps it was with these difficulties in mind that Graham Parker wrote of "The Masochism of the Legal Historian"! (Parker, 1974). And yet, for all the difficulties of such an enterprise, there are heartening signs that an inter-disciplinary history of law, economy and the state is beginning to develop more vigorously than at any previous point in time. Several people have observed a sudden blooming of wild flowers (for example, Gordon, 1981b, p. 1055). Hopefully, this work will tempt others to join in the labour of cultivating flowers in the wilderness, even though the varieties we succeed in producing will not all be the same.

Notes

1. I am grateful to Douglas Hay for his comments. I should also like to thank Gerry Rubin for allowing me to extract part of my contribution from Sugarman and Rubin (forthcoming) and for his comments.

2. The rise of freedom of contract as the pre-eminent legal doctrine in the mid-nineteenth century facilitated and legitimated *both* the qualification of absolute private property and its enhancement. In other words, significant tensions arose as between the concepts of freedom of contract and absolute private property and the ostensible values they exhaled. For examples of the tensions between new property rights and freedom of contract see Cornish, 1981, pp. 297-298 and 499-500.

   It is important to note that the abolition or retention of particular classes of multiple use-rights in law could affect different social groups very differently. The strict settlement and the doctrine of estates were not all of land law—only that law important to the rich. Co-existing alongside the rise° of qualified conceptions of property was the abolition of common rights in thousands of cases on enclosure.

3. However, the discretion to use or not to use the state law order may be exercised so as to secure a degree of social control (see Hay *et al.*, (Eds) 1975, pp. 17-63).

4. Of course, the impact of freedom of contract cannot be simply deduced from the content of the law. Freedom of contract may in theory ". . . signify a decrease of

constraint and an increase in individual freedom"; but in practice the degree of freedom or coercion is determined ". . . above all by the differences in the distribution of property guaranteed by law" (Weber, 1954, p. 188). Weber, therefore, warned against the error of assuming that freedom of contract necessarily implied a decrease in the coercion exercised within the state legal order. In fact, as Weber showed, despite a formal regime of freedom of contract a state legal order ". . . can nonetheless in its practical effects facilitate a quantitive and qualitative increase in coercion in general . . ." (Weber, 1954, p. 191). (See generally, Dawson, 1947; Simon, 1954; Weber, 1954, pp. 188-191; Friedman, 1972, pp. 119-160; Horwitz, 1977, pp. 188-210; Stevens, 1979, pp. 138-143 and 160-164).

5. Cf. Pashukanis (1978) who treats the commodity form of law as *the* capitalist form of law. This view is inconsistent with that espoused in this essay. To equate 'capitalist law' with either a contractual, commodity or absolute private property form of law is to overlook the extent to which the rise of the interventionist state in the later nineteenth century undercut and problematized the supposed pre-eminence of these forms of law. See, for example, Atiyah, 1979, Pt III.

References

Abel, R. (1977). From the Editor, *Law and Society Review,* **11**.

Abel-Smith, B. and Stevens, R. (1967). *Lawyers and the Courts.* Heinemann, London.

Abrams, P. (1982). *Historical Sociology.* Open Books, Near Shepton Mallet.

Althusser, L. (1977). "Ideology and Ideological State Apparatuses". In *Lenin and Philosophy and Other Essays.* New Left Books, London.

Anderson, A. (1971). The Political Symbolism of the Labour Laws. *Bulletin of the Society of Labour History* No. *23*, 13-15.

Anderson, B. L. (1972). The Attorney and the Early Capital Market in Lancashire. In *Capital Formation in the Industrial Revolution* (F. Crouzet, Ed.). Methuen, London.

Anderson, S. (1981). The Lawyer as Historian. *Modern Law Review* **44**, 227-233.

Anonymous. (1980). Tortious Interference with Contractual Relations in the 19th Century. *Harvard Law Review* **93**, 1510-1539.

Arthurs, H. W. (forthcoming). Special Courts, Special Law: Legal Pluralism in 19th Century England. In *Law, Society and Economy: Essays in the History of English Law, 1750-1914* (G. R. Rubin and D. Sugarman, Eds). Professional Books, Abingdon.

Atiyah, P. S. (1979). *The Rise and Fall of Freedom of Contract.* Clarendon Press, Oxford.

Bailey, V. (1980). Crime, Criminal Justice and Authority in England. *Bulletin of the Society for the Study of Labour History* No. **40**, 36-40.

Bailey, V. (Ed.) (1981). *Policing and Punishment in 19th Century Britain,* pp. 94-125. Croom Helm, London.

Bartrip, P. W. J. and Fenn, P. T. (1980). The Conventionalization of Factory Crime. *International Journal of the Sociology of Law* **8**, 175-186.

Beale, H. and Dugdale, T. (1975). Contracts Between Businessmen. *British Journal of Law and Society* **2**, 45-60.

Beckett, J. V. (1977). English Landownership in the Later 17th and 18th Centuries. *Economic History Review* **30**, 567-581.

Birks, M. (1960). *Gentlemen of the Law.* Stevens, London.

Bonfield, L. (1980). Marriage Settlements and the Rise of Great Estates. *Economic History Review* **33**, 559-563.

Bouwsma, W. J. (1973). Lawyers in Early Modern Culture. *American History Review* **73**, 303-327.

Bowen, Lord. (1907). Progress in the Administration of Justice During the Victorian Period. In *Select Essays in Anglo-American Legal History* (various authors), Vol. I. Little, Brown and Co., Boston.

Brenner, J. F. (1974). Nuisance Law in the Industrial Revolution in England. *Journal of Legal Studies* **3**, 404-434.

Brewer, J. (1980). The Wilkites and the Law 1763-74. In *An Ungovernable People* (J. Brewer and J. Styles, Eds). Hutchinson, London.

Brewer, J. and Styles, J. (Eds) (1980). *An Ungovernable People*. Hutchinson, London.

Burrow, J. W. (1966). *Evolution and Society*. Cambridge University Press, Cambridge.

Burrow, J. W. (1974). "The village community" and the uses of history in late 19th century England. In N. McKendrick (Ed.) *Historical Perspectives*. Europa, London.

Cain, M. (1975). Rich Man's Law or Poor Man's Law? *British Journal of Law and Society* **2**, 61-66.

Cain, M. (1983). Where are the Disputes? A Study of a First Instance Civil Court in the U.K. In *The Study of Disputes* (M. Cain and K. Kulscar, Eds). Hungarian Academy of Sciences and Pergamon Press, Budapest and London.

Carson, W. G. (1974). Symbolic and Instrumental Dimensions of Early Factory Legislation. In *Crime, Criminology, and Public Policy* (R. G. Hood, Ed.). Heinemann, London.

Chaytor, M. (1980). Household and Kinship, *History Workshop* No. **10**, 25-60.

Cohen, G. A. (1978). *Karl Marx's Theory of History*. Oxford University Press, Oxford.

Cornish, W. R. (1979). Legal Control over Cartels and Monopolization 1880-1914: A Comparison. In *Recht und Entwicklung der Großunternehmen im 19 und frühen 20 Jahrhundert* (N. Horn and J. Kocka, Eds). Vandenhoeck and Ruprecht, Gottingen.

Cornish, W. R. (1981). *Intellectual Property*. Sweet and Maxwell, London.

Corrigan, P. (1977). *State Formation and Moral Regulation in 19th Century Britain: Sociological Investigations*. Durham University Ph.D.

Corrigan, P. (Ed.) (1980). *Capitalism, State Formation and Marxist Theory*. Quartet, London.

Corrigan, P. (1981). (Book review). *Sociological Review* 465-470.

Corrigan, P. and Sayer, D. (1981). How the Law Rules. In *Law, State and Society* (B. Fryer *et al.*, Eds). Croom Helm, London.

Cosgrove, R. A. (1980). *The Rule of Law: Albert Venn Dicey, Victorian Jurist*. Macmillan, London.

Cover, R. (1978). *Justice Accused*. Yale University Press, New Haven.

Danzig, R. (1975). *Hadley v. Baxendale*: A Study in the Industrialisation of the Law. *Journal of Legal Studies* **4**, 249-284.

Dawson, J. P. (1947). Economic Duress — An Essay in Perspective. *Michigan Law Review* **45**, 253-271.

Dicey, A. V. (1885). *Introduction to the Study of the Law of the Constitution*. Macmillan, London.

Dicey, A. V. (1914). *Law and Public Opinion in England During the 19th Century*. Macmillan, London.

Duman, D. (1982). *The Judicial Bench in England 1727-1875*. Royal Historical Society, London.

Duman, D. (1983). *The English and Colonial Bars in the Nineteenth Century*. Croom Helm, London.

Engels, F. (1902). *The Origin of the Family, Private Property and the State*. Free Press, Chicago.

Ferguson, R. B. (1980). The Adjudication of Commercial Disputes and the Legal System in Modern England. *British Journal of Law and Society* **7**, 141-157.

Fifoot, C. H. S. (1936). *Lord Mansfield.* Clarendon Press, Oxford.

Fifoot, C. H. S. (1950). *Judge and Jurist in the Reign of Victoria.* Stevens, London.

Finer, S. E. (1952). *Life and Times of Sir Edwin Chadwick.* Methuen, London.

Flaherty, D. (Ed.) (1982). *Essays in the History of Canadian Law.* University of Toronto Press, Toronto.

Foucault, M. (1979). *The History of Sexuality Vol. I.* Allen Lane, London.

Foucault, M. (1980). *Power/Knowledge.* Harvester, Brighton.

Friedman, L. M. (1965). *Contract Law in America.* University of Wisconsin Press, Madison.

Friedman, L. M. (1973). *A History of American Law.* Simon and Schuster, New York.

Friedman, W. (1972). *Law in a Changing Society.* Penguin Books, Harmondsworth.

Frug, G. (1980). The City as a Legal Concept. *Harvard Law Review* **93**, 1059-1154.

Galanter, M. (1981). Justice in Many Rooms. *Journal of Legal Pluralism* **1**, 1-48.

Gatrell, V. *et al.* (Eds) (1980). *Crime and the Law.* Europa, London.

Gordon, R. W. (1975). J. Willard Hurst and the Common Law Tradition in American Legal Historiography. *Law and Society Review* **10**, 9-55.

Gordon, R. W. (1978). Some Thoughts on Legal Form and Social Practice in American Legal Historiography. Unpublished.

Gordon, R. W. (1981a). (Book Review). *Harvard Law Review* **94**, 903-918.

Gordon, R. W. (1981b). Historicism in Legal Scholarship. *Yale Law Journal* **90**, 1017-1056.

Griffith, J. (1979). Is Law Important? *New York University Law Review* **54**, 339-374.

Hall, J. (1952). *Theft, Law and Society.* Bobbs-Merrill, Indianapolis.

Hall, S. (1979). The Great Moving Right Show. *Marxism Today.* January, 4-8.

Harding, A. (1966). *A Social History of Law.* Penguin Books, Harmondsworth.

Hart, H. L. A. (1961). *The Concept of Law.* Clarendon Press, Oxford.

Hay, D. (1980). Crime and Justice in 18th and 19th Century England. In *Crime and Justice Vol. 2* (N. Morris and M. Tonry, Eds). Chicago University Press, Chicago.

Hay, D. *et al.* (Eds) (1975). *Albion's Fatal Free.* Allen Lane, London.

Heuston, R. F. V. (1964). *Lives of the Lord Chancellors, 1885-1940.* Oxford University Press, London.

Hilton, R. (1980). Individualism and the English Peasantry, *New Left Review* No. **120**, 109-111.

Hirst, P. (1979). *On Law and Ideology.* Macmillan, London.

Hogg, R. (1979). Imprisonment and Society Under Early British Capitalism. *Crime and Social Justice* No. **12**, 4-17.

Holdsworth, M. W. (1965). *A History of English Law.* 16 volumes. Methuen/Sweet and Maxwell, London.

Horwitz, M. J. (1973). The Conservative Tradition in the Writing of American Legal History, *American Journal of Legal History* **7**, 275-294.

Horwitz, M. J. (1977). *The Transformation of American Law, 1780-1860.* Harvard University Press, London.

Hurst, J. W. (1956). *Law and the Conditions of Freedom in the 19th Century United States.* University of Wisconsin Press, Madison.

Hurst, J. W. (1964). *Law and Economic Growth.* University of Wisconsin Press, Madison.

Hutchins, B. L. and Harrison, A. (1903). *A History of Factory Legislation.* P. S. King, Westminster.

Ignatieff, M. (1978). *A Just Measure of Pain.* Macmillan, London.

Ignatieff, M. (1981). Theorising the Facts. *New Society*, 237-238.

Jones, D. (1982). *Crime, Protest, Community and Police in 19th Century Britain.* Routledge, London.

Jones, G. S. (1972). History: The Poverty of Empiricism. In *Ideology in Social Science* (R. Blackburn, Ed.). Fontana/Collins, London.

Jones, G. S. (1977). Class Expression *Versus* Social Control?, *History Workshop* No. 4, 163-170.

Joyce, P. (1980). *Work, Society and Politics.* Harvester, Brighton.

Kennedy, D. (1975-6). Form and Substance in Private Law Adjudication. *Harvard Law Review* **89**, 1685-1778.

Kennedy, D. (1979). The Structure of Blackstone's Commentaries. *Buffalo Law Review* **28**, 205-382.

Kennedy, D. (1980). Toward an Historical Understanding of Legal Consciousness. *Research in Law and Sociology, Vol. 3* (S. Spitzer, Ed.). JAI Press, Greenwood.

Kirk, H. (1976). *Portrait of a Profession.* Oyez, London.

Klare, K. E. (1978). Judicial Deradicalization of the Wagner Act and the Origins of Modern Legal Consciousness, 1937-1941. *Minnesota Law Review* **62**, 265-339.

Klare, K. E. (1979). Law-Making As Praxis, *Telos*, 123-135.

Landes, D. (1969). *The Unbound Prometheus.* Cambridge University Press, Cambridge.

Larson, M. S. (1977). *The Rise of Professionalism.* University of California Press, Berkeley.

Lewis, R. A. (1974). (Book Review). *History* **59**, 116. Quoted in Corrigan (1977) p. 2.

Macaulay, S. (1963). Non-Contractual Relations in Business. *American Sociological Review* **28**, 55-66.

Macfarlane, A. (1978). *The Origins of English Individualism.* Blackwell, Oxford.

Malcolmson, R. W. (1973). *Popular Recreations in English Society 1700-1850.* Cambridge University Press, Cambridge.

Macpherson, C. B. (1978). *Property.* Blackwell, Oxford.

Maitland, F. W. (1898). *Township and Borough.* Cambridge University Press, Cambridge.

Maitland, F. W. (1908). *The Constitutional History of England.* Cambridge University Press, Cambridge.

Manchester, A. H. (1980). *Modern Legal History, 1750-1950.* Butterworth, London.

Marx, K. (1954). *Capital Vol. I.* Lawrence and Wishart, London.

Marx, K. (1973). *Grundrisse.* Penguin Books, Harmondsworth.

Marx, K. (1976). *Capital Vol. I.* Penguin Books, Harmondsworth.

Marx, K. (1980). *Capital Vol. III.* Penguin Books, London.

McBarnet, D. and Moorhouse, H. F. (1977). Business Law and Bourgeois Ideology. Unpublished.

McGregor, O. R. (1981). *Social History and Law Reform.* Stevens, London.

Mensch, B. (1981). Freedom of Contract as Ideology. *Stanford Law Review* **33**, 753-770.

Miller, P. (1966). *The Life of the Mind in America.* Victor Gollancz, London.

Mitchell, J. (1975). *Psychoanalysis and Feminism.* Penguin Books, Harmondsworth.

Moorhouse, H. F. and Chamberlain, C. W. (1974). Lower Class Attitudes to Property. *Sociology* **8**, 387-405.

Neale, R. S. (1975). The Bourgeoisie Historically Has Played a Most Revolutionary Part. In *Feudalism, Capitalism and Beyond* (E. Kamenka and R. S. Neale, Eds). Edward Arnold, London.

North, D. C. and Thomas, R. P. (1973). *The Rise of the Western World.* Cambridge University Press, Cambridge.

Offer, A. (1981). *Property and Politics 1870-1914.* Cambridge University Press, Cambridge.

Parker, G. (1974). The Masochism of the Legal Historian. *University of Toronto Law Journal* **24**, 279-317.

Parris, H. (1969). *Constitutional Bureaucracy.* Allen and Unwin, London.

Pashukanis, E. B. (1978). *Law and Marxism.* Ink Links, London.

Philips, D. (1977). *Crime and Authority in Victorian England.* Croom Helm, London.

Polanyi, K. (1944). *The Great Transformation.* Beacon Press, Boston.

Pollock, F. and Maitland, F. W. (1898). *The History of English Law* Vol. **I**. Cambridge University Press, Cambridge.

Prest, W. R. (1978). The Art of Law and the Law of God. In *Puritans and Revolutionaries* (D. Pennington and K. Thomas). Clarendon Press, Oxford.

Prest, W. R. (Ed.) (1981). *Lawyers in Early Modern Europe and America.* Croom Helm, London.

Purcell, E. A. (1973). *The Crisis of Democratic Theory.* University of Kentucky Press, Lexington.

Radzinowicz, L. (1956-1968). *A History of the English Criminal Law,* 4 volumes. Stevens, London.

Richards, P. (1979). The State and Early Industrial Capitalism. *Past and Present* No. **83**, 91-115.

Risk, R. C. B. (1973). The 19th Century Foundations of the Business Corporation in Ontario. *University of Toronto Law Journal* **23**, 270-306.

Risk, R. C. B. (1976). The Golden Age: The Law of the Market in Ontario in the 19th Century. *University of Toronto Law Journal* **26**, 307-346.

Risk, R. C. B. (1977a). The Last Golden Age: Property and Allocation of Losses in Ontario in the 19th Century. *University of Toronto Law Journal* **27**, 199-239.

Risk, R. C. B. (1977b). The Law and Economy in Mid-19th Century Ontario: A Perspective. *University of Toronto Law Journal* **27**, 403-438.

Roeber, A. G. (1980). Authority, Law and Custom: The Rituals of Court Day in Tidewater Virginia, 1720-1750. *William and Mary Quarterly* **47**. 29-52.

Rubin, G. R. and Sugarman, D. (Eds). (Forthcoming). *Law, Economy and Society: Essays in the History of English Law, 1750-1914.* Professional Books, Abingdon.

Sarat, A. (1977). Studying American Culture. *Law and Society Review* **11**, 427-462.

Scheiber, H. A. (1981). Regulation, Property Rights and Definition of 'The Market'. *Journal of Economic History* 103-109.

Scheiber, H. A. (1982). (Book Review), *Journal of Economic History* 103-104.

Seed, J. (1981). (Book Review). *History Workshop* No. **11**, 176-178.

Simon, D. (1954). Master and Servant. In *Democracy and the Labour Movement* (J. Saville, Ed.). Lawrence and Wishart, London.

Simpson, A. W. B. (1975). Innovation in 19th Century Contract Law. *Law Quarterly Review* **91**, 247-268.

Simpson, A. W. B. (1979). The Horwitz Thesis and the History of Contracts, *University of Chicago Law Review* **46**, 533-610.

Skocpol, T. (1979). *States and Social Revolutions.* Cambridge University Press, Cambridge.

Spitzer, S. (1979). Notes Towards a Theory of Punishment and Social Control. In *Research in Law and Sociology, Vol. 2,* (S. Spitzer, Ed.). JAI Press, Greenwich.

Spring, E. (1964). The Settlement of Land in 19th Century England. *American Journal of Legal History* **8**, 209-223.

Stevens, R. (1979). *Law and Politics: The House of Lords as a Judicial Body 1800-1976.* Weidenfeld and Nicholson, London.

Stevenson, J. (1979). *Popular Disturbances in England, 1700-1870.* Longman, London.

Stinchcombe, A. (1978). *Theoretical Methods in Social History.* Academic Press, New York.

Sugarman, D. (1980). (Book Review). *British Journal of Law and Society* 297-310.

Sugarman, D. (1981). Theory and Practice in Law and History. In *Law, State and Society* (B. Fryer *et al.*, Eds). Croom Helm, London.

Sugarman, D. (1983). The Legal Boundaries of Liberty: Dicey, Liberalism and Legal Science. *Modern Law Review* **46**, 102-111.

Sugarman, D. and Rubin, G. R. (forthcoming). Towards A New History of Law and Material Society in England, 1750-1914. In *Law, Economy and Society: Essays in the History of English Law, 1750-1914* (G. R. Rubin and D. Sugarman, Eds). Professional Books, Abingdon.

Sugarman, D., Palmer, J. N. J. and Rubin, G. R. (1982). Crime and Authority in 19th Century Britain. *Middlesex Polytechnic History Journal* **I**, Nos. **2-3**, 28-141.

Summers, R. S. (1977). Naive Instrumentalism and the Law. In *Law, Morality and Society* (P. M. S. Hacker and J. Raz, Eds). Clarendon Press, Oxford.

Supple, B. (1973). The State and the Industrial Revolution, 1700-1914. In *The Fontana Economic History of Europe, Vol. 3* (C. M. Cipolla, Ed.). Fontana/Collins, Glasgow.

Thomas, M. W. (1948). *The Early Factory Legislation.* Thames Bank, Leigh-on-Sea.

Thompson, E. P. (1968). *The Making of the English Working Class.* Penguin Books, Harmondsworth.

Thompson, E. P. (1971). The Moral Economy of the English Crowd in the 18th Century, *Past and Present* No., 76-109.

Thompson, E. P. (1975). *Whigs and Hunters.* Allen Lane, London.

Thompson, E. P. (1976). The grid of inheritance. In *Family and Inheritance* (J. Goody *et al.*, Eds). Cambridge University Press, Cambridge.

Thompson, F. M. L. (1981). Social Control in Victorian Britain, *Economic History Review* **34**, 184-208.

Tushnet, M. V. (1977). Perspectives on the Development of American Law. *Wisconsin Law Review* 81-110.

Urry, J. (1981). *The Anatomy of Capitalist Societies.* Macmillan, London.

Vandevelde, K. J. (1980). The New property of the 19th Century. *Buffalo Law Review* **29**, 325-367.

Various authors. (1909). *Select essays in Anglo-American Legal History.* Little, Brown and Co., Boston.

Ward, J. T. (1970). *The Factory System.* David & Charles, Newton Abbot.

Weber, M. (1954). *Max Weber on Law in Economy and Society.* Harvard University Press, Cambridge.

White, G. E. (1980). *Tort Law in America.* Oxford University Press, New York.

White, M. (1957). *Social Thought in America.* Beacon Press, New York.

Williams, R. (1977). *Marxism and Literature.* Oxford University Press, Oxford.

Further Reading

Although the period 1750-1914 is undoubtedly of central importance to our understanding of law, economy and the state in contemporary England, like all periodization there is an element of artifice about it. As Pollock and Maitland emphasized, one can always go back earlier. "Such is the unity of all history that any one who endeavours to tell a piece of it must feel that his first sentence tears a seamless web" (Pollock and Maitland, 1898, p. 1). In terms of the relation between law and capitalism (and the foundations of the modern legal system), it could be argued that the fifteenth, sixteenth and seventeenth centuries were also significant. It is important, therefore, not to conflate the historical development of an industrialized economy in England with the historical development of capitalism. The latter continually pushes one back into the seventeenth century and earlier.

Two seminal works spring to mind as appropriate texts for the reader approaching the period 1750-1914 for the first time. Abel-Smith and Stevens (1967) is a pioneering study unequalled despite its age. Atiyah (1979) constitutes the most important intellectual history of a central area of private law in England, 1770-1970. For a useful assessment of Atiyah (1979) see Mensch (1981).

Other major works devoted to the modern period include: Dicey (1914); Fifoot (1936 and 1959); Heuston (1964); Holdsworth (1965), esp. volumes 10-16; Stevens (1979); various authors (1907).

Manchester, (1980) is substantially flawed and must be treated with caution: see Anderson (1981). Baker (1979) and Harding (1966) are learned texts primarily concerned, however, with the period prior to 1800.

As regards modern criminal law, crime and its institutions, the literature has grown enormously in recent years. Important texts include: Radzinowicz (1956-1968); Philips (1977); Thompson (1975); Ignatieff (1978); Brewer and Styles (Eds) (1980); Gatrell *et al.* (Eds) (1980); Hall (1952); Bailey (Ed.) (1981); Jones (1982); Malcolmson (1973); Stevenson (1979); Hay *et al.* (Eds) (1975).

For overviews of the current state of the history of crime, criminal law and allied institutions see: Bailey (1980); Hay (1980); Sugarman *et al.* (1982).

On the theme of law and economy, see Rubin and Sugarman, (Eds), (forthcoming). North American studies are particularly suggestive for future research on law and economy in England. As regards Canadian work, a series of papers by Risk (1973), (1976), (1977a), (1977b), are recommended. Also important is Flaherty (Ed.) (1982)—the first of several promised volumes. In respect to the United States, the relevant material is enormous. Some of the most useful and important texts include: Hurst (1956 and 1964); Friedman (1965 and 1973); and Horwitz (1977).

Much work remains to be done of the historical emergence of the legal professions and their role in economy and society. Some of the leading studies include: Anderson (1972); Birks (1960), Duman (1982 and 1983); Kirk (1976); Larson (1977); Prest (Ed.) (1981).

On the questions of theory, method and historiography, Gordon (1975, 1978, 1981a, 1981b) are rich in learning and insight. They constitute an excellent guide to many of the major issues. See also Horwitz (1973); Scheiber (1981); Sugarman (1980, 1981 and 1983); Sugarman and Rubin (forthcoming); and Tushnet (1977). See generally, Abrams (1982) and Weber (1954).

10 Anarchism, Marxism and The Critique of Law

Zenon Bankowski

Introduction

Anarchism, as a form of political activity, does not seem to be very noticeable at the moment. Its last great flowering, if we discount the student revolt of Paris '68, was in Republican Spain. In truth, anarchism as a political movement has never been strong or large — political victory has never been its criterion of success. But it has always cropped up as a distinctive strain in major political upheavals and has thereby made a distinctive contribution to political theory.

Marxism has tended to see anarchists as, at best, reactionaries who hark back to peasant and primitive communities. There is truth in this view but anarchism is not a monolith. This paper is not the place to give a complete history and analysis of the diverse strands of anarchism but nevertheless I will start by giving a brief conspectus so as to show the spectrum of anarchist theories.[1]

At one end stands individualist anarchism and a vision of the community of ruthless egoists, a good example of which would be Stirner. Here also come people like Nozick whose theories can be seen as a kind of anarcho-capitalism. The individual is supreme. It is he alone who is important. His freedom and his right to property justly acquired is supreme and can best be protected through a form of market arrangement which requires no or only a minimal state. The individual is the only thing to count — the collective and well being of the society as a whole is only important in so far as that is understood as the sum of the individuals comprising it.

Proudhon is a mutualist anarchist. His vision was that of a society where people were bound by relations of exchange and mutual credit. It was based on

Law, State and Society Series: "Legality, Ideology and the State", edited by D. Sugarman, 1983.
Academic Press, London and New York.

individuals and small groups possessing but not owning the means of production.

We now come to strains of anarchism which are more obviously socialistic, that of collective and communist anarchism and anarcho-syndicalism. Bakunin and Kropotkin tended to eschew the class politics of the Marxists. Their claim being that the state exploits everybody, giving power to only a few. The aim of the state was to 'divide and rule' and to break up the solidarity of the oppressed. Anarchism's aim was to unite them and to broaden the struggle from that of merely the class to everyone; from the strict class analysis of the later Marx to the more humanistic consciousness of the earlier Marx. Again there was an insistence that the germ of the organizations of the new society lay in the dispossessed; the state and 'civilisation' suppressing it. There is in these strains a concentration on organization for the future. Within this general stream of ideas Kropotkin moved to forms of literal communism. The communes and local organization were the base units but there was to be no wage labour and everyone gave what he could and took what he needed. Syndicalists on the other hand, concentrated on the point of production and took as their base units the workers' own organizations, the unions. Maletesta, the Italian communist anarchist, went further and was concerned to build up proletarian organization to seize power by the working class in the name of all mankind.

One of the key themes in this group of theories was that we all have freedom and sociality within us but are repressed in this sociality by the false community that the state offers us. In this we have the strong moral thrust of anarchism — that it is our duty as humans to live the anarchist way.

Anarchists do tend then to concentrate on small groups and produce sometimes an almost religious fervour in these experiments. This is not to say that they are irredeemably bound to peasant communities. However, because anarchists believe that, to an extent anyway, people have that freedom and sociality within them it does imply that they will look to all human organizational forms for clues on how to organize in a free manner. It is here that we can find the common factor uniting all anarchist theories. They are voluntaristic and anti-authoritarian and demand immediate action in that direction. This contradicts with many trends in Marxism and social science where the desire for 'scientific' understanding makes it more plausible to concentrate solely on structures which can far more easily be fitted into causal webs. Anarchism is not necessarily anti-Marxist and much of what I have to say will be accepted by Marxists. It does, however, provide a valuable corrective to some more 'scientistic' theories which concentrate too much on production and the 'iron laws of capital'.

I start then, with some notion of the collective. There are two reasons for this. Firstly, in the extreme sense, it is logically impossible to be an individualist for no-one is truly human himself alone. We cannot start off in a state of nature as atomic individuals for we would have no notion of what it is to be human. Our concept of humanity is not something that comes uniquely from our biological makeup but is something that can only be understood from within a community and social structure. Robinson Crusoe might exist on his desert island as the prototype of classical economic man but the only reason he could be known as Robinson Crusoe and a man was because of his origin in the English community whence he came. It was that community that gave him the identity we know him by. This then is what Aristotle and Marx mean when they see men as communal and social beings and this entails the belief that one cannot justify society by the needs of atomic beings coming together. If they are human then they must already be in some form of community to be seen as such. This does not, however, imply the collectivization of everyday life and denial of individuality that some commentators see in the phrase 'man is a communal being'. If one sees man as social in the way that I have been describing him then that does imply that his individuality and private space is not something that is uniquely fixed but rather it is something to be determined by the concept of humanity that a particular society will have. 'Social man' can be quite individualistic in his public definition. A society justified in terms of a social contract with atomic individuals coming together from some form of chaos will assume that individual space is of primary importance because those are the basic and prior units of the society. Within that society the public definition of man will make him less of a social and public being and more of an individual and private one so that what seem to be very public affairs are gone about in a highly privatized way. This sort of view will go against the collectivist sentiments that follow, to some extent at least, from the fact that humanity is a creation of the public realm. The political forms that it will express itself in will be those of the right in Nozickian and other varieties of anarcho-capitalism. One can see their inspiration also in the activities of the Reagan and Thatcher administrations.[2]

The second reason for using some notion of the collective is a moral one. This consists in the belief that people only display their true humanity when they work for and with each other. This collective communitarian belief is what Strawson (1961) has called an ethical ideal. Something that does not belong to the everyday world of morality but rather represents an almost aesthetic vision which permeates one's whole morality. This then is in opposition to the ethical idea of the strong individual.

Anarchists with the collective ideal tend to side with the political left. What we are concerned with then is an anarchism that locates itself within the socialist political current. It might be called the libertarian wing of socialism. Adolf Fischer, one of the Haymarket martyrs,[3] said that every anarchist was a socialist but that not every socialist was necessarily an anarchist. According to Rocker (1938) these forms of anarchism and socialism were alike in that they both opposed the exploitation of man by man. Where they differed was that only anarchism necessarily opposed the dominion of man over man.

Anarchism is not about disorder but its aim is to construct an egalitarian society which is also free. Here it differs from the anarcho-capitalists who believe only freedom is possible. The word stems not from 'no order' but from 'no ruler' and it is how to organize on a free and equal basis that it is concerned with. As Voline (1955), a twentieth century anarchist put it:

> A mistaken — or, more often, deliberately inaccurate — interpretation alleges that the libertarian concept means the absence of all organization. This is entirely false: it is not a matter of 'organization' or 'nonorganization', but of two different principles of organization . . . Of course, say the anarchists, society must be organized. However, the new organization . . . must be established freely, socially, and, above all, from below. The principle of organization must not issue from a center created in advance to capture the whole and impose itself upon it but, on the contrary, it must come from all sides to create nodes of coordination, natural centers to serve all these points . . . On the other hand, the other kind of 'organization', copied from that of the old oppressive and exploitative society, . . . would exaggerate all the blemishes of the old society . . . It could then only be maintained by means of a new artifice. (Quoted in Guerin, 1970, p. 43)

It is this sort of thinking that engenders the attack on those currents in communism which think that all that is necessary is to get rid of exploitation in the economic sphere. Domination, or hierarchical organization will then naturally cease or is, to some extent, necessary. (See for example, Lenin's acceptance of Taylorism as a system of factory management.) It was these authoritarian tendencies in socialism that Bakunin criticized and which occasioned his split from the First International. For how can you, he argued, build a free, a direct society on the organizational methods of an unfree one. His prophecy has proved all too tragically correct.

> I believe that Mr Marx is an earnest revolutionary, though not always a very consistent one, and that he really desires the revolt of the masses. And I wonder how he fails to see how the establishment of a universal dictatorship, collective or individual, a dictatorship that would in one way or another perform the task of chief engineer of the world revolution regulating and directing an insurrectionary movement of the masses in all countries pretty much as one would run a machine — that the establishment of such a dictatorship would be enough of itself to kill the revolution, to paralyze and distort all popular movements. (Dolgoff, 1972, p. 278)

But anarchists need not necessarily be anti-Marxists and Chomsky, in a quotation from Pannekoek — a leader of the council communist movement — shows how the strains can coalesce.

The consistent anarchist, then, will be a socialist, but a socialist of a particular sort. He will not only oppose alienated and specialized labor and look forward to the appropriation of capital by the whole body of workers, but he will also insist that this appropriation be direct, not exercised by some elite force acting in the name of the proletariat. He will, in short, oppose

> 'the organization of production by the government. It means state socialism, the command of the State officials over production and the command of managers, scientists, shop officials in the shop . . . The goal of the working class is liberation from exploitation. This goal is not reached and cannot be reached by a new directing and governing class substituting itself for the bourgeoisie. It is only realized by the workers themselves being master over production.'

These remarks were taken from "Five Theses on the Class Struggle" by the left-wing Marxist Anton Pannekoek, one of the outstanding theorists of the Council Communist movement. And in fact, radical Marxism merges with anarchist currents. (1970, p. v)

What then is wrong with law as a means of organizing our collective undertaking? Kropotkin purported to show the uselessness of laws. He divided them into three categories: protection of property, government and persons. Laws concerning property are made either to rob the producer of all or part of what he has produced or to secure for others what they have stolen from the producer or society as a whole. The vast bulk of our laws, he says, fall into this category. Laws for the protection of government i.e. constitutional laws are also merely there to protect those who have the power. The third category, laws against the person, seem more problematic. But, according to Kropotkin, most crimes in this category, at base, are concerned with someone trying to gain wealth and this is natural in inegalitarian societies. Punishment has never, ultimately, stopped crime. Most importantly, for our purposes, the vast apparatus needed to maintain these laws is itself morally corrupting both for those who staff it and for those subjected to it and in itself creates more crime and law. We can see this by looking at the scandal and corruption that lies over the law enforcement machinery even in the big 'democratic' states (cf. USA and UK). The fact that law creates more law might seem a strange idea at first. But what this means is that the more law is seen as the way of solving problems the more this creates a pressure to legalize all sorts of problems in society. In doing this we have, of course, to create more lawyers, courts, etc. to service the necessary legal problems that have been thrown up. This feeds on itself and we get a drive to legalize more and more. In *Images of Law* (1976), a book written from a socialist anarchist perspective, we studied a scheme to make legal aid more available and found that the most measurable outcome was increase in business for lawyers.[4] Indeed, that was one of the pressures that started the scheme in the first place.

We must, Kropotkin ends, treat people humanely, let our natural fellow feeling come out and not treat them barbarically by law and legal punishment.

> The main supports of crime are idleness, law and authority; laws about property, laws about government, laws about penalties and misdemeanours; and authority, which takes upon itself to manufacture these laws and to apply them.
>
> No more laws! No more judges! Liberty, equality, and practical human sympathy are the only effective barriers we can oppose to the anti-social instincts of certain among us. (In Woodcock, 1977, p. 117)

Tolstoy in similar vein, says that law is based on violence; is in the interests of the ruling class; involves mystifying through the 'science of legislation' that instead of making things clear builds up a huge opaque apparatus of its own, comprehensible only to its acolytes. Finally direct responsibility is evaded in that anyone can deny responsibility for what they have done as merely carrying out the law.

> And so the essence of legislature does not lie in Subject or Object, in rights, or in the idea of the dominion of the collective will of the people, or in other such indefinite and confused conditions; but it lies in the fact that people who wield organised violence have power to compel others to obey them and do as they like.
>
> So that the exact and irrefutable definition of legislation, intelligible to all, is that: *Laws are rules, made by people who govern by means of organised violence, for non-compliance with which the non-complier is subjected to blows, to loss of liberty, or even to being murdered.*
>
> This definition furnishes the reply to the question: What is it that renders it possible for people to make rules? The same thing makes it possible to establish laws, as enforces obedience to them, namely, organised violence. (p. 47)

Law then is a robbery and involves the domination of the few over the many. As a way of organizing social life it is itself corrupting. This is because it prevents sympathy and fellow feeling from coming through. It feeds on itself creating more crime and legal apparatuses which in turn solidify the power of those experts controlling them, preventing people from acting directly but rather through the coils and excuses of the law. It is, then, an aspect of domination and authoritarianism. Many legal ways of trying to change society are unhelpful because they retain the domination of law. This confirms the power of experts who would know best how to run a society and so prevents any direct political action leading to the anarchist ideal of a self managed society. Action towards this end is prevented by going through law and the experts. People give up their own power to those who control the society and the law.

The Marxist Critiques of Law

In what follows I propose to defend this view of law against various Marxists critiques of it. These are those that consider that it is wrong, as I have done, to put forward a view which sees law (1) as a sham and illusion entailing an instrumentalist view of law; (2) as just naked class power; (3) as one of class conspiracy; (4) as a complicated theft where one section of society steals from another. Marxist theorizing of late has been concerned to show how law cannot just be seen as exploitative and dominating and it is such a potent force precisely because it is not.

These arguments take two forms: first there are those who see the law, in some aspects at least, as a liberating and useful tool for radical political action. They attack those anarchists and others who attack its political use from principled rather than tactical reasons. Second there are those who, while attacking the view that sees law as exploitative and dominating, nevertheless want to show how law is, as a form of organizing social life, specifically bourgeois. I will argue that the first group beg the question for the anarchist and that some of their arguments in fact adopt the theories they attack. The second group are unable to show what is wrong with law unless it is exploitative and dominative. Though they claim to concentrate on the law as a form of social life, in the end they seem to argue in terms of its content. Their arguments in the end seem to imply that the form of law is good if the content is, and so they begin to sound like the first group. I go on to try and develop an anarchist view of why this form is itself morally dangerous and corrupting. In this anarchists are better enabled to get somewhere because, as I mentioned above, they see organization as important *per se* and not necessarily connected with the exploitation of production.

I turn then to look at (a) the first group as represented by E. P. Thompson and Alan Hunt who might be considered to have 'liberal' Marxist theories and (b) the second group, consisting of the 'form' theories of Richard Kinsey and Bob Fine. The problem with the arguments of the first group comes out clearly when we look at what positive assertions they make about law. E. P. Thompson (1977) sees the Rule of Law as an unqualified human good; something that the bourgeois have to respect to legitimate their power. But in adopting its standards of justice and the like they will be forced to inhibit their power or run the risk of being exposed. By exploiting these contradictions the working class can advance. Further, by pursuing the unqualified good as an independent end, the working class can secure victories in its own right. This then is the justification for using law in radical political action.

From this position then they criticize the views I have put forward. Thus Hunt
(1980) says of *Images of Law*:

> It is exclusively an *instrumentalist* view of law. Law is the instrument of a
> ruling class which functions directly at the behest and control of dominant
> economic and political interests as an instrument of oppression and
> domination; it is all the more successful because it is able to do so in such a
> way as to disseminate 'false consciousness', for example, spreading the
> illusion of neutrality and impartiality. Liberals and radicals connive,
> consciously or unconsciously, because in proclaiming the possibility of
> 'using law' they bind the subordinate classes more closely to capitalist values
> and "exacerbate the feeling of powerlessness". In general the use of law "has
> the effect of increasing the domination of law over people's lives". (p. 41)

All of which Hunt disagrees with because for him legal values, ideals and
principles cannot be reduced to falsity since they have a reality. Doing this
would reduce law to an ideology seen in terms of a crude dichotomy of truth and
falsity. Is Hunt's argument correct? No-one is denying that legal values etc. have
a reality — of course they exist. The point is that these ideals, no matter how well
meaning, create situations where solutions to political problems are taken outside
of people and given to the external force of law. I do not disagree with Marxists
such as Kinsey that "law is embedded inextricably in the organisation and
culture of our social existence and just as that social existence presents a many
sided reality so does the law" (1978, p. 202). But one must be careful of the
notion of 'real'. The fact that something is real doesn't mean to say that it cannot
be false, as Hunt implies. Monetarism, for example, is a real economic policy but
arguably a false one. Thus it is no contradiction to say that the law does what it
claims to do but that what it does is not especially good in that it prevents people
from organizing in a libertarian mode. Thus in the discussion of the Industrial
Relations Act in *Images of Law* (pp. 27-27) we were concerned to point out how
this could strengthen official trade union leadership at the expense of shop floor
organization — not an outcome we would support. Our point is the simple one of
'beware of Greeks bearing gifts'. The gifts may be real but that is not to say that
they do not have strings attached. The reality of the law then masks some of its
more important functions and in that sense it is a false friend. That was the point of
our analysis of the 'law for the poor movement' — law did help but at what cost?[5]

The views of Hunt and Thompson seem to assume some sort of mask and
conspiracy theory which, in others, they strongly criticize. For the law is being
forced upon the bourgeois who then accept and use it to legitimate their underlying power — its goodness masks the underlying violence. The effect of the law
is then to constitute a liberal society of representative democracy where law
inhibits power somewhat but, as I shall argue later, still leaves it intact in the
hands of the few. Law is only an 'unqualified good' if one accepts the liberal

democracy to which it pertains. This may be better than many conceivable societies but that is not to say that there might not be societies where more free organization is possible. Their arguments stop, it appears to me, at the point where those of anarchists and many Marxists would begin. Often, when these arguments are used to promote the radical use of law all that is being done is looking to what, in the short term, are the effects of a particular law. Thus if something gives relief immediately the argument is to accept it with open arms even though, in the long term, it might enmesh people in the coils of this particular society even more—something which our theorists do not want. We move one step forwards and two back. When unpacked the theory looks like a conspiracy theory and a belief in the value of liberal society. It doesn't tell us what is wrong with law because it seems to accept it.

I now come to that group of objections, which while critical of the position held by Thompson and others, says the anarchists have got it wrong because they essentially see law as some form of illusion hiding the reality of naked exploitation, and expropriation or 'rip-off'. This is the implication of a Pashukanian view of law which rejects "any analysis which reduced law to the status of mere ideology, a confidence trick, the civil liberties lie" (Kinsey, 1978, p. 202). This view is concerned to claim that law is not an unqualified good but that the anarchist view that it is authoritarian is wrong. What is important, they argue, is to look not at the content of law and state action but at its form. It is with the form of law rather than its content that we see what is wrong and this is where both the anarchist and Thompsonites go astray.

What then is the form of law and what is wrong with it? Kinsey begins his analysis with the following quotation from Marx (1970):

> It is plain that commodities cannot go to market and make exchange of their own account. We must therefore have recourse to their guardians who are also their owners. Commodities are things and therefore without the power of resistance against men. If they are wanting in docility, he can use force. In other words he can take possession of them. In order that these objects may enter into relation with each other as commodities, their guardians must place themselves in relation to each other as persons whose will resides in those objects and must behave in such a way that each does not appropriate the commodity of the other, and part with his own except by means of an act done by mutual consent. They must therefore recognize in each other the rights of private proprietors. This juridical relation, which expresses itself in a contract, whether such a contract be part of a developed legal system or not, is a relation between two wills, and is but a reflex of the real economic relation between the two. (p. 88)

He goes on to argue that:

> . . . the social-economic relation of commodity exchange can only obtain in so far as the juridical relation is expressed through "informal" means of "consent" or morality, *or* through the formal mechanism of private law . . .

> In conclusion to this section I will only add that so far as the commodity
> structure "penetrates society in all its aspects and remoulds it in its own
> image" so the juridical relation obtaining between separate and abstract,
> right and duty bearing subjects, expresses that economic relation in all its
> aspects either through legal institutions such as property and contract, or
> through what may be termed positive morality. In that sense, the civil
> society of a capitalist social formation is a juridical society; this is the full
> meaning of the rule of law (cf. Tonnies, "gesellschaft"; Weber, Legal
> rational and so on). (pp. 217-218)

The form of the law then, has a very close relation to atomic individualism either
constituting it, reflecting or expressing it (I will return to this ambiguity later).
Each individual stands before the law as an abstract holder of rights and duties,
as a legal person and not somebody trailing status and history behind him. Law
in its standard expression is the contract form—the free exchange of rights
between equivalent parties. This equivalence, and equality, is achieved by the
fact that everyone who comes before the law comes not as what he is but as a
legal person, a juridical subject, and in that respect equal to every other who
comes before the law as a juridical subject (the only way that one can come before
the law). This is what equality before the law means. No one can call on any
special status to defend themselves when arraigned—they are juridical subjects
the same as everyone else. The key thing about law then, is its universality for
this is the means whereby everybody can be treated abstractly and equally. Law,
seen in this way, has close affinities to the Kantian categorical imperative: act
only according to that maxim by which you can at the same time will that it
should be a universal law of nature. It is in this way that the law becomes the non
arbitrary means of organizing society and totally implicated with commodity
exchange:

> The exercise of legal right must be both private and free but also socially
> guaranteed. This requires that the juridical order is expressed as external
> legal authority, in that the exercise of will must be constrained precisely
> because commodity exchange is also a necessary social transaction. (p. 224)

Or, as Pashukanis says, constraint cannot take the form of domination subordination:

> . . . the more systematic the development of the principle of authoritarian
> regulation (which excludes any inkling of separate and autonomous will) the
> less ground there is for the application of the category law . . . [for] exchange
> value ceases to be exchange value, commodities cease to be commodities if
> the exchange-ratio is determined by authority situated outside the inherent
> laws of the market. Constraint as the command of one person addressed to
> another and confirmed by force contradicts the conditions precedent to the
> intercourse of commodity possessors.

Law then is not authoritarian but 'the reverse side of commodity fetishism', that is to say part of the universality and equality of the exchange relation.

If all this is true, what then is wrong with the form of law? On the face of it there seems nothing to hold against it. One might even be tempted to see it as the unqualified human good of Thompson and others for the tendency will be towards juridical freedom and formal equality at law. But this, according to Kinsey (p. 222):

> . . . ultimately makes visible in the law the disparity between the universal juridical equality of the sphere of circulation, and the economic inequality of the particular level of the labour process.

As Engels (1970), p. 501) says:

> . . . in the industrial world . . . the specific character of economic oppression that weighs down the proletarian stands out in all its sharpness only after the legal privileges of the capitalist class have seen set aside and complete juridical equality of both classes is established.

But where does all this leave their arguments against those who claim law is a 'mask' and a 'rip off', part of the 'civil liberties lie'? Their argument now becomes remarkably similar to that of the first group I mentioned. They both imply that the theory has a wrong view of ideology forcing us to see law as an illusion and ignoring its reality. But there is a difference and that is that the commodity exchange theorists are not prepared to see law as an unqualified human good since its form is specifically bourgeois. What is wrong with it then? The 'reality' of the law for them is in its being the site of, or 'constitutive' of, commodity exchange and that masks the inequality of production relations. But if that is the case then law, though 'real', is no more than a real mask which masks inequality and that is what, fundamentally, is wrong with it. Thus for Kinsey it:

> . . . allows the maintenance of the appearance of justice and the belief that law holds good for all. To that extent it is true that all law is nothing more than a gigantic confidence trick. (p. 227)

Having started his paper by denying the proposition that law is a 'rip-off' he is forced to assert it is with the qualification that it is more complicated than one might think.

One way of getting round this is to argue that one cannot look at the form of law in isolation but must also advert to its changing content for they are inextricably (or dialectically) connected. In *Capitalism and the Rule of Law*, Fine (1979) criticizes Pashukanis for concentrating too much on the exchange connection and says:

> For if we consider the exchange relation and the legal form from the point of view of its derivation from social relations of *production*, we see the entirely different content it has in a society of petty-commodity production, based on independent producers whose interconnections are established through the exchange of the products of their labour, from that which it has in a capitalist society, based on the expropriation of the working class. For in the former case, the fetishism and the competitive antagonism which lay hidden behind the form of law do not erase the real character of the exchange and its real equality in terms of a flow back in one form of what flowed out in another. But in the capital-labour relation, the exchange is illusory in that what flows back to the worker is not an equivalent in another form (money) of what he or she has put in in the form of labour; nor is it merely an 'unequal exchange' in which the labourer gets back less than he or she puts in. Rather, the content of the exchange is quite illusory, since what the worker gets back is only what he/she puts in in an earlier period. The bourgeois class character of law, as opposed to its fetishized and atomistic character, only becomes apparent when we analyse its determination by relation of production, and not by circulation alone. (pp. 42-43)

Legality then is not a mere mask for class exploitation and remains the form through which social relations of production are mediated. Legal relations do have an objective basis in exchange, the equivalence breaking down in the relation of capital to labour. But this 'spurious' exchange is 'the objective basis for bourgeois legal right' and the freedom and equality posited with it. These rights in themselves, however much extended, cannot erase the class relation for the exchange remains a mere semblance and illusion.

What is Fine trying to do with this argument? He is intending to show what is wrong with law without being forced to say, as Thompson does, that it is an unqualified human good which the bourgeois use to legitimate their power and thus inhibit it. He does this by connecting the form of law with class oppression in production. In this way he can show how law is specifically bourgeois power and oppressive as such without having to deny its reality. And so law is neither naked class power nor a rip-off but rather the form in which bourgeois society is organized.

Does he succeed? I think not for various reasons. Firstly, Fine is saying that the capital labour relationship is fundamentally an expropriative one because though the form through which it exchanges is equal the exchange itself is not. Thus no matter how hard you extend the form of the exchange it will always be based on that fundamental expropriative relation. The form and the content dialectically interact and change each other to make the whole exploitative. But granted this analysis, what is wrong with the bourgeois form of law? At the end of his article Fine seems to be going back to Thompson. He talks of the contradictions and problems that the legal form of regulation gives to capital and how the political problem is to use them; i.e. law inhibits bourgeois power. But he parts company from Thompson in that he does not believe it is the best way of organizing society. So what is wrong with the legal form of regulation as bourgeois power? What is wrong is its implication in productive relations which, as we saw, are fundamentally exploitative. This is the case because the worker is getting back less than he put in and the surplus is being expropriated by the capitalist. What is wrong with that is that it is not fair in the sense that it is no longer an equal exchange, the capitalist getting more than his share. In other words, the workers' labour power, or part of it, is being expropriated or, to put it more bluntly, stolen.

The property of the capitalist is, then, based on a form of theft which is based on the private ownership of the means of production.[6] So what is wrong with the society is that the producers do not have, or have a say in, their product. It is in this respect that law is wrong because it institutionalizes, supports and defends this state of affairs. But this does not show why this is necessarily the case for law — its bourgeois class character, as Fine puts it. What Fine seems to be arguing is that one cannot understand the law except in its setting of providing and institutionalizing generalized commodity exchange which cannot be understood except in the context of an exploitative productive system. But that, though it might explain the entire social formation does not say why law, as a component of it, is necessarily wrong. For one can, on the E. P. Thompson model discussed earlier, imagine non-exploitative schemes wherein law is instantiated.

The argument here is two-fold: exploitation is expressed in capitalist societies through the value form, i.e. generalized commodity exchange. Law, since it is implicated in this, is part of that exploitation. There are a number of points that can be made here. First, though exploitation might be expressed in this way it does not have to be necessarily the case. Exchanges need not necessarily work like this (see the mutualist system of independent cooperatives of Proudhon, for example) though a particular society such as capitalism, might be stipulatively defined as being a society where that is the case. But the relationship would still be contingent. Seeing the expropriation of surplus value in the value form as the central relation tends to lead, however, to certain political consequences. One might think, for example, that in abolishing this expropriation the central problem of capitalism has been solved. But though expropriation, in the sense of expropriation of surplus value, would have been stopped the repressive organization of social life would not necessarily thereby come to an end. People might no longer be exploited in the sense of being victims of unequal exchange but could still be exploited in the sense that humanity, dignity and autonomy have been taken away from them. As Rocker (1938) put it (cf. *infra*) the problem of the domination of man over man is separate from that of his exploitation. Now I am not arguing that this problem is not recognized by Marxists but rather that they tend not to see it as a separate problem. Anarchists, as we saw, tend to see this as the most important problem whether they accept the Marxian analysis of economic exploitation or not. That, for them, is a separate issue.

Marxists will tend to relate the problem of domination back either to its base in the exploitation of production or to the value form in general. In the arguments about law which we have discussed one can see this happening. For they trace law, in so far as it is bad, to production, the exploitation of surplus value or to the value form as a way of organizing social life which ultimately is wrong because of the expropriation of production.

What has happened is that while questions of the relation of exchange to production have been explored, the relation of law to the economy has been left vague. Words such as reflect, express and constitute show up this vagueness. If we say that the law is caused by the economy, this does not of itself show what is wrong with law. War causes acts of heroism but this does not imply that because war is bad, acts of heroism are also. This seems to be precisely the sort of position that the first group of Marxists would adopt. Law is bad in so far as it is captured by the bourgeois and legitimates their power but is not of itself a repressive and exploitative social form. Words like express and reflect show there may be similarities but they have to be argued for. Those who argue that law is related to the economy in the sense that it constitutes exchange relations do not thereby show what is wrong with law. Though law may constitute exchange relations, it does not necessarily do so in the unequal way that, it is argued, capitalism does. For the equality that law constitutes is equivalence and not the measurable equality of quantities which, Marx argues, does not obtain under capitalism. In law things are equal because they are reduced to legal persons and as such are the same as any other legal person, while commodities are equal when there is an exact equation between labour times. Now the institutionalization of commodity exchange in law guarantees their equivalence but not that exact equation in terms of quantities of labour times for commodities may exchange in numerous differing ways.[7] The law with its equivalence will tend to mask the real inequality of any particular productive scheme. So law might be a mask and illusion. What is wrong with that mask, however, Fine cannot say and so has to have recourse, as was shown, to Thompson-like theories. We do not get an argument which shows what is wrong with law as a form of social life.

An Anarchist Critique of Law Exemplified

Paradoxically, though the Marxist theories we have been considering have argued that law is non-dominating and non-authoritarian, they have been unable to show why it is a bad method of organizing social life except for arguments that claim its connection with class power or its nature as a mask obscuring the reality of that power. If this is the case then it would, these unfortunate circumstances being taken away, be a good method of organizing social life. This then is what Thompson argues for. Fine and others want to deny this but they cannot produce an argument that does so without coming down to some version of the Thompson argument.

Now anarchists have not themselves been clear as to what is wrong with law. But the main thrust in those like Kropotkin and Tolstoy at least, was to see law as a dominating force in the hands of a few which suppressed our fellow feeling. So far I have been somewhat negative and have merely denied that some strands of Marxist thinking can get beyond the anarchist (and 'vulgar' Marxist) rhetoric that they attack. I now intend to go beyond the rhetoric and argue, more specifically, for the truth that lies within it. In much of what follows Marxists will not find much to disagree with for the arguments go to the heart of liberal society itself. I think, however, that some of the methodological implications will not be welcome and it is with those that I will conclude. The first part of my argument is more moral, the second more epistemological (though, of course, the two cannot be separated).

In an article entitled Despotism and Legality, Kinsey (1979) tells of how productive relations in advanced capitalism become more and more legalized. I am not concerned here with his main argument but rather with what he sees as the deadening effect of the 'despotism of Legality'. He quotes Bagehot as showing most clearly law not "as a spider's web of conspiracy but as a concrete practise of routinized social relations . . . it is precisely this taken-for-granted, routinized expression of everyday relations which informs the analysis of the fetishism of legal subjectivity as the basis of the voluntary contract of employment." (p. 6):

> [for ante-political man] morality . . . was to be found in the wild spasms of 'wild justice', half punishment, half outrage—but anyhow, being unfixed by steady law, it was intermittent, vague, and hard for us to imagine. Everybody who has studied mathematics knows how many shadowy difficulties he seemed to have before he understood the problem, how impossible it was when once the demonstration had flashed upon, ever to comprehend these indistinct difficulties again, or to call up the mental confusion that admitted them. So in these days when we cannot by any effort drive out of our minds the notion of law, we cannot imagine the mind of one who had never known it, and who would not by any effort have conceived it. [1965, p. 16]

In this quotation one can also get a flavour of the anarchist attack on law as something that places outside of oneself the important everyday decisions. Law helps to construct the automatic man necessary for the automatic production processes of modern capitalism. In this sense legal relations are the relations of a capitalist society and contractual relations of this sort best fit capitalist society. But to say that does not mean we have to link them necessarily with production.

For the anarchist then, law is something which makes men automatic movers in the world, doing things outside the range of decisions that they are allowed to make. Law connects people by the abstract categories of right and duty rather than by love or fellow feeling. Kant's moral philosophy is a good example. At one level his emphasis on duty and right seems the ideal and humane moral philosophy of our time. But is it really such a good way to live? We can pose the question, as Elizabeth Anscombe (1958) did, in the following way. What would be the more worthy action? Visiting my dying mother in hospital because I wanted to or because it was my duty. This problem at the least establishes that the morality of right and duty is not unquestionable. I would go further, however, and say in contradistinction to more Calvinist moralities, that it is more worthy to be naturally good rather than to do the right thing having triumphantly conquered the everpresent desire to do otherwise. Otherwise one has a morality resting on the irony that you can only be truly good if you have evil within you. It is a poor morality that lifts right and duty to such high esteem that it forgets or downgrades people's feelings. It is precisely this that happens in systems of contractual relations. Our relations with each other are governed by the rights and duties engendered by this over-arching system and by nothing else. This then is legal society, one that enables us to have a large amount of freedom—more than in the despotic régimes of the past—but lets us have this freedom at the cost of losing our souls.[8]

I will illustrate this by an example which, at first sight, might seem unusual for an anarchist. Hegel (1976), when discussing marriage in the *Philosophy of Right*, attacks *inter alia* Kantian morality claiming that applying it to marriage makes marriage a mere contract for sexual use and that this is a perverse way of looking at it. Much of modern reforming legislation strengthens this view of marriage and, in so doing, strengthens the unsatisfactory nature of a relationship more and more merely a contractual one. And so, in trying to find freedom from the bonds of patriarchy, the fundamental relationship is destroyed and made to rest on the bonds of law where the protagonists are governed by claims of right and duty and not by love.

But according to Hayek (1976) the overarching system of rules, implying the Kantian moral philosophy of right and duty and equal treatment under equal abstract rules is the only rational way that man can live in community. It may be unnatural but that is all to the good for it is a step above our primitive emotions and need for security. It is a move from the morality of the tribe to the solidarity of the small group to the great society where everyone is equal, united by abstract rules. We do not have the same depth of feeling and emotion in such a society but that is the price one has to pay for civilization. It is no wonder such a society is very fragile.

> It would therefore not be really surprising if the first attempt of man to emerge from the tribal into an open society should fail because man is not yet ready to shed moral views developed for the tribal society; or, as Ortega y

Gasset wrote of classical liberalism in the passage placed at the head of this chapter, it is not to be wondered that 'humanity should soon appear anxious to get rid of . . . so noble an attitude, so paradoxical, so refined, so anti-natural . . . a discipline too difficult and complex to take firm root on earth.'

. . . .
. . . .
This conflict between what men still feel to be natural emotions and the discipline of rules required for the preservation of the Open Society is indeed one of the chief causes of what has been called the 'fragility of liberty': all attempts to model the Great Society on the image of the familiar small group, or to turn it into a community by directing the individuals towards common visible purposes, must produce a totalitarian society. (pp. 146-147)

Now in some ways we can agree with Hayek's view if what he means is that feeling *per se* is not necessarily a good thing. This seems to me to be true for one cannot just say that any contingent feeling is important. What is important is to live in a society where one can act out of rational feeling and not out of the right and duty engendered by contractual relations. We can see this again in marriage. For love *per se* is not enough, marriage is also a rational undertaking and it is perverse to think, as Hegel points out, that contingent feelings can ground stable relationships. All we need is not love but a community where human feelings can be rationally expressed. Does law give us this through the abstract equality of right and duty? Hayek, though seeming to agree that to some extent it smothers feeling and instinct in the contract of right and duty, thinks that in the end law engenders a more rational way of acting towards one's neighbours. But does law give us this rational objective order? I think not and in the end it dissolves into the subjectivity of personal preferences and gives no stable basis for community. It is to this point that I now turn for it brings me to my second argument against law.

It might be objected that, leaving aside the moral point that I have made, law is in fact the way of trying to rationalize and objectify our feelings. I have argued that it is at least a morally questionable way and now I wish to go on to claim that the enterprise is doomed to failure and, in the end, rests on the power of the few. Law then, is the classical liberal way of trying to bring objectivity to social relations; to construct some sort of unity from the mass of competing and logically subjective private desires. It is only thus that a society such as ours can survive and at the same time believe that people have differing values which can be freely expressed but that there is no objective standard for determining their correctness. For the law ranks our competing desires and gives us order and within that order the ability to express them freely. So the legal order allows me to express my desires in so far as they do not conflict with someone else's. In this way the law creates order out of chaos. Does this way of objectifying feelings and solving the problem of freedom and order work? The solution of generalized norms does not work since these have to be instantiated in particular decisions with respect to individual ends and that devolves into a mess of contingent value choices. Put simply this means that law does not give us a rational objective base because the old Blackstonian picture of the legal universe does not work. The rules cannot, in themselves, determine all possible outcomes. This argument is well put by Hart (1961) in *Concept of Law*:

> ... there is a limit, inherent in the nature of language, to the guidance which general language can provide. Law may sometimes be indeterminate in its application because of its open texture. Our relative ignorance of fact and relative indeterminacy of aim in framing general rules in advance makes it necessary and desirable to exercise choice in subsequent application of the rules. (pp. 121-123)

Now this, as Dworkin (1977) and others saw, cannot be the solution because it destroys the premise on which this theorizing is based; that law solves the problem of freedom and order by enabling rational objective decisions. The classic way out of the dilemma is to adopt a form of purposive reasoning. The aim of this sort of reasoning is, recognizing that language is conventional, to try to put into effect the intention or purpose of the legislator and in this way get non-arbitrary choice. Quite apart from the profound technical problems of this solution, it implies that in the end a regime of prescriptive rules does not exist. This is so because all rules can be questioned with reference to their purpose and the ultimate criterion of adjudication is whether the ends of the legal rule in particular and the legal order in general are served by the particular judgement. This must always be the case because the decision whether to apply purposive reasoning or not is not itself clear and must be a purposive judgement. The decision as to whether something is a hard or easy case has always to be taken before any rule can be applied and that decision can rest on no objective base— rather it rests on a view of whether in the end the rule in particular and the legal system in general is served. This implies that every decision is a political one because it opens up, again, the question of general norms.

In a sophisticated attempt to get out of this maze of subjectivity, Neil MacCormick (1979) recommends a procedure which tests competing legal rules by seeing what their universalizable consequences are within the context of the coherency of the legal system as a whole (consequentialism). This gives a procedure for testing but the ultimate guarantee of rationality of this decision making procedure is the coherence and 'fit' within the legal system itself. This solution is very similar to that of Popper. Popper's theory of falsifiability—the process whereby a scientist makes a hypothesis which rationalizes a part of the world and then attempts to test it by falsifying it—presents a problem about how the hypotheses are to be generated. Since the non-falsified hypothesis is our guarantee of fit with the world then there must necessarily be some procedure of selection—otherwise we could pick any crazy hypothesis we like, and that, if not falsified but logically able to be, would have as much truth-value as any other one. The guarantee of fit that Popper in fact uses is its acceptability as a coherent hypothesis within the community of science. MacCormick is saying much the same thing in his account of legal reasoning. The generation of the rules and their ultimate guarantee of fit rests upon their having a 'legal warrant' — his term for coherence and consistency. When unpacked this comes down to precedent, statutes and the like which are themselves to be looked at and justified in terms of consequentialism. So what emerges finally from his project is a system that turns in on itself and gains whatever objectivity it has from the reflexive equilibrium that the judges construct. If this is the case it follows that the legal system that the judges are bound by is binding only because they agree to it. Just as science is ultimately, in Popper's theory, what scientists do, so law is what judges do and its guarantee of objectivity or 'fit' in Popper's terms, is that they are a caste who have for centuries been socialized in a particular way. One can see this clearly in Simpson's (1973) essay of common law and legal theory. They decide 'rationally' and 'coherently' because they have all been socialized into that same way of thinking.

This, then, is the classic legal way of trying to create an objective community and unity out of a mass of seeming conflict. But, as we saw, this solution, that of generalized norms is at base contingent and arbitrary. The rationality and justice of decisions stemming from generalized norms can only be maintained coherently if they are given to the socialized few. Thus the aim of this sort of society, the government of laws and not men, is not only morally suspect but doesn't and cannot happen in practice. What we really have is a government of a few men.

However, this is the only way that the image of the law as giving order out of a mass of competing desires can be maintained. But since this is the case, then whatever the rhetoric of freedom, law cannot be democratized and opened to everyone. Lay participation in the process is a problem precisely because the system operates only if those skilled and socialized in it man it. The more the socialized group that gives law its coherence is subverted, the more likely that the decisions that stem from generalized norms become incoherent and contingent.[9]

Law then cannot be the organ of the anarchist dream of an order of people taking part in their own solutions because, as I have shown, it only works if a few skilled in its lore do it. You need professionals skilled in the law. Law then is one form of professional control among many, its justifying base being not the 'science' of the social worker but the 'freedom' of universality and contract. This is why law, in the way that I have described it, is unacceptable to anarchism, precisely because it is a mask and an illusion. Its reality is a version of sociality and community which is morally questionable; it contractualizes relationships and can only operate in its universal and rational way by having a skilled professional cohort running its machine. Law as a form of life is wrong because its apparent universality is purchased at the cost of domination by a particular class.

Conclusion

What I have done is to defend a socio-anarchist view of law both positively by putting forward what I take to be its critique of law and also through criticizing various Marxist theories which either cannot coherently explain what is wrong with law or end up by loving it. The question now is, can one put something better in its place? It is not my intention, in this paper, to go into the precise formulations of a new society. The point of this paper has been to understand the anarchist, and sometimes Marxist, critique of law more clearly. What I have said so far would not necessarily disagree with some Marxists. Indeed Pashukanis does make similar moral criticisms of bourgeois law that I have been making and many Marxists are concerned with participatory organization. That is to be expected since I have been concerned with socialistic anarchism. There are, however, some methodological implications which do point to a difference. What stems from my discussion is that the basic organizing concept or prior sociological category is for anarchists organization or what Gurvitch (1947) calls forms of sociality. As Young (1980) in his discussion of Gurvitch says:

> . . . his work presumes that all forms of social life imply some form of organisation and that the nature of this organisation can be discerned in the context of the social relationships of which they are composed. (p. 121)

The basic principle of this society is that life and work are organized in such a way that some control the many.

In this paper I have been talking of law as an instance of society organized on that principle. We need here, however, to be careful of an ambiguity in the term law. As I have been using it, it has meant the generalized norm system of bourgeois society described above. In this sense law is not necessarily present in all societies. But if, on the other hand, it is used as a synonym for organization or form of sociality, it will be present in all societies but in different forms. What this implies is that it is not contradictory for anarchists to speak approvingly of law if, by that, they understand law in the generic sense as a form of administrative regulation or sociality. What they are against is that form of administrative regulation which, although its aim is to bring objectivity to our social life by providing an overarching framework of generalized norms, can only do so at the cost of the domination of the many by the few. This then, is what is known in our society as law and what Marxists and some anarchists call the bourgeois form of law.[10] Anarchists have to look to ways other than the

domination of this form of law for bringing justice and objectivity to social life—
of making rational our feelings. To some extent this means, in value conflicts,
allowing for participation of all actors, direct and indirect from the community.
This would be a version of the ideal speech situation of Habermas, where norm
conflict is made rational by free and democratic discussion and that is the only
rationality there can be (see Sumner's paper in this book). In practical terms this
would involve what Christie (1978) has seen as giving conflicts back to the
people. He seeks a forum where conflicts would be restored to those centrally
affected by them rather than, as now, being confiscated and turned over to
lawyers and behaviour modification experts. This would give opportunities for
more clarification where the norms can continually be debated and changed.
Again it would mean more voluntary arbitration schemes and more humane
alternatives to merely custodial imprisonment. When some of these ideas are yet
more concretized as for example decarceration, small claims arbitration schemes,
attempts, as in Scotland, of non-legal juvenile justice schemes, then we can see
some of the difficulties involved—not least in the expansion of state and
professional control that often, in the name of the community, follows these
schemes. Organizing communally in this way does not inevitably lead to no
domination. Historically it has often led to more either because it was planned
for or because people thought that 'collectivity' and the 'rational' planning of
managers was enough. That this is so is not surprising. In a system based on
privilege the state will use the democratic aspirations of its subjects and under
the name of the community extend its control still further. These developments
will then be incorporated into official legal institutions and function in the
manner of the form of law that we described and anarchists object to. Again
given the principle of control in the system, control may be extended to
professional groups other than lawyers—those whose scientific ideology is one
way of making rational and just our value conflicts.[11] Indeed historically far too
much faith was placed in the scientific rationality of planners, social workers and
the like. It is planning against this form of control that is now given special
attention.[12]

The key factor in all of this is organizing so that people can run their own lives.
One cannot, however, as some Marxists do, separate organization from control.
Organization and control of production, for example, do not oppose each other.
This mistake leads to the myth that organization of the factory isn't important as
long as, through the party, 'workers' have control. It is because anarchists do not
see this dichotomy that they are, ironically, a good deal less Utopian than
Marxists. For anarchism believes that the key problem is one of organizing to
prevent the authority and control of the few whereas for Marx, at times, and
Marxists more generally, the problem has always been one of abolishing private
ownership of the means of production or commodity producing society—once
that is done everything else will follow. But of course it does not and Bakunin is

quite right when he says (in Dolgoff, 1972, p. v): "Liberty without socialism is privilege, injustice; socialism without liberty is slavery and brutality." This then takes us back to the beginning of the paper where we saw that anarchists were not just concerned with egalitarian organization but with non-dominating organization. The dictatorship of the proletariat might improve the society in many ways but it would still leave people as slaves and anarchists want a society where people can be truly human.

Domination is the central problem for it is domination, according to anarchists, that prevents the finding of the true community where objective human value can be expressed. A true human morality, they claim, is only possible when relations of superiority and inferiority no longer exist and shared community is possible. The more dominance is rooted out the more likely this community is to come into being and people be enabled to live in groups which express both their individualism and their society. Thus Unger (1975):

> The more these shared ends express the nature of humanity rather than simply the preferences of particular individuals and groups, the more would one's acceptance of them become an affirmation of one's own nature; the less it would have to represent the abandonment of individuality in favour of assent and recognition. Thus, it would be possible to view others as complementary rather than opposing wills; furtherance of their ends would mean the advancement of one's own. The conflict between the demands of individuality and sociality would disappear. (p. 220)

What does this sort of society entail? Firstly it means the politicization of everyday life—society is so organized that everything, including economic efficiency, is subordinated to equality and the free and critical discussion of what to do. Society and its production is organized in such a way that it does not rest on the decision of the few. We can see these embryonic forms in the history of the anarchist collectives, the workers' councils and soviets that spring up during times of revolutionary upheaval.[13] Anarchists would claim that this shows the mass of people struggling to attain their humanity only to be put down by relations of subjugation.[14] It is these 'forms of sociality' that anarchists claim should be studied and emulated in order to see how a whole society might be democratized rather than concentrate on changing one form of production for another with the naive hope that this might prevent domination.

In this paper I have defended an anarchist critique of law against the Marxist attack. I have argued that anarchists are more realistic in that they think that the central problem is how to organize an expressive and free way of life. For Marxists this is a problem because, if seen as important, it has to be related to the central organizing concept of the economy. I showed that the 'rule of law' fails to give true community because it leads to the dominance of the few and because of the moral way of life it presupposes. It may be argued that, granted all of this, it is still the best chance we have of achieving a fair peace and we should take it as the best compromise. The domination is after all only in the ultimate instance. That may be but the compromise is not likely to be stable. I have argued that it is precisely because this form of life cannot satisfy people's moral instincts that it becomes unstable as people seek to realize their true selves and escape their moral ambiguity.

Anarchists think that we should study the embryonic organizations that are thrown up to ensure a lasting way out. Whether that is possible is another matter — the road may be littered with failure but it is at least arguable that we ought to try.

Notes

1. See the further reading section at the end of the paper for a more detailed reading list on the spectrum of anarchist theories considered here.
2. See Bankowski (1977) for a full account of this.
3. Fischer and other American anarchists organized massive strikes and demonstrations as part of the campaign for an eight-hour day. During one such meeting in Haymarket Square, Chicago in May 1886 a bomb was thrown at the police. Fischer and his comrades were charged and convicted of this, and he was one of those executed. The trials were the occasion for mass demonstrations and the convictions caused great controversy.
4. Cf. Bankowski and Mungham (1976) especially Ch. 3.
5. Cf. Bankowski and Mungham (1976).
6. Cf. Cohen (1980).
7. For a similar argument though used to somewhat different purpose see Cutler *et al.* (1977).
8. Pashukanis himself makes similar criticisms of bourgeois law though this is not often taken up (see Warrington's paper in this book).
9. See Bankowski and Nelken (1981) especially S.v. for a fuller version of this argument.
10. Some anarchists, the anarcho capitalists, think a constrained form of this sort of law is the only freedom possible for it is the only way that everyone could, without chaos, express their individual subjective desires. My argument has been that this is doomed as dissolving into the rule of a few men (cf. Bankowski, 1977 and *infra*).
11. For some discussion of the problems associated with this see Bankowski and Mungham (1978) and (1981), Scull (1977), Brown and Bloomfield (1979), Cohen (1979), Hirst (1980).
12. See Illich (1975) and (1977).
13. Hirst argues against this by claiming that this would not solve the problems of coordination and the like. He goes on to say that the point of democracy is not to represent, for the ideas of bodies ultimately representing the 'sovereignty of the people' is a useless concept and can lead to domination by those representatives. Rather the point is to provide personnel to run a system. His arguments are very similar to anarchist ones against the notion of representative democracy but his solution seems to be to replace domination by the domination of the rule of law.

14. Space does not permit me to go into some detail on anarchist organization. I hope to do that elsewhere. See the further reading section at the end of the paper.

References

Anscombe, E. (1958). A Modern Moral Philosophy, in *Philosophy*, Vol. 33, p. 1.

Bagehot, W. (1956). *Physics and Politics*. Beacon Press.

Bankowski, Z. (1977). Anarchy Rule O.K., in *Archiv für Rechts und Socialphilosophie*, Band LXIII.

Bankowski, Z. and Mungham, G. (1976). *Images of Law*. R.K.P., London.

Bankowski, Z. and Mungham, G. (1978). Law and Lay Participation, in *European Yearbook in Law and Sociology*. Nijhoff, Hague.

Bankowski, Z. and Mungham, G. (1981). Lay people and Law people in the Administration of the Lower Courts, in *Intern. Journal of Sociology of Law* 9, 85-100.

Bankowski, Z. and Nelken, D. (1981). Discretion as a Social Problem, in *Discretion and Welfare* (Adler and Asquith, Eds). Heinemann, London.

Brown and Blookfield *et al.* (1979). Legality and Community. Aberdeen Peoples Press, Aberdeen.

Carroll, J. (1974). *Break-out from the Crystal Palace*. R.K.P., London.

Christie, N. (1978). Conflicts as Property. In *Sociology of Law: A Conflict Perspective* (Reasons, C. and Rich, R., Eds). Butterworths, London.

Cohen, G. (1980). *The Labour Theory of Value and the Concept of Exploitation in Marx, Justice and History* (Cohen, M., Nagel, T. and Scanlon, T., Eds). Princeton University Press, Princeton.

Cohen, G. (1981). Freedom, Justice and Capitalism, in *The New Left Review* **126**, 3-16.

Cohen, S. (1979). The Punitive City, in *Contemporary Crises* **3**, 339-363.

Cutler, A., Hindess, B. *et al.* (1977). *Marx's Capital and Capitalism Today*, R.K.P., London.

Dolgoff, S. (1972). *Bakunin on Anarchy*. Random House, New York.

Dworkin, R. (1977). *Taking Rights Seriously*. Duckworth, London.

Engels, F. (1970). *Marx-Engels Selected Works in One Volume*. Lawrence and Wishart, London.

Fine, B. (1979). Law and Class, (in Fine *et al.*, Eds) *Capitalism and the Rule of Law*. Hutchinson, London.

Guerin, D. (1970). Anarchism. Monthly Review Press, London.

Gurvitch, G. (1947). *The Sociology of Law*. Kegan Paul, London.

Hayek, F. A. (1976). *Law, Legislation and Liberty*. Volume One. University of Chicago Press, Chicago.

Hirst, P. (1980). Law, Socialism and Rights in Radical Issues, in *Criminology* (Carlen, P. and Collison, M., Eds). Martin Robertson, Oxford.

Hunt, A. (1980). The Radical Critique of Law: An Assessment, in *International Journal of the Sociology of Law* 8, 33-46.

Kinsey, R. (1978). Marxism and Law: Preliminary Analysis, in *British Journal of Law and Society* **15**, 202-227.

Kinsey, R. (1979). Despotism and Legality (in Fine *et al.*, 1979).

Illich, I. (1975). *Tools for Conviviality*. Fontana/Collins, Glasgow.

Illich, I. (1977). *Disabling Professions*. Calder and Boyars, London.

MacCormick, D. N. (1979). Legal Reasoning and Legal Theory. Clarendon Press, Oxford.

Marx, K. (1970). *Capital*. Lawrence and Wishart, London.
Nozick, R. (1974). *Anarchy, State and Utopia*. Basic Books, New York.
Proudhon, P. J. (1966). *What is Property?* H. Fertig, New York.
Rocker, R. (1938). *Anarcho-syndicalism*. Freedom Press, London.
Scull, A. (1977). *Decarceration*. Prentice-Hall, Anglewood Cliffs, NJ.
Simpson, A. W. B. (1973). Common Law and Legal Theory, in Simpson (Ed.) *Oxford Essays in Jurisprudence* (2nd series). Clarendon Press, Oxford.
Stirner, M. (1971). *The Ego and his Own*. Jonathan Cape, London.
Strawson, P. (1961). Social Morality and the Individual Ideal, in *Philosophy* Vol. **36**.
Tolstoy, L. (1972). *The Slavery of our Times*. John Lawrence, London.
Unger, R. M. (1975). Knowledge and Politics. The Free Press, New York.
Woodcock, G. (1977). *The Anarchist Reader*. Fontana, Glasgow.
Young, P. (1980). Punishment and Social Organization, in Bankowski, Z. and Mungham, G. (Eds), *Essays in Law and Society*. RKP, London.

Further Reading

(I) There are many and various anarchist writings. The best way to get a grap of the different varieties is to look to the anthologies.
Woodcock, G. (1971). *The Anarchist Reader*. Collins/Fontana, Glasgow.
Horowitz, I. (1964). *The Anarchists*. Dell Publishing, Oxford.
Both these books give extracts from the main anarchist theories; in addition Horowitz provides a good typology of anarchist theories in his Introduction.

(II) Here I give a selection of the writings on or about the main strands of anarchist theory mentioned in my paper.
Bakunin on *Anarchy*: Dolgoff, S. (Ed.) (1972). Vintage Books, New York.
This is a good English selection of his writings.
Bakunin, (1970). *God and State*. Dover Books, New York.
Kropotkin's Revolutionary Pamphlets (Ed. Baldwin, R.) (1970). Dover Books, New York.
There is no satisfactory anthology of Kropotkin's writings—most have important pieces missing. This is the best for our purposes as it contains much of his writings on law and crime.
Kropotkin (1969). *The State: Its Historic Role*. Freedom Press, London.
Malatesta: His Life and Ideas (Ed. V. Richards) (1971). Freedom Press, London.
Proudhon, P. J.: *Selected Writings* (Ed. Edwards) (1965). Macmillan, London.
Tolstoy, L. (1962). *The Slavery of our Time*. His pamphlet denouncing law and government.
Tolstoy, L. *Resurrection*: His last great novel written after his conversion to anarchism.
Godwin, W. (1978). Enquiry Concerning Political Justice, Pelican. A utilitarian anarchist of the 18th Century. Has interesting comments on legal organisation.

Nozick, R. (1974). *Anarchy, State and Utopia*. Basic Books, New York. This is an important book in the anarcho-capitalist tradition.

Carroll, J. (1974). *Breakout from the Crystal Palace*. RKP, London. Deals with Stirner, Nietzsche and Dostoevsky.

(III) More general works on anarchism include:

Woodcock, G. (1963). *Anarchism*. Penguin Books, Harmondsworth.

Carter, A. (1971). *The Political Theory of Anarchism*. RKP, London. An introduction to anarchism and political theory.

Wolff, R. P. (1976). *In Defence of Anarchism*, Harper. A rigorous philosophical defence of an anarchist position with some thoughts on anarchist organization.

Anarchism, Nomos, 19. The American Association of Legal and Social Philosophy. This is their annual symposium devoted to all strands of anarchism.

Law in Anarchism, 1980 (Holterman, van Maarseven, Eds), Erasmus Univ. Press, Rotterdam. A symposium of anarchist academics representing all strands.

Tift, L. and Sullivan, D. (1980). *The Struggle to be Human*. Cienfuegos Press, Orkney. A modern attempt to deal with crime and criminology from an anarchist perspective. Clear but not wholly successful.

(IV) Here I include some works more specifically on anarchist organization. However, these cannot really be separated and you will get much of value from the main reading list.

Guerin, D. (1974). *Anarchism*, Monthly Review Press, London. Is a general book but deals mainly with syndicalist organization.

Dolgoff, S. (1974). The Anarchist Collectives, Black Rose Books, Montreal. Deals with the Spanish experience.

Brinton, M. (1976). *The Bolsheviks and Workers Control*. Black and Red, Detroit. An anti-bolshevik account of organization during the Russian Revolution. Perhaps a bit tendentious.

Kropotkin (1972). *The Conquest of Bread*. Allen Lane, London.

Kropotkin (1972). *Mutual Aid*. Allen Lane, London.

More modern works on anarchist organization include:

Ward, C. (1973). *Anarchy in Action*. Allen and Unwin.

Baldelli, G. (1971). *Social Anarchism*. Penguin.

Bookchin, M. (1979). *Limits of the City*. Harper and Row, New York.

Bookchin, M. (1980). Towards an Ecological Society. Black Rose, Montreal.

Index

J

K